NAUGHT ESCAPES US

The Story of No. 206 Squadron
Royal Air Force

by
Peter B. Gunn

THE 206 SQUADRON ASSOCIATION

Printed and bound by
Witley Press Limited, Hunstanton, Norfolk PE36 6AD

ISBN
0-9547553-0-8

Front Cover:
Then and Now – Nimrod photographed in November 2002 flying over site of original foundation of No. 6 Squadron Royal Naval Air Service (RNAS) at Dover in November 1916. (*Dover Mercury* via Graham Tutthill)

Back Cover:
Top to bottom: Nieuport Scout; Hudson; Liberator

DEDICATED TO THE MEMORY OF

Captain Alan Denzil Burness Smith MRAeS
1924 - 2002

Without his indefatigable enthusiasm, drive, fundraising and hard work over many years this historically important and very necessary record of the history of 206 Squadron would not have been produced.

Fg Off. A.D.B. Smith taken 1945/46
at Transport Command Development Unit, Brize Norton.
(Pete Smith)

Contents

ACKNOWLEDGEMENTS

A new history of 206 Squadron was first suggested to me by the late Alan Smith at a Squadron Association lunch in the RAF Club, and as always with Alan, a request from him was very difficult to turn down. The rest is history, so to speak.

From the start Alan supplied material, photographs, advice and much encouragement, as well as hospitality at his home in the Isle of Man, only a few months before his untimely death. J. J. V. Glazebrook (the writer of the original 206 Squadron history in 1945) and the late J. C. Graham were invaluable sources of help and advice, as was Mrs Betty Beaty, widow of the late Squadron Leader David Beaty DFC and Bar, MBE.

Air Vice-Marshal David Emmerson, former Association President and overseer of the project, has made himself constantly available for my many queries and appeals for information. He also checked through my script and enabled me to fill many gaps in the recent history of the squadron. I am also grateful to him for writing the foreword to the book. Air Commodore R. W. Joseph (President of the Association) read the later chapters and provided much additional information about the Nimrod era. Air Commodore S. D. Butler (Chairman) also checked the later chapters, making many useful suggestions as well as supplying photographs. Ian Grant, former chairman, assisted me in reading the section on the Association's history. Robin Woolven provided information and drew the maps. My sister Elspeth Mackinlay proofread the complete script with her usual meticulous attention to detail.

I was very fortunate to be granted almost unlimited access to the squadron archives at Royal Air Force Kinloss on several occasions, with the kind permission of Wing Commander Andy P. Flint, OC 206 Squadron, and that of his predecessor Group Captain Tom Cross. Wing Commander Flint also submitted a fascinating report on the squadron's role in the Gulf. Permission was granted for me to reproduce many of the photographs and other material from the archives, for which the acknowledgement 'Crown Copyright, 206 Squadron archives' has been abbreviated in the text to 'CC/206'.

The present station commander Group Captain G. R. Porter contributed some reminiscences of his time on the squadron. The squadron historian Flight Lieutenant Tom Talbot and his predecessors Flight Lieutenants I. D. Macmillan and Richard Frick were a source of help and advice, along with Flight Lieutenant Duncan Milne and Squadron Leader Graham House.

It has been a privilege for myself and my wife Janet to be invited to several squadron reunions, and there to share the memories of many members of the squadron, past and present. Those who have supplied information and in many cases photographs include the following:

Bill Balderson; Bill Alborough; Leslie 'Sid' Banks; Kenneth Beere; J. D. Beresford; Jack Blackburn; Mrs Alix Donald (widow of the late Professor Ian Donald); G. V. Donald; Bryan Doughty; Dr Charles Eaton (son of the late Charles Eaton, 206 Squadron 1918); Jack Farley; David Fellowes; Ernest E. Fitchew; M. J. 'Jack' Frost; Lewis M. Glanville; H. C. F. Goff; Laurie Hampson; George Hart; John S. Hart; Edwin C. R. 'Ted' Hill; Jack Holywell; James R. Hood; Mrs Brenda Laird (widow of the late Squadron Leader P. E. Laird); Eric Lake; Charles Lowe; Frank R. MacManus; Bill McColl; John McCubbin; Allan Monaghan; Malcolm Morris; Ted Nelson; Charles Peacock; Janet Ratcliffe; Vic Reynolds; S. 'Robby' Robilliard; Alan Rowe (son of Sgt Observer L. H. Rowe DFM); Dick Scrivener; L. A. Smith; Pete Smith (Alan Smith's son) and family; P. G. Smith; Charlie Staples; D. P. E. Straw (Association Secretary); Frank Stubbs (former Treasurer); Dusty Sworder; Colin H. Taylor; Richard Thomas; Mitchell Williamson and John Young.

Other individuals who have supplied information and advice include Tony Arter, Mrs P. Bancroft, Librarian, Lichfield Cathedral; Chaz Bowyer; Nick Forder; Maurice Gardner, artist; Mike Seymour; Roger Sheldrake and Graham Tutthill of *The Dover Mercury*.

I am also indebted to the following organisations in researching for this book:
The National Archives at Kew (formerly the Public Record Office); The Commonwealth War Graves Commission; Air Historical Branch (RAF), Ministry of Defence; The Royal Air Force Museum, Hendon, and in particular the Curator Gordon Leith, Senior Keeper Peter Elliott and staff of the Department of Research & Information Services; The Fleet Air Arm Museum, RNAS Yeovilton, and in particular Jerry Share, Assistant Curator; The Warship Preservation Trust, Birkenhead; The Shackleton Association and journal 'The Growler' and John Botwood (President and Founder), John Cubberley (Chairman), Peter J. Dunn (Secretary) and Norman Thelwell.

Permission to use photographs and other material was kindly granted by the M. J. G. Hunter Collection; Gluvian Art Ltd and by the editor of *Cross and Cockade International*, Paul S. Leaman.

Crown copyright material is reproduced by permission of the Controller of Her Majesty's Stationery Office.

Financial contributions which have made this history possible were generously contributed by the following: A. Armstrong; J. D. Beresford; J. W. Blackburn; J. E. Bury; Mrs Alix Donald; B. Doughty; David Emmerson and Mrs M. K. Emmerson; D. Ford; H. S. Frost; J. J. V. Glazebrook; the late J. C. Graham; Ian Grant and Mrs J. Grant; W. H. T. Hallett; M. J. Hughes; M. W. Jones; E. E. Lake; J. Murdock; P. O'Riordan; J. S. Oakes and A. T. Oakes; J. Ratcliffe; Abe Shamas; the late A. D. B. Smith; D. P. E. Straw; M. Sweeney; Colin and Mrs E. J. Taylor; T. C. Williamson.

Finally, I am grateful to Colin Marsters and staff of Witley Press for their efforts in the production of this book.

Every effort has been made to trace and acknowledge the copyright of photographs and other material published but I would welcome any fresh information if it becomes available. I have done my best to produce an accurate and comprehensive account of the squadron's history, but I apologise in advance for any errors or omissions.

Peter B. Gunn,
Docking, Norfolk.
March 2004

About the Author

Peter B. Gunn is an indexer by profession and in his spare time researches and writes aviation history. His interest in 206 Squadron resulted from his study of the early history of the squadron when it was based at Bircham Newton in Norfolk. He then undertook the task of compiling a comprehensive history for the 206 Squadron Association. The author of two previous books on local airfield history, he lives in Norfolk with his wife Janet.

Foreword by
Air Vice-Marshal David Emmerson CBE AFC

Alan Smith was the driving force behind the 206 Squadron Association, and for over 10 years he was the Association. He was tireless, innovative and meticulous in taking the Association forward, acting as Secretary, Treasurer and event organiser across a broad spectrum of activities until his untimely death in 2002. He was a much admired person, sadly missed by so many, and the Association all felt that this book should be dedicated to the memory of Alan.

In the late 1990s Alan first discussed with me the possibility of sponsoring a History of 206 Squadron. I was supportive but felt that finding an author and the cost would be major problems. Alan, as always, saw the problems as little more than an administrative hurdle to be crossed and immediately set about locating a volunteer to research and write the history. He also persuaded the Association at its 2000 AGM to raise the funds for the project and blazed the trail with a healthy donation. Over the next two years Alan extracted some £5000 from members, enough to fund the research and a paperback version. Alan was determined that the book should appear in hardback form, and was about to launch a further fundraising push when he was so tragically taken from us. However, his final bequest to his beloved Association was a major donation to fill the gap, and Peter Gunn and I have attempted to bring the project to a successful conclusion over the past two years. I hope that he would have approved the end product.

Alan was the driving force, but in finding Peter Gunn and persuading him to take on the enormous research, writing and compilation tasks was an enormously important act. Without a fee, Peter has worked tirelessly to bring together the strands of nearly 90 years of history from many sources. His research has been thorough and tremendously time consuming, and without his hard work, skills and experience the project would have failed. So, our enduring thanks go to Peter, and his so patient wife Janet. Peter has produced a book that should interest anyone with a connection to 206 Squadron, and there is more than enough information – left out because of space restrictions – to fill a follow up version in due course. Enjoy the read.

David Emmerson

MAP (drawn by Robin Woolven)

Squadron Bases from November 1916 to May 1919

CHAPTER I

'NAVAL 6'

Let me go out to meet my fate
As all men do, so I may be
One of your knightly company.

From *An RFC Prayer* by Capt. R.N.G. Atkinson

No. 206 Squadron originated from a small group of naval personnel who assembled in Dover on 1 November 1916. During December they moved to Petite Synthe in the Dunkirk area and on 31 December, No. 6 Squadron Royal Naval Air Service was established from this nucleus. The new squadron, nicknamed 'Naval 6', was commanded by Squadron Commander John Joseph Petre and equipped in the fighter role with Nieuport Scouts. Petre came from Ingatestone in Essex and had joined the Royal Naval Air Service in September 1914, gaining his pilot's certificate the following month at the age of 20. He became an exceptional and brave pilot who was soon in action over Ostend and Zeebrugge in reconnaissance and bombing operations, being awarded the Distinguished Service Cross (DSC) and the French Croix de Guerre during 1916. In October, just before he took command of No. 6 Squadron, he had destroyed an enemy LVG aircraft.

At the end of 1916 and the start of 1917 the army had appealed to the Admiralty for naval squadrons to reinforce the Royal Flying Corps to match the increasing numbers of fighting aeroplanes the Germans were deploying. Accordingly, four naval squadrons were earmarked for this role, Nos 1, 3, 6 and 8 Squadrons. Thus, on 15 March 1917 No. 6 (Naval) Squadron moved to the aerodrome at La Bellevue, soon followed by the aerodromes at Chipilly and Flez, as part of No. 13 (Army) Wing) in the Third Army Area to reinforce the Royal Flying Corps in the Battle of Arras which began on 9 April. Among several casualties sustained by the squadron during that period was the squadron commander himself on Friday 13 April, but in his case by a tragic accident due to his Nieuport Scout N3206 breaking up during a practice in firing at ground targets. The wings of his machine broke off in a dive at around 300 feet. Apparently the early Nieuport Scouts had a weakness in the wing structure which caused a number of accidents during certain manoeuvres, usually with fatal results.[1] Petre was replaced as CO by Squadron Commander C. D. Breese, who had previously served as an Engineer-Lieutenant. In June the squadron moved back to the Dunkirk area at Bray Dunes to re-equip with the Sopwith F1 Camel, being the first naval squadron to completely equip with this type. Other aircraft used by the squadron during its short life in this period included the Sopwith 1½ Strutter and the Triplane. In July the unit was in action intercepting Gotha bombers returning from raids over England. This was followed by a further move to Frontier Aerodrome, where the squadron was disbanded towards the end of August.

The squadron was re-formed on 1 January 1918 at Dover as a day-bombing and reconnaissance unit under the command of Major C. T. MacLaren. The unit was equipped initially with De Havilland DH4s mainly for training, and by February with

---

1 *Airfields and Airmen – Somme* by Mike O'Connor, Leo Cooper (Pen & Sword) 2002 pp180-2

Nieuport 24 Scout – No. 6 Sqn RNAS, 1917.
(Fleet Air Arm Museum, Yeovilton)

Senior Officer.

    R.N.A.S., H.Q.,   Director of Air Services,
                              Hotel Cecil.
    Dunkerque.   Strand, W.C.

19th. November 1917.

Submitted.

    In view of the approval given for next year's requirements,
which include two D.H.4 Bombing Squadrons, it is proposed,
subject to your approval, to form the second Squadron about
the 1st. January 1918.

    2.- The necessary Squadron Commander and Flight Leaders and
ratings have been detailed, and arrangements made for the engine
ratings to go through a course in the B.H.P. engine at Messrs.
Siddeley Deasy's.

    3.- All that is required will be about eight or ten pilots
trained in D.H.4 machines at Manstone to be drafted to DOVER
COMMAND during the month of December.   These will then be
divided between the two Bombing Squadron and experienced pilots
mixed between the two Squadrons.

    4.- It is proposed to call this Squadron No. 6. Squadron.

                    Signed C. L. Lambe.
                      Captain. R.N.

No.6 Squadron re-formed end of 1917 (CC/206)

the new De Havilland DH9s, powered by the 230hp Siddeley Puma engine, which was a development of the 230hp BHP (Beardmore-Halford-Pullinger) engine. Personnel came from the Walmer Defence Flight and No. 11 Squadron RNAS and were largely inexperienced in aerial warfare. They included the Flight Commanders J. S. Wright DSC, and I. N. C. Clarke DSC, both from No. 5 Squadron RNAS, and G. L. E. Stevens from No. 13 Squadron RNAS. The Recording Officer was Sub-Lieutenant B. H. Rook RNVR who recalled these early days at Dover:

'No. 6 Squadron was getting ready to proceed to France, and on the night before departure the Mess produced oysters to mark the occasion. We considered ourselves fortunate in having as our mess cook one who had been a chef at a leading London hotel. We kept quiet about this but eventually higher authority heard about it. However, we successfully resisted ensuing efforts to steal our cook! On 14 January those members of the squadron travelling to France by sea were mustered at the aerodrome and proceeded down the narrow path cut into the side of the cliff, en route to the Marine Pier, where a naval vessel was waiting to embark the party for Dunkerque. The journey was uneventful and the ship made good time, for there was no deviation from course on this occasion to carry out a minefield patrol.'[2]

Corporal Observer Horace W. Williams recalled the passage on the *Marshal Soult* to Dunkerque 'snowing all the way over, and after landing we were conveyed by lorry to Petite Synthe. Some huts had just been put up, no doors, no windows, no water, but plenty of mud.'[3]

The squadron was based at Petite Synthe to cover a sector of the front ten miles north of Ypres to 20 miles south-west. The first operation was on 9 March 1918 when DH9s made a bombing attack on St Pierre Capelle, led by the squadron's senior flight commander Captain I. N. C. Clarke DSC, an Australian. On the return trip an enemy Gotha bomber was sighted in a field, having just forced-landed. When this was reported to Major MacLaren back at the airfield volunteers were asked for to return to bomb it later in the day. An enemy Pfalz Scout was another victim of the first day's operations. This was the first time the DH9 aircraft had been used operationally against the enemy. Lieutenant Rook retained some memories of the days at Petite Synthe:

'I remember my first flight ever with V. C. Tiarks. I also recall that J. S. Wright, regardless of the hubbub around him in the Mess, would park himself on the floor against the wall and immerse himself in what appeared to be music scores. The black cocker spaniel I. N. C. Clarke brought out from England must also be mentioned for on the ground, Clarke, his Observer St John and the dog were almost inseparable. As soon as planes landed from operations the dog had an uncanny ability to single out Clarke's DH9 and was the first to greet him when he climbed out.'[4]

When he arrived on the squadron Captain Clarke had amassed considerable experience as a bomber pilot with No. 5 Squadron RNAS during 1916 and 1917 and trained No. 6 Squadron RNAS in tight formation flying to provide maximum protection against enemy fighters by concentrating their defensive firepower. The tactic was to bomb from 13-14,000 feet, make a sharp turn and dive back to allied lines at 120mph, a speed well able to match even the best fighter opposition. However, there were some instances of trouble with the new Puma engine, which could lead to a machine lagging behind in the formation and exposing itself to enemy fighters. But the DH9 was a rugged aircraft, well able to defend itself and it has been claimed that during the ten months of operations 52 enemy aircraft were confirmed destroyed for a loss of 30 of the squadron's

2   Rook, Lt B. H., Personal Narrative 6 RNAS & 206 RAF 1918/19 (206 Sqn Archives, RAF Kinloss).
3   Cpl Obs. (later Sgt) Horace Walter Williams DFM (206 Sqn Archives, RAF Kinloss).
4   Rook, ibid.

aircraft – two of which fell to ground fire.[5] Captain Clarke remained with the squadron until the end of June, handing over to Captain Anderson MC, another bombing veteran. However the bombing tactics developed by Clarke with Nos 6/206 Squadron were to be of importance for future bombing tactics, even up to World War Two.

For its bomb load the DH9 carried twelve 20 lb high explosive Cooper bombs or two 112 lb bombs, or one 230 lb bomb. Another alternative was to drop a cardboard container in which were six Mills bombs. On contact with the ground the containers split and the Mills bombs exploded, their safety pins being removed before fitting into the containers. Armament on the DH9 consisted of two Vickers guns, firing through the propeller. These were controlled by a mechanism timed with the propeller, but a late firing could hit the blade which happened from time to time, resulting in an almost certain engine failure and inevitable crash with no parachutes to save the crew. In addition, the Armament Officer Captain J. M. Beddall had designed a special twin Lewis gun mounting for the observers which had independent twin thumb triggers. This was later adopted as standard RAF equipment.[6]

At this stage in the war there appears to have been much rivalry if not intense dislike between the personnel of the RNAS and RFC squadrons. Although the former had originally been formed for naval work, several squadrons were now engaged over the Western Front and the different service traditions often seemed to be not far below the surface. There was greater rank and class consciousness among RNAS compared to the RFC squadrons such that at Alquines, for example, officers and other ranks were accommodated at opposite ends of the airfield and there was no inter-mixing, even of aircrew, outside daily flying operations.[7]

Further bombing raids followed during March which included an attack on Bruges Docks which resulted in the sinking of three cement barges, a submarine, two torpedo boats and a cargo ship, as well as damage to the quays. Corporal Observer Horace Williams recalled the prize money he received on three occasions for success in these raids. There was a further move to the airfield at Ste Marie Cappel, and at the end of the month the squadron was transferred from 5 Wing RNAS to 11th (Army) Wing, 2nd Brigade, Royal Flying Corps. A new era in the squadron's history was about to begin.

DH9 D7222 – operated by the squadron during 1918.

5   Rowe, Alan, 206 Squadron RAF – 'Some Australian Connections'
    (Cross and Cockade International Vol 28 No. 1)
6   Rowe, Alan, ibid.
7   Rowe, Alan, letter to author 14/5/01.

CHAPTER 2

THE FINAL OFFENSIVES

'When he (the CO) asked me if I would double up and go,
there is always one answer and that is "Yes Sir!".'

Lieutenant H. A. Schlotzhauer, US Army Air Corps, attached 206 Sqn 1918.

On 1 April 1918 the Royal Air Force came into being and the squadron was redesignated No. 206 Squadron RAF, but continued to operate with the 2nd Brigade. Lieutenant B. H. Rook remembered the occasion:

'When the squadron was re-numbered 206 Squadron RAF on 1st April, a number of ex-RFC mechanics were transferred to 206 and provided an unrehearsed diversion at the first pay parade. Hitherto, more or less complying with naval practice, a man about to receive his pay stepped forward to the pay desk, removed his cap smartly and held it out in front of him. The money was then placed on the cap and removed by the man, who replaced his cap and saluted before withdrawing. When the first of the ex-RFC mechanics presented himself at the pay desk and saluted smartly with his cap on, Sergeant-Major Wiggins ordered "cap off"! The merger of the RNAS and RFC personnel in 206 at first produced much banter and for some time the ex-RNAS men proceeding out of camp on short leave by lorry spoke of "going ashore" on the "liberty boat".'

With almost no time to spare 206 Squadron was plunged into the Battle of Lys which began on 9 April with the attack by the German Sixth Army on a line between Armentières and the La Bassée Canal. By 11 April the squadron was in the thick of the battle, carrying out a succession of bombing raids on enemy lines. On the 12th Sir Douglas Haig issued his famous Order to the British Troops: 'Every position must be held to the last man: there must be no retirement. With our backs to the wall, and believing in the justice of our cause, each one of us must fight on to the end.' On that same day 206 was continuing its operations with 19 pilots flying a total of 76 hours. The next day the squadron bombed German lines of communication at Comines, Quesnoy, Frélinghein, Haubourdin and Merville. Later in the day 21 x 112 lb. bombs were dropped on targets between Armentières and Estaires. Bad weather hampered bombing activity for much of the rest of the battle, as described by Corporal Observer H. W. Williams on a fog-bound day at Alquines on 17 April:

'Our 18 machines were ready loaded with two 112 lb bombs each waiting for the fog to clear sufficiently. Our orders were to attack Bailleul which the Germans had captured two days before, and where they were now reported to be massing fresh troops for a further push forward. When we took off at last we flew in at 500ft, just under the clouds, and were so low we could hear our bombs explode and feel their concussion. This raid was so effective that the enemy attack was wrecked before it could start, and they never did succeed in pushing on any further in this Sector.'

By the end of the month the German drive to the coast had been halted. More unit movements followed during the month, to Boisdinghem and then to Alquines, returning to both airfields in May and June. Squadron tasks were now being expanded to include reconnaissance and photographic work and the unit was to become the reconnaissance squadron of the Second Army with the duty of mapping the Army area.

206 Sqn members visiting Alquines, November 2002.
Left to right: Sgt Jake Thackeray; Sgt Paul Marr; Sgt Ian 'Ski' Sinski; Sqn Ldr Graham 'Sheds' House; Flt Lt Tom Talbot; Flt Lt Duncan Milne (kneeling).

When bad weather intervened and operations were cancelled trips would be arranged to Calais and Boulogne, as recalled by Lieutenant Rook:

'On these occasions, a meal at the Officers' Club or at Monières provided a welcome change of scene. After one of these excursions we were just settling down in the COs car for the return journey, but J. M. Beddall had other ideas and insisted on stopping for a last drink. When we returned to the car, we missed Beddall and our driver went back to the place to find him. After a pause, an upstairs window was thrown open, an arm reached out and emptied a jug of water over the car. It required our united efforts to get Beddall back into the car, but we reached the aerodrome without further incident.'

Another personal account of life with the squadron during 1918/1919 was recorded by Second Lieutenant John S. Blanford (later Major, DFC)[1]. After being commissioned from Sandhurst in 1917 into the Buffs (East Kent Regiment) he was seconded to the newly-formed Royal Air Force and trained as an observer before being posted to 206 Squadron at Boisdinghem, France, on 29 May 1918, aged 19 years four months. His detailed day-to-day account of life with the squadron at the time has been freely used by kind permission of *Cross & Cockade International*. In his original manuscript sub-titled 'Reminiscences of Service with 206 Squadron Royal Air Force in France, Belgium and Germany, 1918/19' he dedicated his work to 'All Members of 206 Squadron, Past, Present, and Future.'

Lieutenant Blanford and three other newly-trained observers disembarked at Boulogne for the first time on 29 May, and Blanford proceeded to join 206 at Boisdinghem. His introduction to the squadron was not particularly auspicious as the first things he noticed were the bomb craters resulting from a crash two weeks earlier when an aircraft with bomb load had come to grief on take-off and caught fire.

1   Blanford, Maj. J. S., DFC, 'Sans Escort' (*Cross & Cockade International*, Pt I Vol 7 No. 4 & Pt II Vol. 8 No. 1)

However, lunch in the mess was a jolly affair consisting of bully beef, 'dog biscuits' and large spring onions, the latter finding a new role as missiles being hurled from one side of the table to the other, with the padre in the direct firing line. After lunch Blanford was interviewed by the CO Major C. T. MacLaren and introduced to his pilot, Second Lieutenant Heron.

Although Blanford does not name him the padre in the Mess must have been Captain M. E. Spinney, who was posted to the squadron at Boisdinghem at around this time from the 13th East Surrey Regiment. Captain Spinney's reception on 206 was far from being a warm one, as he related:

'Regrettably, it must be said that too often the wrong type of padre had been assigned to the flying services. There was, for example, the padre who wielded a wigger-wagger as he walked among the pilots and observers about to set out on operations, exhorting them to "give 'em hell, chaps!" – and then, himself, going off to the Mess for a drink. It was not surprising, therefore, that on my arrival at Boisdinghem it was made abundantly clear to me that chaplains were not welcome; and more than one attempt was made to move me elsewhere. Fortunately, apart from being a University Scholar, I was also a Bachelor of Music and my piano playing in the Mess came to my rescue. Thereupon the ex-RFC elements changed their minds and conceded that I could remain with the squadron! Their baiting continued, however, until I shut them up by asking them if they had ever been up a front line – which I certainly had. In time I got to know these brilliant young men well and they were very decent to me once I had gained their confidence.'

The padre remembered that among that number was Rupert Atkinson and his Observer John Blanford – 'both were budding poets, like so many soldiers in those days; while Tiarks was an artist.' Another artist was Lieutenant Clayton Knight, US Army Air Corps, who specialised in aviation subjects and survived the war to become well known in America in later years. Captain Spinney recalled a flight with Victor Tiarks, who 'with a dangerous grin' flew him over to Ypres and Dunkerque. The engines were not powerful enough in those days to cope with a wind of any strength and the aircraft could do little more than hover over the shore at Dunkerque. Captain Spinney remained with the squadron until the war's end and on his demobilisation and return home was appointed Dean's Vicar and assistant organist of Lichfield Cathedral and subsequently a parish priest.[2]

The squadron's sector of operations was part of Second Army's Front stretching roughly from 10 miles north of Ypres as far as Nieppe Forest, about 20 miles SW of that city, a total of about 30 miles. By this time the German offensive in the Battle of Lys had ground to a halt and the front stabilised for the time being, but there was no shortage of activity in the air. Blanford set out on his first operation on 31 May with Heron, a bombing raid on Comines on the River Lys. The trip to the target was uneventful but on the way home they found themselves in the middle of a dogfight and in the confusion lost sight of their formation. They got through unscathed but had to search their maps for landmarks before finally reaching the home base later than expected, a case of 'beginner's luck'! The atmosphere at the time was well expressed in Rudyard Kipling's epitaph 'RAF (aged 18)';

Laughing through clouds, his milk-teeth still unshed,
Cities and men he smote from overhead.
His deaths delivered, he returned to play
Childlike, with childish things now put away.

2 Info from Library of Lichfield Cathedral states his name as Revd. Montague Herbert Spinney, parish priest until 1958 (letter to author 18/7/2001).

More raids on Comines followed until the squadron moved to Alquines, between St Omer and Boulogne on 4 June. A few days later, on 9 June, Blanford was detailed to fly a long reconnaissance with Lieutenant Gillett as pilot, which proved to be the longest and highest he ever undertook. They took off just over an hour before dawn and crossed the lines as it became light. Climbing to 17,000 feet they had a grandstand view of the lines stretching across Flanders. Towns and other landmarks were easily identified. 'We continued to climb steadily. Gillett had had a new engine installed in his aircraft the day before, and it must have been a Siddeley Puma in a thousand, for it ran like a dream. We passed over Roulers at 19,000 feet, Thielt at 20,000 (which was supposed to be a DH9's ceiling without a bomb load), and had reached 21,000 feet by the time we were half way to Courtrai on our second leg, which could well have been a record for a DH9 – at any rate I don't recall anyone else in 206 ever getting so high'. The main objective was to report on road and rail transport movements, and their aircraft was well above the range of 'Archie' and hopefully of enemy fighters. But the strain began to tell: 'By the time we changed course I was feeling bloody cold after standing up so long in the cockpit….my fingers were so stiff and numb I could hardly write my notes. Both Gillett and I were starting to feel the lack of oxygen, so we had recourse to our primitive oxygen apparatus. This involved sucking the stuff through a rubber tube that always tasted foul. I doubt if this really did us much good, as we were both feeling rather groggy by the time we began to lose height after crossing the lines. Moreover, by this time, as the circulation began to return to my frozen fingers I suffered excruciating pain for a short time. However, we got home safely in a long and slow glide, landing four hours 20 minutes after take-off, which was very near our petrol endurance limit.'

A few days later Blanford had his last flight with Lieutenant Heron, who was sadly killed the following month. He was now assigned to Lieutenant T. Roberts, a 30-year old ex-farmer from South Africa. By the end of June Blanford had flown 20 missions and amassed nearly 50 hours' combat flying, being then recommended for his Observer's badge. His appointment appeared in the London Gazette as 'Flying Officer (Observer)' – in those days 'Flying Officer' was an appointment, not a rank, which in Blanford's case was Second Lieutenant. Being a seconded officer he now held a temporary commission in the RAF which ran concurrently with his permanent commission in the Buffs.

Another member of the squadron at this time was Temporary Lieutenant (Flying Officer) Charles Eaton who arrived in May 1918 as a pilot, having served with the Royal West Surreys since enlistment as a private in 1912 at the age of 17, and remaining with his battalion throughout the early part of the war. He endured the Battle of the Somme before transferring to the Royal Flying Corps for pilot training.[3]

In the five weeks he saw service with 206 he was credited with two enemy aircraft destroyed, but his luck was soon to run out. On 29 June, a Saturday morning, he carried out a special reconnaissance of Tournai aerodrome in DH9 C1177 but he had engine failure and immediately tried to get back to Allied lines. In his own words:

'The day stands out in particular. It was clear over the target and as we approached the lines the cloud base obscured the ground at 3,000 feet. On entering the clouds, still making west, they were about 1,500 feet thick and on coming out I found that I was right on top of the end trench lines. Whether I was on the German or British side I did not know until I found the aeroplane surrounded by bursting ack-ack, and in front of me I could see the forest of Nieppe which I knew was on the British side. The aeroplane was headed west until it crashed into a shell hole. The aircraft turned over and I was thrown out. My Observer was under the wreckage and while attempting to get him out some men came running towards the crash. Immediately they were called to assist and

---

3   Information about Lt Eaton from Dr Charles Eaton (son) and Mitchell Williamson.

did so, and it was not until we dragged the Observer from the wreckage that I had another shock in finding that my helpers were Germans. The Observer was not badly injured and we were taken into the trenches, when it was found that we had come down 800 yards from the British front line and just behind the German first line of trenches.'

After his capture Eaton made a thorough nuisance of himself, escaping three times and being court-martialled twice, but he was at large near the Dutch border at the time of the Armistice. He went on to have a distinguished career in the Royal Australian Air Force and in civil aviation, serving in World War Two and later in Australia's diplomatic service making an important contribution to Australian-Indonesian relations.

It was late in June 1918 that a young Lieutenant J. B. Heppel, an observer, was posted to the squadron at Alquines. He quickly teamed up with a Canadian pilot called Russell and they were called to be interviewed at Wing HQ by the Wing Commander Van Rysveld. The conversation was brief but to the point:

'Can you shoot straight?' The airmen said they thought they could.

'You'll damn' well need to!' And that was that.

The next morning they were rostered for a bombing raid on enemy lines. They picked up the technique from the other crews, who tended to keep their eyes on the leader's aircraft and when they saw his signal, a Very light fired by his observer, they would release their bombs in a salvo. The fairly primitive bomb sights, not notable for their accuracy, and screwed on to the outside of the fuselage on the right-hand side of the observer's cockpit, were usually not to be relied upon.

Russell and Heppel did a forced-landing some time later, after they had attacked a German observation balloon. Anti-aircraft fire from the ground opened up as the balloon was winched down and the pilot was wounded in the leg. The engine conked out and they glided towards a field covered with bushes and scrub, landing through the undergrowth but tipping on the aircraft's nose. Luckily an Army Service Corps horse-drawn wagon appeared and the pilot and observer were taken to a nearby collection of dugouts which served as an HQ. An ambulance arrived which collected Russell and took him to Poperinghe Hospital where his wound was not found to be serious. The next day a Crossley tender was sent by the squadron to collect Heppel. Soon both airmen were back on operations but fortune smiled again when the engine was damaged in a fight with a German two-seater over Dunkirk. The radiator was pierced and this caused a fine spray which led to icing of the pilot's windscreen and Heppel's goggles. To make matters worse the exposed parts of Heppel's face began to be affected by frostbite but they were able to find a friendly field occupied by a French squadron flying Spads and landed safely. They were royally entertained, helped by the presence of a French Canadian officer, one of Russell's compatriots, and the aircraft was repaired. After an enormous breakfast the entire squadron turned out to bid them farewell![4]

The Squadron's success in those early days owed much to the work of the mechanics, who had to deal with the vagaries of the new BHP engine with which 206 Squadron's DH9s were among the first to be equipped:

'.........they were all experienced and skilled men, the majority of them having served with the RNAS since the first year of the War. During the months of May and June the squadron was carrying out on many occasions three raids a day, two long reconnaissances and photographic work, the last two operations being carried out by seven machines. It was necessary to strip the cam boxes after each day's work, as owing to faulty manufacture, since rectified, the exhaust valve springs were continually breaking. This meant a three hour job. It must be remembered that the squadron's work started at 3 a.m. and did not finish until 9 p.m.. The mechanics worked all night, night

---

4 Lt J. B. Heppel: personal narrative (206 Sqn Archives).

after night, and anyone walking around the hangars would see them sleeping, dead beat, for an hour whilst one of the squadron raids was in progress. On many occasions, when fine weather was continuous, this was the only sleep they got. In the annals of the squadron, these men should always be remembered as being one of the largest factors contributing to the reputation earned by the squadron.'[5]

During the summer of 1918 Sergeant Air Mechanic Leslie Holman Rowe was one of the RFC personnel posted to the squadron (to 'B' Flight) and he took part in many of the raids undertaken during the months of June and July. An account of his service has been provided by his son, Alan Rowe[6]. Sergeant Rowe's pilot was Second Lieutenant Brock MM, who had transferred from the Royal Artillery. 'Brockie was very cool in a fight but a holy terror when landing our aircraft. His reputation would often have the Mess gather outside to watch him kangaroo hop the aircraft across the field on return from a raid.' The DH9's flat glide path made it difficult for pilots to master a three-point touchdown. In case of emergencies an extra joystick was carried in the rear cockpit so that the observer could land the aircraft if the pilot had been killed or wounded.

Lieutenant Blanford's new pilot at Alquines was the Senior Flight Commander Captain Rupert Atkinson MC, a highly experienced veteran who was later to be awarded the DFC and bar and the Croix de Guerre. The war continued to be static on the Second Army Front during July but aerial activity was enlivened by the presence in the sector of the famous fighter 'circus' of von Richthofen, now led by Hermann Göring. Some tasks for the squadron were cancelled during July owing to bad weather, as Blanford explains: '…it must be remembered that aircraft in 1918 (whose sole navigational instrument was a not always reliable compass) were far more at the mercy of the elements than modern aircraft.'

Lieutenant V. C. Tiarks and his observer Sergeant W. S. Blyth were caught in a severe storm during a dawn long reconnaissance flight on 16 July, as related by Tiarks:

'Just before take off (at 3.40 a.m.) the flashing and the flickering on the southern horizon heralded an approaching storm. The CO, Major MacLaren, who at that horribly early hour came into the Mess to drink a cup of cocoa and see us off, said, looking at the flickering sky "You please yourself, but I don't think you should go, this is going to be a storm."

"Oh," I said, "It's coming from the south, by the time we get back it will have passed over."'

The CO accepted this and they took off, climbing to 17,000 feet and then crossed the Line at Roulers, where they were to start the reconnaissance, working their way south and noting all railway, road and canal movements. Then the storm hit:

'This wasn't rain, it was a deluge of falling water. It got rather dark and gloomy and occasionally we heard a sharp crack of lightning. Visibility was nil, so we went down to tree-top height; I kept my eye on the compass and kept as south-westerly as conditions permitted – I had no wish to get lost on the wrong side of the Line. Two or three times some hardy Hun, braving the elements, gave us a burst of machine gun fire; I doubt if he could see us well enough to have a chance of hitting us.' Eventually the rain stopped and they turned west and flew for some time to ensure they were on the right side of the Line, until finally spotting a large field with a concentration of Nissen huts. They landed and taxied up and a sentry with rifle came up but refused to say where they had landed, but led them to the Adjutant's Office where after a brief introduction they both enjoyed hearty breakfasts. After telephoning the squadron to say they were safe the airmen returned to their DH9 for take-off. Tiarks continued:

'I had never even swung a prop! However, I'd seen it done often enough…..as it happened it wasn't too bad. I had to do without the chokes that were usually pushed

5   History of 206 Squadron (unfinished): Compiled at RAF St Mawgan 1958.
6   Rowe, Alan, 'Some Australian Connections', Cross & Cockade.

into the inlet pipes and also I had to swing several times with the switch ON. However, she fired after five or six swings, and I climbed in.' The field had corn standing three to four feet high and the ground was very muddy after the storm but the airmen waved goodbye and got away with some anxiety, with the tail down to avoid tipping over onto the nose. When they got back they found that the radiator was stuffed with corn and green straw had wrapped itself around the undercarriage axle, and the tail skid had some souvenirs of the day!' Lieutenant Tiarks was fond of hedge-hopping, a stunt for which the DH9 was none-too suitable owing to its unreliable 240 hp Siddeley Puma engine, but on this occasion his flying prowess proved its worth.

On 24 July Captain Atkinson and Lieutenant Blanford were on a photo-reconnaissance when an oil pipe fractured. Atkinson just managed to nurse the aircraft back to the nearest airfield at St Omer, without further incident. The next day there was a combat involving enemy Pfalz fighters in which one was shot down by an American pilot on the squadron Lieutenant H. D. Stiers USAS and his observer Corporal J. Chapman. Sergeant Pacey and Sergeant Rowe forced two other enemies out of the combat area but in the low cloud they were not able to confirm these as 'kills'. On 29 July 206 formations were attacked by up to 20 Pfalz fighters on two raids to Courtrai. In the ensuing combats four of the enemy were shot down, making a total of six for that day, as two others had been shot down during a morning encounter. The squadron suffered three killed and two wounded that day. One of the victims of the morning dogfight was Lieutenant Brock and his observer Sergeant Rowe in DH9 C6289. They were part of a formation of seven aircraft which was attacked by eight Pfalz fighters. Because of engine trouble Brock's machine fell behind the others and was picked on by four enemy aircraft. In the ensuing fight Rowe was wounded but continued firing until an enemy machine appeared to turn over and plunge earthwards. Brock took violent evasive action and managed to reach Allied lines, forced-landing his machine (which turned over) alongside the 1st Australian Casualty Clearing Station at Hondeghem near St Omer, with his severely wounded observer.

The events of that day were recalled by Colonel Harry A. Schlotzhauer, US Air Force (retired), at the time a Lieutenant in the US Army Air Corps attached to 206 Squadron:

'We were on an early bombing raid at 0645 hrs that day, and from all indication it was a pretty rough trip for all concerned. I remember how worried MacLaren was over his lack of experienced personnel in making up the roster for the late afternoon raid on Courtrai, and when he asked me if I would double-up and go, there is always only one answer, and that is "Yes Sir".'[8]

The formation of seven aircraft took off at 1745 hrs for the raid on Courtrai railway station and, climbing to 15,000 feet (without oxygen), they were attacked by at least 20 Pfalz fighters just before dropping their bombs. The first victim was B7668 of Lieutenant Galloway C. Cheston, another US Army pilot, and his Observer Sergeant J. W. Pacey, pursued by four or five enemies resulting in the only fatal crash that day. Both men were killed. Another victim was the DH9 of Lieutenant Schlotzhauer, with his observer Corporal Horace W. Williams, whose aircraft was damaged by a hit in the oil tank and the observer wounded in the left arm. Continuing to fire in spite of his wound, Williams shot down one fighter and then tossed the Lewis gun overboard, hoping to get it in the way of the enemy. Schlotzhauer takes up the story in a letter to his observer in later years:

'........after the first shock of realising that I was still alive I raised my glasses and found I was covered in oil, and the pressure had dropped to zero. We had been shot

---

7   V. C. Tiarks, letter 28 Sept. 1974 among memorabilia of Sgt W. S. Blyth DFM. (206 Sqn Archives, RAF Kinloss).
8   Letter from Col H. A. Schlotzhauer to Sgt H. W. Williams (Memorabilia of Sgt H. W. Williams: 206 Sqn Archives)

Cpl (later Sgt) Observer Horace W. Williams DFM.
(CC/206)

through the oil tank. It was then that my knowledge and experience with internal combustion engines stood me in good stead – babying that engine down without the pistons or main bearing freezing......The best thing you did at that moment was to toss over the empty Lewis drums, in hopes that they would get into the slipstream of the Huns and crash their propellers – and they were that close, believe me.'

Eventually a big Red Cross was sighted west of Poperinghe 'with fields galore around it, until I got low enough to see telegraph wires and ditches, but the dear old Siddeley Puma gave two final gasps and froze....' They managed to land near the field hospital but by now Williams had lost a lot of blood but was revived by an injection, two whiskies and some rabbit pie! The following day he was taken to hospital at Bergues for an operation but began to make a rapid recovery. The CO Major MacLaren wrote to Mrs Williams commending her son for his 'fine spirit and great devotion to duty' in spite of his wound, for his actions that day. On 7 August 1918 the award of the DFM was announced in Army Orders for Corporal Williams and subsequently he was repatriated to Ripon in Yorkshire and promoted to Sergeant.[9] The citation in the London Gazette on 2 November 1918 stated that Corporal Williams 'has taken part in forty-three successful raids, showing at all times devotion to duty and affording the most valuable support to his pilot. In a recent engagement having shot down an aeroplane out of control, he continued in action although wounded in the left arm, until his ammunition was exhausted, thereby enabling one of our machines that was heavily attacked to regain the lines in safety.'

Sergeant Rowe, one of the morning's victims, was left for dead at the Casualty Clearing Station until an alert nurse spotted signs of life and he was operated on and survived, spending the next six months convalescing until discharge in December 1918. The surgeon who operated on Rowe the day he was shot down was Dr George Bell,

---

9   Sgt Williams' memorabilia are displayed at 206 Sqn, RAF Kinloss.

who later became a distinguished surgeon in Sydney. By a lucky chance Leslie Rowe went to Australia to meet that surgeon and the 'alert' nurse in 1968 to offer his personal thanks for saving his life![10] Sadly, fate was less kind to Lieutenant Brock and his new observer, who disappeared without trace over enemy lines two weeks after the forced landing. They had probably received a direct hit from enemy anti-aircraft fire.

The London Gazette of 3 June 1919 lists four awards for NCO observers of 206 Squadron. Sergeants George Betteridge, William Blyth and Holman Rowe received the DFM. Sergeant James Chapman (also 'B' Flight) received a bar to his DFM. His first DFM had been awarded in July 1918, and the citation in the London Gazette on 21 September 1918 had stated: 'During a recent raid four of our machines were attacked by twelve enemy aeroplanes. The pilot of this observer's machine was badly wounded and lost consciousness. The machine fell out of control, but Private Chapman took control from his seat and flew the machine back to the aerodrome, and landed without breaking a wire, exhibiting skill and presence of mind worthy of the highest praise.' Sergeant Chapman was one of only two Observer/Air Gunners in the RAF's World War One history to receive the award of the DFM twice.

The ground war remained quiet throughout August on the Second Army Front but further south Haig was beginning his final counter-strokes on 8 August, later called by Ludendorf 'The Black Day of the German Army'. The Hindenburg Line was finally breached by the Allies and the RAF maintained its supremacy in the air. For Lieutenant Blanford a highlight of the month was being chosen as one of the squadron representatives in 2nd Brigade RAF to meet King George V on one of his visits to the Front on 6 August.

On the operational side the crews were organised in three flights, each of six aircraft, and the daily routine alternated between at least one reconnaissance patrol per day, with the rest of the time being taken up with bombing operations. The squadron was probably not unusual in the varied composition of its personnel, including some US Army pilots who were posted to British squadrons to gain combat experience while their own units were being prepared for the Western Front.[11] John Blanford recalled how well the Americans fitted into squadron life:

'........it would have been surprising had this not proved so, in view of the heterogeneous nature of 206, already a mixture of Navy and Army traditions and habits, and composed of personnel from the UK, Canada, South Africa, Australia and Rhodesia. It was this very diversity of the elements composing 206 which produced that happy blend that was a basic reason for our success as a squadron. I need hardly add that our American comrades played their full part both in the air and in the mess, and made a great contribution to our success.'

Of the four American pilots who joined the squadron in May 1918, two became casualties shortly after Blanford's arrival. First Lieutenant John W. Leach was shot down and badly wounded on 12 June, and First Lieutenant Galloway C. Cheston was killed along with his observer during the raid to Courtrai on 29 July.

Blanford was sent on leave in mid-August after less than three months' active service, returning at the end of the month to the news that his tent-mate Lieutenant John and his pilot Captain Mathews had been killed during an attack by the crack German fighter wing 'Richthofen's Circus' led by Hermann Göring. Even at this late stage of the war there still lingered an old-fashioned chivalry among aircrew of opposing sides to exchange news about the fate of missing personnel, but on this occasion there was no word. Later, by what seemed a remarkable chance, Blanford joined a small group on a

---

10 Rowe, Alan, Cross & Cockade article.
11 America had declared war in 1917.

sightseeing trip in what had been enemy territory, now vacated by the Germans in their headlong retreat, and the crash site was found along with the two graves and a small memorial to the airmen.

September and October 1918 saw the final offensives against the German Army on the Western Front, and the day-to-day pressure on the aircrews was unrelenting. John Blanford resumed operations after his leave on 3 September with two bombing raids, on Quesnoy and Perenchies, totalling four hours 30 minutes in the air. The next day he was on a Line Patrol lasting one hour 35 minutes. On 7 September another raid on Quesnoy resulted in the engine being hit by AA fire and a forced landing on the way back. Bad weather intervened on several occasions throughout the month to hamper bombing operations which at that stage were very much a 'hit-and-miss' affair. Techniques were in their infancy and the crew of the lead aircraft in the formation had to use their judgement on approach to the target, sometimes with the aid of a crude bombsight, and the observer would fire a white Very light as a signal for the others to release their bombs.

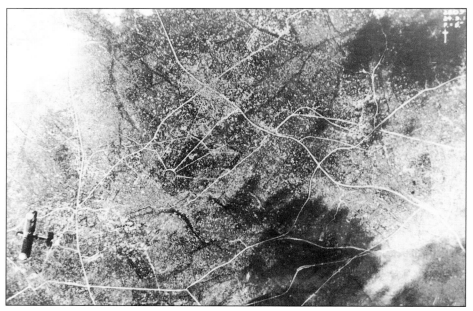

Aerial photography near Courtrai, 24 September 1918. Note the DH9 in bottom left of the photo.
(CC/206)

Aerial photographic techniques were more precise, and usually the operational height was around 16,000 to 18,000 feet. 206 Squadron was often praised at Brigade level for the good quality of photographs taken, a considerable compliment when one considers that the aircraft carried only a very limited oxygen supply and no parachutes.

There were several raids on enemy ammunition dumps in the Courtrai area during the latter part of September, such as on the 24th when Blanford and his pilot Lieutenant J. S. Cumming were detailed for a raid. On the return home they had engine trouble and only just made it back to Alquines. On the 28th the Second Army began its final offensive but the low cloud and heavy rain kept the squadron grounded until later in the day. With steadily improving weather the 29th saw John Blanford acting as observer on a dawn Special Reconnaissance with pilot Captain Rupert Atkinson, 206 Senior Flight Commander, along the entire front to ascertain the extent of the previous day's breakthrough. This together with two bombing raids made up a total of six hours' operational flying that day. It was clear that at long last and after four years of war the

Allies had broken through and were advancing. Rupert Atkinson, already the holder of the Military Cross, was awarded the DFC during the month for his work in photo reconnaissance and for his leadership of bombing raids. In the citation for his DFC (London Gazette 2 November 1918) the occasion of an attack by eight Fokkers on his solitary machine was described, during a reconnaissance at 15,000 feet, and his shooting down of one of the attackers.

John Blanford survived being shot down by AA fire on 5 October. This was one of the squadron's unluckiest days during Blanford's time as four out of ten aircraft detailed for a raid on Courtrai were shot down. Courtrai was well known as a dangerous spot for 'Archie' so the target was to be attacked from the rear to achieve maximum surprise from a height of about 10,000 feet. Atkinson and Blanford were in the lead aircraft and as they began their bombing run the Germans opened up with the deadly 88 mm Skoda AA guns, accurate at 10,000 feet. They got through and with bombs gone Blanford looked astern and saw the rear formation being pounced on by at least a dozen Fokkers. Atkinson slowed to 80 mph instead of the planned 120, to enable the formation to catch up but they were now caught by the German gunners and took a hit from AA directly below the aircraft. Severely damaged but uninjured they limped home with a pronounced list to port and losing petrol. The flying controls were jammed and to attempt to correct the list Blanford leaned over the starboard side as far as he could, jamming his heels against the gun mounting (Scarffe mounting). Eventually Atkinson's skill brought them over friendly lines and they crash-landed near St Jean, north-east of Ypres. Although still shaken they were taken in hand by a nearby Army Service Corps (later RASC) unit, given a hot meal and fortified by tea and rum before being collected later in the day for the new squadron base of Ste Marie Cappel. Later, in 2nd Brigade's recommendation for the immediate award of the DFC to Lieutenant Blanford, his pilot Captain Atkinson stated that it was entirely due to Blanford that the machine was brought down safely and without injury to either of them.

Another casualty on 5 October was DH9 D560 with pilot Lieutenant Knight USAS, and observer Second Lieutenant J. H. Perring. The aircraft was shot down at 0830 hrs near Aelbecke by Oberleutnant H. Auffahrt (his 23rd 'kill'), and was last seen gliding west towards British lines but too far away to reach them. The CO Major MacLaren

Schedule No. (to be left blank)	Unit	Regtl. No.	Rank and Name (Christian names must be stated)	Action for which commended (Date and place of action must be stated)	Recommended by	Honour or Reward	(To be left blank)
	ROYAL AIR FORCE. 206 Squadron.	--	2nd.Lieut. JOHN STEPHEN BLANFORD, The Buffs (East Kent Regt.) and R.A.F.	When returning from a raid on COURTRAI on the 5th. October, 1918, the machine in which he was flying had all the controls shot away, bar those of the rudder, and started to fall out of control. 2nd.Lieut. BLANFORD jammed his heels against the Scarffe Mounting and leaned over the side from his knees upwards, and brought the machine back into a straight glide. He remained in this position from 12000 feet until the machine crashed in some shell holes N.E. YPRES. The Pilot, Capt. ATKINSON, MC.DFC., states it was entirely due to the Observer that he was able to get the machine down and land it without injury to himself and the Observer. In addition, on 14-10-18, he destroyed one FOKKER biplane in flames, when returning from a raid on SWEVEGHEM DUMP.	Brigadier General, Commanding 2nd. Brigade, ROYAL AIR FORCE.	THE DISTINGUISHED FLYING CROSS.	

Recommendation for award of DFC for 2/Lt Blanford, 5 October 1918.
(CC/206)

Date and Hour. 1918	Wind Direction and Velocity.	Machine Type and No.	Pilot Lt.	Time. Mins	Height.	Course.	Remarks.
Sep. 5	S×5b20	5750	Knight	75	2500	Line Patrol - with	Cabin Natters
6	8.40 A			60	9000	Raid	Cloudy W.O.
7	7.05 A			120	15000	Do Quesnoy (3/12)	escort misty
16	10.05			195	16200	Escort long recon chased by 3+	
						one down our patrol	
						Roulers Courtrai Menin Lille	
18	1.25			45	6000	Raid W.O. clouds	
20	11.45			-	-	Do Courtrai S.O.S.	
24	11.30	8878		40	3000	Engine test	
	4.0			10	2000	Raid engine vibrating	
25	4.05			170	15000	Escort long recon chased by 3+	
27	11.30			170	15000	Raid Courtrai 9 Coopers AA the place	
28	1.15			120	10000	Menin 3/112	
28	4.15			105	10000	Courtrai 3/112	
29	1.35			90	11000	Menin 3/112	
	4.45			105	11500	Halluin 3/112 where they are	
	1.30			20	4000	W.O. AA the place	
				105	4000	Menin 3/112 Shot up roads	
						Came on return Down at 149 Sqdn	
31	5.10			20	3000	149 Sd to home Thunderstorm	
				1145			
				24-K			

Extracts from Log Book of 2/Lt J. H. Perring
(CC/206)

wrote to Mrs Perring the next day regretfully announcing that her son 'failed to return' from the raid. However the news came through later that both men were prisoners-of-war.[12]

On the 14th Atkinson and Blanford were leading in a raid on Sweveghem ammunition dump near Courtrai and on the way home were attacked by three Fokkers, one of which closed in on the formation only to be shot down by Blanford. This episode played a part in Blanford's recommendation for a DFC.

Meanwhile the Second Army was advancing steadily. Lille collapsed on 18 October and Courtrai on the 20th. Later in the month there was another squadron move, this time to Linselles, recalled by Lieutenant B. H. Rook:

'The vehicle in which some of us had set out when the squadron was about to move from Ste Marie Cappel to Linselles was held up overnight by an element of a Guards Regiment because the area was said to be still harbouring Germans. In fact, when our squadron finally took possession of the aerodrome the following afternoon we learnt that the enemy had vacated it only that morning. We were warned to beware of booby traps, but the enemy appeared to have left in a hurry. Flowers had been left on the table in the Officers' Mess and in the evening we had our first meal in former enemy territory. In the middle of the meal the ticking of some mechanical device became noticeable and we quickly cleared out of the Mess – only to discover that the ticking had emanated from an alarm clock which an unknown wag had placed against the side of the hut.'

Lieutenant Heppel recalled the move to Linselles, and the mud due to the heavy rain which caused the lorry containing all the officers' stores and baggage to slide off the road into a ditch. 'We therefore had to forage for food that night in the surrounding countryside but as the Germans had been there only a few days before there was

---

12 *DH4/DH9 File* by Sturtivant & Page (Air-Britain) p159.

practically none to be had anywhere......Russell and I, with a few others, walked several miles and found a farm where, with many apologies for having nothing better to offer, they regaled us with beer – very sour! – potatoes (fried) and slices cut from their last old horse!' Having no bedding they were forced to sleep in their Sidcot suits.

As the Germans retreated there was a great welcome for the Allies among many of the people who had endured four years of occupation. Heppel recalled an occasion after he and Russell had made a lucky escape from a dogfight with several enemy fighters, later discovered to be the Fokkers of von Richthofen's 'Circus', now led by Hermann Göring:

'We landed in a turnip field near the Franco-German frontier. Several children came running out to us from a nearby farmhouse and invited us to go back with them. The farmer's wife and eldest daughter welcomed us effusively as the first Allied troops they had seen since the departure of the Germans, but were distressed that they had no coffee or food to offer us! The enemy had been there up till only a few days previously and on leaving had taken all food supplies and all the young men – including her son. The farmer himself had been shot by Uhlans at the beginning of the war.' Later the crew of an observation balloon arrived and in due course the aircraft was collected and taken away for repairs. Before they left the airmen promised the family that they would return later and drop coffee, chocolate, soap and other essentials from the air, an undertaking that they were able to carry out. A few days before the Armistice the airmen flew low over Lille and found the whole town decorated with blue, white and red bunting and crowds of people in the streets waving handkerchiefs as they passed over!

It was from Linselles that one of the last major bombing raids of the war was carried out by the squadron, on 30 October against Sotteghem. The objective was about 35 miles from Linselles and 24 miles due west of Brussels, and an important road and rail junction along one of the German Army's main escape routes. On the morning of the 30th John Blanford had taken part in an unopposed raid on Grammont. At around 1415 hrs he took off again with Captain Atkinson as his pilot leading a formation of seven aircraft heading for Sotteghem. They flew unopposed to the target and dropped their bombs from 14,000 feet in poor visibility. Turning for home they sighted at least 20 Fokkers and were attacked from astern and then from both sides. In the fierce dogfight which followed, lasting for nearly half an hour, all the ammunition was exhausted and two of the observers had to fire Very lights at the attackers. Four Fokkers were claimed to have been shot down and the 206 aircraft sustained damage only, and made it back to base as the light faded. John Blanford had a lucky escape as he discovered later that a burst of Spandau bullets had passed through the floor of his cockpit and out through the side of the fuselage. After the Armistice, the crews met some of their German adversaries that day when they were stationed at Bickendorf, Cologne, and the Fokker pilots recalled the combat and that they were overwhelmed by the better side!

By 4 November the Second Army had forced the Germans back across the River Scheldt and the war was obviously nearing its end. In spite of a lack of serviceable aircraft Atkinson and Blanford led another raid on Sotteghem on the 4th and on the 11th they led the last raid of the war for 206 Squadron, on Lessines. A raid on the 10th was cancelled because of the rapidity of the army advance and that evening news of the Armistice came through, effective from the 11th.

There is little detail available on the 1917 fighter squadron but taking stock of the squadron's operations during the period from 9 March to 11 November 1918, 156 successful bombing raids had been carried out, with $116^1/_4$ tons of bombs being dropped. The number of successful reconnaissance missions had been 478 and 12,000 photographs had been taken. Twenty-six enemy aircraft had been destroyed with 23 being reported out of control. One enemy observation ballon had been destroyed. Of

Air and ground crews of 'A' Flight taken on Armistice Day, 11 Nov. 1918, at Linselles. Aircraft is DH9 serial D569. Note the Bessoneau marquee-type hangar in rear which the RAF used when moving forward behind our advancing armies.
2nd row left to right: Ground Crew Sgt; 2/Lt Byrne; Lt G.A. Pitt; next unknown; Capt. R. N. G. Atkinson (died during 'flu epidemic 1919); 2/Lt Garside; 2/Lt J. S. Blanford; 2/Lt Learmont. Sgt George Betteridge (Pitt's Observer) in 4th row 7th from right.
(CC/206)

squadron casualties, 26 men had been killed with 13 wounded and 22 personnel unaccounted for. Squadron awards and decorations in this period included one award of the OBE, one bar to the DFC, nine DFCs, one bar to the DFM, four DFMs, twelve Allied Decorations and eight Mentions in Despatches.

The work of the squadron received fulsome praise from Major-General Sir John Salmond KCB, CMG, DSO in January 1919 who said in an address to the officers: '….that the squadron had one of the finest reputations in France, and was regarded as the finest squadron of its type. The photographic work has been wonderful; on some occasions the Army requesting the squadron to stop, as they could not cope with the supply. The formation flying has been the finest for a squadron of its type, machines reaching their objective, and in doing so beating off many attacks, destroying quite a number of enemy aircraft, and not suffering heavy casualties themselves. It was a record to be proud of.'[13]

None of this would have been possible without the sterling work of the ground crews, often working in the most appalling conditions in bitter cold at all times of the day and night, in muddy fields, using tents and stables as workshops and dealing with battle damage as well as routine servicing. 'No. 206 was also the first to receive the BHP engine and had to discover its foibles and weaknesses in battle conditions; there were many. At the end of every day the cam boxes on all aircraft had to be stripped to replace the exhaust valve springs which were continually breaking. The mechanics were all working from 5am to 9pm every day and it is fair to say that without them the squadron could not have maintained its operational effectiveness.'[14] Among that distinguished band of ground crew were Chief Mechanics Morris and W. T. 'Lofty' Bates whose names should rank highly in the annals of the squadron.

---

13 75th Anniversary history (1991) pp15-16
14 ibid. p16

CHAPTER 3

PEACETIME ROLE AND DISBANDMENT

'Owing to the breakdown of transport – both road and rail – across the areas devastated by shell and bomb, the turkeys and plum puddings sent out to us from Blighty never reached us – which boded ill for the 25th!'

Lt J. B. Heppel, Observer 206 Squadron, Bickendorf, December 1918.

With the fighting over there was the inevitable period of rejoicing after the tension of over four years of war, but very shortly the squadron were on the move again in the wake of the advancing Second Army which was now to form part of the allied occupation in Germany. So on 26 November the squadron left Linselles and were now to be based at Nivelles, south of Brussels, formerly a large German airfield and aircraft supply depot. Lieutenant B. H. Rook described the journey:

'During the journey from Linselles to Nivelles we passed through the populated district of Lille and our car was held up by the excited inhabitants. On arrival at Nivelles a wonderful repast of steak was produced at the station restaurant. Later, we learned that we had been regaled with meat from a horse slaughtered by the retreating Germans.'

The hangar and hut accommodation at Nivelles were excellent and the Germans had only just vacated the base as 206 were arriving, leaving behind various items of equipment and even a few aircraft. As we have seen, the Belgians proved generous hosts and were able to produce quantities of steaks, lager beer and many other treats which had mysteriously been in short supply during the German occupation. Lieutenant Heppel recalled that the town was celebrating the disinterment of the famous reliquary

'Hun machines' scattered around Nivelles.
(CC/206)

Group of officers of the squadron at Bickendorf, Cologne, January 1919. Some 8 or 10 were absent on leave or sick (Spanish 'flu)

Left to right – front row: Lt J. S. Cumming (Canadian) – later killed flying Army Air Mail; Lt B. H. Rook, Recording Officer (Adjutant) & ex-No. 6 RNAS; Capt R. E. Burn (Canadian); Capt. R. N. G. Atkinson; Maj. C. T. MacLaren, CO and ex-No. 6 RNAS; Capt. T. Roberts (South African); Lt G. A. Pitt, ex-No. 6 RNAS; Capt. 'Daddy' W. A. Carruthers (Canadian); 2/Lt A. J. Garside

Second row: Unknown; 2/Lt H. H. Seddon; 2/Lt Campbell (Canadian); 2/Lt Trevor Evans; 2/Lt 'Duggie' Haig (Canadian); 2/Lt R Ramsay (Rhodesian); 2/Lt Denny; unknown; Chief Master Mechanic Morris, ex-No. 6 RNAS

Third row: 2/Lt Thompson; 2/Lt Knee; 2/Lt H. P. Hobbs; Lt J. S. Common (Canadian); 2/Lt 'Pop' Welch (Canadian); Lt J. B. Heppel; 2/Lt J. D. Russell (Canadian); 2/Lt (ex-Sgt) G. Packman

Fourth row: 2/Lt Byrne (Australian); 2/Lt H. McLean; Lt E. B. Green; Lt H. O. F. Berrington Blew (South African); 2/Lt Morgan.   (CC/206)

'206 does it again' or '206 rules – OK!'
2nd Brigade Soccer Cup, 1918/19, at Cologne.
(CC/206)

of St Gertrude, who was the foundress and first abbess of the beautiful Benedictine Abbey which was the pride of the town. This treasure had been hurriedly buried in a deep pit just hours before the Germans had arrived at the beginning of the war, a sensible precaution owing to its reputed value of six million francs! Throughout the war the Germans had searched in vain for this and other reliquaries. On the festive day these treasures were carried shoulder high in procession to the great abbey amid much rejoicing, a not-to-be-forgotten spectacle.

It was during December that there were the first signs of the outbreak of the so-called Spanish 'flu which was in the end to lead to more than 20 million deaths in the post-war period, more than had been killed during the Great War. Most of the squadron went down with it, one of the first being Lieutenant Blanford, and such was the severity of his illness that it was early in 1919 before he fully recovered. On 20 December the squadron moved to Bickendorf, Germany, on the outskirts of Cologne. There was the inevitable friction with certain elements in the local population from time to time but living accommodation was provided in the homes of local people. Many of the German population were somewhat formal but not unfriendly, although a few continued to carry illicit weapons. They were beginning to realise that they were more fortunate here than in other parts of Germany where food was short and there was communist-inspired agitation. The Officers' Mess was in a large baronial mansion nearly opposite a huge equestrian statue of Kaiser Wilhelm I. John Blanford recalled that the atmosphere in the Mess was not quite what it had been, with the start of demobilisation and many new personnel posted in from another DH9 unit, 211 Squadron. There were a few familiar faces like Rupert Atkinson but 'the old 206 was no more.'[1]

After the excitement of war there was a general feeling of anti-climax, even boredom. Flying was confined to air tests and the new task of operating on the Second Army Air Mail Service between Cologne and GHQ at Spa, starting on 1 January 1919 and continuing until the service ended on 7 July. This mail service was part of an ambitious pioneering scheme devised towards the end of 1918 to convey official army as well as ordinary mail by air to the troops stationed in France, Flanders and Germany. In effect, it was the first organised aerial post and one of the purposes was to utilise the experience gained in aerial navigation during the war in a peacetime role – a classic example of the application of advances in military aviation for civilian uses.[2] There were many problems to contend with, not least the European winter weather. The pilots flew solo with the mail bags stored in the observer's cockpit. Sadly on one of these flights on 31 January Lieutenant Charles Cumming and his observer 2nd Lt Andrew Waters were killed when their DH9A E8877 caught fire in the air and crashed. They are both buried in Cologne Southern Cemetery. On 4 March Brigadier-General Ludlow-Hewitt of the Air Staff sent a letter of appreciation to the commanding officers of the squadrons taking part in the scheme, Nos 57, 99, 103, 120 and 206 Squadrons: 'The GOC wishes to convey to you his high appreciation of the postal work carried out by your squadron. The weather conditions have been very unfavourable, but in spite of the fact that pilots have had to fly at extremely low heights and often in actual mist, a high measure of success has been obtained in the delivery of mails throughout the entire route.'[3]

Cologne's nightlife helped to lift the gloom and there were some memorable squadron parties, as on the night the squadron were entertaining No. 4 Squadron Australian Flying Corps. As events reached their climax the Australians turned their attention to the nearby large equestrian statue outside and painted the Kaiser's charger with aircraft dope in full Zebra colours, including every detail of what had been the

1 Blanford, 'Reminiscences'.
2 Report on 'Aerial Postal Services', Maj. E. E. Gawthawn, 1919
3 Quoted in L. W. C. Pearce-Gervis, *Britain's First Aerial Mails* (MS, RAF Museum).

stallion's anatomy! As a grand finale the CO's chamber-pot was 'borrowed' and ceremoniously placed as a crown on top of the Kaiser's head! The local Germans were definitely not amused and given the resistance of aircraft dope to normal removal by water and even petrol there were still faint signs of the zebra stripes on the statue for some time afterwards. Other off-duty activities included soccer in which 206's team won the Second Brigade Cup in the 1918-1919 season.

In March 1919 the sad news reached the squadron that Captain Rupert Atkinson MC, DFC and Bar, Croix de Guerre (Belgium), had died as a result of Spanish 'flu. There were many moving tributes to this courageous veteran who had enlisted at the beginning of the war in the Middlesex Regiment before transferring to the Royal Flying Corps in 1916, finally joining 206 Squadron in June 1918. A lesser known fact about him at the time was his poetry writing, some of which was published in the *Daily Mail*. *A Royal Flying Corps Prayer*, written by him in 1917, sums up the quality of his life as well as the sacrifices made by many of his comrades at the time:

O Spirits, who for ever fly,
Banish the fears that terrify,
Stifle the horror of being afraid,
Still the conscience that would upbraid.
Give me no chance to hesitate,
Let me go out and meet my fate
As all men do, so I may be
One of your knightly company.
(Rupert Atkinson 1917[4])

As demobilisation continued most of the war veterans were no longer with the squadron. Lieutenant John Blanford rejoined his regiment, the Buffs, in the very different role of a platoon commander in Fermoy, Ireland, where the 206 days seemed like an age away though never forgotten. By now the days of the squadron were once again numbered. In May it moved back to Maubeuge in France, and in the following month to Heliopolis and then Helwan, Egypt, to undertake a policing role in that part of the Empire. On 1 February 1920 the squadron was redesignated No. 47 Squadron, bringing to a close this illustrious early period of its history.

Westland-built DH9A F1051 of 206 Sqn, Cologne 1919.
('Sans Escort', *Cross and Cockade International*)

4 75th Anniv. History p15 & Blanford, 'Reminiscences'.

CHAPTER 4

COASTAL COMMAND AND THE LAST DAYS OF PEACE

'The squadron pilots were very excited at this time – September 1936 – as they had been equipped with one of the most modern aircraft, the Avro Anson Mark I – a beautiful silver bird. Believe it or not a monoplane had been introduced in the RAF.'

AC2 Bill Parkes, Bircham Newton 1936.

It was against the background of the rise of the dictators, Hitler and Mussolini, and increasing threats to international peace that the Royal Air Force began to reorganise and expand by the middle of the 1930s. After 1934 Hitler had announced Germany's rearmament programme, and during 1936 Mussolini was engaged in his aggressive war in Abyssinia and in March of the same year Hitler had re-occupied the Rhineland. The League of Nations seemed powerless to act in the face of armed threats in Europe. New aircraft, new squadrons and new airfields were planned for the RAF, and a new 'Command' system was established during 1936, Training, Bomber, Coastal and Fighter Commands.

Thus No. 206 Squadron was re-born on 15 June 1936 at Royal Air Force Manston from personnel of 'C' Flight, 48 Squadron, under Squadron Leader A. H. Love, being designated No. 206 GR (General Reconnaissance) Squadron, initially within Training Command. The unit took delivery of 24 Avro Anson aircraft, each powered by two Siddeley Cheetah IX engines, and the following month moved to Bircham Newton in Norfolk under the command of Wing Commander F. J. Vincent. In August the squadron was transferred to No. 16 (Reconnaissance Group) Coastal Command, beginning its long and proud maritime tradition. As one of the earliest units of its type, the squadron acted as a training unit for flying boat, GR and Blenheim squadrons and in due course helped to establish what were to become the core Hudson units of Coastal Command, 224, 233, 220 and 269 Squadrons, the latter two serving with 206 for a time at Bircham Newton. The Anson, or 'Faithful Annie' as it became known, represented a major step forward in aircraft design   as the first monoplane to enter squadron service and the first with a retractable undercarriage, although the latter operation was only achieved by hundreds of manual backward turns on a winding handle.

Those early days at Bircham Newton were recalled by Bill Parkes, then Aircraftman Second Class (AC2), who was posted to the Station in 1936 after passing out from Uxbridge. He claimed that he was only posted to Bircham Newton by default as his original posting was cancelled owing to injuries received during celebrations after the passing-out parade! His arrival at Bircham was not particularly auspicious:

'I arrived at a small town called Docking, about 3 km from Bircham, and I discovered there was no transport to Bircham so I phoned the Station and was informed by the RAF Police that there was a Stand-Down and all the staff were away and the transport section closed. Therefore I had to make my own way and decided that I could not walk and carry a kitbag, suitcase etc so I decided to look for some other method of travel. I saw a man driving a horse and cart outside the railway station and asked him if he knew of anyone going to Bircham. Now the cart was covered in manure as he had been

MAP (drawn by Robin Woolven)

Squadron Bases from 1936

delivering a load to a field nearby. He was very friendly and told me he was passing the Station and would be delighted to take me there. He had some straw to cover the manure so I joined him. I had a little difficulty understanding his speech (an Irishman and a Norfolk speaker) but we arrived at the Guardroom, close up to the door to ensure that the staff had the full benefit of the scent.....I booked in. The staff did not appreciate my carriage.'

As 'the lowest form of life' – an AC2 - Bill Parkes was given the job of manual control to raise and lower the Anson's undercarriage – well over 100 revolutions – but he got what he wanted – plenty of flying hours!

He was posted to 220 Squadron but well recalled the rivalry between 206, 220 and 269, the latter soon to be posted to Abbotsinch in Scotland (now Glasgow Airport). There was intensive training on the new Mk I Ansons and there were some mishaps:

'The pilots were never used to having an aircraft which had a retractable undercarriage and a landing speed a little higher than what they were used to, so with all the other instruments and those not in the same position they had a difficult task. No warning e.g. horn sounded for the new retractable undercarriage – just two green knobs

Anson early mishap c. 1937-38.
(L.A. Smith)

appeared when the u/c was fully up. Now something had to happen and it did! Over a period of about 14 days five Ansons landed with undercarriage fully retracted. Our CO was not too pleased. Fortunately both squadrons were guilty so the rage was shared!'

In October 1936 Wing Commander Vincent was replaced by Wing Commander H. O. Long. A period of hard training followed while the squadron established itself with new aircraft in a new role. There was a chance to show off the Ansons to the general public during the Empire Air Day on Saturday 29 May 1937, but maritime reconnaissance over the North Sea took up the bulk of training time, along with gunnery and bombing practice, and formation flying. At this stage little attempt was made to equip the Ansons for an anti-submarine role as it was felt that Asdic fitted to destroyers would be sufficient in a future war[1]. In July 1937 the squadron was employed on coast defence exercises, operating from Woodsford, Dorset, and in September there was an exercise with the

---

1 Asdic – ship-borne sonar detection equipment.

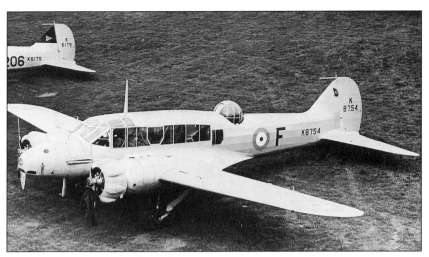

Anson K8754 of 206 Squadron at Bircham Newton, pre-war.
(CC/206)

Home Fleet, the first of many, in which aircraft had the task of locating, shadowing and practice-bombing of cruisers.

On 4 January 1938 16 aircraft and 27 officers with 114 other ranks were detached to Leuchars for the squadron's first Armament Training Camp, which lasted until the 31st. In the same month King George VI approved the new Squadron Badge and on 11 March this was presented to the Squadron by Air Vice-Marshal H. M. Cave-Brown-Cave DSO, DFC, AFC, Air Officer Commanding No. 16 Group. This consisted of the 'octopus' symbol in the centre of the badge, with the motto 'Nihil Nos Effugit' ('Naught Escapes Us'), appropriately summing up the maritime role of the squadron.

Exercises with the Home Fleet returning from Gibraltar took place during March and in July a detachment of 16 aircraft was sent to Boscombe Down to transport 116 OTC cadets to various locations – the first and by no means the last use of Coastal Command aircraft for the transport role.

According to some eyewitnesses at the time there was something of the atmosphere of a 'Gentleman's Club' at permanent pre-war RAF stations like Bircham Newton, at least for the officers. There was a new officers' mess and accommodation was generally of a high standard. Batmen were available to cater for most needs of the officers and there were the weekly dining-in nights, even if this might prove somewhat irksome to married officers living at some distance from the station in places like Old Hunstanton. The most serious crimes seemed to be getting into debt, being unable to pay the mess bill, followed by damaging aeroplanes. Shooting parties and dinner invitations with local landowners were commonplace and with up to 51 days' annual leave allocated plus one long weekend every month there was ample leisure time to pursue sports like golf, sailing and tennis at nearby Hunstanton and Brancaster. For evening entertainment there were the local village pubs and facilities in towns like Hunstanton and King's Lynn. Given Bircham Newton's relative isolation from the more populated areas of the country it was not impossible to combine cross-country training flights over a weekend with the need to collect a consignment of wine or champagne, or turkeys at Christmas.

Training needs were not neglected, and several exercises during the summer months tested the efficiency of the air arm and ground defences against air attack. One of these was planned for 5 to 7 August, 1938, involving much of eastern England and the Midlands. There was to be a complete 'black-out' on the ground with two opposing forces, the 'Westland' defending force and the 'Eastland' attacking force. The former included 23 fighter squadrons and 14 bomber squadrons, along with ground defences and the Observer Corps. The attacking 'Eastland' force comprised 36 bomber squadrons plus Nos 206 and 220 Squadrons from Bircham Newton. Other stations taking part included Marham, Feltwell and Mildenhall. In the event cloud and thick fog prevented the Bircham squadrons from taking part at all and tragedy occurred when a Harrow bomber from Feltwell crashed at Bury St Edmunds with the loss of the entire crew.

The War Defence Scheme was brought into operation on 25 September and all personnel were recalled to be available for immediate operations, and camouflaging of aircraft and other similar tasks were carried out. The two weeks from 31 October saw daily visits from Spitfires of No. 19 Squadron, based at Duxford, for fighter affiliation exercises.

Later in the year tragedy struck 206 Squadron when an Anson (K8836) failed to return from a night navigation exercise in bad weather off Flamborough Head in Yorkshire, on 1 November, no trace of the aircraft ever being found. The crew were posted missing, Pilot Officer M. A. Scott, AC1 R. W. S. Rae and AC2 D. A. Wilson.

A vivid account of squadron life at the time has been provided by the late Vernon Buckman who was posted to the squadron in December 1938. In his *Memories of Life with 206 (GR) Squadron* he recalled how he left No. 6(B) Squadron based at Ramleh in Palestine without regrets but on the homeward journey on the troopship Somersetshire in a northerly blizzard he pondered his new posting:

'Hearing that I was to join 206 Squadron caused me no qualms for I knew nothing about it, but the dreaded words "Bircham Newton" reduced me to the depths of despair for it was the most feared posting in the UK in those days.' He arrived at Docking Station, close to the airfield in the evening in snow three feet deep. No transport was available that day so he spent his first day back in 'Blighty' in front of a fire in the station waiting room. The next day, in desperation, he followed the horse-drawn snow plough for the two miles to Bircham Newton on foot, with his kitbags balanced on the boards of the plough!

'I was warmly welcomed at 206, particularly by Corporal Harry Miller, who ran the squadron orderly room with remarkable efficiency (an early "Radar" from M.A.S.H.?), and who from that moment on looked after me as he did the rest of the squadron. That warmth stayed with me throughout my four years with 206 – the longest time I spent with any one unit in my 40 years of service.' His hopes for a long spell of leave to see his fiancée were dashed by the CO, Wing Commander D'Aeth[2], who informed him he could have a long weekend but it was essential he accompanied the squadron to Leuchars early in the New Year for the annual firing practice, as he was the only gunner on the squadron with active service experience.

On returning to Bircham late in January 1939 Vernon was promoted to sergeant and put in charge of the squadron radio section, which included responsibility not only for the equipment but also for the training of air wireless operators and for the maintenance of carrier pigeons. The squadron was honoured by being allowed to fly the King's birds from the lofts at Sandringham.

Serious training continued through the months of 1939, as the international scene darkened. Vernon continues: 'We did much more refuelling and rearming, navigation exercises much further out to sea, intensive fishery patrols and much more night flying. Each aircraft had two pilots, generally both "astronav" qualified, because even at this stage the only navigation aids required radio transmissions from the ground or from the

---

2   Sqn Ldr D'Aeth had replaced Sqn Ldr H. H. Martin as CO on 9 January 1939, the latter being posted to the Staff College, Andover. D'Aeth was promoted to Wg Cdr on 1 April 1939.

aircraft. However, many very complex navigation exercises were staged over the North Sea using astro or dead reckoning, with extremely detailed logs having to be kept. Some time after debriefing, the squadron received most searching queries regarding position, time, heading and height. Although few knew then that they were under trial radiolocation (later radar) surveillance, such snooping certainly raised eyebrows![3] Also in early 1939 I attended a course to learn about Standard Beam Approach (SBA) which was later installed at Bircham as our first introduction to bad weather landing aids. It was a copy of the German Lorenz system.'

Vernon regarded the Anson as a 'pansy' aeroplane compared to 'proper' machines like the Hart and Vildebeest. However, he acknowledged that it was manoeuvrable and rugged, these qualities being just about its only defence, and it was useful for reconnaissance. It was to the chagrin of the squadron that their sister unit, No. 220 Squadron, moved to Thornaby in August 1939 to re-equip with the Hudson:

'During 1939 and until we converted to Hudsons in early 1940 we lost about ten aircraft. Of these, two were missing, one ditched off Calais (probably K6187 on 9 September 1939), two flopped on Bircham airfield (which was of grass), and one was lost in a bad mid-air collision in full view of the airfield, resulting in many fatalities' (possibly N9897 which collided with a 235 Sqn Blenheim 25 May 1940).

As the months passed, preparations for war seemed to involve the painting and re-painting the aircraft for camouflage, and indeed anything else that moved. How much this extra weight burdened the already under-powered Ansons is open to question. The other visible sign of impending crisis was the continual posting-in of reserve personnel for training who were then posted-out, and the process began again. Some 'Class C' reservists were veterans of the Great War. Most reservists were very keen but lacked formal training and the complexities of the Anson were very baffling for the trainee electricians. However, one bonus for Vernon was that he was relieved of the daily supervision of the pigeons: 'This was no sinecure, for not only did they need to tend the birds in their loft in the hangar, but had to provide a cage with two birds for collection by the wireless operator when proceeding on all maritime flights. The regal source of these birds and their very high intrinsic value, made me extremely careful!'

The last full month of peace, August 1939, saw 206 on a home defence exercise over the North Sea on the 8th, locating and shadowing high speed launches and on the 11th there was a search for a missing Wellington which had been lost at sea. The days of peace were almost over as international tension built over the German-Polish question. On the 20th a state of emergency had been declared for the RAF and on 1 September, the day German troops marched into Poland, general mobilisation was ordered by the Air Council. On 3 September at 11 a.m. the country was once again at war.

---

3 Bawdsey Research Station was pioneering radar trials at this time.

CHAPTER 5

THE WAR AT BIRCHAM NEWTON 1939-1941

*'We landed at Bircham. It was a lovely June evening.......The position looked hopeless.
It worried me that I was to belong to a generation that was beaten.'*

Jack Holywell: Memoirs of Life with 206 Squadron 1940-41.

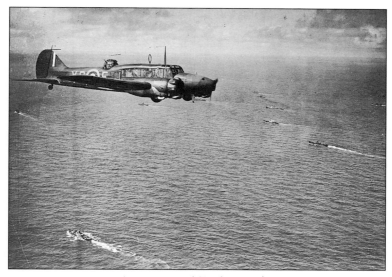

Anson on patrol, North Sea 1940.
(Imperial War Museum Photo Ref. HU63066)

As the AOC-in-C Coastal Command, Air Marshal Sir Frederick W. Bowhill, surveyed the scene from his headquarters at Northwood, Middlesex, in September 1939 he might have been forgiven for a passing doubt or two about the resources at his disposal and the formidable opponent they faced. He had four groups under his command comprising 19 operational squadrons, with 298 aircraft on strength of which around 170 were serviceable at any one time. This was to guard the shores of a maritime island nation with an enormous coastline, facing a threat from a Luftwaffe which numbered well over 4,000 aircraft, compared to a total strength of the Royal Air Force of some 2,451 aircraft. These figures illustrate the comparative starvation of resources which was the lot of Coastal Command but there was also the fact of the obsolescence of the aircraft which were the backbone of the command, the Avro Anson and the Vildebeest, the latter possessing a design that dated back to 1928. Bomber Command was able to claim the lion's share of resources of longer-range and multi-engined aircraft.

Bircham Newton was part of No. 16 Group Coastal Command, commanded by Air Commodore R. L. G. Marix DSO, with headquarters at Chatham. The two squadrons present at the station, No. 206 and the Vildebeests of No. 42 Squadron, had responsibility to provide air cover for convoys between Flamborough Head and Orfordness, handing over to aircraft based at Thornaby (north) and Detling (south). Also there would be anti-submarine sweeps to the enemy coastline, and continual vigilance to assist the Royal

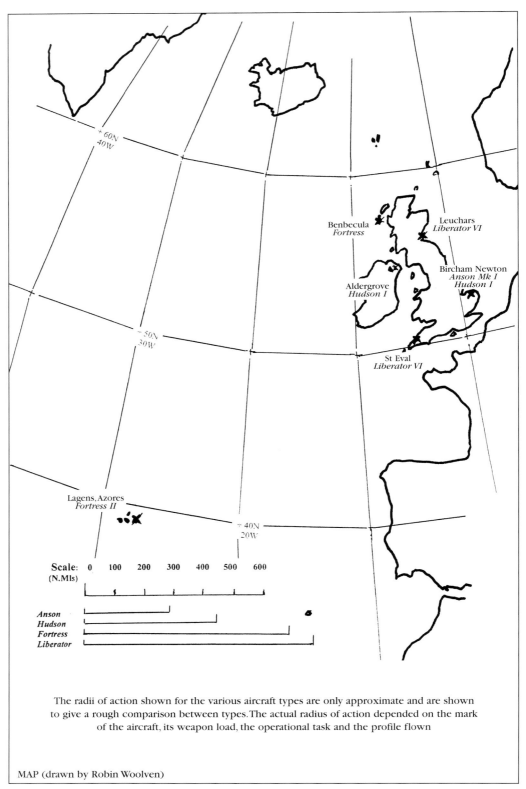

The radii of action shown for the various aircraft types are only approximate and are shown to give a rough comparison between types. The actual radius of action depended on the mark of the aircraft, its weapon load, the operational task and the profile flown

MAP (drawn by Robin Woolven)

Squadron Bases in the Second World War

Navy in combating the threat from the German Battle Fleet and preserving the sea lanes. In addition there were the unspectacular 'Kipper Patrols' protecting the fishing fleets of Humberside and East Anglia, for which consignments of free fish were often gratefully received by the airmen. And there was the threat of invasion which became a serious possibility during 1940.

The onset of war saw unit equipment brought up to its war establishment of 24 aircraft and squadron strength totalled 32 officers and 206 airmen. Throughout the period just before the coming of war and for a few months afterwards experienced personnel were being drawn from 206 to form the first crews of Nos 200, 220, 224, 233 and 269 Squadrons. War routine at Bircham Newton was recalled by Vernon Buckman:

'Operations just slid from peacetime to war. One day we were unarmed, the next complete with ammunition and bombs – the latter as I recall being a quantity of 25-pounders under wing and two 100 lb or 250 lb anti-shipping bombs under the wing roots.' Another change was that the squadron code on the side of the aircraft changed from WD to VX.

By the end of the first day of the war 206 had carried out its first operation, with three Ansons on an anti-submarine sweep for a U-Boat. The crew, relying on purely visual detection, failed to find their quarry and returned safely to base. The following day navigators from the squadron guided aircraft of Bomber Command on the first RAF bombing raids of the war against naval targets in Kiel and Brunsbüttel. One of those seconded was Sergeant Ernest Fitchew, who was attached to No. 83 Squadron Bomber Command and took part in that first raid of the war. He recalls that the Kiel raid was aborted due to bad weather, making it impossible to identify the target and avoid civilian areas. He was absent from 206 for several days at Scampton, Feltwell, Honington and Marham on standby navigational duties for further raids against the German Fleet.[1]

On 5 September Pilot Officers R. T. Kean and H. M. F. Barnitt in K6187 sighted and attacked an enemy U-Boat 85 miles north-east of Lowestoft, the first attack of the war by an RAF aircraft on a U-boat. Two 100 lb bombs were dropped just as the submarine had submerged but it was impossible to estimate damage. During the attack Kean had flown so low that a column of water from the explosion of one of the bombs split his aircraft's tail. This experience seemed to confirm the misgivings about the inadequacy of the bomb load carried by the Anson, especially as U-Boats on the surface could survive even a direct hit of a 100 lb bomb. None of this detracted from the letter of commendation of the two officers written by their CO Wing Commander D'Aeth to the Station Commander, praising their swift actions on that day in spite of the comparative inexperience of the two men. Sadly, Pilot Officer Kean was killed along with Pilot Officer R. Rustom on 5 August 1940 when their Hudson (VX-D P5133) stalled and crashed in flames near Syderstone, Norfolk.

That same day, 5 September, 206 suffered its first loss of the war when K6183 was reported missing from a patrol to the Dutch coast. Pilot Officer L. H. 'Jumbo' Edwards, a New Zealander, and navigator Sergeant Heslop, with LAC J. Quilter and AC1 G. Sheffield had fallen victim to a Heinkel He115 float plane. Four Ansons carried out a sea search but no trace was found of the missing aircraft. Accounts vary about the fate of Pilot Officer Edwards who was at first listed as 'missing' along with his crew but was then reported by the Air Ministry as being on the list of the first probable prisoners of war. Ernest Fitchew, newly returned from secondment to Bomber Command, takes up the story:

'On return to Bircham Newton I was informed of the loss of 'Jumbo' and crew, who were shot down soon after the declaration of war. Being a good swimmer 'Jumbo' was

---

1   Fitchew, E. E., letter to author 12/00.

able to survive after ditching – his crew were lost, but he was picked up by a surface vessel (submarine?)........I always say that 206 Squadron had the first PoW!'. Another version is that Edwards was picked up by a German flying boat and found himself in a Bremen hospital, the first officer of any of the services to become a prisoner of war. He acquired something of celebrity status in Germany and while in hospital was reputedly visited by Marshal Göring!

Pilot Officer Kean and his crew ran out of luck on the 9th when they were forced to ditch their aircraft K6187 four miles off Calais, after getting lost. Fortunately the aircraft stayed afloat for five hours, enabling the French crew of the nearby Dyck light ship to rescue the RAF men and duly transport them back to Folkestone.

Operational routine continued with a search for suspected mines off Aldeburgh on the 11th, and on the 16th an Anson sighted a submarine and dropped bombs only to realise from the reception signals five minutes later that the submarine was British!

Later in September six crews were on detachment to Carew Cheriton in Pembrokeshire and on the 20th Pilot Officer R. C. Patrick spotted a periscope near Lundy Island and attacked with one 100 lb bomb which was seen to explode ten feet from the periscope. A few seconds later large bubbles and patches of oil appeared on the surface and a further attack was made but there were no further signs of any damage. The submarine was clearly damaged but was never confirmed as being sunk but Pilot Officer Patrick was later awarded the DFC for the attack. He wrote a letter from Carew Cheriton to the CO at Bircham Newton dated 27 September outlining the events of the day.

During October the squadron flew 123 operational sorties, mainly fishery protection and convoy escort. On the 10th seven aircraft were detached to Hooton Park, Cheshire, for convoy patrol work in the Irish Sea. The work in those early weeks of the war seemed fairly routine, with a dawn take-off from Bircham Newton, convoy escort duties, and mostly there was little sight of the enemy. At other times, as on 30 October, flying was cancelled owing to the 'thick ground mist' of a type not unusual in that part of Norfolk.

There were a number of duels with enemy seaplanes during November, for example during a diverging search in Terschelling territorial waters by four Ansons on 7 November when Pilot Officer Henderson in K6190 sighted a Dornier 17 and attacked it with one burst of the front gun. The aircraft made off in an easterly direction. The following day Pilot Officer Featherstone's Anson K6195, one of a formation of three aircraft, was attacked by an enemy seaplane at the extremity of a parallel track search over the North Sea. The air gunner Pilot Officer C. A. S. Greenhill got to work and the enemy was seen to fall into the sea and break up. Then Pilot Officer R. H. Harper in K6190 with Pilot Officer Henderson as air gunner, spotted a Dornier flying boat close to the water and bombed it, following that up by gun actions, when they were then attacked by a similar flying boat and fought back until all their ammunition was exhausted and they had to use evasive tactics to escape. For their actions that day Pilot Officers Henderson, Harper and Greenhill were recommended for the DFC.

As autumn turned to winter another enemy became the weather during 1939/1940. By November there was fog to contend with and then snow falls which swept across the airfield and blocked all the approach roads. Operations continued in these very difficult days, but not without loss as on 6 December when Pilot Officer J. H. Grimes, Sergeant V. D. Macmillan, Corporal H. J. Cockayne and AC1 J. C. Bagley in Anson K6189 were reported missing from a North Sea patrol.

At around this time there was very nearly a spectacular 'own goal' when a 206 aircraft dive-bombed what was identified as a U-Boat on the surface. A hit was claimed at the base of the conning tower but the sub dived and disappeared. It turned out to be

HMS *Snapper* but fortunately the only damage done was to four light bulbs inside the vessel.[2] There was a marked increase in the signal communications between the Admiralty and Coastal Command as a result, but the episode illustrates the fact that only one per cent of attacks on submarines by aircraft during this period of the war caused any damage, thanks mainly to the ineffectiveness of the standard weapon, the 100 lb anti-sub bomb. Moreover, with its unreliable fuse and tendency to skip over the surface of the sea the bomb could do more damage to the aircraft than to the submarine. It was to be 1942 before the squadron killed its first U-Boat. Wing Commander J. C. Graham later maintained that the best result which could be generally achieved by an Anson attacking a U-Boat was 'the rattling of the teacups'. However, Pilot Officer R. H. Harper succeeded in engaging an enemy submarine on 3 December, an attack for which he was later awarded the DFC.

By the end of the year the squadron had flown 3,000 hours, ninety per cent of this total accomplished from Bircham Newton, with 'A' Flight being detached to Hooton Park and afterwards to Silloth. Anti-submarine and north- and south-bound convoy escort patrols continued throughout December although flying was cancelled on several days towards the end of the month as the weather enveloped the station with fog and snow showers. Bad weather continued well into January proving an added hazard. On the 26th it was reported that Anson K6207 had forced-landed at Morston near Wells-next-the-Sea owing to the illness of the crew and snow storms. The aircraft hit the top of some trees and was wrecked on landing in a ploughed field. Fortunately the crew escaped uninjured. Right into February there were reports of the airfield being unserviceable due to bad visibility and snow and ice conditions turning to a thaw, with waterlogging of the landing area.

By the spring of 1940 the occasional enemy aircraft in the form of high flying Dorniers would make sporadic attacks in the vicinity of the airfield, dropping sticks of bombs usually around midday. Later the attacks were at low level, using as an aiming point the three 'C'-type hangars and firing all the time. Vernon Buckman remarked that hangar doors had always been left open as the pundits believed that this would lessen blast damage from direct hits. With three hangars full of holed aircraft it was decided in future to close the hangar doors! This new threat led to the urgent need to disperse aircraft around the field and to open a satellite airfield at Docking, a few miles from Bircham Newton, by May 1940.

Apart from operations, various events intervened to vary station routine. On 5 March there was a full parade with march past when AC1 L. J. Britton was awarded the DFM by Air Commodore Marix, AOC 16 Group, for his actions as rear gunner in Pilot Officer Featherstone's crew on 8 November when an enemy aircraft was destroyed. On the 16th lifeboatmen from Sheringham paid a liaison visit to the station. Later in March Lord Trenchard, Inspector-General of the RAF, visited the station along with the AOC No. 16 Group, Air Vice-Marshal J. H. S. Tyssen. LAC 'Robby' Robilliard recalled the occasion, in particular Trenchard's arrival at the camp cinema, when the roof leaked so badly that half the seats were full of water.[3]

By this time there were signs of improved prospects for the squadron when Vernon Buckman was among a group of senior NCOs sent on detachment to Speke, near Liverpool, to work alongside a team of engineers from Lockheed in preparing the first Hudsons Mk1 for RAF service. Each night the team drove Fordson tractors through the city to Garston docks where they hitched the fuselage, wings and tailplane parts to trailers and took them to Speke for assembly. 'Night and day, with short breaks to the

---

2 Puzzle about date/time/circumstances of this.
3 Robilliard, S., letter to author 27/8/91.

Adelphi for food, drink and sleep, the teams assembled the aircraft and flight tested them ready for collection by ATA (Air Transport Auxiliary) pilots who delivered them to the squadrons.'

The first two Hudson MkIs arrived at Bircham Newton for 206 Squadron on 26 March and over the next few weeks the numbers built up until the full complement of around 16 aircraft was reached. The Ansons continued to operate until June on anti-submarine patrols when they were finally removed from squadron charge. With the arrival of the

Cartoon drawn by S.J.'Robby' Robilliard (LAC Ins/Rep) while serving with 206 Sqn
at Bircham Newton 1940-41.

Hudsons there was no doubting the technical leap forward that they represented, but some of this had drawbacks as Vernon Buckman recalls:

'Whilst the Anson had barely a mile of electric cable the Hudson had over ten miles! Wing loading went from a few pounds to 14 lbs per square foot and Fowler flaps were quite awesome. The Anson had been a roomy aircraft, particularly when compared with Blenheims and Hampdens but the Hudson, being of civil airline origin, was comparative luxury. One blatant error was to use such an aircraft on grass when its forbears were obviously meant for runway use. However, all crew positions were comfortable and the large cabin not only made room for a bed, but also made for a rapid exit especially with the novel passenger door which could be jettisoned complete with its built-in dinghy. One major snag was that the gun turrets did not arrive for at least three months during which time the only armament was the front gun and a single Vickers K hand-held gun where the turret should have been.'

At first Vernon found the electrical system 'a terrible headache' but gradually the problems were overcome. A major step forward was the introduction of the first radar in the form of ASV (Air-to-Surface Vessel) Mk1 although this took some time to become effective. No. 206 Squadron was the first Coastal Command squadron to use ASV operationally. As with all new technology there was scepticism among the crews at first and this was only gradually overcome. Another item of equipment was the IFF (Identification Friend or Foe), which detected friendly radar and returned an enhanced echo, thereby indicating that the aircraft was 'friendly'. Vernon Buckman continued:

'To prevent this device falling into enemy hands it was fitted with a destructive charge operated by an inertia switch. This device caused untold headaches. Crews were to test that its circuit was operational before take-off, but repeatedly they set off the charge. Eventually they were warned that they might have to contribute to the cost of the IFF if they destroyed it. We had no more destruction but I have often wondered how many sets were plugged in after that threat!'

On the performance side the Hudsons could boast an increased range and well over five hours' endurance, which brought the north German coast easily within operating distance. This meant more hazardous operations as well as an increased threat from enemy fighters. This was all happening just at the moment when, on 9 April, German forces in the west struck a fresh blow first at Scandinavia, followed by the invasion of Belgium and Holland on 10 May. The 'Phoney War' was well and truly over.

The first Hudson operation by 206 was carried out on 12 April when Flight Lieutenant W. H. Biddell in N7312 flew a reconnaissance patrol of Texel and Borkum in the Frisian Islands group. At least by now the aircraft was being equipped with the long-awaited Boulton & Paul electro-hydraulic gun turrets, so that greater defence was now available against enemy fighters. This came into its own on 3 May when Pilot Officer R. T. Kean's Hudson N7319 was attacked by three Me109s as he dive-bombed an enemy ship off the Elbe estuary. The gunner LAC Ernest Townend shot down one of the enemy only to be killed himself. The remaining two aircraft continued their attack and Kean was severely injured, but he managed to escape from the scene by going down to wave level and flying homewards at zero feet. It is related that the two enemy pilots acknowledged Kean's skill and daring by flying in formation and rocking their machines laterally. The navigator Sergeant E. A. Deverill had to take over for the landing at Bircham Newton, where it was discovered that the aircraft had received 242 bullet holes and 12 cannon shell strikes. Pilot Officer Kean was awarded the DFC for this exploit on 10 July and Sergeant Deverill the DFM. Sadly Kean was killed on 5 August 1940. LAC Townend's bravery went unrecognised. During this action the crew had tried and failed to replace the rear gunner by rotating the gun turret, so after this a cable was attached to the hydraulic release lever in the turret of all Hudsons to enable it to be rotated into a position

This Lockheed Hudson III shows well the camouflage effects. VX was the unit code letters, in this case No. 206 Squadron, and the serial number T9444 its official R.A.F. registration.
(Chaz Bowyer)

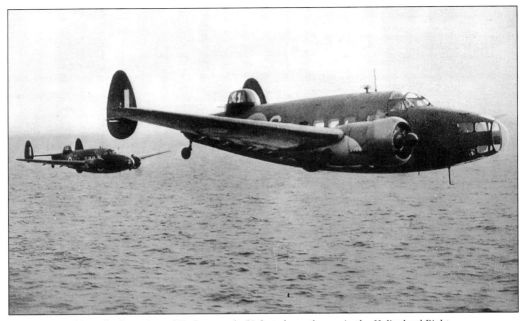

Two of a formation of Hudsons, only 50 feet above the sea in the Heligoland Bight.
(Chaz Bowyer)

Hudson with battle damage.
(Chaz Bowyer)

Interior shots of Hudson – Navigator and Wireless Operator.
(Chaz Bowyer)

that a gunner could be replaced if wounded.[4] Sergeant Deverill was subsequently to have a distinguished career as a bomber pilot, being commissioned in 1941 and posted to No. 97 Squadron. He took part in the famous Augsburg daylight raid, winning a DFC on that occasion, and later a Bar to the DFC. In December 1943 he was captain of a No. 97 Squadron Lancaster on a major Berlin raid but crashed on return near Graveley in Cambridgeshire due to bad weather and lack of fuel. Posthumously awarded the Air Force Cross, Squadron Leader Deverill is buried in St Mary's Churchyard in Docking.[5]

In an effort to reduce the threat from fighters the Hudsons were often provided with an escort of Blenheim Mk IVs from 235 Squadron, also based at Bircham during April and May, but the Blenheim was no match for the Me109. May 1940 was one of the worst months for 206 Squadron with no fewer than six Hudsons being lost due to enemy action. One of these was N7353 on the 12th with Pilot Officer I. L. Gray and crew, who failed to return from a reconnaissance flight after being attacked by Me109s north of Baltrum off the German coast. Two other aircraft failed to return from Hamburg on the 18th, piloted respectively by Flying Officer G. Hutchesson and Flight Sergeant G. A. Turner. A third aircraft was lost on the 20th with Sergeant E. A. Judge and crew and on the 22nd Pilot Officer M. J. Giles in Hudson N7402 failed to return from an anti-shipping patrol.

A hazard closer to home was the number of Hudson accidents on take-off or landing, a total of five in six months. This was partly due to heavy landings damaging the undercarriage mounting which was riveted near the wing petrol tanks. The result was that petrol from the ruptured tank deluged the hot engine and a fierce fire would ensue, a problem confirmed by Vernon Buckman:

'Because of the excellent exit arrangements, as far as I can recall no casualties occurred and 206 aircrew became expert sprinters!' This drawback was complicated by the tendency of the airfield to develop gault holes due to steady pressure from above

---

4   For this latter information I am indebted to Jack Holywell: Memoirs of Life with 206 Squadron
     1940-41.(206 Sqn Archives, RAF Kinloss).
5   Info from Gp Capt. D. Maddox, Docking.

Hudson on patrol at Dunkirk
(Chaz Bowyer)

which led to aircraft causing a minor ground collapse and sinking into the ground.

Towards the end of May the German advances in Belgium and France led to the collapse on the western front and the retreat of the British Expeditionary Force to Dunkirk where it awaited evacuation in Operation *Dynamo*. 206 Squadron, along with 220, the latter having briefly returned from Thornaby, flew crossover patrols codenamed 'Sands' to prevent interference from German warships. The evacuation started on 26 May and continued until 3 June. It was during this operation that Flight Lieutenant Biddell led a formation of three Hudsons into an engagement between Fleet Air Arm Skuas and Me109s. In the ensuing dogfight Flight Sergeant W. D. Caulfield, the lead gunner, shot down two of the enemy and the other 109s made their escape. As a result of the actions that day Biddell received the DFC, Caulfield the DFM and another gunner, Sergeant K. 'Tich' Freeman, was awarded the DFM for his persistence in maintaining fire in spite of being wounded.

Jack Holywell recalled his posting to 206 at Bircham Newton at around this time after training as an air gunner at Penrhos in North Wales. With a dozen others for the journey to Norfolk they were given rations which included some tins of bully beef dated 1917! However, when the tins were opened they smelt all right in spite of that. Jack took part in the operations covering the Dunkirk evacuation and its aftermath:

'I well remember the last flight to Dunkirk. The Channel was empty. We had been looking for stragglers making their way back on rowing boats, oil cans or anything they could get hold of. Normally we would have directed a Naval boat to pick them up, but on this flight it was all over; the sea was empty.

'We landed at Bircham. It was a lovely June evening. We walked back to the Married Quarters that we were living in at the time. I know I was very depressed. The position looked hopeless. It worried me that I was to belong to a generation that was beaten, and looking back on the history of our nation, that hurt. Some WAAFs were sat out in a garden we were passing. They called to us to stop and listen to a broadcast by Winston Churchill that was about to come on the radio. We listened to that great man and when he had ended that memorable speech we carried on to our billets thinking it was not nearly so bad as we had thought only a short time before. It was, but that was the power of that man. How lucky the nation – no, even the world – was to have had him at that time.[6]

During June there was a change of command. Wing Commander N. H. D'Aeth was posted to Command Headquarters and was replaced by Wing Commander J. Constable-Roberts. Now that the Germans seemed to be carrying all before them there was no let up in the pressure on operational RAF squadrons. A new task was to evacuate General Sikorski from France and Flight Lieutenant Biddell flew from Northolt in Hudson P5120 to Bordeaux on 18 June where Sikorski and his staff were taken aboard the Hudson and flown to England across occupied France. Many French officers had been eager to come too but there was insufficient space in the Hudson for them all. Sikorski was now on friendly territory and was able to set up a Polish government-in-exile in London. Biddell was awarded the Polish 'Cross of Valour' for this exploit, the investiture being carried out by General Sikorski himself.

A fresh danger was now Hitler's Operation 'Sealion', the plan to invade Britain and the assembly of invasion barges along the enemy coast became a priority target for both Bomber and Coastal Commands. The Hudson was not specifically designed for low level bombing but the need was so great that several operations were carried out while the threat lasted, as on 12 June when Flying Officer Terry M. Bulloch dive-bombed invasion barges in Boulogne harbour. Other tasks included daily patrols to locate enemy warships and U-Boats and searches for downed aircrew. On the 18th six Hudsons led by Flight Lieutenant J. R. S. Romanes carried out a shallow dive-bombing attack on Norderney airfield and on the same day Flying Officer Hunn's Hudson (P5162) was hit by flak over Ijmuiden while on a reconnaissance of the Dutch coastline. One petrol tank was holed and many hits taken but the aircraft returned safely. As a result of an attack on enemy shipping in Den Helder harbour by some nine Hudsons on the 21st in which some vessels were sunk, Flight Lieutenant F. J. Curtis was later to receive the DFC.

As if there were not troubles enough Vernon Buckman recalls an incident on the night of 29 June when a Hudson (N7299) crashed into a row of neatly lined-up Fleet Air Arm Albacores of 826 Squadron on the airfield, just after the flarepath had been extinguished without warning. The Hudson and two Albacores were destroyed by fire and others damaged but amazingly there were no injuries in spite of the fact that the Albacores had been armed with torpedoes. That same day there had been an invasion scare which proved to be a false alarm.

A major success was achieved on 3 July when Pilot Officer Burne, with crew Pilot Officer Rustom and LACs Deighton and Jack Holywell in Hudson P5143, encountered an Me109 during one of the daily 'recces' of the Dutch and German coasts. In the ensuing combat the rear turret gunner LAC Deighton fired a burst at 500 yards and the enemy's tail fell off. Deighton was later awarded the DFM. The date 4 July was a bleak day for the squadron as two aircraft and crews, Pilot Officers S. R. Henderson and S. J. Lester in N7368 and P5162, failed to return from a sea search for a downed Hampden, probably jumped by fighters. Throughout the month the squadron hammered away at nightly bombing raids on enemy ports like Harlingen and Emden.

Jack Holywell remembered many outstanding airmen during his time with the squadron. There was a wireless operator called Jack Forbes who was awarded the DFM for shooting a Heinkel down by means of one of the side guns (Vickers gas operated). He recalled his flight commander, Rowley, a massive man with a quiet voice who thought the world of his dachshund dog that was always with him. He was a veteran of the Spanish Civil War and a fighter pilot by training, so that he strongly

6 Jack Holywell, ibid.

Photo taken when the squadron was based at Bircham Newton and flying mainly from the Docking satellite, 1940.
(CC/206)

objected to being posted to a Hudson squadron. This showed during bombing missions when he could not get rid of the bombs quickly enough and turned his attention to the search lights on which he would dive with two front guns blazing. He was later posted to a Spitfire squadron in Scotland and was sadly killed after tackling German raiders over the east coast.

Other squadron operations recalled by Jack Holywell included the dropping of spies in enemy territory and supplies to the Resistance. One one occasion his crew were detailed to act on a diversionary operation while a Dutch seaplane picked up a member of the Resistance from a lake on the north side of the Zuider Zee. As their Hudson got through unnoticed the mission failed in its objective!

It was during July 1940 that Graeme V. Donald joined the squadron as a pilot, remaining until June 1942. He recalls the day and night reconnaissance patrols over the Dutch and Belgian coastal areas and in particular the anti-invasion operations, convoy protection and a new adversary, E-boats:

'Reconnaissance was largely the order of the day and night, while attacks on German shipping were one of the best ways to dispose of the four 250 lb bombs carried. The Hudson was fitted with two .303 calibre guns firing forward through the nose, and it had a rear turret also with two .303 guns and some versions were later fitted with a belly gun. For anti-E-boat work I believe it was a Bofors gun of about 25mm fitted within the fuselage and based to fire downwards through a limited arc. It was later believed that if a gun jammed the fuselage would burst.' Graeme Donald also remembered flying by day to the Docking satellite so that by night the flights would take off and land with less chance of interference from the Luftwaffe whose main attacks were directed against Bircham Newton itself. He continued:

'The anti-E-boat patrols were quite interesting, in my log book known as Flares. One

Hudson would fly at about 1,500 feet over the North Sea particularly on the convoy route for UK shipping going north or south. They would unreel a wire rope curling several hundred feet behind and below, and a flare would be attached to this and trailed at the end, with the object of lighting up the E-boats. Then a second Hudson with the pre-mentioned Bofors guns would formate on the flare and shoot the living daylights out of any located E-boats. It was a difficult manoeuvre and probably created more of a distraction than effective damage to E-boats.'[7]

Vernon Buckman also recalled the anti-E-boat campaign: '……the E-boats were not only harassing coastal shipping in the North Sea but were also laying magnetic mines. Attacking them by machine gun was hopeless because long before the aircraft could get within range, they were subjected to fire from the boat's multiple cannons. Bombs were tried with limited success because E-boats operated at night and had great manoeuvrability. As they could be seen by the naval radar at Harwich which could also see the Hudson, it was decided to modify one Hudson with a captive flare capability – the flare being sent down a long cable to ignite and burn at the end – and to install in another Hudson a 3-inch Hispano cannon firing through the floor. For this we cut out a hole approximately eight feet long by two feet wide in the cabin floor and mounted the gun on a swivel which enabled the gunner to stand at the rear of the hole and fire forward, then to swing the gun over and fire to the rear whilst standing in front of the hole. A most dicey operation! The scheme was for Harwich to be in touch with both Hudsons by R/T.'

It was hoped that Harwich would pass on the location of any E-boats to the two aircraft, which would then enable the 'gunship' to destroy the vessel. This ambitious scheme did not take into account the primitive nature of the radar available at the time or the short-range capability of the R/T, designed as it was for aircraft to aircraft communication and between aircraft and airfield control. Vernon Buckman became heavily involved in these trials, making frequent journeys to Harwich. The navy began to use more powerful radio equipment almost to the point that it might have been heard all over Germany, while on the squadron more powerful R/T was fitted. In the end the trials were abandoned when a Lockheed engineer stated that if a cannon shell exploded prematurely the recoil, with as much force as seven tons, would have been sufficient to remove the rear half of the aircraft![8]

Jack Holywell recalled the episode of the (20mm) cannon firing through the Hudson floor and his summons from bed one night with - 'You are the man that knows all about the gun. There's a flap on.' E-Boats were out in force and the two Hudsons took off (the other

Docking's watch office today looking rather forlorn. The faded lettering 'All Visiting Pilots Report Here' barely visible now.

aircraft with flares) heading for the Thames estuary. They neared the end of the patrol without result but at the last moment the other aircraft loosed off its flares revealing a convoy and escort ships, with E-Boats in attack. As he had never used the sights of the

7 Donald, Graeme V., letter to author 3/12/92.
8 Buckman, Vernon, *Memories of Life with 206 Squadron.*

gun at night and had no tracers loaded he more or less had to fire blind at low level without seeing any results of the action. The next morning there was a message of thanks from the navy so the outcome was better than expected! On many occasions there were false alarms, as Jack recalled:

'Bomber Command on their return from raids reported enemy shipping and all ships to them were naval vessels. Attacks on these types of vessels were extremely dangerous and the worst part of the operation was sitting about in the Crew Room waiting for take-off. Once you got in the air there was work to do and you settled down.'

In August and September 1940 patrols over the sea lanes were constant while the fighter squadrons were battling with the Luftwaffe over the southern counties of England. On 10 August a Hudson came under 'friendly fire' from a merchant vessel while escorting a convoy. The flak was 'unpleasantly close' and the aircraft fired three GG cartridges and dived to sea level, making the signal: 'Ships in convoy firing at us', to which the escort vessel replied: 'Thanks, rotten shooting', to which the Hudson replied: 'OK, we can take it!'

Flying Officer Terry Bulloch engaged in an air combat with an He115 floatplane on 28 August west of Texel, and in the course of the fight the enemy was damaged, front and rear gunners knocked out and the aircraft was last seen down on the water just outside Ijmuiden harbour. There was another combat on 6 September when Bulloch was carrying out a dusk sweep of an area of the North Sea on the look-out for enemy surface raiders attempting to slip into the Atlantic. During the patrol he spotted an He115 and engaged in a stern attack. The enemy hit the sea and Terry then dropped two of his 250 lb bombs which narrowly missed their target. The attack was broken off as it was dusk but the Heinkel was severely damaged and listing to starboard by the time the Hudson turned for home. For their exploits during the year Bulloch was awarded the DFC and his gunner Sergeant W. J. Coldbeck the DFM. The crew had been responsible for the downing of several Heinkel 115s.

With the coming of November the danger of invasion had receded and it was felt that the time had come to carry the war right into the enemy's homeland. Accordingly 206 Squadron initiated offensive attacks codenamed RACE aimed at airfields, railway yards and other military or industrial targets in areas like Dunkirk or Gravelines. On one of the first of these operations Flight Lieutenant B. Dias DFC was over enemy territory attempting to attack an airfield when the aircraft was hit by flak which damaged the starboard engine. The other engine began to overheat, the aircraft lost height and the crew nursed the machine back towards the English coast after dropping their bombs on a French invasion port. They ditched in the sea just off Birchington and were able to wade ashore in water only two feet deep. After two hours they managed to find a military post and were at first mistaken for Germans. Luckily there were no serious injuries on this occasion. On 14 November Hudsons were out again, the target being an airfield near Abbeville. During the operation Pilot Officer Ward and his crew were set upon by an Me110 and the gunner Sergeant Garrity succeeded in destroying the enemy. On the 16th three Hudsons of 206 and three Blenheims of 235 Squadron took off to attack an airfield near Arras but they were unable to locate the target. These offensive operations were the forerunners of the 'Intruders' which were to be a major feature of RAF operations in 1941 and 1942.

Graeme Donald recalled the dangers of the time: 'I learned all about the Frisian islands on the night of 26 November 1940. This was quite a pleasant moonlit evening and we circled around Terschelling at about 1,500 feet, spotting several German ships there and finally selecting the biggest to bomb. Dropping the load at 600 feet all hell was let loose and the barrage of light anti-aircraft fire appeared impenetrable. In escaping this it was necessary to dive very smartly to sea level. We ran a little too close to it and the rear gunner who insisted on firing back only shut up when he got covered in spray whipped up by our props from the sea. Settling down ten minutes later, he did observe a glow in the sky but there was no telling whether the attack had been effective or otherwise. Yes it was a danger area and I can well understand the number of bomber aircraft destroyed in that part of the world.'

On 19 November poor visibility led to the crash of Hudson N7300 near West Raynham after the aircraft had been diverted to Coltishall. The aircraft came down on the main Fakenham-Swaffham road and the crew were all killed: Flying Officer H. A. Skeats and Sergeants P. L. Brace, J. H. Moss and S. Bradley.

During the early part of December the winter weather closed in, combined with patchy sea fog. On the 20th there was another loss, of Hudson N7333, which crashed in the early hours on take-off for an EMRO patrol[9]. Pilot Officer R. Ward and all his crew were killed. Other offensive patrols flown during the latter weeks of 1940 and the first part of 1941 included NOMAD, and PAT.

By the end of the year the attrition rate of aircraft and crews was commented on by Vernon Buckman: 'Between the receipt of the first Hudson in April 1940 and the end of the year we had used up 17 Mark Is through accidents and operations. Preparing replacements placed a tremendous extra load on the servicing crews who still had to keep the operational aircraft available. Generally, within hours of an aircraft being written off or missing a new one was delivered. No matter what time of the day or night it arrived (and the ATA delivered night and day), a team would descend on it, install necessary equipment peculiar to the squadron task, calibrate the radios, paint identification or camouflage, flight test the machine, bomb up and arm, swing the compass and hand it over to the appropriate flight. If we had lost a crew there would be the formation of a new crew (as I recall, at that time Coastal Command crews were not formed at OCUs or OTUs[10]), and their initial flight together. All this would take no more than three days, generally.'

Visit to 206 Sqn at Bircham Newton of the King, Queen and princesses, 26 January 1941. AVM Tyssen on extreme left. G. V. Donald (later Sqn Ldr) speaking with the King. On his right Fg Off. Tanner, Flt Sgt Lewis and Flt Sgt Kelly.
(Graeme Donald & CC/206)

---

9 EMRO patrols involved flying the entire length of the Dutch coast just before dawn to trace enemy shipping.
10 Operational Conversion Units and Operational Training Units.

Thus the second year of the war ended on a sombre note. The Battle of France was over, but the immediate danger of invasion had passed. Britain stood alone facing a hostile enemy. What would the new year bring?

The first day of January 1941 brought a fresh tragedy to the squadron, the loss of Hudson T9287 and all its crew in a low flying accident near Langham, Norfolk. Eight crew were killed. On the 6th enemy aircraft were in the vicinity of Bircham Newton and Docking, bombs were dropped near Sedgeford and a Dornier dropped seven bombs around the airfield near the Watch Office but there were no casualties or damage reported. Towards the end of the month, on 26 January, a ceremonial parade was held at Bircham Newton for a visit by the King and Queen and the two princesses, escorted by Air Vice-Marshal J. H. S. Tyssen, AOC No. 16 Group. Decorations were awarded amongst which was the CBE for Group Captain W. H. Primrose, the station commander. Graeme Donald recalled the event:

'During the visit I had the privilege of lining up my crew in front of our Hudson, supported by Group Captain Primrose. The King wore the uniform of Marshal of the Royal Air Force. It was fun showing the two young princesses over the aircraft. It must have been about the same time that *Flight* magazine visited the squadron and they also did an article and there were numerous photographs taken, particularly at the Docking satellite where our mess was in a tent, all a bit cold and uncomfortable.'

Winter weather during much of January hampered operational flying on many days but this did not prevent an enemy aircraft, identified as a Dornier Do17, flying over the station at 1,100 feet on the 31st. This time there were no bombs or machine-gunning from the enemy and the gun posts were able to open fire, but without result.

A change of command followed in February when Wing Commander Constable-Roberts left and was replaced by Wing Commander D. C. Candy RAAF. 'A very strong but fair boss who later became Chief-of-Staff of the Royal Australian Air Force' commented Vernon Buckman. Another change was the arrival of the Hudson Mk II and later Mk III and soon the Mk V. Vernon could not recall that these types brought any great advantage: 'We had got on well with Pratt & Whitney Wasp engines and were not very happy with the Wright Cyclones, even if they were slightly more powerful.'

There had to be constant vigilance in case of attack by enemy intruders, as happened on 7 April during some practice flying at the Langham satellite at around 2345 hrs, with Pilot Officer Alexander at the controls. The aircraft was attacked simultaneously by a Ju88 and a Dornier Do17 and Alexander had to take rapid evasive action, while fire was exchanged. Luckily the pilot was able to escape by diving to 200 feet and managed to land the Hudson undamaged.

Operational activities, mostly convoy patrols, continued at Bircham Newton in the early months of 1941 but there was a squadron detachment to Aldergrove in Northern Ireland and a second detachment to St Eval in Cornwall on 6 May under the command of Flight Lieutenant Hennock RAAF (to be followed by the rest of the squadron at the start of July). Vernon Buckman continued: 'Soon we received orders to split the squadron to form No. 200 Squadron. From the logistics angle "splitting" entails a lot of extra hard work, but it can also cause a lot of heartbreak from the personnel aspect. Although new members were posted in, nevertheless the only fair way was to split the existing staff right down the middle to ensure that both squadrons would have, as near as possible, equal skills and experience. In this case we were not to know until nearer the day that 200 Squadron was destined for West Africa. Few of my staff volunteered to go although in many cases a step-up in promotion was offered. It was decided to stick to one Mark if possible for 200 Squadron and the Mark V was chosen. We had about five weeks to get them ready. This was a bad choice for me because it was the only mark without the latest R/T so I had a major fitting task. By May all was ready and they left, flying via Gibraltar where they did some escort duty. The ground crew went by sea but were torpedoed with heavy losses.'

A depleted 206 Squadron remained at Bircham Newton for a few more weeks under the command of Flight Lieutenant A. R. Holmes, of Canada. Two crews were lost on successive days in June on sea searches, the second loss in the search for the first. Once again, it was presumed that enemy fighters had shot them both down.

The days at the Norfolk airfield were nearly over, as Vernon Buckman recalled: 'Unlike most Coastal Command squadrons, 206 had been left alone for a long time, having been at Bircham since 1936. However, after waving goodbye to 200 Squadron, we were posted to St Eval, probably so that we could build up our strength, but also to give us a spell on runways. We took the place of a squadron which had had a hard time keeping watch on Brest where the *Scharnhorst* and *Gneisenau* had been sheltering. Also they had suffered two or three severe night attacks on their undefended airfield with heavy aircraft damage. We did not mind the move – at least we could look forward to warmer winters.' 206's move was also recalled by Allan Monaghan, who had only been with the squadron for a few months: 'The moving from Bircham to St Eval was one summer's night, weather marvellous, and most personnel and all equipment were loaded at Hunstanton station, and it took until Sunday night to get to Padstow in Cornwall. We had a halt in Bristol due to an air raid.'[11]

A new era and a wider war was now going to be the lot of 206 to fight, as a new and deadly front opened up in the west, the Battle of the Atlantic.

Hudson being serviced at Bircham Newton.
(CC/206)

---

11 Monaghan, Allan, letter to author 14/10/93.

CHAPTER 6

THE WAR WIDENS: ST EVAL AND ALDERGROVE

'Gentlemen, it has been decided to obliterate Bremen tonight'.

Briefing for the 1,000-Bomber raid at Donna Nook, June 1942.
(Sgt Jack Farley, WOp/AG)

Hitler had undertaken his greatest gamble on 22 June 1941 with Operation Barbarossa, the assault on the Soviet Union, so while the danger of invasion had receded in the west and with Britain still fighting alone, the threat was now from German naval forces to our supply lines in the Atlantic. Thus the strategy was twofold: firstly, to continue the disruption of German sea routes in the North Sea and Channel, which had achieved some measure of success thanks to Coastal Command and No. 2 Group Bomber Command and secondly, to utilise all possible resources air and naval in the west to protect our convoys from German U-Boats and capital ships. Hence the watch on Brest harbour on the French coast assumed some importance, where the capital ships were sheltering. It was against this background that 206 Squadron was relocating to St Eval in Cornwall at the start of July 1941.

"DON'T PANIC, BLOKES, THE SIREN HASN'T GONE, YET."

Cartoon on life in 206 Squadron, St Eval 1941
by 'Robby' Robilliard.

Prior to February 1941 St Eval had come under the control of No. 15 Group Coastal Command, with headquarters at Plymouth, which had the responsibility for convoy escort and anti-submarine patrols in the Western Approaches. In February 1941 there had been a reorganisation of the Command to cope with the increasing threat from the German Navy's use of the Bay of Biscay ports and there was a fresh division of responsibility. The Royal Navy Commander-in-Chief Western Approaches moved to Liverpool and No. 15 Group also transferred there, to cover the Western and North-Western Approaches from the Atlantic, while a new Group No. 19 was formed with headquarters at Plymouth, to take over the stations in south Wales and south-west England, including of course St Eval. This latter Group would have responsibility for coastal convoys in the western English Channel and southern part of the Irish Sea and attacks on enemy shipping in French ports.

A reinforced 'B' Flight from Bircham Newton joined Squadron Leader Hennock's 'A' Flight at St Eval, and with the arrival of the CO Wing Commander Candy on 9 July, the squadron's move was complete. Vernon Buckman recalls these first days at St Eval: 'We were dispersed around the perimeter by the church. Already St Eval was a large complex, with many dispersed messes. I took charge of one of the sergeants' messes in the Bedruthan Steps Hotel. Our officers were mainly in the Watergate Bay Hotel. We worked from our messes to our sites, only visiting the station for briefings etc.'

An early action took place on 4 July when Pilot Officer Wills sighted a U-Boat cruising through the Bay of Biscay towards St Nazaire or La Rochelle. At a range of two miles the sub began to dive but the Hudson dropped high explosive beside its hull and a probable hit was registered. Large patches of oil were later reported. On its way back to base the Hudson was pursued by two Heinkel 115 float planes but no contact was made owing to the superior speed of the Hudson.

Many of the anti-submarine and convoy patrols during those months of 1941 were routine, even unexciting, with a motley collection of vessels being identified. These included crabbers, various fishing vessels, coasters, Spanish merchant vessels, tunnymen and unspecified small craft of various types. The sight of 206 Hudsons from St Eval must have been reassuring for many of these seamen.

Any hint of monotony was broken on 8 July when Hudson AE613 took off from St Eval on a cross-over patrol off the French coast, intending to cover the possible escape of the battle-cruisers *Scharnhorst* and *Gneisenau*. Unfortunately the aircraft had already a bad reputation as events were going to prove. The pilot was Pilot Officer T. Kennan, with crew Sergeants Gibbs, Livingston and Rowley. After over two hours in the air and at a height of 500 feet the starboard engine caught fire but was extinguished and then the port engine failed. The Hudson ditched and sank very quickly, although the crew managed to scramble into the dinghy. Without food, water or cigarettes the crew prepared for a long wait although Kennan had managed to manoeuvre the dinghy to a large patch of seaweed and foam. After some hours the dinghy was spotted by Pilot Officer Wills on an anti-submarine patrol who at first mistook the sighting for a U-Boat's wake but on recognising the dinghy alerted the rescue services and a Sunderland from No. 10 Squadron received the signal to divert from its patrol. The aircraft located the dinghy and attempted to land but in the heavy swell lost its outer port engine and a wingtip float. However Kennan and his crew managed to reach the Sunderland but it was unable to take to the air and instead taxied towards the Scilly Isles. Eventually the occupants were picked up by the destroyer HMS *Brocklesby* and the damaged Sunderland was sunk by gunfire.

On 11 July a Hudson crewed by Sergeants Whitfield, Gauntlett, Last and White were flying off Brest when they sighted what they presumed were three large trawlers. As they closed to photograph them a heavy anti-aircraft shell exploded at close quarters and they realised that they had encountered flak-ships and a 1,200-ton minesweeper. The Hudson dived to sea level and Whitfield flew through an intense 'box barrage' before loosing off three General Purpose (GP) bombs at the minesweeper. Direct hits were achieved and the ship was left in flames, but as Whitfield emerged from the barrage one engine burst into flames and the other failed due to a shell piercing the fuel tank. The ASV equipment had received a direct hit and there were holes in various parts of the aircraft. A rapid change-over of tanks was made, the engines revived just in time and the aircraft was able to reach Predannack.

Heinkel He115 floatplanes were a continual threat to the Hudsons and many encounters took place, as on 7 August when two Hudsons attacked and severely damaged an enemy aircraft during an anti-submarine patrol. The enemy disappeared into a cloud and his SOS was picked up by a wireless station. One of the Hudsons returned with 28 bullet holes and one of its tyres burst. The pilot of the other Hudson had a lucky escape when three bullets ended up between his feet and another had penetrated the navigator's log sheet as it lay on the table in front of him.

Within a few days the squadron moved once again, this time to Aldergrove in Northern Ireland, from which it was to operate on convoy duties, anti-Condor[1] and anti-submarine work. Vernon Buckman recalls the events: 'Having got settled (at St Eval), and having brought my wife down to a bungalow, the squadron was moved to Aldergrove where we were to share the airfield with 311 (Czech) Squadron[2]. Well away from any enemy action, Aldergrove gave us much needed rest and there we developed a very fine social life with the Czechs. Operations were over the North-West Approaches, mainly anti-submarine patrols but also escorts for independently routed ships (ships fast enough to proceed alone) like the *Imperial Star*, *Rowallan Castle* and *Strathaird*. However, this comparative rest came to a dramatic end when a 311 Squadron Wellington taking a contingent of NCO pilots down to London for commissioning crashed with no survivors. We certainly missed these extraordinary colleagues who might not have been the keenest of fighters, but what musicians! Every one seemed to be a maestro. We were very sad.'

There was another tragedy for 206 within a few days of arriving at the new airfield. Hudson AM588 crashed on Lady Hill in Antrim after taking off for a convoy escort patrol on 16 August killing the pilot, Pilot Officer T. L. Hayston and wireless operator Sergeant R. Ramsay, seriously injuring the navigator Sergeant Staite. The gunner Sergeant Mann escaped injury.

Another Hudson (AM664) crashed on approach to Aldergrove on 24 September. Sergeant F. Dunn and his crew Flight Sergeants B. Morgan, and V. C. D. Hayward and Sergeant G. O. Linhart, were all killed. During the month the DFC was awarded to Flight Lieutenant R. C. Patrick for his war service thus far. Jim Glazebrook points out in his squadron history that in September 1941, after two full years of war, only five aircrew members of the original 1939 establishment were still with the squadron. They were: Flying Officer C. N. Crook, Pilot Officer E. E. Fitchew, Flight Sergeant W. D. Caulfield DFM, Flight Sergeant R. Field DFM and Flight Sergeant G. H. Livingston. Some had been posted but many were casualties and missing.

Winter was approaching and there could be no better description of what lay ahead for 206 than the words of Jim Glazebrook in his squadron history:

'With the coming of October the squadron settled down to face the winter. The story of the following months, so well known to Coastal Command crews, so little publicised outside their ranks, is one of grim and continual struggle. Gone were the days of cloudless skies and smooth seas when the convoys sailed serenely, exchanging signals with their escort, and a keen eye at 2,000 feet could spot a U-Boat's periscope eight or nine miles away. In winter the Germans, though none the less sought after, took a secondary place to the airman's greatest enemy....the weather; storm and gale reigned in the Atlantic with turbulent winds and turbulent seas, rain and snow, hail and sleet, low cloud and fog, thunder and lightning and all the phenomena of the air that could spell danger and hazard to those who fly.'

The convoys still needed protection and the U-Boats were an ever-present threat, although they were often hampered in their work by seas too stormy to enable

---

1 FW 200 Condors were operating in long-range strikes against shipping.
2 311 had been recently transferred from Bomber to Coastal Command.

torpedoes to be fired accurately. Jim Glazebrook continues: 'And so the patrols went on, day after day, week after week, through every conceivable kind of weather. When the sea rose, everywhere carried its wind-lashed foam patch which trailed away into the next trough looking for all the world like the wake of a surfaced U-Boat. It was a keen and well-trained eye that was not deceived. Whenever possible the Hudsons flew below cloud, often flying within a few feet of the water in order to maintain an unbroken view of the area they were searching. Sometimes, in poor visibility, they would come suddenly upon a convoy, to find themselves fired upon before they could give recognition signals. The naval gunners had had good cause in the past to fear the sudden approach of an unidentified aircraft, and they could not afford to wait to ask questions.

'Another danger was icing. Several aircraft were forced to turn back due to this menace......It was not uncommon for crews to take off knowing that the weather would not be fit for them to return to their own station and that they might be diverted to any landing ground within their fuel range. That this was involving extra risk they were well aware, and more than one crew lost their lives attempting to land at a strange airfield in conditions of bad visibility.'

There was a brief detachment to Wick of a number of crews on 16 November to carry out patrols seeking out enemy warships on passage around the northern seas. The boast that Coastal Command flew 'when even the seagulls were grounded' held good for the most part and operations were only cancelled in extreme conditions. The squadron averaged over 100 sorties in one month during the winter and in a four-month

Sergeants' Mess, Aldergrove, Christmas 1941.
(CC/206)

period 396 patrols and searches were undertaken, 13 U-Boats were sighted, 11 of which were attacked. Ships were guided to the rescue of two seamen on a raft on one occasion and on 24 October Squadron Leader K. H. Holmes and crew in AM722 located six aircrew from a ditched Whitley, which led to their successful rescue by a destroyer.

On 21 December Hudson AM837 was lost with pilot Flight Lieutenant I. W. Terry, Pilot Officer E. D. Rawes and Sergeants J. W. Durrant and R. L. Watts, during a raid with Bomber Command on an oil refinery at Donge near St Nazaire, in which six 206 Hudsons had taken part. The Germans did not claim any aircraft shot down so it was feared that the Hudson had ditched in the sea. All four of the crew are buried in the Pont-Du-Cens Communal Cemetery, Nantes.

Between the end of December 1941 and the start of February 1942 the operational summary by No. 15 Group Headquarters stated that 206 Squadron had amassed 578 flying hours out of a total of 1719 flying hours for the entire Group (excluding Met. Flights), which consisted of six squadrons at five different Stations. No. 206's nearest rivals were Nos 93 and 502 Squadrons at Limavady. During the same period the squadron made three attacks on U-Boats.

By May 1942 better weather enabled the number of sorties to increase to 157. Four U-Boats were sighted during the month, two of which were attacked. A successful rescue of a downed Whitley crew by a destroyer resulted from the vessel being 'homed' to the dinghy by a 206 Hudson.

Towards the end of June twelve Hudsons of the squadron were detached to North Coates for co-operation with Bomber Command, to participate in the next '1,000-bomber' raid, this time on Bremen. In total 1,067 aircraft took part, including a sizable force of 102 aircraft from Coastal Command. To Sergeant Jack Farley, Wireless-Operator/Air Gunner[3], it was obvious that something 'big' was on as they landed at Donna Nook, satellite of North Coates, which was teeming with crews from other squadrons. The only accommodation there was a large marquee in which all ranks had to bunk down for the night. One of his crew's first tasks was to paint the underside of their aircraft black in preparation for a night operation. Jack well remembers the briefing in a packed Operations Room at North Coates where the only available space was standing room on a radiator. He would never forget the opening remarks of the Group Captain: 'Gentlemen, it has been decided to obliterate Bremen tonight!'.

The Hudsons took off from Donna Nook on the night of 25 June heading for their target of the Deschimag shipyard, accompanied by the squadron commander Wing Commander H. D. Cooke, on his first operational flight with the squadron. Cloud obscured the target and bombs had to be dropped in the vicinity. Flight Lieutenant Roxburgh's aircraft was damaged by flak but he managed to return home. Two aircraft failed to return (AM606 & AM762) with the loss of Wing Commander Cooke, Acting Squadron Leader C. N. Crook DFC, Flight Sergeant R. Hubbard, Pilot Officer J. C. Watson, Flight Sergeant G. McGlynn, Flight Sergeant K. D. Wright, Pilot Officer D. Phillips, and Sergeant R. W. Payze. Sergeant J. H. Peet became a prisoner as did WO J. Speed. The dead were buried in Hamburg and Kiel War Cemeteries. The undamaged aircraft returned to Aldergrove on 27 June.

---

3   Later Flight Lieutenant.

206 Squadron, Aldergrove April 1942.
(Jack Farley)

Some 206 groundcrew, Aldergrove 1942.
('Robby' Robilliard, pictured 3rd from left back row)

Hudson crew, Aldergrove 1942. L to R - A. Brown
(Nav.); J. Farley (WOp/AG); Stan Weir (pilot;)
Powditch (WOp/AG).
(Jack Farley)

Squadron line-up in June 1942 before the Bremen
1000-bomber raid. Wg Cdr Cooke, CO from 15 June,
on left at front, soon to be killed over Bremen.
Wg Cdr Hards, who relinquished command of the
squadron on 15 June and was later killed testing a
German jet. On his right Sqn Ldr 'Butch' Patrick

CHAPTER 7

BENBECULA, THE FORTRESSES
AND THE ATLANTIC WAR

'The only thing that ever really frightened me during the war was the U-Boat peril.'

W. S. Churchill, *The Second World War* Vol 2 'Their Finest Hour'.

By the start of 1942 Hitler's armies were heavily engaged in the war with the Soviet Union on the eastern front, and although the United States had recently declared war on the Axis powers it was going to be some time before any new offensive could be launched against Hitler in the west. In the meantime the major threat to Britain arose from the Atlantic U-Boat campaign of Admiral Karl Dönitz, which aimed to cut off our lifeline of food and essential raw materials. Now that America had entered the war German U-Boats could treat any merchant vessels in the Atlantic as fair game. The devastating U-Boat campaign off the American and Caribbean coasts which the Germans nicknamed 'The Happy Time' was now widened to include the western Atlantic, with the aid of U-Boats operating at longer range and with the first 'milch cows' (tankers) to assist. The figures of merchant shipping losses in the North and South Atlantic speak for themselves, rising from 57,000 tons in December 1941 to 514,000 tons in July 1942 and 544,000 tons in August. Dönitz was able to increase the daily average of U-Boats at sea in the Atlantic from 22 in January 1942 to 86 in August.[1] It was not surprising that Churchill confessed that the only thing in the war that really frightened him was the U-Boat peril. Admiral of the Fleet Sir Dudley Pound, the First Sea Lord, was even more graphic: 'If we lose the war at sea we lose the war.'[2]

At the same time further difficulties arose from the loss of information from 'Ultra' (the secret operation decoding German signals) from February 1942 due to an extra wheel being added to the 'Enigma' code machine used by German U-Boat command, which greatly complicated the process of decrypting at Bletchley Park, the government secret communications centre. This meant that convoys could no longer be re-routed away from the U-Boat 'wolf-packs' although it was true that the Admiralty had by now gained considerable experience of U-Boat operations. On top of this, the German Naval Intelligence Division, B-Dienst, had been able to break into the Royal Navy and Merchant Navy ciphers, a fact not discovered until well into 1943. Thus air power was to assume an ever-greater importance in seeking out and destroying U-Boats, and operating in conjunction with escort ships to protect the convoys. The problem was the 'mid-Atlantic gap', an area hitherto beyond the range of all but the few available VLR (Very Long Range) aircraft, where up to one third of all merchant shipping losses occurred. The AOC Coastal Command, Air Marshal Sir Philip Joubert de la Ferté joined with the Admiralty in the struggle of the 'Battle of the Air' to obtain a greater supply of the VLR aircraft, in particular the American-built B-17 Flying Fortresses and the B-24 Liberators, against the competing demands of the RAF bomber campaign and the needs of other theatres like the Mediterranean (for example the Anglo-American invasion of French north-west Africa in Operation *Torch* in November 1942). In addition there were

---

1   Barnett, Corelli, *Engage the Enemy More Closely* pp 455-7.
2   Terraine, John, *Business in Great Waters* p428.

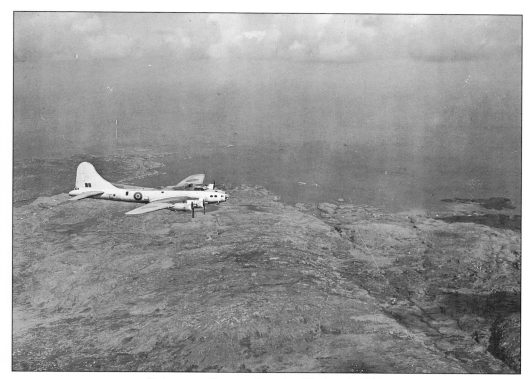

Fortress over the rugged terrain of Benbecula, 1942.
(Sid Banks)

useful advances in technology, such as the new explosive Torpex which improved the detonation of depth charges, and the Leigh Light, which acted as a searchlight attached to an aircraft, enabling it to catch U-Boats on the surface at night. These and other innovations were becoming available but at all too gradual a pace during 1942.

It was against this background that at the end of June 1942 No. 206 Squadron was ordered to move to Benbecula in the Outer Hebrides as part of No. 15 Group, to continue its anti-submarine patrols. There had been some warning of this as far back as April as recalled by Vernon Buckman when the CO at the time, Wing Commander Hards, had flown the heads of section to the Hebridean airfield for a preliminary 'recce':

'......The amazingly blue sea, the white sand and the deep green hills as we approached on that sunny day just looked like the Caribbean and our spirits rose. Even when we had seen the Nissen hutted camp, half completed, a tiny village, five miles to a pub and 25 miles with a sea crossing to the nearest town, we were quite happy.'

The actual move took place from 28 June to 1 July under the command of Squadron Leader R. C. Patrick DFC, consisting of Air and Rail and Sea parties, the latter leaving Aldergrove by train and thence to Larne harbour via Antrim, and by sea to Stranraer, and then on to Stirling and Oban, sailing from Oban to Benbecula (a rather oddly roundabout route). In Movement Order 1/1942 it was laid down for each member of the Rail and Boat Party to carry 48 hrs rations including tea, milk and sugar. Breakfast would be provided at Aldergrove at 0400 hrs on 30 June, a hot meal at Stranraer, tea at Stirling (paid by the OC Party) and breakfast at Oban on 1 July. 'Boiling water for making tea will be available on the ship from OBAN to BENBECULA twice during the journey for which a service charge will be made and for which the OC Party will pay.'[3]

---

3   No. 206 RAF Movement Order No. 1 1942 (206 Sqn Archives, RAF Kinloss)

When the time came for the squadron to move it was depleted by the losses of the June operations. There were initial patrols in the Hudsons. However the news came through that re-equipment was to take place with the American B-17 Flying Fortress, and on 20 July four crews were attached to No. 220 Squadron at Ballykelly to convert to the new aircraft. By the start of August the squadron began to receive its first Fortresses and all the crews began conversion training, with the squadron being taken out of the line until 19 September. Vernon Buckman recalled that for the pilots there were some similarities to the handling of the Anson, except for a rather heavy rudder:

'Our pilots lost no time getting airborne and soon they had mastered the heavy rudder by using the auto-pilot control for rudder when landing! It was an excellent auto-pilot with instant release. Almost immediately we started to receive the Mark II versions which were complete with all the gun turrets, waist guns and ASV Mk V radar. As fast as the crews qualified on the Mk I, operations commenced with the Mk IIs, mainly escorting the independently routed fast liners when they were beyond fighter cover. These ships, including the *Queen Mary* and the *Queen Elizabeth*, chose their own course based on coded information broadcasts of U-Boat positions. Their speed and zig-zagging were considered to be the best defence against U-Boats or surface ships, but despite tremendous firepower on the top deck, they were vulnerable to air attack by Focke Wulf Condor long range bombers which could operate well beyond our fighter cover.'

'The Esquires Last Outpost' – Operational aircrew quarters, Benbecula, July 1942 to August 1943. (CC/206)

Vernon Buckman also recalled life at Benbecula in 1942 as similar to the excitement and discomfort of scout camping:

'We all lived in Nissen huts with primitive coke stoves, for the contractors were still building the station. The nearest pub was a five mile walk and we had to take our own 'jars'! Food was appalling; bread came from Glasgow by coastal steamer. The four pound loaves, having spent four days in transit in very damp weather were thick with mould. Initially we sliced the six sides until we reached bread but as this left us with only about a pound, we later discovered that when toasted a large proportion of mould burned away, giving us a better return! We were permanently hungry until we found a source of self-sown potatoes in what had been the gardens of forsaken crofts. We 'did' our own laundry. With me in my Nissen hut were five flight sergeants. Dirty clothes went into a 30-gallon oil drum with soap powder and the first to have time to spare did the washing. All our clothes developed a uniform battleship hue.

'We were right on the sea's edge and in the long summer evenings we spent any spare time winkling lobsters out of the rock pools and cooking them on the Nissen stove. Our record was one of 8¾ pounds and our sergeant instrument maker insisted on taking it to pieces carefully and assembling the empty shell. This was still residing on the mess mantelpiece when I left the squadron. Mail came in by Dominie when the sea mist allowed. In mid-summer this seemed to last for weeks at a time. It was cold, wet and quite windy. Many a time we heard the mailplane 50 feet above us but after trying for a while it would continue to Stornoway.'

There was the constant danger of severe gales and the Fortresses had to be screw-picketed down at the slightest hint of one. 'However, when one did strike there was pandemonium. It was at night and I drove the senior NCOs down to the airfield (about half a mile) in the Bedford radio servicing van. This was a nightmare for in the half light, sheets of corrugated iron from the huge stacks being used by the airfield building contractors were whipping across in the direction of the airfield like playing cards from a pack. Our van was in danger for the body was constructed of thin fibre board, but we dreaded even more the carnage we expected to find among our new aircraft. When we arrived, some had dragged their pickets (the whole airfield was of peat – even the runway was mainly of rolled tarred sand on peat). Even with tankers at the wings and screw pickets at the tail, the aircraft were still flying at the extent of their tethers and on climbing into the cockpit it was seen that during the gusts, oil pressure was reading normal for flight! The next day we learned that gusts had reached 130 mph. Much damage was done, but as I recall, all repairs to aircraft were within our capability.

'I had not flown much in Hudsons but I took many opportunities to fly in the Fortresses on radar and wireless tests, but also on a few operations. I could not pluck up courage to fly as gunner in the claustrophobic ball turret, although I did get in and play about! My favourite was as rear gunner. This was a manual position, with two .5-inch machine guns. In this position, on 29 June 1942, I experienced the most enjoyable flight since I had left open cockpits! The day was superb, the sea deep blue, picture-book cumulus clouds, and enough wind to provide some 'white horses'. The task was to escort the *Queen Mary*. As we approached her she was doing the usual six-mile zig-zag and the wake could be seen stretching back to the horizon. The rear gun position was well aft of the tailplane, very quiet and comfortable. The flight was of six hours' duration.'

In the meantime Hudsons were still carrying out anti-submarine sweeps, with another loss, this time of Flight Sergeant Ireland and his crew in AM805, who failed to return on 28 July. No signals were received and nothing was sighted of the missing aircraft. But the process of conversion of the squadron to Fortresses continued over the next few days, with a number of aircraft being flown to Benbecula from Ballykelly and Burtonwood for crew training.

The first anti-submarine patrol in a Fortress was carried out by Flight Lieutenant Willis Roxburgh and his crew on 19 September. Roxburgh had worked hard during August and September converting other squadron members to the Fortress Mk II, and he related his experiences with the aircraft: 'The old Fortress MkI was quite a pleasant aircraft to fly although for a four-engined aircraft its bomb load was ludicrously limited. They took a terrible beating on daylight bombing raids over Europe, particularly targets like Brest, but mercifully I was never asked to fly operationally in one of them. Our main problem was with brakes. The braking system in some way incorporated an inflatable bag which presumably pressed the metal shoes against the metal lining. In the event the heat consistently burst these bags and we were always having to replace them.'[4]

On 25 September an anti-submarine escort of convoy QP14 was undertaken, the main part of which consisted of 17 merchant vessels and nine escorts. Four more sorties were flown in the next five days and on 1 October full anti-submarine work got under way with the Fortress Mk II. As the month progressed orders from Group were received to change the load on the aircraft from 12 x 300 lb depth charges and two 250 lb anti-sub bombs to 14 depth charges, for safety reasons in the event of premature release of bombs. Later the load was ordered to be changed again, to replace seven out of the 14 depth charges capable of being loaded in the aircraft by a bomb-bay petrol tank holding 340 imperial gallons, increasing the official endurance to 10.7 hrs and enabling the Fortresses to venture far further into the 'mid-Atlantic gap' than

---

4   Willis Roxburgh, letter 7/11/85 to A. Monaghan.

(7472) Wt. 34220/1650. 180M. 8/40. P.I. 51-7751.

FOR THE MONTH OF OCTOBER, 1942

DATE	AIRCRAFT TYPE & NUMBER	CREW	DUTY	Up	Down	DETAILS OF SORTIE OR FLIGHT	REFERENCES.
6.10. 1942	FL.453(A)	W/C.J.R.S. ROMANES DFC., P/O.A.C.I. SAMUEL, F/S. GRIFFITHS J., SGT. SIMPSON R.L., SGT. THOMAS R., SGT. ELEY D., CHURCHILL J.K.	A.S. SWEEP	0600	1435	A U-boat was sighted at 0905 in position 5745N 1710W but because the navigator had set the operate lever at 'Safe' instead of at 'operate' the attack failed, no DCs being released. U-boat baiting tactics were adapted without success. A warning was passed to 'Empire Tarpon' in position 5720N 1630W and after an unsuccessful search for CV HX 209 the aircraft returned to base at its PLE.	Bec/04/6/10
	FL 457(F)	P/O.R.L. COWEY, SGT. EARL G.A., F/O. J. DUNS., SGT. SMITH J.L., SGT. HOLLINSHEAD L., SGT. MORRIS J.H., SGT. FABIAN R.	A.S. SWEEP	0700	1505	Fortress A circling MV was sighted at 10.00 hours. and at 11.27 in position 5720N 2112W the search was abandoned owing to weather.	Bec/03/6/10
	FL 451 (D)	P/O.L.M. NELSON, SGT. WALMSLEY J., SGT. BENTLEY R., SGT. ROCHE P.J., SGT. LEWIS W.G., SGT. EDWARDS J.G., SGT. BRISTOW L.G.	A.S. SWEEP	0815	1650	In compliance with message from base the aircraft sought and found CV HX 209 carrying out A.S. escort from position 5646N 1525W to 5645N 1508W.	Bec/02/6/10
	FL.454(J)	P/O. J.E. DELARUE, SGT. ROBINSON F.A., SGT. JAEGER J.C., SGT. COUTTS D.S., SGT. HUNT J., SGT. GUPPY J.F., SGT. TAPLIN J.B.	A.S. SWEEP	0603	-	The aircraft crashed into the sea immediately after take-off the survivors Sgts. Coutts and Hunt came ashore in a rubber dinghy.	Bec/01/6/10.
7.10.42						NO OPERATIONAL FLYING.	
8.10.42	FL 460(H)	W.O. L.G. CLARK, SGT. DYER P.P., SGT. ACKERMAN J.D., SGT. JONES G.J., F/S. GARNHAM A., SG. ALLISON F.W., SGT. POLLARD W.E.	A.S. SWEEP	0445	1650	Convoy ONSJ 136 was sighted at 11.18 reassembling in position 5848N 2700W and an unsuccessful search for stragglers was carried out.	Bec/04/8/10

Squadron ORB extract 6/7/8 October 1942.
(CC/206)

had ever been possible before.

The squadron's first tragedy at Benbecula was on 6 October when Fortress FL454 stalled avoiding another aircraft and crashed into the sea, with the loss of five of the crew, Pilot Officer J. E. Delarue RAAF, and Sergeants J. C. Jaeger, F. A. Robinson, J. F. Guppy and J. B. Taplin. Sergeants D. S. Coutts and J. Hunt managed to scramble into a dinghy and came ashore slightly injured. Willis Roxburgh later recalled the tragedy: 'Jack Delarue had taxied to the end of the runway on a very dark morning in his Fortress, and then opened up to take off. About half way along the runway the last aircraft of the detail, thinking everyone had taken off, carelessly broke the perimeter taxying rule and taxied across the main runway in front of Jack. Jack pulled the stick back in his fully laden aircraft, managed to hop over the offending aircraft, hit the runway near the end and went into the sea some 100 yards beyond the beach. I was the senior operational flying officer left on the station at the time (as 'Butch' Patrick was on leave and Romanes the CO had taken off first). I collected John Owen and dashed in a landrover to the edge of the beach. In the dark we could see one wing of the Fortress sticking out of the water so John Owen and I in the absence of a boat of any kind stripped naked and started swimming out towards it. It was winter and the water was freezing cold so unhappily we had to turn back before we could possibly reach the wreck and were taken to sick quarters for a brief treatment to restore our circulation.'[5] Pilot Officer J. E. Delarue's funeral with full military honours took place on 10 October in Nunton Cemetery with the local Church of Scotland minister officiating, the Rev. Neil Mackay. Of the other crew members, Sergeants Taplin and Guppy also lie in Nunton Cemetery, and Sergeant Jaeger was buried in Highgate Cemetery, St Pancras, London. Sergeant F. A. Robinson's body was never found and he is commemorated on the Runnymede Memorial.

The squadron's 'first blood' from Benbecula followed an attack by Flying Officer R.

---

5   Willis Roxburgh, letter 29/8/80 to A. Monaghan.

L. Cowey and his crew in Fortress FL457 on U-627 on 27 October while on escort duty to Convoy SC105, south of Iceland. On sighting the submarine Cowey attacked with seven depth charges and saw oil coming to the surface. Destruction of the U-Boat was not confirmed until after the war, but the action demonstrated that U-Boats could no longer routinely surface and operate with impunity in the areas of the Atlantic which had hitherto been beyond the reach of the Hudsons.

By the end of October 523 operational flying hours over the North Atlantic had resulted in six U-Boat sightings and four attacks. This operational record was achieved in spite of the ground crew strength being only 60 per cent of the full establishment. With the advent of the Fortresses the Squadron was amalgamated into one flight under the command of Squadron Leader Patrick, and existing flight commanders W. Roxburgh and W. Nicholson relinquished their ranks of acting flight lieutenant, reverting to flying officer.

In spite of the onset of winter operational flying hours during November increased to 676, mostly anti-submarine sweeps and convoy escort, although only one U-Boat sighting was reported in the month. It appeared that the number of U-Boats had

All these named crew members lost on 14 December 1942.
L to R: Sgt E. Crowe; Sgt R. Hildred; Sgt W. Shanks;
Fg Off. J. Owen; ?; ?; Sgt W. Parnell.
(CC/206)

decreased in the Benbecula operating area most likely due to Operation *Torch* and the concentration of German naval forces in the western Mediterranean and Atlantic Approaches. Flying Officer Roxburgh and his crew made a visual sighting of a U-Boat and attacked on 25 November, dropping seven depth charges which exploded 120 yards beyond the swirl as the submarine dived. Light-coloured oil appeared on the surface two minutes after the attack. The U-Boat was painted black and appeared to carry the standard periscope. Less fortunate was Flying Officer Owen and his crew who depth-charged a whale, resulting in drinks all round in the mess!

A notable episode on 11 December was the sighting of three U-Boats in succession by Flying Officer John Owen and crew while covering Convoys HX217 and SC111. Owen carried out his attack as the first U-Boat began to crash dive, dropping six depth charges. After the vessel had disappeared the crew sighted the second U-Boat and attacked from dead astern, dropping the remaining depth charge from 30 feet above the surface. A huge explosion was witnessed by the tail gunner and the submarine came to the surface for a few seconds and damage to the conning tower was visible. Two hours later a third U-Boat was seen but with no depth charges left all that Owen could do was to make a mock attack, forcing the vessel to crash dive. Not long after this, on 14 December, John Owen and his crew in Fortress FL453 failed to return from an anti-submarine patrol while covering Convoy ONS152. During the following day parallel track searches were carried out by Squadron Leader Patrick and Flying Officers Roxburgh and Wills but nothing was sighted by the three crews over very rough seas in which the chances of survival in a dinghy were remote. Later in the month the CO wrote:

'Flying Officer John Owen joined 206 Squadron in 1941. His reputation for keenness and thoroughness in everything he undertook was unexcelled. He took part in the third thousand-bomber raid (Bremen, 25/6/42) and made two damaging attacks on U-Boats during his penultimate patrol. With him were lost Sergeants R. N. Hildred, R. Bentley, E. Crowe, W. J. Parnell, G. C. Wilson and W. Shanks.'[6]

On Benbecula itself there had been a change of command on 28 November with Group Captain D. L. Blackford succeeding Group Captain (later Air Commodore) R. C. Field as station commander.

The U-Boat campaign conducted by Dönitz to disrupt Operation *Torch* was being wound down by December so that maximum resources could be concentrated in the Atlantic. This offered a fresh challenge to Coastal Command but at a time when VLR (Very Long Range) aircraft like the Liberator were still in short supply. 206 Squadron was one of three Fortress squadrons available for operations so there was considerable work to do.

On 12 December during an anti-submarine patrol covering Convoy SC111, Squadron Leader R. C. Patrick sighted a U-Boat from a height of 9,000 feet, but the submarine dived before an attack could be made. After some baiting tactics had been employed another sighting was made but the vessel once again crash dived, but not before seven depth charges had been dropped ahead of the swirl and slightly to starboard of the track. Later the assessment of the attack was that the vessel had been 'probably damaged'.

A sea search was undertaken on 18 December after the stern half of what appeared to be a torpedoed ship was sighted by a Liberator of 120 Squadron on passage from the United Kingdom to Iceland. Flying Officer A. E. Bland was diverted from an anti-submarine patrol and carried out a sea search for several hours but without result. A few days later, on 22 December, Pilot Officer P. M. Hill homed on to a radar contact which turned out to be the rear structure and funnel of an oil tanker drifting eastwards, in poor visibility, with a long oil streak stretching out westwards. It was discovered later that the ship was a Norwegian tanker which had been attacked in mid-Atlantic and the crew of 29 had survived for a week in spite of drifting helplessly in violent storms. They were sighted by a number of aircraft and finally rescued when they had drifted to within six miles of allied territory.[7]

A major success for 206 was achieved on 15 January 1943 when Pilot Officer L. G. Clark in Fortress FL452 sighted and successfully attacked U-337 on the surface, during close escort of Convoys ONS160 and ONS161. The vessel appeared to be taken by surprise by the attack which was carried out from the port bow. The first two depth charges fell short, two hit the vessel and exploded and the remaining three failed to release. After the attack the bow or stern was seen at a very steep angle and boiling foam patches were reported before the vessel slid under. After the war U-337 was confirmed as having been lost by the Germans in this area at about the time of the attack.

Apart from seeking out U-Boats the squadron also had a role to play in assisting naval and merchant vessels whenever this was required, as on 23 January when three aircraft on a 'Creeping Line Ahead Search' patrol with pilots Pilot Officers P. M. Hill, R. S. Weir and K. B. Bass, received a signal to seek out and identify the ships of the convoy 'Laconic' which had scattered. Jim Glazebrook took up the story:

'So the Navy's aerial sheep-dogs got to work, backwards and forwards through the area allocated.........and to such good effect that by the end of their patrol 21 merchant

---

6   Quoted in Glazebrook, J, War History of 206 Sqn p16.
7   Glazebrook p16.

vessels had been sighted, identified and their positions logged. Throughout the next few days the ships were watched and guarded, until the convoy had completely reassembled and the surface escorts were once more in position.'[8]

There was a similar turn of events on 9 February when Squadron Leader R. C. Patrick was on an anti-submarine patrol 800 miles out in the Atlantic. The crew sighted a corvette being towed eastwards by a destroyer and the latter requested aerial protection while towing. Accordingly, Patrick began a square search at 30 miles radius of the vessels and after two hours a U-Boat, later identified as U-614, was sighted at a distance of five or six miles ahead, in a position north and east of the vessels. Squadron Leader Patrick went into the attack and his depth charges straddled the submarine forward of the conning tower causing it to lift bodily and sink. An uprush of bubbles and explosions was observed and it was later concluded that the depth charges had caused damage but that there was no further evidence of a 'kill'. Squadron Leader Patrick's diversion from his pre-set patrol at the request of the destroyer's captain was later accepted by Group Headquarters as the right decision. In future the code-word 'Patrick' was introduced into the 'Convoy Escort Code' which could be signalled from aircraft to surface vessels meaning 'I am on independent patrol, but can assist you if necessary'.

In early February 1943 there was a change of command with Air Marshal Sir Philip Joubert de la Ferté being replaced as AOC-in-C Coastal Command by Air Marshal J. C. Slessor. This happened just at the moment that the anti-U-Boat war was given high priority in the combined strategy of Britain and the United States, one of the decisions made at the Casablanca Conference of January. This new emphasis could not have been better timed as Dönitz was deploying large numbers of U-Boats to cause havoc with the Allied convoys, especially in the crucial 'gap' region of the Atlantic. Dönitz, by now Commander-in-Chief of the German Navy, increased the daily average of operational U-Boats in the Atlantic to 116 and on the northern routes to about 60. In the battle of code-deciphering there is some evidence that the Germans were ahead of Bletchley Park GC and CS[9] with their 'B-Dienst' and the results showed in allied losses: during the month of February, in appalling winter weather of snow and hail 63 ships were lost, a total of over 359,000 tons.[10]

A taste of the winter weather was experienced by Flying Officer Roxburgh on 21 February in FK195 when severe icing at sea level at the extremity of his patrol led to reduced power of his port inner engine. He climbed to 12,000 feet before the engine's performance improved but by then fuel was short and Roxburgh had to ignore a signal to divert. It was common for crews to be diverted to Skitton in Caithness or to the Northern Irish airfields of Aldergrove and Limavady when the weather prevented landing at Benbecula.

There was no let-up in March, the worst month for Allied shipping losses since November 1942, with 108 ships being sunk by U-Boats, a total of over 627,000 tons, the Luftwaffe adding another 12 of over 65,000 tons.[11] Ironically the four-week period from about mid-March 1943 was the most successful period for 206 Squadron in the entire war, with a tally of four U-Boats destroyed, all for the first time confirmed by attack results.

The first of these successes was the sinking of U-384, a Type VIIC, by Pilot Officer L. G. Clark in Fortress FK208 on 19 March while shadowing Convoy HX229. The boat was on its second patrol in the North Atlantic, having sailed from La Pallice on 6 March, skippered by Oberleutnant zur See Hans-Achim von Rosenberg-Gruszczynski.

---

8 Glazebrook p18.
9 Government Code and Cypher School or 'Ultra'.
10 Barnett pp 594-5.
11 Barnett p 597.

Its last message was recorded on 19 March. The official report on the incident recorded that the sea was calm with visibility of 20 miles when the vessel was sighted on the surface on port beam at a distance of ten miles. The submarine 'was dirty green colour with slatted wooden upper deck, one gun forward of conning tower, and what was thought to be a light gun lying horizontally in the conning tower'. In the attack, carried out at low altitude from the boat's starboard quarter, four Mark XI Torpex depth charges were released from 50 feet which straddled the vessel. An explosion was witnessed and a heavy black substance appeared as if there was still an object on the water's surface. Then there was a large circular patch in the centre of which were long black streaks of oil. The aircraft returned to its patrolling position and the oil patch persisted for some time afterwards. There was a suggestion that the U-Boat was later claimed by a Sunderland crew of 201 Squadron operating out of Lough Erne, but this was most likely the result of an attack by a Sunderland on U-631 on 20 March, which damaged the vessel.[12]

A few days later on 25 March, Flying Officer W. Roxburgh in Fortress FK195 'L for Leather', known to be the squadron's lucky aircraft, sighted a surfaced submarine from a height of 3,500 feet. The aircraft was put in a steep dive and the depth charges were released at 200 feet while the front upper gunner opened fire as they got closer. The submarine was straddled and was submerged when there was a massive underwater explosion, leading to a large quantity of debris coming to the surface and a long oil slick appearing. The submarine later turned out to be U-469 on her first patrol from Kiel and skippered by Oberleutnant zur See Emil Claussen, and was confirmed to have been sunk in the action. Flying Officer Roxburgh later received the DFC.[13]

The same aircraft was on patrol only two days later, with Flying Officer Ian Samuel at the controls, when a surfaced U-169 (commanded by Oberleutnant zur See Hermann Bauer) was sighted at about three miles distance from a height of 2,000 feet. As the aircraft went into the attack the Germans opened fire and tracers were seen but no hits sustained. Six depth charges were released from less than 100 feet causing an explosion amidships and forcing the vessel to heel over to starboard, then it submerged for several seconds only to re-appear with bows upright at an acute angle. Samuel began his second attack and released the final depth charge into the foam around the submarine, with the tail gunner firing at the keel as the aircraft drew away. Men were seen scrambling about on the conning tower as the U-Boat sank at almost a vertical angle but in the roughness of the sea it was impossible to observe their fate.

The fourth 'kill' of early 1943 was by Flying Officer Bob Cowey in FL451 on 24 April. As he approached the end of his patrol a periscope was sighted at a distance of eight miles. On the aircraft's approach the U-Boat U-710 surfaced, a Type VIIC commanded by Oberleutnant zur See Dietrich von Carlowitz, and the Germans opened fire. Cowey straddled the vessel with six depth charges and an explosion followed, the bows being lifted out of the water. On a second attack with the remaining depth charge the U-Boat sank, stern first. About 25 survivors were seen among the wreckage. After the attack the aircraft landed at Reykjavik. For this attack and for his previous work with the squadron, Bob Cowey was awarded the DFC on 1 June.

The Herculean efforts of aircrews, combined with technical advances in radar and growing experience of working with convoys was beginning to blunt the edge of the German U-Boat weapon as 1943 progressed. Innovations like escort carrier groups by the US and Royal Navies were able for the first time to combat the threat against Allied

---

12 See Loose Minute dated 20 May 1983 AHB (RAF) confirming sinking of U-384 by 206 Sqn. (206 Archives, RAF Kinloss). A. Price in *Aircraft v. Submarine* claims kill for 201 Sqn Sunderland. (p131).
13 Willis Roxburgh was posted to No. 86 Sqn in May 1943, and was later appointed Assistant Air Attaché to the staff of Lord Halifax, British Ambassador in Washington, USA.

Fortress over Benbecula.
(Sid Banks)

convoys. The results began to show in April with U-Boat losses from all causes on an upward trend.[14] Also, 56 Allied ships of a total of 328,000 tons were sunk, just over one half of the March tally.[15] Counter-measures were beginning to pay off.

Early in May a detachment of the squadron flew to St Eval to shadow a convoy in the Western Approaches and fly anti-U-Boat patrols in the Bay of Biscay. A new hazard appeared in the shape of long-range fighters which Flying Officer Lovell had a taste of when he fended off no less than nine Junker Ju 88's on one occasion, the largest number of enemy fighters that had been seen in the Bay during that period. But the U-Boats were facing their first really serious crisis of the war as the losses increased steeply to 38 during May or 32.2 per cent of boats operating, compared with 12 in March and 13 in April. This was in return for 42 allied ships being sunk.[16] It is no exaggeration to say that the power of the U-Boats to range at will over the Atlantic was being broken once and for all. Aircraft of Coastal Command, at their extreme range, were sighting and attacking more enemy submarines than ever before with nearly three-quarters of total U-Boat losses being attributed to air attacks[17]. The air threat faced by the Germans was such

14 4.3% losses of boats operating Jan. 1943, 13% in Feb., 10.3% in March, 11.7% in April.
   (*U-Boat War in the Atlantic* (MOD (Navy): German Naval History Vol I Plan 59).
15 Barnett p 603.
16 MOD: German Naval History (Plan 59 above).
17 Ibid. p112.

that by 24 May the North Atlantic was effectively abandoned and the remaining boats moved southwest of the Azores, to operate against the US-Gibraltar convoys.

There was a change on 16 May when Wing Commander J. R. S. Romanes DFC was posted to Headquarters and Acting Wing Commander R. B. Thomson DSO took command of the squadron. On 11 June the CO took off from Benbecula in Fortress FA704 'R' at 0710 hrs and in the course of the patrol sighted U-417, a Type VIIC, skippered by Oberleutnant zur See Wolfgang Schreiner.[18] The sub was spotted from 1,500 feet about seven miles distant, fully surfaced and at full speed. The aircraft made a number of evasive manoeuvres as it approached and Thomson decided to attack from 50 feet. The submarine opened fire at 600 yards and made a number of hits before it was straddled with four depth charges. Flight Sergeant A. F. Chisnall, one of the crew, recalled that at first Thomson thought he had missed but then the sub's bows rose, almost vertical, and sank back into the sea, leaving 20-30 sailors in the water shaking their fists at the passing aircraft. Before they had a chance to set course for home three out of four engines were pouring smoke and only one engine was functioning well, so the Captain decided to ditch and to take up crash positions. Chisnall continued:

'About a minute later we crashed and were scrambling out of the aircraft into an ice cold sea, making us gasp for breath; only one of the two dinghies inflated, and soon all eight of us were sitting in it and watched the aircraft sink which happened very quickly. Then we considered our chances of being found and were very relieved to hear that the wireless operator had managed to get out an SOS.' Unfortunately the packs containing rations and distress signals had been swept away along with the paddles. There were seven crew on board plus the station armourer who had gone 'for the ride'. The next eight hours were spent shivering and being violently sea-sick.

A faint SOS had been received at about 1130 hrs, sparking off a major sea search. The crew had in the meantime managed to board their dinghy while several Fortresses were diverted to look for the survivors. At 1900 hrs a US Navy Catalina of 84 Squadron signalled that it had located the dinghy but by then the Fortresses had reached the limit of their endurance and had to head for base. Flying Officer Hill took off from Benbecula at 2222 hrs and received a signal that the Catalina would attempt a landing. Sergeant Chisnall described how their spirits rose at the sight:

'The Catalina circled around for about 20 minutes and then put down its floats and came in for a landing. We all held our breath as the sea was very rough indeed. The Catalina touched down on the water and tore into a big wave which rose up in front of her causing one of the propellers

Wg Cdr Thomson and crew being rescued by a Catalina in June 1943, after surviving in the sea for three days. (CC/206)

to fly off. The aircraft began to settle down by the nose. It was agonising to see the Americans climb into their dinghies as they had made a gallant and heroic attempt to pick us up. The Catalina took about a quarter of an hour to sink and we tried very hard for about an hour to get to the Americans but found it impossible owing to the state of the sea. That night a gale blew up, the waves were about 40 feet high and the wind tore around our dinghy. We pulled the covers up over us and tied them in the centre, but still the water came in, making it necessary to bail about every quarter of an hour. For bailers we used the navigator's shoes, as the bailer was missing and the rest of us had

18 Glazebrook pp 25-7 & *206 Sqn History* (75th Anniversary) pp 30-3.

flying boots on. It was a very slow and tedious operation in such a cramped position'.

Nothing more was heard but the search continued overnight, fortunately in a latitude where at this time of year there was no complete darkness. The weather worsened, and the following morning a Catalina of 190 Squadron sighted at least five survivors, which turned out to be the crew of the Catalina which had attempted a landing and had been wrecked in the process, now separated from the Fortress crew in the stormy weather. Flight Lieutenant Wills continued the search into the early evening and sighted Wing Commander Thomson's dinghy but was forced to abandon the sortie due to shortage of fuel and divert to Reykjavik. Flight Sergeant Chisnall recalled that they spent that day and night huddled together and although the wind had died down a little there was still a very heavy sea.

On Sunday 13 June, the third day of the search, three Fortresses took off from Benbecula, joined by Flight Lieutenant Wills from Reykjavik, and Thomson's dinghy was sighted. Another Catalina of 84 Squadron, a Sunderland of 330 Squadron and later a Hampden of 51 Air-Sea Rescue (ASR) Squadron circled while the Sunderland made several fruitless attempts to land. Chisnall recalled that 'wind had calmed down considerably but the swell was as heavy as ever. We were all feeling very thirsty and began teasing one another by describing in detail the local pub, and one standing against the bar with a lovely pint of beer in front of him – it was agonising but it caused a good laugh. That afternoon we were sighted by a Fortress and we cheered and waved as it dived down and flew low over us, dropping two bags containing water and bully beef. We soon had them on board and were tasting the first drop of water we had had for over two days. The Wing Commander took charge of the water ration and allowed us to open one tin, which was about a mouthful each. Later a Catalina arrived and dropped us containers with more water, some cigarettes, matches and Horlicks tablets. Then came a Sunderland, flown by a Norwegian crew, which made two very brave attempts to land – but the swell was too heavy. That night we all felt much happier and some of the crew managed to get a little sleep.'

The next morning and the fourth day, 14 June, a Lindholme dinghy was dropped and picked up by the survivors at 0555 hrs. Flying Officer Hill was joined by three Hampdens and a Catalina of 190 Squadron. Sergeant Chisnall recalled the fresh water and food they obtained and a signal flashed by lamp from a Fortress: 'Keep smiling, help coming soon'. 'We did not realise at the time we were in a minefield and thought help would come by ship......About an hour later a Coastal Command Catalina joined the Fortress and started circling us. Then two Hampdens from a New Zealand squadron arrived and dropped more food supplies. We had so many containers by now that we had to string them in one long line behind the dinghy – it was quite a comforting sight!'

The Catalina of 190 Squadron, FP102, was flown by Squadron Leader J. A. Holmes DFC, having mustered a volunteer crew and stripped the machine down to improve the chances of take-off in difficult sea conditions with a full load of survivors. Sergeant Chisnall continued: 'About midday the Catalina put down its floats and started to make dummy runs across the water; we realised that it was going to attempt a landing and were very anxious about it........it made a perfect landing, and we all cheered loudly and waved a flag we had obtained from one of the containers. The aircraft taxied very slowly towards us and when it was close enough threw us a line which we managed to catch and so pulled ourselves alongside. Some of us were put on bunks and we soon had hot coffee and orange juice handed to us; nothing had tasted better in all our lives. For take-off we were told to brace ourselves and how to get out of the aircraft if anything went wrong. I heard the "Cat's" motors open up, and felt her gathering speed; there was a slight bump and we were in the air. Just over three hours later we were all in nice warm beds.' The crew had been in the water for three days, two hours and twenty-four minutes.

The Catalina took the eight survivors to Sullom Voe where they were safely installed in the sick quarters. The American survivors of the Catalina were still adrift until two dinghies were sighted on the 16th in a minefield, one of which contained two survivors. A US destroyer threaded its way through the minefield to reach them but of the eight crewmen who had attempted the original rescue only one had survived.

Shortly after this a signal was received at Benbecula from 15 Group Headquarters:

'The attack by Fortress 'R'/206 on 11 June 1943 has been assessed by the Admiralty as 'U-Boat known sunk'. The following message from the C-in-C Western Approaches begins: 'Please convey to Wing Commander Thomson and surviving crew of R/206 my warmest congratulations on their success on the 11th of June. I greatly admired the gallant manner in which the attack was pressed home.' Shortly after this the DFC was awarded to Wing Commander Thomson.

In the light of these events more attention was being paid to the forward armament of the Fortress as the Browning .303 machine gun was considered inadequate to combat the cannon and machine guns of U-Boats on the surface. Eventually the aircraft were fitted with a single .5 gun in a flexible mounting, but not the new 'chin turret' mounting twin Brownings that the USAAF Fortresses were being armed with. No further progress was made on this by the time the squadron started to convert to Liberators in March 1944.

Another success in June was achieved by Flying Officer L. G. Clark in FL457, flying on a 'Musketry' patrol from St Eval[19] on the 17th when he attacked U-338 with depth charges on two bombing runs. The submarine opened fire but then immediately dived, damaged in the encounter. It later transpired that the vessel was forced to return to St Nazaire for repairs. On a later patrol in September she was sunk by a Canadian warship.

No. 220 Squadron had arrived at Benbecula in March also with Fortresses, but by August 206's time there was coming to an end and the squadron was taken out of the line to prepare for a new base, the destination of which was not revealed until the move got under way in October 1943.

The memories of the squadron at Benbecula were to remain fresh even after 50 years, and recalled at the Association's reunion there in May 1995. Alan Smith, Secretary of the 206 Squadron Association, was an 18-year old when he first set foot on the island. The *Oban Times* reported the successes the squadron achieved against U-Boats and the many memories of the remote base. At first there was some reluctance to be posted to that far-off place but many firm roots were established to last for a lifetime. Tom Blue, then military transport NCO, remembered driving round the island in 1942 attempting to convince cautious Gaelic-speaking crofters that they should allow their daughters to attend RAF dances and occasionally he had to beat a hasty retreat! Alongside that were the sad memories of losses summed up by a poignant religious service at Nunton Cemetery. There was always the battle with the weather both in the air and on the ground, and it was a huge challenge to keep the aircraft in flying condition day after day so that sorties could be launched deep into the Atlantic leading to 'countless hours peering into the distant haze, searching, praying, protecting our supply routes, hunting the U-Boat enemy.'[20]

---

19 Biscay patrol area, which lay astride U-Boat transit routes.
20 *Oban Times*, Thursday 25 May 1995.

Final farewell to the RAF Station 1997. Flypast by Nimrod from 206 Sqn.
(CC/206)

Graves at Nunton Cemetery and final tribute by
Wg Cdr J. Romanes OBE, DFC and Alan Smith, 1997.
(CC/206)

CHAPTER 8

AZOREAN INTERLUDE: THE FIGHT GOES ON

'The squadron they joined was in far-off Azores:
They weren't very keen to leave England's fair shores,
But were fully persuaded 'twas in a good cause....'

Extract from 'Azorean Interlude' or 'Beaty Does it Again'
by Jim Glazebrook, 206 Squadron 1943.

The tide had turned against the U-Boats in the North Atlantic during the summer of 1943 but the struggle was by no means over. The net had yet to be closed further against U-Boat operations in the central North Atlantic, in the region of the Azores, where the vessels were able to rest, refuel, and recharge their batteries *en route* to their Bay of Biscay bases. During most of 1943 the resources of the Americans had been stretched in the use of surface hunter/killer forces in the area and land bases were now being urgently sought, especially for the Very Long Range aircraft of Coastal Command. To this end there had been protracted diplomatic negotiations with the Portuguese government during the year with a view to the use of a base in the Azores and to gain permission for refuelling naval escorts at either San Miguel or Fayal. Additional protection was now also required for Gibraltar-bound convoys supplying forces in the Mediterranean theatre.

An agreement was finally reached with Portugal in August 1943, based on a treaty dating back to 1373! The use of facilities was granted to enable merchant shipping to be better protected, but this was to be a temporary arrangement and in no way was Portuguese sovereignty to be curtailed.The outcome for Coastal Command was the building of an airfield on Terceira Island on the Azores. The island of Terceira, meaning 'Third', was thus named as it was the third island to be colonised in the group of nine islands. The capital, Angra, had earned the right to add 'do Heroismo' to its name because

Laying the PSP runway at Lagens, Terceira – all personnel joined in.
(Alan Smith collection via Edwin Hill)

Above: 206 Fortresses at Lagens, 1943.
Below: Lagens, 1943.

of heroic fighting of its troops during the Portuguese Civil War of 1828.

No. 206 Squadron was on notice to move from the end of August and after a number of false starts the main party embarked on 1 October. It was only after two days at sea that the destination was revealed to be the mid-Atlantic base of the Azores with the squadron forming Force 'F' at the new location. The convoy arrived on 8 October off the port of Angra do Heroismo, an event commemorated by a plaque (see photo on page 76), and personnel and equipment were brought ashore by lighters. There was then an 18-mile journey by road through a narrow valley to the airfield, which was about 2,000 yards long and 1,500 yards across at its widest point. On the airfield's westerly side were the lower slopes of a mountain which rose to a peak of over 3,000 feet only eight miles away. To the east a four-mile long ridge, up to 400 feet in height, separated the airfield from the sea. The airfield, named Lagens (now Lajes), was grass-covered and both air and ground crews were given the urgent task of laying a metal strip runway 2,000 yards long and converting an old (and unfortunately disused) distillery ('the alcohol factory') to become the new squadron headquarters. The runway was of the PSP (Pressed Steel Plank) variety which was hooked together by means of interlocking lugs to form a firm surface which could withstand the impact of the Fortresses.[1] In addition there were Nissen huts constructed to form living quarters, cookhouse and offices.

Air Vice-Marshal G. R. Bromet became the AOC of No. 247 Group, Azores, and within days the preparations had been completed to receive the first aircraft on 18 October. Two Fortresses set out from St Eval to make the 1,300 mile non-stop flight, one from 206 flown by the OC Wing Commander R. B. Thomson, DSO, DFC[2], and the other with the OC of 220 Squadron, Wing Commander P. E. Hadow, at the controls.

The arrival of the Fortresses on the island was an historic occasion, photographed by the RAF Film Unit. The aircraft were sighted at 1510 hrs in bright and sunny weather and in good visibility, with no trace of a cloud. After making a double circuit Wing Commander Thomson made a perfect landing on the field, followed a few minutes later by the 220 Squadron aircraft. There were warm greetings from Air Vice-Marshal Bromet

1 F. MacManus, *Memoirs of Six Years in the RAF.*
2 Later AVM and AOC No. 18 Group.

Lagens, 1943.

and the welcoming party, which included Group Captain Reynolds (SASO[3]), the station commander Group Captain Oulton with their respective staffs. Not least, the men from 206 who were watching the scene from the operations block were delighted to see their CO and his crew.

The formalities over it was down to the serious work again of hunting down U-Boats in what was left of the Atlantic 'gap'. Morale was high, and the airfield proved more than adequate for the other Fortresses which soon followed, flying from RAF Benbecula via Thorney Island and out to Lagens. On 21 October the first operational sortie was flown by Flying Officer Rigg and his crew but the first confirmed 'kill' fell to a 220 Squadron Fortress a week later. Other units began to arrive, including detachments of Leigh-Light Wellingtons of Nos 172 and 179 Squadrons and No. 269 ASR Squadron, a former stable-mate of 206 at Bircham Newton, comprising a flight of Hudsons, two Walruses and two Spitfires. Jim Glazebrook summed up the task which lay ahead:

'......Much work remained to be done on the airfield. One or two buildings previously used by a unit of the Portuguese Air Force were taken over, but most of the British Force was accommodated in small tents, and messes were marquees. There were no modern conveniences of any kind, and water pipes had to be laid, wash-houses built and latrines dug before the squadron could settle down to a more normal existence. Detachments from the Royal Engineers and the RAF Regiment did most of the heavy work, but for a time it was "all hands on deck" with a vengeance!'[4]

During November the 'wet' season had arrived and the red volcanic dust which made up the topsoil on the islands was becoming a thick layer of mud, and to add to the difficulties there was almost continuous cloud cover of the 3,000 foot mountain peaks and even the top of the ridge. With few radio aids available, bad weather proved an added hazard for crews trying to locate their base after a long patrol, situated as it was in a vast expanse of sea. The nearest base for diversion was Gibraltar, over 1,000 miles away, as Flight Sergeant D. J. Mitchener and his crew in FK208 found on 28 November when they were diverted after a convoy patrol. When they reached Gibraltar, short of fuel, they found the base closed by fog and crashed off Carnero Point in the

---

3 Senior Air Staff Officer.
4 Glazebrook, *War History of 206 Sqn* p30.

early hours of the 29th with the loss of the entire crew. This was 206's first loss from the Azores.[5]

There were also diplomatic constraints on the military use of the islands which made life more difficult. The British Force was granted the use of Terceira only and the neutrality of the other islands had to be respected so that the RAF was not permitted to fly within three miles of them. Included in the 'Instructions for anti-submarine (A/S) patrols' issued to the crews were orders to avoid flying over the high ground of Terceira and not to infringe the territorial waters of the other islands. Thus it was not uncommon for aircraft returning in the darkness from a patrol to be fired at by Portuguese anti-aircraft gunners based on San Miguel, the biggest island in the Azores. There was also a small airfield here which could be used in an emergency but only by the granting of prior permission from the Portuguese Military Governor. There was a small British servicing unit on the island but the personnel were treated almost like prisoners, being confined to camp unless accompanied by a Portuguese military escort. Jim Glazebrook recalled being among a party of aircrew who were permitted to visit the small airfield of Santa Anna to familiarise themselves in good weather with the landing ground, should it be required in the future. Two Fortresses flew to Santa Anna but one became bogged down in soft ground and the crew and passengers had to remain overnight while the aircraft was freed. As there was no local accommodation the personnel were conducted across the hills to Ponta Delgada and were delivered into the hospitality of the British Consul. But the next morning it was back to Lagens!

Frank MacManus recalled that the strict neutrality of the islands enabled a small German presence to remain on San Miguel island although no visits to Terceira were permitted. Many items of German manufacture were available in the shops of Angra do Heroismo and Frank bought a folding bellows camera quite cheaply, a lucky find.[6]

By January 1944 the squadron headquarters buildings were fully refurbished thanks to the muscle-power of everyone concerned, and Air Vice-Marshal Bromet commended the squadron's work in a minute to the Station Commander on 27 January 1944. He congratulated the OC 206 Squadron on 'the enterprise and industry' shown and how impressed he had been with the result. He went on: 'This sort of thing is the "hall mark" of a good squadron.....and Wing Commander Thomson can have every confidence in achieving a high standard of administration and training in his squadron.' Many VIP visitors were proudly shown around the squadron headquarters in the coming months, including the AOC-in-C Coastal Command Air Marshal Sir John Slessor, Air Chief Marshal Sir Frederick Bowhill, and Marshal of the Royal Air Force Viscount Trenchard, who gave a lecture to aircrew personnel. The Azores station was not to be a forgotten backwater in the Command.

Operations continued in the grip of Azores winter weather. By this time the range of the Fortresses had been extended by loading extra fuel into the two bomb-bays, the four depth charges being mounted externally on the wings. In this way endurance could be increased to $13^1/_2$ hours, and even as long as 16 hours. The latter achievement was by an aircraft of 220 Squadron during a Search and Rescue patrol for a downed Wellington.

The fact that U-Boats on the surface were by no means passive victims when it came to air attack, was demonstrated on 6 January 1944 when Squadron Leader A. J. Pinhorn DFC in Fortress FA705 encountered U-270, a type VIIC, commanded by Oberleutnant zur See Heinrich Schreiber. Pinhorn sent a sighting report but after that there was silence. It appeared later that the Fortress had attacked and been shot down by one of the

---

5 Crew are named on the Gibraltar Memorial: Flt Sgt D. J. A. Mitchener, WO D. B. Brown,
  Flt Sgt R. Burnett, WO D. S. Coutts, Fg Off. A. E. Moule, Sgt R. A. Senior, Flt Sgt J. Stones, Flt Sgt J. Wilson.
6 F. MacManus.

submarine's gunners. No trace of the crew was ever found.[7] The award of the DFC for Squadron Leader Pinhorn had only been announced the day before his final sortie. The submarine was, however, damaged in the attack and was forced to return to St Nazaire. Later that year the U-Boat became the victim of an aircraft of 461 Squadron RAAF .

Jim Glazebrook joined the squadron at around this time as a flight sergeant, fresh from crew training in Nassau in the Bahamas and the UK. He was second pilot in the crew of Flight Lieutenant David Beaty who had previously served in a Special Duties Flight of Wellingtons in the Mediterranean theatre, and latterly in Britain with the Coastal Command Development Unit. His choice of Coastal rather than Bomber Command was governed by his preference 'to fight men who were wearing uniform'. Other members of David Beaty's crew included Sergeant Frank R. MacManus, a WOM/AG[8], Sergeant Norman S. Draper, Sergeant Leo Meaker RAAF and the navigator Flight Sergeant J. L. Johnston, all of whom had trained together at Nassau with Jim Glazebrook as their captain before arriving in the UK for conversion training from the Liberator to the B17 Fortress at No. 1 OTU at Thornaby in September 1943. There they were joined by their new captain David Beaty and by Sergeant J. Cunningham, their new flight engineer. The second part of their conversion training was at Longtown from October to November before the posting to the Azores and 206 Squadron came through. The crew was completed at Lagens by the addition of Flying Officer Peter Laird (WOp/AG) in mid-January 1944.

Fortress on patrol from the Azores, 1944.

Frank MacManus recalled the long anti-submarine (A/S) patrols from the Azores in early 1944 as lasting anything up to 12 hours, with inevitable tedium but yet the need to be constantly alert as 'the radar was the rather primitive ASV Mk II, so searching was by means of the Mk I eyeball'. Staring at the empty ocean for hours at a time was made more tolerable by the wireless operator/gunners spending only up to an hour in the one crew position and moving between radio set, top turret, rear guns and beam guns. He recalled the pre-operation routine:

'Before each operational flight, the cookhouse staff prepared packed meals of sandwiches, of which we could usually select our choice, cakes, biscuits, chocolate and fresh fruit. Fresh pineapple was a popular choice but a bit messy to eat with gloved

---

7   Also missing Sqn Ldr R. Brown, Fg Off. J. H. Duncan, Flt Sgt T. Eckersley, Sgt R. Fabian,
    WO1 D. L. Heard RCAF, WO1 O. A. Keddy RCAF, Fg Off. F. D. Roberts, and WO R. N. Stares.
8   Wireless Operator/Mechanic/Air Gunner.

Squadron Leader 'JC' Graham and crew outside 206 HQ (formerly the Old Winery – alcohol factory) in the Azores. L to R (back row): Sgt Edwards (WOp/AG); Plt Off. Bryan (WOp/AG); Flt Sgt Nicol (co-pilot); Sqn Ldr 'JC' Graham; Fg Off. L. F. 'Sid' Banks (Nav.); Fg Off. Pimblott (Nav.); Sgt A. D. B. Smith (Eng/AG). Front row L to R: WO Duffus (WOp/AG); WO Hine RAAF (WOp/AG).
(Alan Smith collection/Sid Banks)

Local villager and wife outside SNCOs Quarters selling pineapples and lamps. Wife also collected washing. Sgt Jim Cunningham right of village man; Sgt Ginger Baxter centre; Bill Thompson (Nav.) RCAF at right end.
(Alan Smith collection)

Post card from official RAF photo, Azores 1943. Sid Banks recalls: 'This was apparently a PR set-up which included several members of my crew scraped together for the photo. I'm the sleek one peering over the shoulder of the mysterious man in the big hat – probably the official RAF PR man sent out to build up our morale.'
(Sid Banks)

fingers. There were also a lot of flasks of tea and coffee – and Benzedrine 'stay-awake' amphetamine tablets if we really needed them. There was an RAF tradition of an 'operational meal' for aircrew. This was always a fry-up of bacon, beans and various other ingredients, sometimes kidney or even a tiny steak but it always included a fried egg. Fresh eggs were a rarity in wartime UK and were not to be seen in an RAF mess other than part of crew 'operational meal'. (Actually the Azores were an exception to the general rule since there were plenty of eggs always available). We always chose to eat our Ops meal after the flight, wherever we were based, but Bomber Command crews often elected to have their eggs before the flight, on the basis that there was a fair chance of their not coming back!' Squadron Leader J. C. Graham remembered these greasy 'fry-ups' before the long patrols and speculated as to the long-term effects on the digestive system these must have had!

Frank MacManus had served initially as an apprentice and found that the RAF had been reluctant to approve aircrew training for apprentices at first. Most bomber sorties tended to be of relatively short duration but as Very Long Range aircraft became available for Coastal Command in the course of 1942 and 1943 it was found that longer patrols increased the risk of radio or electrical failures in the air, which could have fatal results. As there were few navigational aids, a radio problem could be potentially serious as the navigator did most of his calculations by dead-reckoning (compass heading, airspeed and computation of wind speed and direction). In this much depended on the skill of the navigator and the weather conditions. The rear gunner would often assist in checking wind speed and direction. A smoke float (or flame float at night) was dropped and the gunner followed the float as it receded, then read off the drift angle from a calibrated scale on the turret or gun mountings. Aircrew with a mechanical background therefore proved an important asset in a crew and ex-apprentices like Frank MacManus usually became WOM/AGs (wireless-operator/mechanic/air gunners) 'almost exclusively on long-range ocean patrol squadrons, where odds on survival were vastly better than on bomber squadrons.'

The training of Flight Lieutenant David Beaty and his crew was put to the test on 13 March 1944, when they were about to take off from Lagens in FA700 on an anti-submarine patrol and were tasked to assist a Leigh-Light Wellington of 172 Squadron which had attacked with depth charges what later turned out to be U-575, skippered by Oberleutnant zur See Wolfgang Boehmer, in a location some 500 miles north of the Azores. By the time the Fortress had reached the estimated position just before dawn the Wellington had been forced to leave the scene, having reached the limit of its endurance and marking the spot with flares, some 75 miles from Convoy ON 227 which it had been covering. The sky was overcast and a further marker was dropped, and the Fortress began to circle the area as dawn was awaited, with the second pilot Jim Glazebrook at the controls. Suddenly, at about 0740 hrs, he sighted a submarine surfacing in the flat glassy sea just in front of the Fortress but the aircraft was too high and too close to make an immediate attack and the second pilot made a steep diving turn to get into position, by which time the element of surprise had been lost and the U-Boat's guns were manned and firing. David Beaty was unable at this point to send a sighting report back to base due to their low altitude and realised that if they gained the necessary height to get a message through the U-Boat would probably escape. So it was decided to risk an attack without the security of radio contact and David Beaty, by now at the controls, manoeuvred the aircraft to an attacking position at a height of 50 feet, and 30 degrees to port of line astern. They flew through a storm of cannon and machine gun fire while the navigator Sergeant Johnston fired the single 0.5-inch Browning in the nose which appeared to strike home at the conning tower and the gun platform, and Frank MacManus operated the twin Brownings from the mid-upper turret. The four 250 lb

Fortress with David Beaty and crew after returning from attack on U-575, 13/3/44.
Close-up L to R: Cunningham, MacManus, Johnston, Draper, Glazebrook, Beaty, Meaker.
(Jim Glazebrook)

depth charges were dropped three to one side of the boat and one to the other, and exploded, leaving the U-Boat on the surface for a few seconds before she disappeared under the water stern first, leaving behind two large oil patches on the surface. Markers were again dropped and the Fortress remained in the area for five hours to the maximum extent of its endurance, homing in Fortress 'J' of 220 Squadron, with pilot Flying Officer W. R. Travell, and the escort vessel HMCS *Prince Rupert*.

By the time the 220 Fortress reached the position an oil slick was visible, which appeared to move in relation to the smoke marker they had just dropped, suggesting that the U-Boat was already severely disabled. Depth charges were then dropped and the Fortress crew homed to the area HMCS *Prince Rupert* and two US destroyers to administer the *coup de grace* with their deep depth charges, followed up by an attack by three aircraft from the US escort carrier *Bogue*. The U-Boat was finally blown to the surface before disappearing for the last time. Fifty-two survivors, including the captain, were taken on board the ships. Later it turned out that the vessel was one of the first to be fitted with the *Schnorkel* tube, which was basically an air pipe, enabling the boat to remain underwater and travelling on diesels almost indefinitely, without the need to surface to re-charge batteries.

Credit for this remarkable success was shared between the Wellington and the two Fortresses, the Canadian frigate and the US ships and aircraft. Warm congratulations were relayed to 206 Squadron from the Commander-in-Chief Western Approaches and Flight Lieutenant David Beaty was to receive the DFC for the exploit. Flying Officer J. P. Finnessey, the Wellington pilot of 172 Squadron, received the DFC, as did Flying Officer W. R. Travell of 220 Squadron. Later, Jim Glazebrook was commissioned and awarded the DFC. He wrote about some of the lighter aspects of his time in the Azores in his poem 'Azorean Interlude' or 'Beaty Does it Again'. This was in the style of (and with apologies to) The Western Brothers (popular radio comics of the 1930s.):[9]

Now this is an epic of war in the air –
Jolly good show, chaps, jolly good show!
The tale of a Fortress crew doing their share –
Jolly good show, chaps, jolly good show!
They'd done all their 'drills' and they'd got all the 'gen':
They knew how to send a 'first sighting', and when,
In fact – you might say – a fine body of men!
Jolly good show, chaps, jolly good show!

---

9   Quoted with permission of J. Glazebrook.

An experienced skipper was Beaty (D.B.) –
Jolly good show, chaps, jolly good show!
He'd done his first 'tour' out in Malta, you see –
Jolly good show, chaps, jolly good show!
The squadron they joined was in far-off Azores:
They weren't very keen to leave England's fair shores,
But were fully persuaded 'twas in a good cause –
Jolly good show, chaps, jolly good show!

They did several 'Ops' and saw nothing but sea –
Jolly good show, chaps, jolly good show!
They got a bit 'browned off', between you and me –
Jolly good show, chaps, jolly good show!
They practised attacking again and again:
'The thing is'[10], said Beaty, 'You never know when
The chance of a lifetime may come to us, men' –
Jolly good show, chaps, jolly good show!

Well, Beaty's crew sighted a U-Boat one day-
Jolly good show, chaps, jolly good show!
It was surfacing 500 miles from the Bay-
Jolly good show, chaps, jolly good show!
They circled it first, then went in to attack:
The blighter put up quite a barrage of flak,
But they damaged it so that it never got back-
Jolly good show, chaps, jolly good show!

Now it's back to old England they're sending this crew,
Jolly good show, chaps, jolly good show!
They've done all that they were sent out to do,
Jolly good show, chaps, jolly good show!
The Second Front's coming, or that's what they say,
And it wouldn't surprise me to see it one day,
With old Beaty's crew there, in the thick of the fray!
Jolly good show, chaps, jolly good show!

Officers' Mess which used
to belong to the Portuguese
sergeants. A good stone
building with two
anterooms, a card room
and a large dining hall.

---

10 A favourite phrase of Beaty's (J. Glazebrook).

Azores forces 1943/44.

In late March the squadron was preparing for a return to the UK and conversion to B-24 Liberators. By then a major transformation was taking place at Lagens as the Americans were developing the base for use by their large commercial aircraft like the DC4, as a stopping-point on transit across the Atlantic. The US Navy 'Seabees' (construction battalions) were hard at work with bulldozers and other heavy machinery carving a wide gap through the ridge between the airfield and the sea. A new runway was built to allow some protection for aircraft landing against the severe crosswinds and in the process the site of the 206 Squadron HQ and the latrines was obliterated.

The plan was for 220 Squadron to remain in the Azores for the time being, with some of the crews from 206 who were nearing the end of their operational tour being absorbed in that squadron, while the remaining eight crews would fly their Fortresses back to England and leave them at Bircham Newton. Then they would move direct to No. 1674 Heavy Conversion Unit at Aldergrove for conversion to the B-24H Liberator Mks V and VI. There was no time to spare – the allied invasion of Europe was only weeks away.

206 at Lagens, 1944.

Frank MacManus recalled his crew flying back to the UK to leave their Fortress at Bircham Newton, well known to 206 from the early war years, for conversion to a meteorological role. One bonus was that he brought back several bottles of fine local wines and brandy as well as pineapples and bananas, exotic fare which had not been seen in England for years. 'On the train, crowded as usual, from King's Lynn to Liverpool Street, I took a banana from the branch in my kit bag and offered it to a small boy of about five or six years. He didn't know what to do with it, but his mother's eyes opened wide!'[11] A lighter moment to savour before the serious work resumed.

A great adventure lay ahead for the squadron as the momentum built up for the greatest invasion in history that would finally seal Hitler's fate!

Late winter 1944: all that was left of Camp Lagens, Azores.

Photo from collection of John Blackburn, 206 Squadron Azores 1944, and his return visit in 2000. He stands beside a photo of the memorial erected to commemorate the arrival of British forces in the Azores.

11 F. MacManus.

CHAPTER 9

LIBERATORS, ST EVAL AND LEUCHARS

'We knew that something big was brewing and, not surpisingly, guessed that an invasion of France was coming soon......'

Frank MacManus, May 1944.

By the start of 1944 the initiative in the Atlantic had passed to the Allies but the U-Boat remained a considerable threat and Dönitz was looking for every opportunity to exploit weak points in the Allied maritime strategy. It was at this point, in January 1944, that the AOC Coastal Command Air Marshal Sir John Slessor was appointed Deputy Allied Air Commander in the Mediterranean theatre, and Air Chief Marshal Sir Sholto Douglas was appointed in his place. By now the notion that Coastal Command had purely a defensive role was relegated to the history it belonged, with some 430 Allied aircraft available in the Command for anti-U-Boat operations. The major task ahead was in the planning for Operation *Overlord*, the Allied invasion of Europe, and Coastal Command's Nos 16 and 19 Groups were to have a crucial role in the weeks before and after D-Day itself. There were early signs that Dönitz was redeploying his resources away from the Atlantic in the direction of the western approaches to the British Isles and the ports in the Bay of Biscay as the number of U-Boat sightings during March dwindled. It was against this background that Sir Sholto Douglas had to counter the threat of an increased U-Boat presence along the south-western approaches and the Channel, and this meant increasing day and night patrols by No.16 Group in the North Sea and eastern Channel, by No. 19 Group in the western approaches and by No. 18 Group over the northern sea routes. Continual 24-hour a day patrols would make it almost impossible for U-Boats to surface undetected to get into an attacking position or to re-charge their batteries. Moreover, the plan by the Germans to fit their boats with the *schnorkel* breathing device, making them almost invulnerable to air attack, had been delayed by Allied bombing of the French railway system which disrupted the supply of essential equipment to the dockyards. Thus in June 1944 only nine out of 49 counter-invasion boats had been suitably equipped.[1]

Thus the AOC No. 19 Group Air Vice-Marshal B. E. Baker planned to cover the south-western approaches with interlocking patrol areas in the shape of 'corks' – hence the term *Cork* patrol - to be scanned by radar every 30 minutes by means of 30 aircraft continuously on patrol – a massive task encompassing over 20,000 square miles. To bolster the number of aircraft available No. 206 Squadron had been withdrawn from the Azores and No. 179 Squadron from Gibraltar.

Towards the end of March a new CO, Wing Commander A. de V. Leach DFC, arrived on the squadron to replace Wing Commander Thomson. The process of conversion to Liberators starting at Aldergrove in April continued when the squadron moved to St Eval during the month for a period of intensive training to join three other Liberator squadrons, Nos 53 and 224 (fitted with Leigh-Lights for night operations), and 547. The Consolidated B24H Liberators had entered service with the RAF under the Lend-Lease agreement, and were designated Mk V and Mk VI (the later version). The aircraft

---

1 Price, Alfred, *Aircraft versus Submarine* p210.

promised much greater range and endurance than the Fortresses with uprated engines, improved radar and a power-operated gun turret in the nose instead of manually operated guns in that position. During the course of May St Eval became an exceptionally busy place with four Liberator squadrons at the station, as Frank MacManus recalled:

'There was barely space at the station for all these aircraft, let alone ground staff. We knew that something big was brewing and, not surprisingly, guessed that an invasion of France was coming soon.'

Sqn Ldr Mike Fleetwood and crew, St Eval 1944.
(Alan Smith collection)

The first operational sortie by a Liberator of 206 was carried out on 23 May when Squadron Leader J. J. K. Fleetwood (father of the lead singer Mick Fleetwood of the pop group 'Fleetwood Mac') and his crew, accompanied by the CO Wing Commander A. de V. Leach DFC, flew an anti-submarine patrol in the Bay of Biscay in BZ962, but without incident. The first U-Boat sighting was on 28 May by Flight Lieutenant J. J. Fisher in BZ972 when he homed in on a radar contact to spot a 'black conning tower' but the submarine was submerging and the distance was too great for the aircraft to make an effective attack.

As D-Day drew near it had been feared that Dönitz would take advantage of the allied invasion preparations to mount attacks on Atlantic convoys again, so No. 18 Group had its work cut out tracking U-Boat movements in the northern seas, with some success. In the 19 Group area from D-Day on 6 June and for the following six weeks, 24 hours a day, the St Eval squadrons had the task of covering three patrol belts, two between Cornwall and Brittany and a third between Ushant, off the west coast of Brittany and the Scillies. An average of 25 sorties a day were flown from St Eval and 206 was unable to operate on only two days during that period, due to the severity of weather conditions at the airfield. On these days cover was maintained by units based in Northern Ireland.

The enormous effort involved in these *Cork* patrols was more than justified by the results, as within hours of the D-Day landings in Normandy, some 15 U-Boats had set sail from Brest followed by several from other Biscay ports. Most were not fitted with the *schnorkel* tubes. There was no doubt that Dönitz was employing his resources to the full at a critical moment for the allied landings in Normandy and their subsequent supply lines. One early outstanding success was that of Flight Lieutenant K. Moore RCAF of 224 Squadron in the early hours of 8 June when he achieved two confirmed U-Boat 'kills' in just over 20 minutes.

On 10 June it was the turn of Flight Lieutenant Alexander D. S. Dundas of 206 Squadron in Liberator 'K' EV943, during a daytime patrol near Ushant. A radar contact was picked up and the crew sighted U-821 under attack by four Mosquitoes of 248 Squadron led by Flight Lieutenant S. G. Nunn. By the time the Liberator arrived the U-Boat had already sustained severe damage to its conning tower and gun positions and seemed out of control, with some of the crew already taking to the water. Dundas made his attack at 50 feet, releasing five depth charges. Two more attacks were carried out but

Attack on U-821 by Flt Lt Dundas in Liberator 'K', 10 June 1944.
(CC/206)

the DCs failed to release but on the fourth attack six depth charges were dropped, straddling the boat, which sank stern first. Three survivors were seen in the water. At this point Flying Officer O'Halloran's Liberator was close to the scene, having picked up the sighting report, and attacked a 'lean grey shape' which turned out to be a German Air Sea Rescue launch on its way from Brest to pick up the sub's survivors. The crew on the launch opened fire, putting out of action O'Halloran's number one engine. Then two of the Mosquitoes joined in the action, raking the launch with cannon and machine-gun fire. Subsequently the launch was sunk and only one wounded sailor survived from the the entire crews of the U-Boat and launch. Credit for the sinking of U-821 was shared between Nos 206 and 248 Squadrons and DFCs were awarded to Flight Lieutenants Dundas and Nunn.

Within three weeks of the invasion the battle had been won. The *Cork* patrols and their follow-up had proved outstandingly successful. Not a single non-*schnorkel*-fitted U-Boat had got through to the invasion routes, at least seven had been sunk by Coastal squadrons and the survivors were withdrawn from the battle. Of the few *schnorkel*-fitted boats only one was able to sink an allied ship and was then forced to withdraw to its home port. The invasion supply lines were secure.[2] In recognition of the part played by the squadron in this great enterprise Flight Lieutenant (later Wing Commander) L. F. (Sid) Banks, senior navigator, was chosen to be decorated with the

---

2 Price, pp213-15.

Croix de Guerre for 'Gallantry in the Liberation of France'.

As the summer of 1944 progressed the Bay of Biscay ports were becoming less secure for the U-Boats, and there was a gradual transfer to bases in Germany, Norway and the Baltic, from which it was planned to harry Allied shipping in the northern seas and break out into the Atlantic. It was for this reason that some of the long-range squadrons like 206 were moved to the 18 Group operational area. Already there had been a brief detachment to Tain in northern Scotland in April and there was to be a further detachment in July, while the main squadron transferred to Leuchars in Fife during the same month to continue with anti-submarine patrols.

There was no shortage of activity. During the month there were five U-Boat sightings and four attacks and there was more evidence of enemy fighters from their bases in Denmark and Norway. On the 14th an attack was made on a submerging submarine by Flight Lieutenant Green and on the following day Flying Officer B. W. Thynne and his crew in Liberator GRVI/'E' EV947 failed to return from a patrol off the Norwegian coast. Thynne had joined the squadron at St Eval and had only just taken command of his own crew. After an extensive sea search a dinghy was located with one survivor but by the time a high speed launch managed to reach it the occupant had died. He was Pilot Officer Norman Hilton, one of the wireless operator/air gunners. It later turned out that Thynne had engaged U-319 of the 11th Flotilla based in Norway, commanded by Oberleutnant zur See Johann Clemens. In the ensuing fight the boat had been sunk but not before its gunfire had claimed the attacking aircraft. At the same time Flying Officer M. J. Frost in Liberator 'R' had attacked U-299 from the same unit, which had intended to help U-319 but the boat escaped with a damaged conning tower and the Captain and a seaman wounded. M. J. Frost later commented:

'The attack on U-299 failed because the bomb aimer in new gloves was late in operating the depth charge release. Code books sent flying by the pilot's evasive actions hit the electrical master switch of the intercom during the second run, isolating the crew.......I think there is a Scottish proverb covering these mishaps.'[3]

On the 20th there was a second loss, this time when Liberator EV873 crashed on take-off at the end of the runway and exploded. Flight Lieutenant J. D. Hancock and most of his crew perished, with the exceptions of Flight Sergeants W. R. Hoyle and J. A. Nadeau who were thrown clear and survived. Jim Glazebrook recalled the massive explosion that shook the whole station caused by 2,000 gallons of petrol and twelve 250lb depth charges and the miracle that anyone survived the accident. The cause was obscure, but may have been due to the phenomenon of 'nose-wheel shimmy'. Jim also commented on the huge comparison between safety margins now commonplace on civil airliners and their absence in war conditions at the time:

'When we took a Liberator off from a standard 2,000-yard runway, if there was no wind to help shorten the run, then even when all four engines were delivering the maximum rated power, we could often be within 100 yards of the end of the runway before the main wheels left the ground, and the initial rate of climb was very shallow. There was no margin of safety at all.'[4]

In August the squadron was beginning to convert to the Liberator Mk VI equipped with the Leigh Light under the starboard wing. This essentially simple but ingenious device invented by Squadron Leader Humphrey de Verde Leigh as far back as 1940 and first tested by Coastal Command in 1941, enabled crews to illuminate targets at night having homed in on an initial radar contact. Shortage of materials and the need to train aircrew in the skills required meant that the device was very slow coming into service

---

3   Frost, M. J. letter of 1/7/96 in 206 Sqn Archives, RAF Kinloss.
4   Glazebrook, Jim, *War Time Memories of a B24 (Liberator) Pilot*.

'OUCH!' – Collision with a brick hut! Photos of damaged Liberator EV882 at Tain, dated 19 August 1944 where 206 Sqn was operating a six-aircraft detachment away from the main base at Leuchars. Not all serious damage to Liberators was done by enemy U-Boats! James Hood writes that repairs to RAF Liberators were the responsibility of Scottish Aviation Ltd (SAL) at Prestwick and when a repair team was sent out to damaged aircraft a photographic record was made of the damage and the repair work, presumably to properly assess and cost the repairs.

(M. J. G. Hunter Collection via James R. Hood)

and it was only now that it was being made available to 206 Squadron. For the U-Boat commanders it meant that they could no longer charge their batteries on the surface in safety at night – so it was nicknamed *das verdammte Licht* – that damned light![5] The downside was that there was an enormous degree of skill required for a successful attack using the Light, and the obvious drawback that the aircraft itself became an illuminated target. There was an intensive training programme to ensure the correct co-ordination between pilot, radar operator and Leigh-Light operator-cum-bomb aimer.

However, the increasing use of the *schnorkel* U-Boats around the British Isles made them almost undetectable from the air, coupled with the fact that the vessel could submerge to a depth well out of range of depth-charges as soon as an attack threatened. But the advantage was by no means one-sided, as the Allies were gradually introducing the three-centimetre wavelength ASV Mk X which was a great improvement on previous radars in detecting *schnorkels* and periscopes providing the sea was reasonably calm. Training was also under way from about July in the newly-introduced *sonobuoys*, code-named *High Tea*, which when dropped into the sea could detect underwater sound from a submarine, for example the engine noise from the diesel-powered *schnorkel* boats, but this in turn depended on the ability to locate the U-Boat's operating area in the first place. It was not until the arrival of the Liberator Mk VIII in the spring of 1945 that the *sonobuoy* became fully operational.

Quite apart from its potential in the destruction of U-Boats the *sonobuoy* concept did not go unnoticed by the young medical officer of 206 Squadron, Flight Lieutenant Ian

5   Price, p93.

Flt Lt (later Professor) Ian Donald, 206 Squadron Doctor 1943-45.

Donald. He had been posted to the squadron at Benbecula in March 1943 and was to serve in the Azores, St Eval and Leuchars until the end of the war. His interest in psychiatry caused him to study the impact on aircrew of casualties and of the long and stressful patrols over the Atlantic. He had been awarded the MBE and a mention in despatches for bravery in saving airmen from a blazing aircraft. Also his observation of the development of radar and *sonobuoys* for anti-U-Boat warfare led him to pioneer in the post-war years the diagnostic use of ultrasound in medicine. He began his work in this latter field when he became Reader in Obstetrics and Gynaecology at St Thomas' Hospital, London, in 1951 and later as Professor of Midwifery at Glasgow University. It is largely thanks to him that ultrasound scanning of pregnant mothers has become commonplace. Because of his commitment in the field, he became one of the founders of the Society for the Protection of the Unborn Child.

The squadron's anti-submarine patrols continued relentlessly as the summer of 1944 turned to autumn. The fact that most of the hours spent on patrol were uneventful should not make us underestimate the *deterrent* value of so much of the squadron's effort, which is more difficult to quantify than actual scores of sinking or damage caused to U-Boats. Jim Glazebrook recalled this often-forgotten aspect of the work:

'Searching for U-Boats involved long weary hours of flying over the sea (13½ hours was the standard patrol length for our Liberators) often with nothing to show for it. But such patrols were not wasted for the submarines of those days could not travel very far (or at any speed) under water – so if the presence of a patrolling aircraft kept them submerged, they were prevented from getting to where they would do their deadly work.'[6]

The techniques employed in locating and attacking U-Boats required skills of the highest order from pilot and crew, as rapid action was needed before a vessel did a 'crash-dive' to avoid danger. Patrolling was normally carried out at 800 feet and depth charges had to be dropped from only 50 feet above water. If a boat remained on the surface and decided to fight it out, the 20 and 37mm cannon fitted on the conning tower could put up a terrifying barrage and in several cases (as we have seen) led to the destruction of the aircraft. Jim Glazebrook summed up his feelings and those of many of his crew about the dangers they faced: '......there are no atheists in an earthquake.'

Another adversary was the weather, especially from the vantage point of the eastern Scottish base as winter approached:

'.......the machines we flew in the 1940s were a long way from the "all-weather aircraft" we boast today. Some conditions were quite unflyable and we had to be prepared for this over the north Atlantic particularly in winter. Of the aircraft my squadron lost during the last year of the war, half were due to the weather. And, of course, meteorological forecasting was very limited. There were no satellite pictures then and no radioed reports from out at sea (ships and aircraft kept radio silence, except in emergency). So, when we set off – alone – on patrol, we didn't know what conditions

---

6 Glazebrook, op. cit.

we would meet – we had to learn to assess them and make our own decisions accordingly.'[7]

It was a formidable challenge to be captain of a Liberator in 1944, setting off on a typical anti-submarine patrol from Leuchars at four o'clock on a wintry morning, as Jim Glazebrook recalled:

' We carried a crew of ten, including two pilots, and I had served for some months as a second pilot, but now I had been given a command of my own. The responsibility was awesome: remember this was more than 50 years ago and I was 'nobbut a lad' as they say in these parts!'

Liberator crew at Leuchars, August 1944. Flt Sgt Jim Glazebrook had just taken over as captain. He writes that within six months six were commissioned.
Back row L to R: Flt Sgts Johnny Boorman (WOp/AG) and Nick Nicholson (WOp/AG); Jim Glazebrook; Sgt George Ellison (AG); Flt Sgt Jock Bain (WOM).
Front row L to R: Flt Sgt Hartwig (2nd pilot); Flt Sgt Doug Riley (1st Nav.); Sgt Frank Angel (Eng.); Sgt Frank Smith (2nd Nav.); Flt Sgt 'Mac' McLean (WOp/AG).
(Jim Glazebrook)

206 Squadron, RAF Leuchars, September 1944.
(Alan Smith collection)

---

7   Glazebrook, op. cit.

September brought a deterioration in the weather and another reminder of the hazards described above. On the 14th, Liberator VI BZ961 captained by Flying Officer J. W. Bayard RCAF was returning from Tain to which the aircraft had been diverted after a previous night's 'ops', and on approach to Leuchars in bad visibility crashed into Lucklaw Hill killing all twelve personnel on board. An extra pilot had joined them for experience as well as a civilian meteorological officer from Tain who was on his way home on leave. Two other crew members were buried alongside Bayard in Leuchars Cemetery, the navigator Flying Officer G. J. Dunn and one of the wireless-operator/air gunners Warrant Officer G. J. Forbes RNZAF. Frank MacManus recalled the danger to crews of Lucklaw Hill:

'Immediately to the west of Leuchars and almost in line with the runway was a notorious hill (not really high enough to be called a mountain) which was often shrouded in cloud, and unfortunately there were some cases in which crews found, too late, that this cloud had a hard centre.'

The Leuchars area seemed to be particularly susceptible to bad weather at various times of the year, with prolonged sea mists being common. This inevitably led to frequent diversions to Tain in the north of Scotland, something not welcomed by the crews on account of the discomfort and remoteness of the Highland base. By comparison Leuchars was a large and well-appointed peacetime camp, with every facility close to hand and very much of a 'home' feel for the 206 personnel.

In the light of the losses sustained a replacement Liberator was flown in during the month, Mk VI 'D'/EW288, of which more will be described later (see photos). The reinforcement was more than timely in the light of the events that were shortly to follow.

There was a narrow escape for the CO Wing Commander Leach and the crew of Flight Lieutenant Jennings on 19 September when they were unable to land after six attempts at Leuchars in bad visibility and lacked the fuel to reach their diversion airfield. The crew buckled on parachutes as the aircraft climbed to 6,000 feet, with only minimal fuel remaining, but as it turned out they were able to make a safe landing at Milltown in Morayshire with only ten minutes' fuel left and after a flight of 15 hours, 25 minutes!

On the same day Flying Officer Peter F. Carlisle in Liberator BZ984 engaged the surfaced U-865 close to the Norwegian coast, straddling the vessel in two attacks with eight depth charges as it attempted to submerge. The U-Boat was sunk and about 20 survivors scrambled into dinghies. After this episode Carlisle was diverted to Tain. It was tragic that only a few days later, on the 29th, Flying Officer Carlisle and his crew in EV885 failed to return from a patrol and no trace of the aircraft or crew was ever found. Jim Glazebrook described the events that day:

'I had spent nine hours in darkness flying a long rectangular patrol parallel to the coast of Norway: twice fighters from Sola (Stavanger) came up after us, and I avoided them by getting down low on the water, knowing that they would not risk firing their guns so close to the surface at night. Flying Officer Carlisle relieved me at the end of my patrol, and by the time we were half-way back to Leuchars daylight had come, and my wireless operator picked up Carlisle's SOS. As I put in my 'Memories', the fighters that didn't dare shoot at me in the dark came out in the daylight and shot my relief into the sea. It was tragic, really.'[8] It was a sad irony that the two survivors of Flight Lieutenant Hancock's crew (20 July) Flight Sergeant W. R. Hoyle and Pilot Officer J. A. Nadeau were also crew members that day. Within a few days news was received of the awards of the DFC to Flying Officer Carlisle and the DFM to his navigator Flight Sergeant Hoyle.

The Liberator patrols close to the Norwegian coast had not gone unnoticed by the Luftwaffe as was proved on 15 November during a Leigh-Light and anti-submarine

---

8   Glazebrook, op. cit. & letter to author 15/7/02.

Crew of EW288 of 15 November 1944 captained by Fg Off. M. J. 'Jack' Frost: Back row L to R: Sgt E. E. Lake (Flt Eng.); Flt Sgt C. F. Scott, RNZAF (WOp/Radar); Fg Off. M. J. Frost; Sgt K. D. Conway (AG); Fg Off. W. F. Harris (2nd pilot). Front Row L to R: Flt Sgt J. A. Nicholson, RNZAF (WOp/Radar); Sgt J. Webb (WOp/Radar); Sgt D. W. Knight (AG); Plt Off. E. L. Seymour, RAAF (Nav.); Flt Sgt M. Gollan, RNZAF (WOp/Radar).

Ken Conway killed in action; John Nicholson severely wounded (leg amputated). Flt Sgts Nicholson & Gollan awarded DFMs. Fg Off. Frost awarded DFC. Sgts Lake & Webb commissioned retiring post-war as Gp Capt. (Engineer) and Wg Cdr (Signals).

EW288 at Sumburgh after attack by three Me110s.
(M. J. Frost)

David Beaty and crew at Leuchars, winter 1944.
Back row L to R: Frank MacManus; Leo Meaker; Jimmy Cunningham; Norman Draper; Pat Philip.
Front row L to R: John Johnston; Len Cogan; David Beaty; Peter Laird; Johnny Baugh.
(CC/206)

sweep by two aircraft, 'B' captained by Squadron Leader J. C. Graham, and 'D', the recently delivered EW288, captained by Flying Officer M. J. 'Jack' Frost. The latter aircraft was approximately three miles off Bergen when three Messerschmitt 110 twin-engined fighters attacked from dead astern. Cannon shells hit one engine and put it out of action, the hydraulic systems were rendered useless, the wireless receiver was hit and the 'intercom' knocked out. The damage done made it more difficult to take evasive action and it was impossible to jettison the depth charges and the guns could only be operated manually. The port beam gunner, Sergeant K. D. Conway, was killed early in the encounter and the rear gunner Flight Sergeant J. A. Nicholson was badly wounded in the leg but continued to fire until the gun ceased to operate. In the ninth attack, after nearly an hour, the mid-upper gunner Flight Sergeant M. S. Gollan hit the port engine of one of the enemy aircraft and smoke and flames were seen coming from it. After this the enemy broke off the attack and the Liberator limped back to Sumburgh in the Shetlands. Luckily the flight engineer was able to open the bomb doors manually to jettison the depth charges and a successful crash landing was made. After landing, the massive damage was assessed: holes in the fuselage and wings with large sections of the control surfaces shot away. For their actions that day Flying Officer Frost was awarded the DFC, Flight Sergeant Gollan the DFM, and Flight Sergeant Nicholson the DFM, the latter unfortunately having a leg amputated in hospital.

The fact that the aircraft and all but one of the crew survived at all owed everything to the courage and skill of the individuals involved and also to the ruggedness of the Liberator. The lessons were outlined in 'Air-Gunners "Gen" Sheet No. 11', briefing notes issued at regular intervals to keep crews up to date:

'The Me's opened fire at ranges well outside 600 yards, which coupled with the ever-present menace of the third Me110 laying off astern and slightly to port left the crew of 'D' for Dog little, if any, alternative but to corkscrew. So they did the right thing and are consequently still on the Squadron. One more proof that: - PILOT-GUNNER CO-OPERATION PAYS.........One more point. Don't get <u>much below</u> 200 feet. You offer a splash target if you do, and particularly if you stay there.'[9]

Throughout the autumn and winter operational activity was cut back in order to accommodate Leigh-Light training, which was carried out using as marker points for the low-level runs the Bell Rock Lighthouse, a training buoy, and any shipping that happened to be in the right place at the time. Later, exercises were arranged with a submarine and a naval trawler from the Forth. There was also a chance for the submarine crew to have air experience on a Liberator and for the flying crews to go to sea in a submarine. This was the opportunity that arose for David Beaty and his crew when they were sent for two weeks to No. 39 joint RAF/RN anti-submarine course at Maydown near Londonderry in November. The Liberators were stationed at RAF Ballykelly and flying exercises took place off the coast of Northern Ireland. One of the more interesting aspects of the course was the mutual experience the sailors and airmen had of their respective crafts. The results were not wholly unexpected, as Frank MacManus related:

'We found the subs a bit claustrophobic and we didn't care for the violent rolling when the boat was surfaced in a very moderate sea.' However when submerged below the surface the boat was rock steady and there was no sense of motion. All this changed when an aircraft was detected and the vessel dived at a steep angle. Everyone enjoyed the course which seemed 'as good as a holiday' but 'we aircrew thought that submarines were nasty things and we would be frightened to go to war in them. The submariners thought that we were fools to fly many hundreds of miles out to sea in fragile land planes.' And then it was back to Leuchars to resume the routine work.[10]

The routine training resulted in another accident on the night of 2 December, when Liberator GRVI (EV887) of Squadron Leader R. H. Harper DFC caught fire and crashed into the sea off Crail while making low level runs over Bell Rock. Harper had been with the squadron since 1940 and many of his crew were Azores veterans. No trace of the aircraft or crew were ever found except for one of the main wheels of the aircraft.

Any thought that the war 'would be over by Christmas' had been dispelled by the dogged resistance of the Germans on all the major fighting fronts. Although the eventual outcome could not be in doubt there was no room for complacency, as was demonstrated by the German offensive in the Ardennes in December, the 'Battle of the Bulge', not defeated until early January. The equipment and technology available to Coastal Command was more advanced than at any time in the war but the Luftwaffe was still a potent threat and Dönitz was introducing new more powerful U-Boats into his fleet, the Type XXI and Type XXIII which were becoming operational by the end of the year. The difficulty in detecting the *schnorkel* boats from the air meant that a daring U-Boat commander could still get through to attack shipping around the British coastline. In short, the enemy were still capable of inflicting heavy losses on equipment and manpower and at worst, as Churchill warned, 'It is always in the last lap that races are either gained or lost'.

9 *Air Gunners' Gen Sheet No. 11*, via E. J. Casswell to OC 206 Sqn, 22/3/82 (206 Sqn Records, RAF Kinloss)
10 Beaty, Betty, *Winged Life* pp100-1. Also F. MacManus, *Piece of Cake*.

CHAPTER 10

LEUCHARS: THE FINAL RECKONING

'All ranks must realise that for Coastal Command the war goes on as before.
We started first we finish last. I call upon all squadrons for a great final
effort against our old enemy.'

Signal from Coastal Command HQ to all Groups and Stations, 5 May 1945,
Air Chief Marshal Sir W. Sholto Douglas, AOC-in-C Coastal Command, Northwood.[1]

There was a change of command on 9 January when Wing Commander A. de V. Leach was replaced by Wing Commander J. P. Selby. A fresh challenge in the grip of winter arose with the need to protect the convoys heading for Russia, and this called for flights lasting up to 11 hours or more in the most appalling weather, when even the U-Boats were unable to operate effectively. It was a test of endurance for crews in a freezing cold aircraft when even the extra warm flying kit proved inadequate and clumsy to wear. Frank MacManus, in David Beaty's crew, recalled one such patrol in February when they operated from Tain in the Moray Firth to give them the extra endurance to cover the convoy which was well within the Arctic Circle. After an eight-hour flight against a fierce headwind they managed to locate the convoy scattered over hundreds of square miles, in spite of rough sea conditions and poor visibility, in which the radar had not been 100 per cent reliable. They managed to find the escort carrier to signal the SNO (Senior Naval Officer) but by then the aircraft had reached the limit of its endurance and they had to turn for home. The strong tailwind got them back to Tain in three hours!

With the collapse of German resistance over much of continental Europe except for the German mainland and Scandinavia, and the Soviet advances in the east which had closed off the ports of Danzig and Königsberg, there were few ports and training areas now secure for the U-Boats. What little there was, in the Baltic for example, became a target for Bomber Command's mine-laying or 'gardening' operations, which claimed several U-Boats, and during January and February there was also the seasonal icing-up of parts of the Baltic to contend with. It was against this background that the AOC, Sir Sholto Douglas, devised a daring plan to use his long-range aircraft to hit one of the last remaining Baltic areas of U-Boat training, north-east of the island of Bornholm and almost due north of the German/Polish border, where up to 30 submarines were believed to be exercising by night. Code-named Operation *Chilli*, the plan was to use the Leigh-Light Liberators of Nos 206 and 547 Squadrons assisted by Halifaxes of Nos 58 and 502 Squadrons in diversionary attacks. There was going to be nowhere to hide for the U-Boat commanders, as Sholto Douglas related: 'In addition to administering some nasty shocks, we hoped that there might also be a chance of bagging a few U-Boats.'[2]

The details for Operation *Chilli* had taken many weeks to work out, in total secrecy as surprise was crucial. The plan was for 14 aircraft in two waves to head through the Skagerrak and Kattegat at low level keeping equal distance from the German radars in Denmark and Norway, and then on across the southern tip of Sweden and into the Baltic, to attack in parallel tracks the (hopefully) unsuspecting U-Boats. Losses were

---

1   Sholto Douglas with R. Wright, *Years of Command* p277.
2   Sholto Douglas p275.

expected as the Skagerrak and Kattegat areas were closely guarded by enemy fighters based in Norway and Denmark and the Baltic was heavily defended. Spot-on navigation and meticulous timing were essential to the success of the operation.

On the night of 3 February 14 aircraft took off from Leuchars on *Chilli I* in a blinding snowstorm within a few minutes of each other. Squadron Leader J. C. Graham's Liberator (Mk VI 'D' EW 301) had an engine fire and he was forced to jettison his Leigh-Light and depth charges, eventually having to divert to Wick.[3] A second Liberator, captained by Flight Lieutenant G. R. Haggas, was shadowed by enemy aircraft on his way up the Skagerrak and was forced to take evasive action for nearly an hour, using up so much fuel that insufficient was left to complete the operation and a course had to be set for home. The remaining 12 aircraft approached from the east of Bornholm and a number of surface vessels and U-Boats were attacked in the face of some intense anti-aircraft fire.

Pilot Officer Jim Glazebrook had first attacked a 2,000-ton coaster with six depth charges, but then the radar operator detected a large contact ten miles away, which turned out to be a group of five U-Boats with a destroyer as escort. As the aircraft homed in on the target the intercom system short-circuited due to a fault, which meant that none of the crew heard the radar operator's call for the Light to be switched on at the 'one mile' point, and the call was only heard at the three-quarter-mile position from the target, by which time the Light's beam overshot and the bomb aimer failed to see the U-Boats. As a consequence the depth charges were not dropped and there was as yet no response from the ships. Jim Glazebrook continued:

'As I flew on I thought "That's torn it! They may have been asleep just now, but they won't be when I come back." But I figured that the alarm had been given and the U-Boats would have been ordered to dive. To do that they would first have to get under way, and might show wakes (Met. had forecast that we would have had a moon to attack by – we didn't, but it wasn't quite black, and the U-Boat wakes would be visible). So, mindful of the presence of the destroyer I told the bomb-aimer not to use the Leigh Light and if he could see anything at all to bomb visually. This he did, and the moment he called "bombs gone" I flung the Liberator to starboard and as I did so all the flak from the destroyer came up past my left wing-tip! It was only then, after we had dropped all our remaining depth charges, that I broke off the engagement and got away from the area as quickly as possible.'[4]

Flight Lieutenant David Beaty and crew arrived on the scene a few minutes later as part of the second wave of attackers, having homed in on a substantial radar echo and switched on the Leigh-Light preparatory to an attack. By this time the U-Boats had submerged but the destroyer's gun crews were ready and waiting. Beaty ordered the Light to be switched off as he went into the attack and the aircraft received multiple hits in the process but the depth charges were released just as the aircraft itself became difficult to control. David Beaty and his co-pilot Gerry Clements fought to regain control as the flight engineer assessed the damage sustained. The rudder cables had been severed, No. 4 engine (starboard outer) had stopped so the propeller had to be feathered, No. 3 engine (starboard inner) was damaged as were the port wing, aileron, fuselage and starboard beam gun. The bomb doors would not close and the compass had failed. To keep the aircraft in the air all heavy equipment was jettisoned and gradually Beaty managed to gain height sufficient for the crew to bale out if necessary. Frank MacManus related how he tried to send an SOS signal to Leuchars which the Germans jammed, but eventually was able to transmit a signal using a medium frequency (MF) which reached a Lincolnshire station. With the aircraft now only just

---

3   A family in Carnoustie had a lucky escape when the Leigh Light crashed into their house! The jettisoned depth charges were later recovered by the Navy from the River Dee.
4   Jim Glazebook, letter to author 25/8/01.

controllable the option of baling out was complicated by the accidental release of the radar operator's parachute inside the aircraft which added to the confusion. There were only two options now available and David Beaty characteristically sought the consensus of the crew before making his decision. First, they could attempt a landing in neutral Sweden with all that might mean for the secret equipment on board the aircraft and the inevitable internment of the crew. Secondly, they could attempt to struggle back to a home base, risking the marauding night fighters along the notorious Kattegat and Skagerrak in a damaged aircraft in no fit state to take evasive action. It was decided to risk the second option and they set off for home with the two pilots struggling to retain control and Frank MacManus obtaining fixes from MF/DF stations at intervals to keep them on course, which turned out to be for Banff on the Moray Firth. Even the guns and ammunition were jettisoned when they arrived within the normal fighter cover zone. By the time they reached Banff the second engine had failed but they made a safe landing at 0930 hrs on 4 February. Amazingly, none of the crew were injured but all concerned were staggered at the amount of punishment the aircraft had sustained.

After his own encounter the night before, it was with immense relief that Jim Glazebrook learned that David Beaty and his crew had made it home in spite of the severe damage to his aircraft: 'David's navigator, John Johnston, who had been my navigator originally before David took over this crew, was already married and living out at a cottage (with no telephone) a couple of miles from Leuchars. So when I heard that David had crash-landed at Banff and that all the crew were all right, I borrowed some RAF transport and drove out to the cottage to let John's wife know that he was safe.'[5]

Repairs to EW322 carried out by SAL at Leuchars February 1945. Notice also Liberator BZ984 carrying 206 Squadron code PQ-S. EW322 is a B-24J or Liberator Mk VIII which retained the American tail turret. BZ984 was a B-24H – RAF designation Liberator Mk VI – and in RAF service the Mk VI had its American tail turret with 2 x 0.5 in. Browning machine guns replaced by British Boulton & Paul turret housing 4 x 0.303 in. Brownings.
(M. J. G. Hunter Collection via James R. Hood)

5   Ibid.

Within two weeks David Beaty had been awarded a Bar to his DFC for his skill and daring in bringing his aircraft safely back, and DFCs were also awarded to Pilot Officer Jim Glazebrook and Flight Lieutenant E. N. Jennings. In spite of the damage done, all the aircraft had returned safely from the *Chilli* operation, but the results were disappointing with no confirmed sinkings reported. Other *Chilli* operations were flown in March but were thereafter called off. However the psychological damage to the U-Boat crews was undoubted as nowhere was now safe for them to operate or train with impunity.

Liberator L/206 flying off Scottish coast, March 1945. (Jim Glazebrook)

The first positive result in the use of the *sonobuoy*, codenamed 'High Tea', came on 9 February when Pilot Officer J. Glazebrook detected a *schnorkel* U-Boat on return from a patrol near the Orkneys. An attack was carried out but soon broken off as the aircraft had reached the limit of its endurance. A second aircraft in the area was also nearing the end of its patrol limits and could not follow up the attack. It was never possible to assess the extent of any damage inflicted on the vessel.

The aircraft had already been fitted with what was then a revolutionary navigator-operated low-level visual bombsight (LAB) to replace the standard manual system of pilot release of bombs or depth charges. But on 2 March the squadron was withdrawn from operations to re-equip with the Liberator Mk VIII fitted with an even more revolutionary radar bombing system (LABS –'Low Altitude Bombing System'). This had its own independent mini-radar and was linked to the auto-pilot so that the navigator controlled the aircraft directionally during an attack (height control remaining with the pilot), and the bomb was released automatically by the system.[6] A period of intensive training was required to enable crews to undertake low altitude night bombing against U-Boats and surface vessels. No. 206 Squadron was to be the only unit to use the LABS device operationally in the war with the first recorded attacks taking place in April. It was during that month that news came through of the award of the DFC for Squadron Leader J. C. Graham for outstanding service during three tours of operations.

Operations resumed in what was another very intensive period for the squadron. Alan Smith recalled that the squadron's task at the time was harassing enemy ships and U-Boats in the Skaggerak and Kattegat and flying up the Norwegian coast escorting the Russian convoys on their way to Murmansk and Archangel in north Russia: 'The system of doing this was to keep the convoys in our sights – they were quite a way off the Norwegian coast heading north – and we would patrol between them and the Norwegian coast to make sure that the subs which were then based in Bergen and in north Denmark did not get at the ships.' Once the convoys were well north of Bergen they were relatively safer from submarine attack. But if an aircraft was forced to ditch in those chilly waters the chances of survival for any length of time were slim.

During those final weeks of the war U-Boats were attacked by Flight Lieutenant E. N. Jennings DFC, Flight Lieutenant Haggas, Captain Prinsloo SAAF, Flying Officer K. J. Ayrton, Flying Officer J. A. Elviss RCAF, Flying Officer Fisher RAAF, and Flight Lieutenant C. R. Alexander DFM. Merchant ships were targeted by Flight Lieutenants Richards, Jennings, Harbot and Flying Officer Grant. Flight Lieutenant Markham DFC dropped

---

6 Sid Banks – information supplied to author.

bombs on a destroyer. There was no doubting the dangers in those Baltic operations even at this late stage as the final two operational losses occurred during the month, the first on 9 April when Flight Lieutenant Brian L. Howell and his crew in Liberator Mk VIII KK259 failed to return from an anti-U-Boat patrol in the Kattegat. The aircraft and crew disappeared without trace except for Sgt George A. Ellison, air gunner, later buried in Kviberg Cemetery in Sweden, and Flying Officer John A. W. Heatlie, navigator/bomber, who was interred in Skagen Cemetery in Denmark. It was one of those tragic quirks of fate that Sergeant Ellison had been flying that night, as Jim Glazebrook recalled:

'Sergeant Ellison was my gunner and should not have been with Flight Lieutenant Howell at all. What happened was that for some unremembered operational reason I and my crew were asked to take leave a couple of weeks earlier than originally scheduled. George Ellison came to me in some distress to say that he had fixed his wedding for the first day of our (scheduled) leave and the change was upsetting his plans. I took him to see the Squadron Gunnery Leader, who said not to worry - he would use George in the Gunnery Office while the rest of us took our leave, and then he would find a spare gunner to fly with us until George came back from his honeymoon. Sadly while we were away George volunteered (or was asked) to fly with Flight Lieutenant Howell and so was lost.'[7]

On 20 April Lieutenant-Commander Nicodême Guilonard (Mk VIII KK410) and Flying Officer Elviss (Mk VIII KK335) and their respective crews were briefed for anti-U-Boat patrols in the Baltic. Guilonard was a Dutch naval airman who had joined the squadron in September 1944, and was determined to become operational as soon as possible to avenge the damage done to his country. Both aircraft were airborne just after 2000 hrs from Leuchars and set course for Danish waters. During the patrol Elviss sighted and attacked a U-Boat, managing to evade a marauding enemy aircraft in the process and returned safely at 0618 hrs on the 21st. Nothing further was heard of Guilonard's aircraft and the crew of eleven were posted missing. Alan Smith recalled the events:

'Lieutenant-Commander Guilonard had trained with Squadron Leader Graham and his crew (which included myself) before getting his own crew. His flight engineer was Pilot Officer W. T. 'Ginger' Gale who roomed with me in the mess at Leuchars. The usual navigator was Tommy Thompson but he was having a minor operation in hospital and did not go on that fateful trip. Ginger Gale woke me up before he went and insisted that I went through the emergencies with him because they knew they were on a very dangerous mission, which was to go back into the Baltic where the *Chilli* operation had taken place to see if there were any subs lurking about which could be sunk in their training grounds. However the Germans were waiting for them and they were shot down over the Danish coast, most likely by enemy fighters as they would be too low for heavy AA fire (although even fighters would have had problems with the low altitude at night). The crew were all killed in the crash. Before Ginger had left he asked me if I would go with him to have his photograph taken for his mother. He never did collect it but I subsequently went and sent it to his mother. Commander Guilonard was married and had two daughters who were all living out at Leuchars at the time he was killed, but after his death Wilhelmiena and her daughters returned to Amsterdam.'[8]

The full story of this episode emerged after the war. There had been a rumour that the aircraft had been on a secret mission to drop weapons to the Resistance movement and/or deliver a mystery passenger into Denmark, but there was no evidence for this.

7   Jim Glazebrook, letter to author 15/7/02.
8   This event was recalled in 1997 when Alan Smith visited Amsterdam on behalf of the 206 Sqn Association to see Mrs Wilhelmiena Guilonard, then aged 85. Her daughter Corry (only a young girl in the Leuchars days) accompanied Alan and he presented Mrs Guilonard with an 'Octopus Brooch' on behalf of the Association.

DATE	AIRCRAFT TYPE & NUMBER	CREW	DUTY	TIME		DETAILS OF SORTIE OR FLIGHT	REFERENCES.
				UP	DOWN		
20.4.45.	LIBERATOR VIII L/L LAB KK.262	F/L ALEXANDER, C.R. F/L BATHURST, M.E.S. P/O HARGRAVES, A. F/S JOHNMAN, A.R. F/S McLOUGHLIN, A.E. W/O RUSSELL, E.G. F/S STAHL, F.J. F/S McMILLAN, J. F/S SANDFORD, R.D. F/S CURTIS, G.R. SGT. WRIGHT, L.	A/U Patrol	0327	1411	At 0605 on Patrol in position 6110N 0219E. No incidents.	Leu/03/20 Apr.
20.4.45.	LIBERATOR VIII L/L LAB "O" KH.418	S/L MARTIN, M.J.P. F/O COLLYER, J.J.W. F/O CLOUGH, M. P/O RNID, H.D. W/O THOMAS, A.J. W/O ASBURY, A.G. F/S WEAKING, A. F/S MERCER, R. F/S WELFORD, J. SGT. LEE, J.N.	A/U Patrol	1041	2130	On Patrol at 1323 in position 6102N 0229E. During patrol one radar contact was obtained at 13 miles distance, but disappeared at 12½ miles and not regained.	Leu/04/20 Apr
20.4.45.	LIBERATOR VIII L/L LAB "L" KK.335.	F/O ELVISS, J.A. F/O MILLER, R.D. P/O THOMSON, T.J. F/O BROOKS, J.M. W/O KING, B. W/O O'MALLEY, F.J. F/S HARPER, W.D. F/S CORBETT, C.T. F/S PARTRIDGE, W.A. SGT. DODGSON, R.	A/U Patrol	2048	0618/21	On patrol at 0001 in position 5757N 1102E. At 0144 poss. 5711N 1135E (after homing on a radar contact) a fully surfaced U/Boat approx. 700 tons was sighted. An attack was carried out, the first bomb being 130 feet from the port beam of the U/Boat and the remainder straddling. 7 minutes after the attack an orange flash was observed from the target area. At 0301 radar contacts were obtained and a few minutes later the dark form of an enemy A/C was observed. L/206 took evasive action and nothing further was seen.	Leu/01/21 Apr
20.4.45.	LIBERATOR VIII L/L LAB "T" KK.410	L/C GUILONARD, N. F/L LAYCOCK, P.S. Welsh F/O SMITH, A.R. N.Z. F/O GALE, W.T. Welsh W/O LONG, G.C.K. English W/O TOPLISS, G.H. Australian W/O SPENCER, W.W. Canadian W/O EMERY, K. English W/O TURANT, T.K. Canadian W/O HARDING, C.P. English F/S ORITT, F.R. English	A/U Patrol	2011	-	A/C failed to return to base. No signals received.	Leo/02/21 Ap

ORB extract fateful 20 April 1945.
(CC/206)

The aircraft had crashed in flames in woodland and the Germans had buried all 11 bodies in secret on 22 April to the immediate west of the crash site. The graves were found in June 1947 and the remains removed to Aarestrup Cemetery in Denmark where the burials took place on Sunday 22 June 1947 in the presence of several dignitaries including the British Air Attaché E. W. R. Saddler and representatives from the Danish forces and the Dutch Government. A monument to the airmen was erected at the crash site in Torstedlund wood. Alan Smith pointed out that their names are also listed in the Commemoration Book in St Clement Danes in London, but because Lieutenant-Commander Guilonard was not in the Royal Air Force, he is not mentioned in any of the Commonwealth War Graves records or in the Church.[9] Just as a postscript there was a brief entry in Grand Admiral Dönitz's war diary which suggested that enemy air activity over Danish airspace had ruled out the transference of German resistance to that theatre.

However, in spite of the advances of the Allied forces a considerable threat remained from the U-Boats in those final weeks of the war. As the Soviet forces advanced there was a desperate scramble to leave the Baltic area and stream through the Kattegat in a bid to reach the Norwegian bases. Many of the craft remained on the surface due to the danger from mines, thus offering Coastal Command a number of tempting targets. On the night of 3 May the mass evacuation of ships was witnessed by Flight Lieutenant David Beaty and Pilot Officer Glazebrook from their respective Liberators, at the eastern end of the Skaggerak, where vessels were steaming northwards between the Danish and Swedish coasts, fully visible with riding lights and in orderly rows. There was also a large formation of German fighters some of which shadowed the Liberators but did not attack.

If there were any doubts about the role of Coastal Command at this point these were

---

9   For information on this episode I am indebted to the late Wg Cdr J. C. Graham and the late Sqn Ldr Alan Smith.

U-Boat surrendering to a 206 Sqn Liberator, 10 May 1945.
(CC/206)

soon dispelled by the AOC-in-C of Coastal Command, Air Chief Marshal Sir W. Sholto Douglas in a signal dated 5 May:

'In spite of the surrender of German forces on the continent there is as yet no indication that they contemplate surrender in Norway. We may, therefore, expect the continuance of intense U-Boat operations from Norwegian bases. All ranks must realise that for Coastal Command the war goes on as before. We started first we finish last. I call upon all squadrons for a great final effort against our old enemy. It falls to Coastal Command to strike the final blow against the enemy's one remaining weapon.'[10]

That same day Squadron Leader J. J. Martin DFC, AFC attacked an oil streak caused by a previously damaged U-Boat, and Flight Lieutenant G. Thompson in Liberator 'T' KK250 attacked another U-Boat in the Kattegat which was heading for southern Norway. It was at first believed that this action resulted in the sinking of U-534, a boat captained by Herbert Nollau who survived along with the majority of his crew of 52. However later evidence credited a Liberator of No. 86 Squadron with the kill and Flight Lieutenant Thompson had most probably attacked another U-Boat further north. There was a great deal of press speculation at the time that U-534 was transporting senior Nazis escaping justice along with many valuables, precious stones and currency, to a safe haven like Argentina. Matters came to a head in the press when the vessel was located in 1986 by Aage Jensen, a Danish diver, off the Danish island of Anholt. With the support of Danish businessman Karsten Ree the boat was raised in August 1993, but little evidence was found to corroborate the claims made of a valuable cargo. In 1996 the vessel was taken to a new home on Merseyside, with the Warship Preservation Trust at Birkenhead, to be restored and opened to the public as a permanent memorial to all who died in the Battle of the Atlantic.[11]

Patrols continued for several days in daylight, with aircraft flying low over Danish towns and villages to drop sweet and chocolate rations to the children below. The last operational sortie was completed in the afternoon of 7 May 1945 by Flight Lieutenant Pearce. V-E Day was celebrated on 8 May, but there were still many fully armed U-Boats at sea which were ordered by Dönitz to surface, display a black or blue flag, and

---

10 Quoted in *Sholto Douglas: Years of Command*, Sholto Douglas with Robert Wright p277.
11 Information from the Warship Preservation Trust, Birkenhead.

proceed to a designated Allied port. Coastal Command crews were ordered to act as 'sheepdogs' for this task and attack any boat that did not obey these instructions. Over the next four weeks 206 Squadron received the surrender of nine U-Boats but great vigilance had to be exercised as Jim Glazebrook related:

'On 13 May I found a U-Boat trying to sneak past the north of Scotland at periscope depth and in accordance with our instructions I opened my bomb doors and commenced an attack. But they must have been watching me for as I ran in they came swiftly to the surface and put out their surrendering black flag. When we flew low past them the officers stood in the conning tower giving a Nazi salute. This submarine was the U-1231, 750 tons. We stayed with her to make sure they didn't submerge again until we were relieved by another aircraft.'[12]

U-2326 coming alongside at Dundee, plus two torpedoes and crew, 12 May 1945.
(Eric Lake/M. J. Frost)

Shortly after this Flying Officer Frost and his crew found U-2326 in the North Sea heading towards Denmark. The boat stopped but the crew appeared to have difficulty with the instruction to head towards Scotland until the aircraft had dropped a depth charge in front of the vessel, and minds were speedily changed and a course set for Dundee! Jim Glazebrook recalled that a few Leuchars personnel later visited Dundee and went on board that submarine: 'This was a new submarine and I had some conversation with the captain whose command of English was little better than my German. He boasted that his boat could stay submerged for 81 days. I could think of little worse than being in a tin box under the sea for that length of time, and suggested that it must be a great strain. "Not so", he replied, claiming that the longer they could stay submerged the less danger there was of aircraft attack. So that was their real fear at that time.'[13]

The surrender and gradual handing over of German naval ships continued. On 25 May Flight Lieutenant J. A. Elviss and his crew took part with two No. 547 Squadron aircraft in escorting the cruisers *Prinz Eugen* and *Nurnberg* out of Copenhagen,

---

12 Jim Glazebrook, letter to author 15/7/02.
13 Ibid.

German cruiser leaving Copenhagen 25 May 1945, with escort by Liberators of Nos 206 and 547 Squadrons.
(CC/206)

accompanied by four Royal Navy destroyers.

The end of an era was at hand when at 1135 hrs on 3 June Liberator Mk VIII KH415 'B' captained by Flight Lieutenant D. R. Fray in position 5718 N, 0141 W, was recalled to base when all anti-U-Boat patrols ceased. On that day the squadron was withdrawn from the line in preparation for conversion to a transport role. On 10 June 206 Squadron was transferred to No. 301 Wing Transport Command and was reorganised into 48 crews of five members each (two pilots, one navigator, one wireless-operator and a flight engineer). Royal Australian Air Force and Royal Canadian Air Force personnel were not included and were posted to RAF Bircham Newton (in preparation for repatriation) and air gunners were posted to RAF Dallachy. A three-week period of training followed for transport duties to India. Meanwhile 28 new crews were drafted in, from No. 1674 Heavy Conversion Unit (HCU), No. 547 Squadron, and No. 502 Squadron. Conversion to Liberators was undertaken by some 206 Squadron captains. The squadron became operational in its new role on 1 October 1945.

CHAPTER 11

TRANSPORT ROLE: TROOPING TO INDIA

'The Liberator was very noisy and it must have been an uncomfortable ride for the troops, but at least they were coming home.'

Group Captain John Hart, 206 Squadron 1945-1946.

The war in Europe was at an end at last but the war with Japan still dragged on until the middle of August, and it was towards the Far East and the Middle East that attention was now drawn. One thing was certain, the transport capability of the Royal Air Force was going to have to be reinforced as the need built up for troop rotation, fresh supplies and not least, the repatriation of thousands of prisoners of war as territories were liberated. The crews of Coastal Command with their long-range aircraft and experience of arduous flying conditions seemed ideally placed to meet the new challenge.

Thus 206 Squadron was posted to Oakington near Cambridge on 1 August 1945 as part of No. 301 Wing Transport Command. Wing Commander J. P. Selby had been replaced as CO by Wing Commander T. W. T. McComb OBE towards the end of July, 'a lovable but wild Irishman' according to one description[1]. The flight commanders were Squadron Leader David Beaty, just promoted to command 'B' Flight, and Squadron Leader John Martin of 'A' Flight. The crews underwent a period of training, which in some cases involved conversion from types like the Halifax, and the Liberators had to be modified for the new role. All guns were removed, turrets covered over, bomb bays sealed, and wooden flooring and seating capacity installed in the bomb bay and rear fuselage to accommodate up to a maximum of 26 men.

RAF Oakington must have been a hive of activity during that summer of 1945. The crews were issued with tropical kit and there was a full training schedule organised by Squadron Leader David Beaty, who had undertaken the first training flight to India on 12 July prior to the Oakington move. Other flights followed: Flight Lieutenant Markham in KK375 on the 14th, returning on the 27th; Flight Lieutenant Frost in KK342 departing on the 15th and returning on the 21st; Flying Officer Glazebrook in KK257 from the 16th to the 27th; and Flight Lieutenant Ian Grant[2] in KK377 from the 17th and returning on the 31st. Other captains and crews starting out for India during July included Flight Lieutenant Richards in KL622, Flight Lieutenant Sharp in KG979, Flight Lieutenant Haggas in KL669 and Captain Prinsloo in KL666. There was a lot to learn, new and unfamiliar routes over some very inhospitable territory and the dangers posed by the monsoon weather conditions. There were also health hazards for which anti-malarial medication had to be prescribed.

By August the new work was under way. There was no 'typical' route but there were a number of staging posts depending on the nature of each trip where crews might rest overnight. These included Melsbroek, Brussels; Castel Benito airfield near Tripoli in Libya – usually for aircraft checks and refuelling; then Cairo, with a possible stop for delivery or collection of personnel at Lydda near Tel Aviv, at that time in the British Mandate in Palestine. The average time taken as far as Cairo, not including overnight

---

1   Gp Capt. John Hart, letter to author 2/01/03.
2   later Capt. Ian Grant, Chairman of 206 Sqn Association.

Boldly going on the 'proving flight' to India in the summer of 1945. David Beaty in back row, 2nd from right. Sid Banks on left in back row carrying a roll of navigation charts and included on the flight as he was Navigation Training Officer.
(Sid Banks)

stops, would be around 14½ hours. There might then be the long 11-hour haul over the deserts of Jordan and Iraq, with other possible staging-posts at Shaibah and Habbaniya, both in Iraq, or Abadan, a US base in the Persian oilfields; then down the Persian Gulf and along the coast of Baluchistan to Mauripur, Karachi, which was the eastern terminal, with an occasional extension across India to Dum Dum at Calcutta. After a two-day break the aircraft would return home via Palestine and Libya. The nature of the tasks varied but might include the emergency ferrying of troops from Germany (boarding at Melsbroek) to Palestine, where there was growing unrest among the Jewish population as they demanded their own independent state. The next leg would be to Cairo to pick up Indian troops who had fought in the Western Desert campaign. On arrival in Karachi British troops or ex-prisoners of war would be awaiting the flight home and a welcome demobilisation.

To describe these flights as 'spartan' compared to present-day standards would be an understatement, but to the men returning home there was no comparison between this, a flight lasting for two or three days, and weeks aboard a crowded and uncomfortable troopship. By the end of August, the first full month of these operations, operational and non-operational flying hours totalled 1,107.

Scheduled flights to India continued through September. By October every second day on average saw a crew departing for a trooping flight. On 7 October three captains with their crews, Flight Lieutenant I. C. Grant, Flight Lieutenant M. Frost and Flying Officer J. Milne, left Oakington in Liberator KL595 bound for Castel Benito, to ensure that slip crews would be waiting for homecoming aircraft. They duly returned, KL503 on 8 October (Grant), KL595 also on the 8th (Milne), and KK375 on the 9th (Frost).

As always, adverse weather conditions in tropical regions might pose a sudden and unexpected threat, but hazards could also arise nearer home for fully-loaded aircraft on runways barely adequate for the task, as was experienced by Flying Officer Peter Green and his crew on 13 October in KL595 when their Liberator crashed on take-off at Melsbroek killing the entire crew and the 26 passengers on board. The crew included Flying Officer B. Connor (navigator), Flight Sergeant G. Nightall, Flying Officer J. D. Freckleton (2nd pilot) and Flying Officer H. T. W. Alderton (wireless operator). One RAF officer, Squadron Leader R. C. Rivaz, was numbered among the passengers[3] and the remainder consisted of Army personnel. Squadron Leader David Beaty had been concerned about the situation in Melsbroek for some time and had warned the authorities about the 1,850-yard long runway, too short for Liberators, and the lack of weight restrictions on aircraft, but to no avail.[4] Only two days later on the 15th, Liberator KL351 captained by Flight Lieutenant G. S. Knapp developed engine trouble on take-off from Melsbroek and No. 3 engine caught fire. Tragedy was averted on this occasion and the aircraft was diverted to Orly, Paris.

---

3 Sqn Ldr Rivaz had served in the crew of Plt Off Leonard Cheshire (later Gp Capt., VC) in 102 Sqn in the early part of the war.
4 Betty Beaty: *Winged Life* pp 117-18.

These events must have affected morale as the Squadron Detail issued at Oakington on the 17th included a warning to crews not to discuss technical defects of aircraft 'within the hearing of passengers' as it might shake their confidence. Operational flying hours for October were 1,804 and on 3 November a congratulatory message was sent by the AOC No. 48 Group to the station commander, to be conveyed to all personnel, announcing the success of the large scale trooping programme in its first month of operations, in which target figures had actually been exceeded. This was in spite of the growing problem of operating American aircraft like the Liberator since the phasing out of the Lend-Lease agreement by President Truman only a few days after the ending of the Japanese war. A directive was issued by higher authority laying down that no equipment officer could indent for or sign requests for spares to keep the American aircraft serviceable. In due course this would have grounded the aircraft responsible for the trooping operation to India. Thus 'Keeping off the Q-form' – that is avoiding an aircraft becoming declared unserviceable through lack of spare parts – became a major headache for the equipment and engineering officers. The equipment officer at Oakington along with Betty Beaty, WAAF Section Officer in Stores, and the engineering officers, devised a plan to take advantage of the natural generosity of the Americans in local USAAF bases like Alconbury, and simply request what they were unable to obtain through official channels. They were assisted by the fact that it was standard practice in the USAAF to write off unwanted spares. Unfortunately the equipment officer who had initiated the plan was posted and it was left to Betty Beaty and her colleagues to carry it out, which they did with much success over the succeeding months. As USAAF stations closed, they would ask permission to have a look around and collect anything useful before it was bulldozed into the ground. As time went on supplies began to dwindle and greater distances had to be travelled even as far as Orly, Paris. To save fuel, some of these trips were organised in conjunction with 206 Squadron training flights, thanks to the co-operation of Squadron Leader David Beaty, the training captain. [5]

Pause at Cairo: L to R Fg Off. Webb (later Wg Cdr); Fg Off. Lake (later Gp Capt.);
Flt Lt Frost; Flt Sgt Sheppard.
(M. J. Frost)

5 'Keeping off the Q-Form' by Betty Beaty (WRAF Officers' Gazette).

Liberator KL664 converted for use of 206 Sqn, Shaibah, May 1946.
(Air-Britain *Aeromilitaria* Vol 26 Issue 103 Autumn 2000)

An example of routine scheduling was on 11 November, when Flight Lieutenant Mawdsley with Warrant Officer Sharples, Flying Officer Gregory, Flight Sergeant Kemp and Flying Officer Haslam crewed Liberator VIc KL666 for a 'trooping' from Oakington to Castel Benito. Flight Lieutenant Jennings, Warrant Officer Wright, Flight Lieutenant Christensen and Warrant Officer Evans took the aircraft on to Lydda and from there a new crew, Flying Officers Young and Johnson, Flight Lieutenant Moules, Flight Sergeant Baker and Warrant Officer Watkins completed the journey to Mauripur. The crew on the return trip from Mauripur to Lydda consisted of Flying Officer Sarre, Warrant Officer Scouller, Flight Lieutenant Haynes, Flying Officer Smith and Warrant Officer Gifford. The next leg to Castel Benito was undertaken by Flight Lieutenant Johnson, Flying Officer Neville, Flight Lieutenant Evans, Warrant Officer Major and Flying Officer Hardwick, with the homeward run in the hands of Flight Lieutenant Jamieson, Warrant Officer Jordy, Flying Officer Hudson, Flight Lieutenant Bell and Warrant Officer Law.

Squadron strength at Oakington on 1 December amounted to 307 aircrew and 27 ground crew. From January 1946 it seemed more usual for the same crew to undertake the return flight to Mauripur in stages, as on the 1st when Flight Lieutenant Davenport captained Liberator VIc KL664 with crew Flying Officers Carter and Bradley, Pilot Officer MacManus and Warrant Officer Morse. During the month operational and non-operational flying hours totalled 1,688.

There were a few compensations in spite of the discomfort, the dangers and difficulties. Frank MacManus, as a newly commissioned pilot officer, recalled the luxurious Officers' Club in Tripoli whose staff of Italian PoWs included some top-class chefs and provided him with his first taste of 'real' Italian spaghetti. There were the exotic surroundings of Cairo to savour, with its restaurants and 'Groppi's ice cream parlour', but two of them had a narrow escape when they lingered too long among a potentially hostile crowd of locals. There were terrorist threats in Tel Aviv from Zionist extremists to be on the look out for, and a forced landing at any point during the long haul across desert terrain risked a gruesome fate at the hands of unfriendly tribesmen, for which the 'goolie chits' were carried by aircrew.[6] However, at journey's end in Karachi there was another well-appointed Officers' Club to look forward to and the delights of the bazaars and shopping emporia there.

The duration of a round trip could be anything from eight days to between two and four weeks and because most crews spent so little time in Oakington it was usual for a nest-egg of pay to accumulate in home bank accounts, which Frank MacManus found a godsend when he finally left the RAF in May 1946.[7]

During March 1946 operational and non-operational flying hours amounted to 2,278, but by now the squadron's task was nearly accomplished, and the need for ferrying troops and supplies was diminishing. In the months following the ending of the war in the Far East the RAF faced a rapid run-down in the austere post-war financial climate. As always, there had to be priorities and these amounted to, firstly, developing the atomic weapons of the future and secondly, preserving the 'strike' capability of the Air Force, which in essence meant Bomber and Fighter Commands. Coastal Command was ranked next in order of importance and some way down the list came Transport Command and the other elements. No. 206 Squadron was one of the squadrons listed as being surplus to requirements and was disbanded at Oakington on 25 April 1946.

---

6   Ibid. and F. MacManus.
7   F. MacManus.

CHAPTER 12

TRANSPORT COMMAND,
THE BERLIN AIRLIFT AND DISBANDMENT

'We always had black faces and smelt of fish.....'

Alan Smith, on the problems of transporting coal and kippers to Berlin, 1948-49.

It was challenge enough to maintain strong bomber and fighter arms in the RAF at a time of economic austerity, but the Air Staff were also advocating a broadly-based Air Force with a sound air transport capability. Britain still had extensive colonial possessions and a network of overseas bases which had to be supplied and reinforced. In the longer term improved squadron mobility might reduce the RAF's dependence on these bases and thus enable savings to be made. There was also the hope, expressed in the 1947 Defence Statement, that the shortfall in American aircraft caused by the end of Lend-Lease would in due course be made good by rearmament with a new generation of British-built transport aircraft.

In August 1947 the long struggle for Indian independence was achieved with the passing of the Indian Independence Act which came into force in August of that year, partitioning the subcontinent into two new dominions, a mainly Hindu India and a predominantly Muslim Pakistan. One consequence was the need to transfer refugees between the two states to relieve the upsurge in communal violence in both countries, and Transport Command was required to provide an airlift. Avro Yorks of No. 511 Squadron joined Dakotas in the task from August for three months, but it was then decided that the large squadrons of Transport Command were proving too cumbersome and that more, smaller units would be more appropriate. Thus within No. 47 Group Nos 99 and 206 Squadrons were re-formed at Lyneham in November 1947 followed by Nos 40 and 59 at Abingdon a month later. However, the total number of aircraft operating under centralised servicing on a station basis, remained the same.[1]

It was against this background that 206 Squadron resumed operations from 17 November 1947 at RAF Lyneham in Wiltshire under the command of Squadron Leader F. C. Blackmore, again within Transport Command, and this time equipped with the Avro York C1. At first crew 'slipping' on the long route was attempted but this was not popular and instead the five-man crews would undertake the outward journey, followed by rest, and then fly the return journey home. A typical load for Changi (Singapore) or Dum Dum (Calcutta, India) on a PCF[2] York would be a dozen passengers and up to 9,000 lbs of freight.

But by early 1948 a fresh crisis had arisen over the Soviet blockade of West Berlin which was going to require a massive air supply operation. The Berlin crisis arose from the partition of Germany at the end of the war into zones, to be allocated to the four powers, the United States, the Soviet Union, Britain and France. The former capital Berlin, which lay deep inside the Soviet zone, was also jointly administered by the four powers, with guaranteed access from the west by designated land and air routes. The problem was that the Soviets and Western Allies had conflicting plans about the future

---

1   Ashworth, C: *Avro York in Royal Air Force Service* (*Aviation News* mini-monograph) p24.
2   Passenger cum Freighter.

of Germany, with the Soviet Union determined to resist any attempt by the West to establish democracy. Berlin became the focus for this disagreement between the powers which soon became a trial of strength, as the Soviets viewed the western sectors of Berlin as an obstacle to their own long-term strategic plans for Europe which did not include a reformed and restored democratic, western-orientated Germany. If pressure by peaceful means in the first instance could be brought to bear to bring about the collapse of western authority in Berlin, and perhaps next in the western sectors of Germany, so much the better. Thus by June 1948 matters came to a head with the closure by the Soviets, in defiance of treaty obligations, of all road and rail links to West Berlin, leaving the western allies with no choice but to operate an airlift to ensure supplies of food and essential raw materials to a city of 2.5 million people.

At first the United States Air Force in Europe (USAFE) operated C-47 flights with military supplies for the US Army garrison in the city along the southern air corridor, but by the end of June the basic daily requirements of the population, at a minimum of 5,000 tons of food per day, went far beyond the US Air Force's capability of supplying by air a maximum of 700 tons daily. Even with the use of other allied aircraft a daily total of not more than 5,000 tons could be lifted, so there was a considerable challenge ahead.

Quite apart from that, air access to the city from the west was limited by the Soviets to three air corridors, from the south, central and north. Each corridor was 20 miles wide but flying altitude was restricted to 10,000 feet, mainly to prevent air reconnaissance and interference with Soviet aircraft. The Royal Air Force part of the airlift called Operation Plainfare[3] began with the despatch of eight C-47 Dakotas from Waterbeach near Cambridge, and soon included Sunderland flying boats of Coastal Command from Nos 201 and 230 Squadrons, to be based at Hamburg. By 1 July the entire fleet of RAF

Alan Smith, as Chairman of the British Berlin Airlift Association and representing 206 Sqn, being presented to Prince Charles.

---

3   The USAF airlift was Operation Vittles.

Transport Command Dakotas had arrived in Wunstorf, one of the RAF bases 20 miles (32 km) north-west of Hanover, reinforced by aircrew seconded from the Royal Australian Air Force, the Royal New Zealand Air Force and the South African Air Force. The entire Transport Command fleet of Avro Yorks was also in place which included 206 Squadron under the command of Squadron Leader E. Moody. The full line-up consisted of the Dakotas of No. 46 Group normally based at Oakington (Nos 27, 30, 46 and 238 Squadrons) and at Waterbeach (Nos 18, 53, 62 and 77 Squadrons); the Yorks were on the strength of No. 47 Group usually based at Abingdon (Nos 40, 51, 59 and 242 Squadrons) and at Lyneham (Nos 99, 206 and 511 Squadrons).[4] Later two squadrons of the newly introduced Handley Page Hastings were added, Nos 47 and 297.

It has to be borne in mind that only 30 per cent of the cargo flown into Berlin was food; some 60 per cent was coal vital for the economic life of the city. Given the plight of the Berliners the carrying capacity of the aircraft involved was maximised: for the Avro York the authorised maximum landing weight was increased from 60,000 lbs to 65,000 lbs and with a fuel load of 800 gallons the payload was 16,500 lbs, with all excess equipment stripped out. The usual payload was coal and flour producing a thick dust which was impossible to remove due to the rapid turnaround required, two and a half hours at Wunstorf and between 15 and 45 minutes at Gatow, in the British Sector of Berlin. It is not difficult to visualize the problems of transporting coal by air, as Alan Smith found as a crew member of a York delivering coal and kippers into the city:

'Kippers were taken because they were the most compact form of nutrition, but it meant we always had black faces and smelt of fish.'[5] At one point the air-dropping of coal from hoppers was contemplated to reduce wear and tear but this was rejected when it was found that the coal disintegrated into dust. It was originally planned to operate 30 Yorks daily flying 120 sorties but problems with servicing and the poor weather reduced this to 100 sorties, and even this was difficult to maintain although a rota system of servicing the Yorks in the UK for every 150 flying hours per aircraft was established which stabilised the situation. Apart from Gatow, reception airfields in Berlin included Tempelhof in the American Sector. These were later joined by Tegel in the French Sector.

On 5 August the first manufactured goods were exported from the city, by which time the airlift was delivering more than 4,000 tons daily, rising to over 4,600 tons by the autumn. The carrying capacity of the Avro York at around 8/9 tons was more than double that of the C-47 Dakota, but the frequent take-offs and landings for an aircraft that was designed for long-distance hauls brought with it serviceability and maintenance problems as tyres, brakes, undercarriages and engines bore the strain. Another problem was the stress around the cabin floor so that a false floor was added to assist in weight distribution of the heavy loads. Crews and aircraft were pooled resulting in a 24-day cycle which included four days' leave in the UK. The typical routing for the Yorks from Wunstorf to Gatow was a climb to 3,500 feet to Walsrode, then cruising at 160 knots to Egestorf, Restorf and Frohnau where there was a holding beacon and then authorised descent to Grunewald or Huston depending on the runway in use at Gatow. The final approach was under GCA control. The return flight was usually via Plutzke and Volkenrode. In spite of occasional fog the winter was relatively mild and allied air capacity was gradually building up, resulting in an increase of tonnage carried after an initial dip to 3,800 tons per day in November, to 5,500 tons in January 1949 with a staggering 12,940 tons during the so-called 'Easter Parade' on 16 April.

The blockade was suddenly lifted on 12 May 1949 but the airlift continued, to build up stockpiles for any future repeat of these events. In July Flight Lieutenant L. A. Mather

---

4 *History of the Royal Air Force* (J. D. R. Rawlings as Consultant), Temple Press 1984, p182.
5 The late Alan Smith quoted in the *Manx Independent*, 25 May 1993.

of 206 Squadron was awarded the Air Force Cross for completing 404 sorties, a record for any pilot in the operation. In all the airlift had involved 692 aircraft, with a total of 277,804 flights, and just under 66,000 by the Royal Air Force. The Yorks had carried some 233,145 tons of supplies, more than half the RAF contribution to the airlift, and achieved a higher than average number of sorties per day, compared to other types, making a total of 29,000 flights into Berlin.[6] During the airlift there were 700 cases of harassment by the Soviets, which included the use of searchlights to dazzle pilots, dangerously close flying manoeuvres, flares and occasional ground fire damaging aircraft.

With the end of the airlift 206 Squadron was once again disbanded, on 31 August 1949, although there was a short period from January until 20 February 1950 flying Dakotas from Waterbeach. The squadron was never again used in the transport role.

Avro York at Wunstorf during Airlift.
(CC/206)

6   Ashworth, ibid. p27.

CHAPTER 13

SHACKLETON ERA: ST EVAL 1952-1957

'We rapidly seemed to become oblivious to all those shortcomings because there was such a good spirit within the squadron.'

Sergeant Air Gunner Lewis M. Glanville on his impressions of St Eval, October 1952.

The Squadron Re-born

The post-war maritime role of 206 dates back to 27 September 1952 when the squadron was re-formed at its old wartime base of St Eval under the command of Squadron Leader J. D. Beresford, this time equipped with the new Avro Shackleton MR 1A. The decision to restore the squadron as part of an expansion of Coastal Command had its origins in the growing international tension with the Soviet Union which had if anything worsened since the ending of the Berlin Airlift.

The crisis over Berlin had convinced the western powers of the need to cooperate in the face of Soviet pressure, thus the North Atlantic Treaty was signed in Washington in April 1949 by the western European countries and the United States as a mutual defence treaty. This brought with it joint military obligations and as far as the UK was concerned, a greatly widened responsibility for the sea around Britain and especially in the north Atlantic. This was a task that would have to be shared between the Royal Navy and an expanded Coastal Command. Coupled with this were the plans of the Soviet Union to expand their navy, and in particular the submarine fleet, far beyond the requirements of their own home defence needs. Then, the outbreak of the Korean War in June 1950 and the entry of the Chinese into the conflict at the end of the year, seemed to bring the prospect of a new world war a step nearer.

The expansion of Coastal Command could not be achieved overnight. Apart from the defence cutbacks of the later 1940s and the demobilisation of trained aircrews, the American aircraft the Command had relied upon under Lend-Lease were now being withdrawn, including the Liberators, Catalinas and Fortresses. This left the surveillance and anti-submarine tasks to the ageing Lancasters and Sunderland flying boats with their operating radius of under 1000 miles. A scheme for the replacement of the Sunderland was scrapped but the Air Ministry had issued in 1946 specification R.5/46 for a very long range maritime aircraft, which was taken up by Roy Chadwick, Avro's Chief Designer. The new design was based on Chadwick's Lincoln, which had replaced the Lancaster, but with the wider and deeper fuselage necessary for a crew of ten and the extra equipment needed for lengthy maritime patrols. The aircraft was to be powered by four Rolls Royce Griffon 57 contra-rotating engines, a powerplant design which had already proved its worth in the later versions of the Spitfire, and from which the phrase 'Griffon Growl' arose. Chadwick chose the name 'Shackleton' for the new aircraft as he had become friendly with the explorer in 1921 and felt the name appropriate for an aircraft which was to range over great distances across the world. Sadly, Chadwick did not live to see the first flight of the prototype in March 1949 at Woodford as he was killed in the crash of an Avro Tudor in August 1947.[1]

---

1   Barry Jones: *Avro Shackleton* p25.

By 1950 there was still a gap in Coastal Command's provision as the Shackleton would require another 18 months before it was ready for the squadrons, so a stop-gap had to be arranged with the United States under the Mutual Defence Aid Pact by which 52 Lockheed P2V-5 Neptune aircraft were loaned to the RAF to equip Nos 36, 203, 210 and 217 Squadrons. This aircraft had an effective range of nearly 1,300 miles and powerful search and attack radars but was withdrawn later in the 1950s as the Shackleton became the mainstay of the Command.

Inevitable delays at the testing and production stage before deliveries got under way, dictated the rate of expansion in the Command. The first unit to be equipped with the Shackleton MR 1[2] was No. 120 Squadron based at Kinloss, on 3 April 1951, followed by No. 224 Squadron at Aldergrove in August 1951. No. 220 Squadron re-formed at Kinloss (soon moving to St Eval) in September alongside No. 236 Operational Conversion Unit (OCU) and No. 240 Squadron was re-formed at St Eval in May 1952 before moving to Ballykelly in June. Other units included No. 42 Squadron, re-formed in June 1952 at St Eval, this time with the MR 1A, powered by the slightly modified Griffon 57A engine. In September the re-formed No. 206 Squadron received its first MR 1A Shackleton. The squadron was back in business, albeit the last unit to be formed in this phase of expansion.

Getting Established

Progress at first was slow. By the end of October four Shackletons had been allocated from other squadrons including VP263, WB836, WG528 and WB832 plus one Oxford KB992. Squadron appointments included Flight Lieutenant L. S. Alden as Flight Commander, Flying Officer C. H. Bidie as Adjutant, Flight Lieutenant K. L. H. Allington as Navigation Leader, Pilot Officer W. J. Williams as Weapons Leader, Flying Officer N. A. C. Tibbles as Signals Leader and Flight Sergeant F. A. Painter, Engineer Leader. Eleven aircrew personnel were posted in from No. 224 Squadron to form an experienced

No. 236 OCU crew – all to 206 Sqn, October 1952. John Young is 4th from right.
(John Young)

2 MR (Maritime Reconnaissance) rather than the previous GR (General Reconnaissance) designation. (Ibid. p37).

No. 236 OCU, Kinloss early 1950s. Neptune in background. Shackleton MR1A WB855 in foreground.
(Charles Peacock)

nucleus, and ground crews were similarly drafted in from other units. Later No. 236 OCU became a source of trained aircrew. From the start there were problems of serviceability and shortage of spares, a severe headache for the CO as the squadron was responsible for its own first line servicing as Wing Commander J. D. Beresford recalled:

'The station commander (Group Captain D. M. Somerville) summoned me one month to order me to remove the phrase "chronic unserviceability" from the Historical Record (Form 540) but accepted "recurrent unserviceability"'.[3] The result was that the flying programme was very severely restricted in the period up to December 1952.

Among those joining the squadron in October 1952 was a young conscript who had just qualified as a sergeant air gunner on Shackletons, Lewis M. Glanville. He counted himself lucky to have an AG brevet and 'three stripes on my arm' which would give him the advantage of additional pay and the chance of nearly 400 hours' flying experience which was relatively rare for national servicemen. He felt fortunate to be crewed with Flying Officer Colin Bidie as captain, one of the most experienced and accomplished pilots on the squadron. He had mixed feelings about St Eval:

'Probably St Eval's greatest disadvantages were, firstly, its inaccessibility in those days because the bus service was sparse and motor cars were beyond everybody's financial reach. Secondly, the food in the Sergeants' Mess was awful, due to the necessity for the sergeant WAAF cook to use an open range as part of her cooking equipment. More than once we noticed perspiration falling from her forehead into the food that she was cooking. Thirdly, the accommodation was antiquated, with two sharing a cubicle and the partitioning did not reach the ceiling. Our squadron billet was on the opposite side of the road to the mess hall. We rapidly seemed to become oblivious to all those shortcomings because there was such a good spirit within the squadron. The national service lads seemed to lead separate off-duty lives from their regular colleagues, possibly because they tended to be younger and some of the regulars were married.'[4]

In November a further Shackleton had been delivered bringing squadron strength to five Shackletons and one Oxford. On the 8th three aircraft and crews were placed under the command of Squadron Leader D. H. Sutton to fly to Ballykelly in Northern Ireland as part of a joint detachment of 206 and 42 Squadrons to the Joint Anti-Submarine School (JASS) at Londonderry. The course lasted for about four weeks and consisted of training

3   Wg Cdr J. D. Beresford, letter to author 22/9/2001.
4   Lewis M. Glanville, letter to author 23/11/02.

ship and aircraft crews in combined anti-submarine tactics. This was the first of many such detachments for the squadron. Flying Officer (later Squadron Leader) C. H. Taylor, recalled his experiences at such a detachment in March 1953:

'The crews were accommodated at HMS *Sea Eagle* in Londonderry where we also did the ground portion of the training. The aircraft were based at Ballykelly whence we travelled by bus to do the air exercises. Among the attractions of this detachment was that we had WREN batwomen in place of the wrinkled old batmen at St Eval. Another, not universally welcomed, part of the course was a day at sea with the Navy; the sea off Northern Ireland can be rough in March. Also because sugar was still rationed, a bus trip over the border to Buncrana was favoured for a Saturday afternoon. (This was long before the "Troubles").'[5]

Gradually the number of flying hours increased during December, despite the granting of leave to half the squadron pre-Christmas and the other half post-Christmas. The sorties included navigational exercises, local training flights and a stand-by system of Search and Rescue (SAR) shared with the other squadrons was inaugurated. Squadron strength had now grown to 16 pilots, 19 navigators, 23 signallers, 9 engineers and 16 radar/gunners. Ground crew numbers remained under strength especially in the number of corporals available.[6]

One of those joining the squadron in December was the afore-mentioned Flying Officer C. H. Taylor, a navigator. He arrived as part of a complete crew who were without a senior pilot. The consequence was that they often flew with the CO Squadron Leader Beresford, or 'Gentleman John' as he was known in squadron parlance. On 31 December his crew flew on a seven and a half hour exercise and the next day, New Year's Day, another 14-hour sortie to Rockall. Within two months Flying Officer Taylor had become squadron adjutant and got to know the CO well, soon finding that the latter's reputation as something of a 'killjoy' was not strictly accurate:

'True he rarely if ever visited the bar; true he was never heard to swear; true he expected very high standards of behaviour. But he was always a perfect gentleman; and he did have a sense of humour – a very dry one...'[7]

Even before the Shackleton Mark 1 had been delivered to the squadrons work was already in hand developing the Mark 2 version which was intended to eliminate a number of shortcomings, which included taxying and ground handling problems and the positioning of the radar scanner housing in the nose, making it vulnerable to bird strikes and restricting its all-round scanning range. The Mark 2 variant included a lengthened nose and tail cone, a semi-retractable 'dustbin-like' radome aft of the wings on the underside of the fuselage, and various improvements in ground braking. Improved visual sighting positions in the nose and tail cone were invaluable for the search and rescue role and there was a remotely-controlled Boulton Paul nose turret armed with two 20mm cannon. By the end of 1952 the new version was being delivered to the squadrons alongside the Mark 1s, with 206 Squadron collecting its first Mark 2 WG558 from Aldergrove on 4 February 1953. Flying Officer Freer appears to have been the first squadron pilot to be checked out on the Mark 2. For at least a year this squadron like others operated the two versions side by side, with the inevitable problems for the air and ground crews of two sets of equipment, spares, flight manuals and general operation. But apart from the modifications already mentioned Flying Officer Taylor commented on the 'retractable tail-wheels and the radio compass which enabled the navigator to listen to (somewhat distorted) music while he worked.'[8]

5   Sqn Ldr C. H. Taylor (RAF Ret'd), letter to author 24/1/2001.
6   206 ORB Dec. 1952.
7   Sqn Ldr Taylor.
8   Ibid.

Shackleton MR2 WL742 delivered to 206 Sqn March 1953.
(John Young)

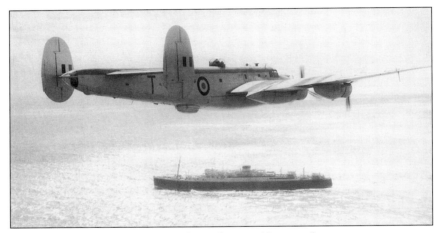

MR2 (serial obscured) on maritime patrol.
(Charles Peacock)

In January 1953 the squadron sent four crews to Luqa in Malta on the first so-called 'Fair Isle' detachment, training exercises working with units of the Mediterranean fleet and other NATO forces. The crews returned to St Eval on 14 February. Closer to home the first 'Co-ordinated Anti-Submarine Exercise' (CASEX)[9] was flown on 9 February by two crews captained by the CO and Flight Lieutenant Barton, in sorties lasting between two and three hours. On the 19th a somewhat unusual task was the ferrying of a Griffon power plant to Luqa for No. 120 Squadron by Flight Lieutenant Pendry and his crew. This was the first time a power plant had been ferried in a Shackleton bomb bay. Unfortunately the bomb doors could not be fully closed and the resulting vibration warped them and fractured both pitot head bases.

Squadron training in the maritime role continued. In March the crews attending No. 50 Joint Unit Course (JUC) Course, JASS, in Londonderry flew a number of sorties from Ballykelly to gain experience with the 'British Directional Sono-Buoy'. During February and March a number of *Fleetex* sorties were flown, exercises with the home fleet.

The squadron was now well established at St Eval, possessing five Shackleton Mark 1s and three Mark 2s. Aircrew strength was 21 pilots, 24 navigators, 12 engineers, 20 signallers and 27 air gunners. There were around 40 groundcrew under a flight sergeant.

---

9   CASEX and other exercises usually were allotted numbers to denote the type of exercise and the
    resources involved e.g. CASEX 43.

Shackleton MR1A WB836 of No. 224 Sqn over Grand Harbour, Malta c. 1952.
Aircraft served with 206 Sqn from July 1954 to March 1957.
(Charles Peacock)

Flying Officer Taylor recalled the sight of the aircraft parked adjacent to headquarters with their colour scheme (which had varied little for Coastal aircraft since 1941) of matt grey above 'which came off all over your battledress if you got near it' and gloss white below. 'This caused no end of grief prior to AOC's inspection time. How we all avoided lead poisoning I cannot think; we dipped rags into 130 Octane fuel and, without gloves, cleaned the brown oil/exhaust stains off the underside, aircrew and groundcrew alike.'[10] As adjutant, Colin Taylor was responsible for drawing up details for Saturday morning Station Commander's Parade, in Station Routine Orders: 'The whole procedure was made difficult by there being far more officers and senior NCOs than was ever envisaged when the RAF drill manual was compiled.'[11]

The introduction of the Shackleton into service with its very long range capability inevitably put quite a strain on crews, on anything up to and beyond flights of 15-hour duration. The problems of crew fatigue due to the lengthy patrols against a background of noise and vibration was investigated by the Institute of Aviation Medicine (IAM), a branch of the Royal Aircraft Establishment at Farnborough. Various crews undertook gruelling tests and the conclusion was no suprise that aircrew got tired flying these operations!

In what was becoming a busy year two crews (20 aircrew and 21 groundcrew) were detached from 8 to 16 May 1953 to Aalborg in Denmark, to participate in exercises with the Royal Danish Navy and the Royal Danish Air Force under the command of Flight Lieutenant K. H. Allington. Things did not get off to a very promising start, as recalled by Colin Taylor:

'Soon after the aircraft arrived one experienced an engine failure. With some difficulty a replacement engine was fitted into a bomb bay and off we went to Aalborg. The exercise was maintained using our aircraft while we watched the amazing procedure of an engine change with virtually no ground equipment apart from hand tools and a Coles Crane. How "Chiefy" managed to cope with removing and replacing both the contra-rotating propellers and the engine under such primitive conditions and entirely in the open I shall never know (and I was originally an engine fitter). Meanwhile we were made very welcome by the Danes, some of us even managing a flight in an RDAF Catalina.'[12]

---

10 In 1955 the whole airframe finish was changed to Dark Sea Grey, and in 1959 fuselage tops became white.
11 Sqn Ldr Taylor.
12 Ibid.

At the end of the exercises there was praise from the Air Attaché in Denmark and the AOC No. 19 Group. The squadron team also manged to beat the RDAF in their national game of skittles!

Royal Review at Odiham

From the middle of June three crews from 206, alongside three crews from each of the other squadrons at St Eval, Nos 42 and 220, were practising formation flying in readiness for the Royal Review at RAF Odiham in Hampshire, on 15 July, the year after the Queen's accession to the throne and six weeks after the Coronation of 2 June.

Three crews were also selected from each of Nos 120, 240 and 269 Squadrons. The Shackleton Wing was to be part of a formation of some 640 aircraft in the flypast. The training flights for the event were of a duration of around three and a half hours and Colin Taylor noticed in his logbook that his crew practised on 18 days:

'For ten of those days we did the complete route as a nine-aircraft formation, dovetailing in with some 630 aircraft in each flypast. The three 206 aircraft formed the rear three of the St Eval formation. Our captain was Flying Officer Norman Allsop and 2nd pilot Pilot Officer Paddy Shorthouse. Formation flying in a Shackleton, in summer, in the rear "vic", was a physical nightmare for the pilots, who were by the end of each sortie physically and, I think, mentally drained having sweated pints in the constant struggle to keep position. The route took us in loose formation over Cornwall, Devon and Somerset to Gloucester where we tightened formation as we passed directly over the top of Birdlip Hill at some 500ft (or below!). There was a field with cows at the top of the hill and judging by their antics the milk yield must have been well down that month. The route continued up to the Watford area where we turned south for the run into Odiham. I must have trusted Norman and Paddy because I spent most of the time, about three and a half hours per sortie, in the nose – only some 15ft away from the tail of a 220 aircraft.'[13]

Left:
Practice for 1953
Royal Review Nos
206/220 Sqns.
(Charles Peacock)

Below
Practice for 1953
Royal Review.
Shackleton MR1A
WG528 nearest to
camera.
(John Young)

13 Ibid.

Royal Review at Odiham, Shackletons of <u>Nos 206/220 Sqns.</u>
(Charles Peacock)

The hard work paid off for, in spite of 15 July being dull and overcast, the Review was pronounced a great success with the Shackleton Wing being singled out for especial praise by the organiser, Air Vice-Marshal The Earl of Bandon.[14]

Busy Schedule

The squadron was also taking its share of SAR standby, as recalled by Colin Taylor:

'The three (later four) St Eval squadrons took it in turn to provide 24-hour SAR cover. During its one-day duty tour the crew had to be ready for take-off at about one hour's notice, which is about how long it took to get briefed, into the aircraft and away. At one time we shared the SAR task with the Sunderlands at Pembroke Dock but as they were scrapped we took over the whole job. The aircraft was fitted with Lindholme gear[15] which comprised five yellow canisters connected by rope and fitted to the bomb carriers in the bomb bay. These contained dinghies and survival kit, and we did practice drops from time to time so that we could position the "stick" correctly relative to any survivors.'[16]

Various SAR sorties were flown during August including four from the 7th to 9th for a US Air Force B36 lost in the Atlantic north-west of Ireland. Also on the 7th Lieutenant Legg RN with his crew were detailed to search for a Vampire downed in the Bristol Channel, but on this occasion the pilot was rescued by a launch.

Another flying commitment during August was Exercise *Momentum*, in which aircraft from the squadron flew from West Malling simulating mine-laying raids on English harbour areas.

The Battle of Britain was commemorated on 19 September by 'At Home' Days at various RAF stations and three crews were detailed to fly in formation over a number of stations in southern England. That month also saw the start of the serious business of the annual NATO exercise, that for 1953 being *Mariner* which began on the 24th. Nine nations participated in the exercise, which lasted for nine days. The squadron flew a

---

14 Barry Jones, *Avro Shackleton* p89.
15 Invented by the Squadron Commander of RAF Lindholme.
16 Sqn Ldr Taylor.

Above: Airborne Lifeboat Mk 3 trials at Farnborough, 1953.
(John Young)
Below: Mk 3 Airborne Lifeboat, St Eval Sailing Club 1953.
Boat designed for use with Shackleton.
(John Young)

total of 200 hours in 20 sorties but these early NATO exercises were not without their 'teething troubles', as related by Colin Taylor:

'These exercises usually involved long sorties, often of 17 hours including convoy escort. There was often the need to communicate with some ships of another NATO nation and these being the early years of NATO collaboration our efforts were not always successful. I recall circling the Dutch aircraft carrier *Karel Dorman* for an hour trying to pass a message by VHF or Aldis in a peculiar code called "LANTCO" – all to no effect.'[17]

Problems of servicing continued to interfere with flying hours, as was evidenced by the failure to attain the flying commitment by over 70 hours during November. Centralised servicing of squadron aircraft had been in place for several months by this date but there were several mishaps including the collapse of the starboard undercarriage in one aircraft, and at least two instances of engine failure one of which resulted in a fire on take-off. (In April 1954 the squadron once again became responsible for its own servicing.) One of two aircraft detached to Keflavik in Iceland from 17 to 21 November on a search for a US Air Force SA 16 amphibian, lost an engine on take-off and a replacement engine had to be flown out by a Transport Command Hastings. The detachment, commanded by Flight Lieutenant J. S. Knight, also had to cope with freezing temperatures and wind speeds of at least 20 knots. Unfortunately no sightings were made by the searching aircraft.

The squadron 'Fair Isle' detachment to Luqa in Malta, from 8 to 30 January 1954 was commanded by Flight Lieutenant J. Jones and included sonic exercises with submarines together with several night attacks with illuminants and some navigational exercises. Some officers and senior NCOs were given experience of life aboard a submarine and in return some RN officers and ratings flew in the squadron aircraft. Serviceability of aircraft during the detachment was compared favourably with that available at St Eval.

The problems of unserviceability were serious enough to be taken account of in the higher levels of command when in June 1954 a decision was reached to end the mix of Shackleton variants within squadrons and return to a uniform type, either Mark 1 or Mark 2. For 206 this meant handing over to No. 42 Squadron three Mark 2 aircraft and

---

17 Ibid.

CASEX MARCH 1954, H.M.S. SEA DEVIL
(Notice bomb bursts,photo taken through

Casex, March 1954. HMS *Sea Devil*. Notice bomb bursts!
(CC/206)

receiving three Mark 1s, bringing the total on squadron strength to eight Mark 1s. The obvious conclusion was that uniformity in servicing and spares was achieved but at the cost of increasing the average age of the aircraft.

Aird Whyte Trophy 1954

At around this time practising got under way for the Aird Whyte Trophy due to be held on 22/23 June. Wing Commander J. D. Beresford recalled the occasion:

'I looked around for something to distinguish the squadron, and lighted on the Aird Whyte Trophy, presented in memory of an air gunner who had been killed while serving in a Coastal squadron[18]. In those days the trophy was awarded for low-level bombing (with simulated depth charges), gunnery and photography. The procedure was to enter three crews from each squadron and for each to fly at 1,000 ft at optimum cruising speed off St Austell on the reciprocal of a launch towing a "submarine" without noticing it until

Aird Whyte Trophy 1954 – the winning crew.
(Charles Peacock & CC/206)

18 Sgt Nairn Fincastle Aird Whyte was killed in 1943 while serving as an air gunner in Coastal Command.

the judges gave the word. Then continuing for, I think, 45 seconds, changing the pitch to increase rpm to 2,400 (2,800?), closing the throttles, lowering half flap and opening the bomb doors, descending to 100 feet and then making three attacks all in 3 minutes 45 seconds, using a five lb bomb to represent each end of the stick of eight depth charges, avoiding range error and line error. We had hardly any time or bombs for practice in 1953 but I determined to win in 1954, so I selected three crews for special training, omitted the 45 seconds stage so that a turn to port began immediately, practised endlessly using two months' allocation of five lb bombs until we could all make the attacks in precisely 3 minutes 45 seconds.'

The training paid off and the squadron won the competition, the trophy being presented by the Air Member for Personnel, Air Chief Marshal Sir Francis Fogarty KCB, KBE, DFC, AFC.

First Goodwill Tour

Gp Capt. Faville taking off in MR1A WG510,
St Eval Church in background.
(Charles Peacock)

Sqn Ldr Beresford and crew for the 1954 Far East tour in 'A' VP293.
(Charles Peacock)

The squadron's first 'Goodwill Tour' was undertaken in August 1954. With the coming of the Shackleton into RAF service came new opportunities to 'show the flag' in locations which would have been difficult in previous times. The aircraft's maximum range of 4,200 miles and its ample carrying capacity for ground crew, stores and spares, made this possible, not to mention the advantages of re-stocking for the return trip with exotic food unobtainable in Britain and of course liquor for the mess bars! Also there was the serious business of exercising with foreign navies and showing off the new maritime aircraft for possible export orders. Inevitably such tours acted as a boost to morale at a time when foreign travel for the general public was almost non-existent.

Preparations were in hand for a combined maritime exercise in Ceylon called *Jet 54* where units of four navies were to join forces in Trincomalee Harbour for their annual exercises. Then word came through that the squadron had been chosen to send a detachment to visit New Zealand and Fiji by invitation from the New Zealand Government. Personnel involved numbered 52 aircrew and 37 groundcrew under the command of Group Captain R. Faville CBE, station commander at St Eval (and a New Zealander), and Squadron Leader Beresford, OC 206 Squadron, as second-in-command. In the last week of July the four aircraft detailed for the trip were prepared, a massive task in which ten engines were changed and new tyres fitted to all the wheels except one. Needless to say, the inevitable 'Sod's Law' (or 'Murphy's Law'?) kicked in and the only tyre to burst was the one that had not been changed!

On 12 August the four aircraft left St Eval, captained by Group Captain Faville, Squadron Leader Beresford, Flight Lieutenant Salmon and Flight Lieutenant Barton. Two routes were flown, two aircraft led by Group Captain Faville via El Adem in Libya and Khormaksar in Aden. Squadron Leader Beresford led the remaining aircraft by Habbaniya in Iraq and down the Persian Gulf in two 17-hour stages, to monitor the effects of successive long flights in a hot climate. It was not only heat that the crew had to contend with but the noise, flying in the Gulf at 1,000 ft with all the windows open and in temperatures of not less than 104 degrees F.

However the two formations met up on time in Negombo, Ceylon, although one of the aircraft had a hydraulic failure and a fifth aircraft had to be flown out from the UK by

A header tank blew up, Negombo, 1954!
(CC/206)

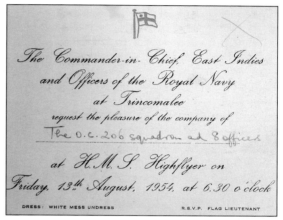

Social life en route!
(CC/206)

Flying Officer 'Pop' Gladstone as a relief arriving on the 23rd. Nevertheless, the exercises were successful and all were struck by the beauty of the island. On the 31st the detachment, together with two Hastings aircraft from No. 47 Squadron set out for New Zealand, stopping at Changi in Singapore, thence via the East Indies to Darwin, and Richmond. It was in the latter location that Squadron Leader Beresford was told, to his horror, that they would be required to lecture without notes or preparation to a number of senior officers. Later, the squadron leader, his own worst critic, described the result as 'disappointing'. It was then on to New Zealand, to Whenuapi (Wellington) where the contrast between the 'English' or 'British' style of the New Zealanders and the more 'American' ways of the Australians was noticed. Many places were visited including Auckland, Hamilton, Christchurch and Invercargill in the extreme south (in a heavy rainstorm) and wherever they went the 206 detachment was warmly greeted and generous hospitality provided. There was a visit in Sunderlands, courtesy of the RNZAF, to Lauthala Bay in Fiji. Any hope that the New Zealanders might be persuaded to buy the Shackleton came to nothing as they had already placed an order for Neptunes.[19]

Back in Australia there was a short visit to Townsville in Queensland, where the RAF

19 Wg Cdr J. D. Beresford.

VP293 served at the RAE Farnborough from 1963-1975 – here photographed in
Farnborough colours.
(via Doug Cook, Shackleton Association)

contingent were unaccustomed to the heat, as Wing Commander Beresford recalled:

'....We went into a pub in Townsville each wearing shirt and tie but not jacket as it
was hot by our standards. We were very courteously asked to leave the saloon bar and
use the public bar, which we much preferred as we were served by a most attractive
young woman who told us all about the place.'

The detachment returned to St Eval on 27 September after a tour of more than 30,000
miles accomplished in seven weeks. As a footnote to the tour Squadron Leader
Beresford had flown in Shackleton 'A' VP293, in which he and his co-pilot Peter Best
reputedly demonstrated some single-engined flying in New Zealand![20] The aircraft was

---

20 According to a letter in 'The Growler' (Shackleton Association Newsletter), Winter 2000 edition.

eventually withdrawn from service in 1975 and became part of the Strathallan Collection in Scotland until that was dissolved in 1988/89. The aircraft was then broken up but rescued from the scrapyard by Norman Thelwell who purchased the nose section, moved it to Chichester and restored and refurbished it. Since then the nose section has been transported for exhibition to various museums and air shows and now resides at the Midland Air Museum, Coventry.

The Squadron Saved (unofficial)!

The usual squadron routine continued into the autumn, with the NATO exercise *Morning Mist* in September, although only a maximum of two serviceable aircraft were available until the return of the Far East detachment on 27 September. In October a crew commanded by Flying Officer March was detached to Thorney Island to take part in a BBC television film on the work of NATO. In November it was back to the primary role of the squadron and Operational Flying Exercises (OFEs) which would often involve outward flights of over 1,000 miles monitoring shipping or submarine movements in the Atlantic, excursions which could take anything up to or beyond a total of 15 hours.

Other tasks such as SAR Standby continued throughout the year, a typical example being the search for a crashed Lancaster from St Mawgan some 60 miles south-west of the Scilly Isles in December. The wreckage was found and ships were directed to the scene, one body being recovered by a Royal Navy destroyer.

There was a change of command on 8 November when Flight Lieutenant R. S. Salmon assumed temporary command of the squadron in place of Squadron Leader Beresford who was posted to Headquarters Coastal Command at Northwood. Squadron Leader E. K. Paine took command of the squadron on 8 December, a navigator, and one of the first navigators to be given command of a Coastal Command squadron[21]. But that is where the history of 206 Squadron might have come to yet another premature end,

Fg Off. 'Pop' Gladstone's crew. Charles Peacock 4th from left.
(Charles Peacock)

---

21 Sqn Ldr Taylor.

had it not been for the vigilance and cunning of its former CO. The background to this was another Defence Review following the ending of the Korean War in 1953 although there was still the growth in the Soviet navy to be taken into account. Squadron Leader Beresford takes up the story:

'On my first day (at Northwood), Bobby Craven[22] handed me a file enclosing a paper on reduction of Coastal Command forces, prepared by my predecessor whom I never met but took to be a socialist wedded to the Last In First Out doctrine of the trades unions, naming No. 206 as the first to be once more "Reduced to Number Plate Only". LIFO seemed entirely inappropriate to the fate of squadrons, so I disregarded his paper and wrote another, insecurely based on the provenance and war record of the existing squadrons and recommending a sequence of disbandment when need arose. Mine was unchallenged, so far as I know, but as I was promptly posted to Malta with an acting rank I might not have known. Whatever may have happened, No. 206 was SAVED and remains to this day.'[23]

New Devices, New Challenges

On a wet and windy night on 11 January the squadron SAR Standby crew were called out on a search for two missing 42 Squadron Shackletons which had lost contact on patrol to the south of the Fastnet Rock off southern Ireland. Colin Taylor was on duty that night:

'I was navigator to Flight Lieutenant Bob Salmon (later Squadron Leader) and we had just about got to sleep in the duty room behind the Mess when the phone rang. We dressed and ran down to Operations where we were told that two Shackletons of 42 Squadron were out of contact. The Duty Ops Officer, Bill Cook, tried to work out from their flight plans where they ought to be and it appeared possible that at some point SW of Ireland the two tracks got close together. We took off (in WB836) at 0130 and did a CLA (Creeping Line Ahead) search south of Cork and at first light got permission from the Irish to fly down the coast looking for wreckage. We found nothing.'[24]

Another aircraft captained by Flying Officer Reid continued the search which was not called off until the 13th. Very little was found except possibly a wheel and it was not until 11 years later that a starboard outer engine was trawled up in the area. The fact that 42 Squadron was 'stable-mate' of 206 at St Eval gave the whole incident a special poignancy, with the loss of 18 men. Colin Taylor recalled attending the memorial service in St Columb Major Church.

The need to track potential enemy submarines led to a number of new devices being introduced to the Shackleton squadrons in 1954 and 1955. The British Directional Sono-Buoy has already been mentioned but in January 1955 some 206 Squadron aircraft were fitted with the 'Autolycus' equipment. This rather odd code-name arose from the Shakespeare play *The Winter's Tale* in which Autolycus was 'the snapper-up of unconsidered trifles', thus the nickname 'sub-sniffer', or more correctly 'Exhaust Trail Indicator'.[25] The claim was that this would detect a submarine via its exhaust while 'schnorkelling' on the surface for a certain distance, that is until the introduction of nuclear submarines in later years. For surface ships the ASV Mk XIII was in theory able to distinguish vessel sizes and identify formations at ranges of up to 40 miles, but there were some complaints about its serviceability at times.

During the year there were exercises with surface ships and with the new Autolycus equipment, known in the squadron as 'Bisto', such as in Exercise *Fishplay* in May, an anti-submarine exercise between Scotland and Iceland. The results were inconclusive as

22 Wg Cdr R. E. Craven (later AM Sir Robert) KBE, CB, DFC.
23 Wg Cdr Beresford.
24 Sqn Ldr Taylor.
25 John Chartres, *Avro Shackleton* pp46-7.

Right: Squadron Standard (CC/206)

Below: Shackleton MR3 XF707
           over St Eval mid 1960s (CC/206)

Bottom: Nimrod deployment to San Diego in
           California, summer 1998, to take
           part in Exercise Joint Fleetex 98-1
           (CC/206)

Top: Final approach into Ascension Island
Middle & bottom: Nimrod MR2 in maritime role (CC/206)

Top: 75th Anniversay of the RAF formation returns to Kinloss (CC/206)
Middle: Nimrod refuelling
Bottom: Nimrod escorted by Tornado in 80th Anniversary year 1996 (CC/206)

Superb shot of Nimrod over Ayers Rock, Australia, during the 1998 Fincastle Competition (CC/206)

Top left: Nimrod XV241 with tail design for 80th Anniversary of 206 Squadron, 1996.
              L to R: Gp Capt. R.W. Joseph (OC 206 1992-94 & Station Commander 1994-96);
              Wg Cdr Paul Lane (OC Eng Wg); Fraser Currie (Nimrod Major Servicing Unit);
              Wg Cdr Stu Butler (OC 206 1994-96 & Station Commander 1998-2000) (Stu Butler)

Top right: 206 Squadron Memorial Window, Kinloss, dedicated in May 1989 (CC/206)

Above: 1998 Fincastle Competition, RAAF Edinburgh

Top: Nimrod detachment in the Gulf, March 2002
Top left: Nimrod releasing flares
Top right: Aircraft over the desert
Above: A night shot of a Nimrod over the Gulf at night
Bottom left: En route to Iraq – Nimrod refuelling from Tristar
Bottom right: Over Iraq

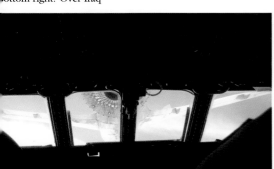

Above: 206 Squadron photograph, Kinloss 2003 (CC/206)
Below: Group at York Reunion 2002, taken at Yorkshire Air Museum, former RAF Station at Elvington (David Fellowes)

although subs were detected it was not with the aid of the new equipment. Further trials were held in June with better results when three US Navy submarines were detected to the north of Ireland using Autolycus, but again it was concluded that much depended on weather conditions and the height chosen to fly.

Another important innovation was the Mark 30 18-inch homing torpedo which had recently been introduced to improve the attack capability. The first tests of this by the squadron took place late in June with the CO and his crew, and a few days later by Flight Lieutenant Salmon, but on neither occasion did the weapon succeed in homing on to the target ship HMAFV *Bridlington*, due to mechanical failure. Initial tracking was aided on several occasions by the use of Anti-Submarine Training Indicators (ASTIs) which were flame and smoke floats released by friendly submarines.[26] At the end of June there was another chance to exercise with submarines in one of the periodic 'Fair Isle' detachments to Luqa in Malta via Gibraltar, on this occasion with Flight Lieutenant J. S. Knight in WG527 and Flight Lieutenant D. S. March in WB832.

During the previous winter the Manpower Study Team had visited St Eval and presumably for this purpose squadron flying hours had been raised until they amounted to 440 hours in February. After the Team left in March it was possible for the target hours to revert to 320, which enabled a more balanced flying programme to take place.

Formation flying practice once again intervened in April as three aircraft were detailed to take part in a flypast of 18 Shackletons in honour of the official birthday of HM The Queen. It was noted with some irritation in the ORB that the flypast was cancelled in June owing to the rail strike of that month, thus some valuable flying hours had been lost to training. More promising was the flypast of nine aircraft, including three of 206, over Farnborough on 9 July in connection with the Jubilee Celebrations of the Royal Aircraft Establishment (RAE). There was less success later in the month in the Aird Whyte Trophy competition in which the squadron failed to retain the Trophy but came third, the culprit being a bomb hang-up at the critical moment.

The September NATO exercise *Center Board* started over the Bay of Biscay with a US Carrier Group, and ships and aircraft from bases in Gibraltar, France, Portugal as well as the UK took part. Captains and crews from 206 taking part included Flight Lieutenants D. Robertson in WB836, D. March in WG510, Flying Officer A. Shorthouse in WG526, Flight Lieutenants J. Staples in WB836, and I. LeGresley in VP293. One sortie by Flight Lieutenant Robinson totalled 17 hours, 50 minutes. The squadron flew 11 sorties totalling more than 160 flying hours and two submarine contacts were made, with two unconfirmed. With the exercise over, the month of October was taken up with the annual JASS course at Londonderry and in November routine CASEX, long-range OFEs and Autolycus training sorties.

Towards the end of the year aircraft from the squadron played a part in an SAR operation to a ship in distress off the Lizard, by illuminating the area to enable ships to complete the rescue of 17 seamen. An additional aid was fitted to squadron aircraft in January 1956, Search And Rescue Automatic Homing (SARAH) but there was some confusion over its use to begin with, as airborne receivers did not seem at first compatible with the transmissions from surface beacons. This was highlighted in March 1956 in a search for a Hunter pilot from Tangmere downed in the English Channel, which proved successful in the event, but all airborne receivers had to be modified.

Trooping

Political instability in many parts of the world where there were British possessions meant that rapid troop movements would be required at any time to reinforce garrisons,

---

26 Ibid. p48.

for example in the Middle East. Thus the squadron was tasked with trooping trials, the first being on 1 November 1955 in an aircraft captained by Flight Lieutenant J. Knight, who flew 26 troops from Lyneham to Malta. It was demonstrated that after a flight of eight hours, troops were fit to carry out normal duties. In December the trials continued, this time with Squadron Leader R. S. Salmon as captain. The number of troops conveyed was increased to 33, once again to Luqa in Malta. This facility came just in the nick of time as events of 1956 unfolded.

The outbreak of violence in Cyprus in early 1956 involving the Greek Cypriot EOKA terrorist organisation left British forces on the island in dire need of rapid reinforcement, so trooping flights by Shackletons in Coastal Command in Operation *Encompass* were ordered during January. Five crews from 206 captained by Squadron Leader E. K. Paine, Flight Lieutenants D. R. Foster, J. Staples, D. March and T. R. Gurr began ferrying 900 troops of the Independent Parachute Brigade from Blackbushe in Hampshire to Nicosia from 12 to 15 January. Each flight conveyed 33 fully equipped soldiers. The experience gained must have been of use when the Suez Crisis erupted later in the year. Colonel Nasser of Egypt nationalised the Suez Canal and Britain and France launched a military operation, *Musketeer*, and once again rapid reinforcement was needed. Thus on 18 October Operation *Challenger* got under way with 206 Squadron aircraft moving personnel and equipment from various UK locations like RAF stations Binbrook, Marham and Wittering to Malta and Cyprus. Captains on these sorties included Flight Lieutenants D. F. Roberston, J. E. Staples, D. R. Foster and A. I. LeGresley, D. March and T. R. Gurr. Flying Officer P. Hanson and Flight Lieutenant N. Prowting were also involved. Apart from the transport of troops, some flights conveyed Valiant ground crews and spares to the Mediterranean theatre. The Suez operation, the failure of which need not detain us here, was over in seven days but the transport arrangements turned out to be flawless in their execution. With the operation being wound up there was the final phase of *Challenger* at the end of the month and the start of November, with participating captains mentioned above together with the new CO (since 10 April) Wing Commander J. E. Preston and Squadron Leader A. Craig. It was not until December that *Challenger* was completed with Flight Lieutenants LeGresley and T. R. Gurr flying out to Nicosia to bring home men of the 16th Parachute Brigade who had seen action in the Canal Zone. The final sorties collected the squadron ground crew.

Final months at St Eval

The last two years at St Eval were dominated by Operation *Challenger* in 1956 and the start of the squadron's role in Operation *Grapple* during the early summer of that year, which will be discussed later. In the meantime the squadron's work went on, frequently as a skeleton unit in terms of aircraft, air and ground crew.

Exercises with submarines were often hampered by lack of available vessels, as in January 1956, by severe weather in March and by lack of submarine availability again in June although during that month 109 hours were flown on 33 submarine exercises. In the meantime Autolycus ('Bisto') sorties helped to keep crews on their toes. Later in the year the training bore fruit when in October, Flight Lieutenant D. R. Foster located, shadowed, and photographed a Russian 'M'-type submarine. Ship surveillance off the north Cornish coast in February by Squadron Leader R. C. Church was part of an exercise involving shore-based radar. Again in March the Antarctic exploration vessel *Theron* was located and escorted on two days on its return to Britain, a story which was covered by the national press and BBC. In the same month aircraft participated in Exercise *Dawn Breeze*, shadowing the return of the Home Fleet and Royal Yacht *Britannia* from the Mediterranean.

Severe gales in July led to several call-outs for the SAR standby crews, most notably when the yacht *Moyana* got into difficulties south-east of the Lizard during a race. Flight Lieutenant D. R. Foster and his crew located the vessel and guided the successful rescue operation which followed. Other SAR duties includes occasional stand-by for Royal flights. There was a more serious incident in October when a US transport RD6 aircraft was reported missing between Land's End and the Azores. Several Shackletons and other aircraft joined in the search which continued for five days. No. 206 Squadron's flying hours amounted to 200 hours, but no crew members were ever found. Later in the month Flight Lieutenants Foster and Gurr and crews helped a Royal Navy frigate to locate some wreckage from a Sea Venom, but sadly no survivors, which had crashed off Portland.

Bad weather affected the performance of radar in *Gamefish* in November 1956, a submarine exercise involving four squadrons, so there had to be more reliance on visual searching for 'snorts'. Also in the month Flight Lieutenants D. F. Robertson and N. Prowting gained experience of a meteorological sortie code-named *Bismuth*[27] in a No. 202 Squadron Hastings flying from Aldergrove, presumably as part of the preparation for the forthcoming *Grapple*. Other training involved the new DECCA navigation equipment which began to be fitted to some squadron aircraft by the end of 1956. This hyperbolic navigation system worked on the principle of having a master station and a number of 'slaves' which transmitted a signal at exactly the same time. The aircraft equipment measured the time difference of arrival of the signal and by the use of charts navigators were able to obtain a 'fix' of the aircraft's position. This system, essential for the precise navigation required in the dropping of nuclear weapons, was installed around the islands in the area of Christmas Island, presumably with the master station on Christmas Island itself.[28]

The start of 1957 saw the build-up for Operation *Grapple*, which together with *Challenger*, had soaked up more than half the training hours during the previous quarter. In spite of new commitments and the growth of the potentially hostile Soviet Navy, all aspects of Coastal Command had been examined in Whitehall with a view to further cutbacks during 1956 and 1957, and Whitehall battles over inter-service rivalry complicated the issue. The Neptune and remaining Sunderland squadrons were disbanded by early 1957, the personnel moving to Shackleton units like 206, but a new SAR dimension was added with the introduction of Whirlwind helicopters.

The first of the Coastal Command Arctic Survival courses started at Kinloss in February, with exercises in the Cairngorm mountains, and two officers from 206 were detailed for this training. Another novel event was the visit by Flight Lieutenant J. E. Staples DFM to RAF Chivenor in Devon during March to assess facilities at that station for possible redeployment of the squadron from St Eval in time of war. This was presumably similar to the dispersal plans as had been seen in the Second World War, in the event of airfields being put out of action. This time, the threat was from an infinitely more devastating nuclear strike. By the same token, later in the year squadron buildings in St Eval were transformed into temporary dormitories to make way for additional personnel from other stations. On a brighter note, though, the squadron won the Aird Whyte Trophy in July 1957!

Among the comings and goings of personnel at around this time was Robin Woolven, a 19-year old Sergeant Air Signaller who arrived at St Eval to join 206 in July 1957 on his first squadron tour. He joined Crew Five captained by navigator Squadron Leader Alex Craig, 'A' Flight Commander. He recalled the Shackleton Mark 1, equipped with ASV 13 search radar which by then seemed 'long in the tooth' given the challenges

---

27 *Bismuth*: pre-planned Met. sortie over Atlantic.
28 Information from Robin Woolven, 23/9/02.

they faced; faster submarines, with nuclear boats coming into service, and the Russian *Sverdlov* class cruisers. The squadron crews were a mixture of World War II aviators, some Korean War Sunderland veterans and youngsters like himself. Robin was impressed with St Eval after the Maritime Operational Training Unit at Kinloss:

'........RAF St Eval was, for me, heaven. The station buildings were of single storey wartime construction and the Sergeants' Mess accommodation comprised single rooms made by dividing the hut with brick internal walls which, presumably for reasons of economy, reached only to just above the tops of the doors so DIY wood and cardboard extension walls were erected by the residents to reach the roof in an attempt to achieve some privacy.'

The hut was in the charge of Flight Sergeant, later Master Pilot, Joe Siekierkowski who flew with the CO Wing Commander Preston. Joe was a colourful character who had escaped, or so the story went, from the German-occupied Balkans firing a machine gun from the back of a motor cycle, heading eastwards to Russia and eventually reached the UK via that route. The squadron buildings were quite a trek from the main camp, being in the lee of the tower of St Eval Church. There were few cars around as only the older and more senior officers and NCOs took their cars to the squadron. Robin managed to club together with three other senior NCOs to purchase a pre-war Ford saloon for Saturday afternoon trips to Newquay, but the vehicle had to kept well out of sight of the authorities because of its dreadful state of repair.

Squadron routine consisted of various NATO exercises and of course frequent SAR commitments. Being the standby crew brought with it some perks 'such as free admission at the St Eval Astra cinema but call-outs generally seemed to come as the big film reached its climax.'[29]

News came through during August 1957 that the squadron was to re-locate to the nearby St Mawgan during January 1958, prior to the planned closure of St Eval. The two airfields were located on top of cliffs but St Mawgan was more suitable for possible expansion with its satellite airfield on the western side of the main airfield. After St Eval's closure in 1958 the married quarters were retained for a time along with hangars for agricultural storage. Thus ended 206's long association with St Eval.

---

29 Robin Woolven, notes, 2002.

CHAPTER 14

OPERATION *GRAPPLE* 1956-1958

'Within seconds the dramatic fireball was seen to be rapidly expanding and rising...'

Robin Woolven as witness to the H-Bomb test, November 1957.

Britain had joined the 'nuclear club' of the United States and Soviet Union in 1952 with the testing of its first device in October of that year. The development of the hydrogen bomb unleashed an even greater destructive power and both the United States and Soviet Union had carried out their first tests in 1952 and 1953 respectively. Britain's tests had thus far been carried out in Australian territory, the most recent deep inside South Australia, but when sites for H-Bomb testing was considered the Australians ruled out their own territory for this much more devastating weapon. The location chosen was now to be Christmas Island, present-day Kiritimati, in the central Pacific, part of what was then the Gilbert and Ellice Islands group, now the Republic of Kiribati. Along with its remoteness, the island's main population consisted of red land crabs.

There was much work to be done preparing the base for the tests targeted for the summer of 1957, codenamed Operation *Grapple*, and Shackleton detachments had already proved their worth in the Australian tests with their long range capacity for the transporting of personnel and stores, meteorological patrolling, aerial photography and general reconnaissance and SAR work.

The squadron was chosen for the support work the first phase of which got under way in June 1956 with the first two crews, captained by Squadron Leader R. C. Church and Flight Lieutenant I. LeGresley, setting off for Canton Island on the 2nd where they were to be positioned for transporting personnel and stores to Christmas Island. This detachment lasted until 14 July when the crews returned to St Eval.

In November training continued in cross country flying using the UK civil airways

Crews and aircraft sittin' and waitin', Charleston, South Carolina!
(CC/206)

routes to undertake radio range training. Met. training included another *Bismuth* sortie in a 202 Squadron Hastings from Aldergrove, this time for Flight Lieutenants D. Roberston and N. Prowting. Three aircraft were withdrawn from normal operations for major servicing and modifications. By January 1957 there were five aircraft being prepared and detailed planning and briefing began for the crews, with lectures on conditions that would be encountered en route.

Flight Lieutenant Robertson and crew made an inauspicious start, departing on 19 January 1957 and flying to Travis AFB near San Francisco where there was an unexpected two-week delay owing to mechanical problems. The four remaining crews for the second wave of *Grapple* continued their training at St Eval before setting out for Christmas Island by the beginning of March via the southern transit route of Lajes in the Azores, Bermuda, Charleston in South Carolina, Biggs in Texas, Travis AFB, and Hickham AFB in Honolulu to Christmas Island. Captains and crews included Wing Commander J. E. Preston in WB821, Flight Lieutenants Gurr in WG528 and Robertson in WG823, Squadron Leader Church and Flight Lieutenant Prowting. Flight Lieutenant Laurie Hampson (later Group Captain), squadron adjutant, recalled that the long overseas legs caused some amusement among the pilots since, although all the aircraft departed more or less simultaneously and arrived together, and all the navigators insisted that they had been on track all the way, none of the pilots reported seeing another Shackleton en route. During the overnight stop in Lajes the detachment was hosted by the Portuguese Air Force, whose base it was, but there were only enough rooms for the officers and the NCOs and airmen were the guests of the US Air Force. This arrangement had some interesting results as the next morning it was clear that the airmen had enjoyed superb USAF hospitality and acquired a few sore heads, while the officers had overdosed on garlic and were unapproachable until they had donned their oxygen masks![1]

On arrival in Bermuda the crews were welcomed by the base commander, a USAF colonel, but a slight contretemps arose when the CO Wing Commander Preston marched straight through the group to shake hands with a khaki-clad customs officer, not realising that the USAF was no longer the US Army Air Force and had changed to blue uniforms. Nevertheless no harm was done to UK-US relations and once again USAF hospitality was of the highest order. The leg to Travis AFB involved flying over the mountains and using oxygen – a rare experience for the 'sea level' Shackleton crews – and then on to Honolulu, in those days less crowded as holidaymakers came by sea and there were few cheap flights. As always the arrangements laid on by the USAF for the crews were impeccable.When the aircraft finally arrived at Christmas Island the transit time was nine days and some 60 flying hours since leaving the UK.[2]

Most of the flying consisted of met. sorties of which 19 were flown, because there was little reliable Met. forecasting available for that region, but there was also the opportunity for some four transport flights to Honolulu due to the unserviceability of Transport Command Hastings. The trips to Honolulu could offer a welcome break with a night out on the town even with 'an uncomfortable return flight with an aircraft stuffed to the gunwales with fresh fruit and vegetables.'[3] Getting accustomed to the local conditions could throw up some challenges for the crews which required 'Heath Robinson' solutions, as recalled again by Group Captain Laurie Hampson: 'The prevailing wind was westerly and pilots invariably found themselves landing into the sun at the end of the Met. flights. Since the windscreens salted up badly during these long flights and there were no windscreen washers on the Mk 1 Shackleton, pilots' vision was

---

1   Gp Capt. Laurie Hampson, letter to author 27/12/02.
2   Ibid.
3   Ibid.

'J' WB828, with Canberra in background, Christmas Island.
(P. G. Smith)

badly limited until, that is, the ground crew invented washers using cans of water and enema tubes "borrowed" from sick quarters. Utilising convenient holes ahead of the windscreens, crews were able to squirt water on to the screen and the problem was solved.'

A shuttle system of crew rotation was operating, for at the end of March Squadron Leader A. Craig in WB510 and Flight Lieutenant D. Foster in WB826 departed for Christmas Island, and on 4 April Flight Lieutenant D. Robertson and his crew returned having been delayed for a week, this time in Bermuda, awaiting a replacement magneto. It is hard to resist the observation that a week's delay in Bermuda cannot have been an exceptional hardship! On the 11th another two crews set off for Christmas Island, Flight Lieutenants J. Staples in VP289 and I. LeGresley in WB828. Considering that the first actual test was conducted on 15 May it is not surprising that for most of June there was only one operational crew left at St Eval, captained by Flight Lieutenant Gurr. Squadron Leader A. Craig assumed temporary command of the squadron on his return from Christmas Island due to the absence of Wing Commander Preston at RAF Worksop on a jet familiarisation course.

Activity on Christmas Island intensified in June due to preparations for the third and final H-Bomb test on the 19th. In the days before, several surveillance sorties were flown as part of the build-up, to monitor shipping movements and to ensure that no unauthorised vessels strayed by accident or design into the test area. Flight Lieutenant Robertson and crew patrolled the area around Christmas Island, Squadron Leader Church and crew the island of Malden, some 400 miles to the south-east, and Flight Lieutenant J. E. Staples and crews undertook photographic tasks. The latter crew was the last to leave Christmas Island in WB828 on the 26th and, in spite of an engine failing while crossing from Hickham AFB to Travis, managed to land safely at Travis, completing the last leg to St Eval by 4 July and bringing this detachment to a close.

But the lull was only temporary as word

WG508 'H' (Sqn Ldr R. Church) with 'Grapple Bird' by Cpl Lester Peart – the first aircraft to be so adorned.
(P. G. Smith)

reached St Eval in August that the squadron would be required for another detachment to Christmas Island in October for further H-Bomb tests, codenamed Operation *Grapple X*, so training was to restart in earnest. Once again aircraft modifications went ahead, including the refitting of DECCA sets in the six aircraft earmarked. In September, after a busy month of preparations and anti-submarine exercises, Wing Commander Preston (Crew 4) and Flight Lieutenant Hampson (Crew 6) set off once again for Christmas Island as the first wave. The other captains involved in the second and third waves were Squadron Leader A. Craig, Flight Lieutenant W. Houldsworth, Squadron Leader R. Church and Flight Lieutenant K. FitzRoy. Flight Lieutenant D. R. Foster captained the reserve aircraft. The overall task force Commander was Air Vice-Marshal Wilfrid Oulton who was responsible for preparing the facilities on Christmas Island. He was no stranger to 206 Squadron having had the task, as a group captain, of opening up Lagens (later Lajes) in the Azores prior to the arrival of 206 in 1943 to harry the U-Boats in the mid-Atlantic gap.[4]

The Mid Pacific News — SPECIAL

BOMB GONE!

H-BOMB PUTS BRITAIN ON LEVEL TERMS

CHRISTMAS ISLAND — ISSUE NUMBER 229 — WED 15th MAY. '57

A flash, stark and blinding, high in the Pacific Sky, signalled to the world today Britain's emergence as a top-ranking power of this nuclear age.

No one saw it! No human eye could survive the hellish glare of white-hot air brought to incandescence by the fantastic heat.

But those who were present on this historic occasion, backs turned to the explosion nearly thirty miles away, could sense the brilliant intensity of the flash through closed eyelids. Even through thick clothing a flush of warmth penetrated to the body.

Ten seconds after the burst, spectators turned to see the dying explosion still threshing with the mighty powers that had been unleashed. High above the sea, and rising rapidly, was an enormous ball of fire that changed swiftly into a bubbling cauldron of coppery-red streaked with grey. A feathery white cap spread over the top of the cloud, extending downwards to form a gigantic snowball poised on a white stem, that appeared in sections between cloud and sea. The minutes that passed while waiting for the following sound seemed endless. All eyes were fixed upon the fantastic yet familiar mushroom, bridging sea and sky like some giant waterspout. And when it came, it came as a double boom like distant gunfire. Along with this conscious feeling, everyone felt a subconscious ripple of relaxing tension.

As the cloud rose up and penetrated the troppause, it flattened off into a round disc, while the stem leaned over drunkenly, and disappeared.

Hours of Preparation

The 24 hours prior to the release of the bomb were tense and dramatic. Long before dawn on the day before D-Day, the first aircraft roared off the runway on a met. flight; and as faint streaks of daylight showed, the ground crew of Valiant 818 and scientific teams began comprehensive preparations for bombing-up. One after another, aircraft were ordered off on their allotted duties. Shackletons of 206 and 204 Squadrons, and Canberras of 76 and 100 Squadrons broke the still morning air with the thunder of their engines as they took off from Christmas Island on weather reconnaissance – with the added duty for the Shackletons of searching vital areas to ensure they were free from shipping.

From HM Ships Narvik and Warrior, HMNZ Ships Rotoiti and Pukaki, from neighbouring islands and stations farther afield, reports continued to arrive in a steady stream. Before noon, the Met Office at Christmas Island had compiled its main forecast for the next 24 hrs – and

Continued on Page 2

The Mid Pacific News, 15 May 1957, with Danger Area warning. (P. G. Smith)

The task of the squadron was similar to the previous commitment, although this time the experience gained was invaluable – maritime surveillance, meteorological reconnaissance and SAR duties. Robin Woolven, as a signaller in Squadron Leader Craig's crew, recalled the experience as being 'an interesting free holiday for a now 20-year old.' – not a surprising observation if one considers the itinerary:

'......the squadron deployed in pairs of Shackletons transiting through the Azores, Bermuda (where we were accommodated in a first class hotel with liveried staff in white wigs), Charleston and El Paso where we sampled the Mexican nightlife in neighbouring Juarez.'[5] Group Captain Laurie Hampson, then squadron adjutant, recalled that El Paso was 'dry' and that the crews were given instructions how to get to Juarez, just across the bridge, and to the area that was out of bounds! Most managed to make it there to enjoy the relaxed atmosphere of this 'pretty wild frontier town'[6].

One unexpected problem was 'Asian flu' which laid low a few crew members on

4 AVM W. Oulton died in 1997 and his ashes were scattered by a 206 Nimrod in the Bay of Biscay.
5 Robin Woolven, notes 2002.
6 Gp Capt. Laurie Hampson, letter to author 27/12/02.

206 Sqn at St Eval, between Operation *Grapple* and Operation *Grapple X*.
(P. G. Smith)

the outward trip. Flight Lieutenant Le Gras, co-pilot in Squadron Leader Craig's crew, had to be taken to hospital in Travis AFB and a replacement, Flying Officer K. McDonald, was despatched by Transport Command. Robin Woolven remembered Le Gras as a former Neptune pilot 'complete with handlebar moustache and with sports cars as his main outside interest.' More seriously, Squadron Leader Craig's aircraft WB826 was struck by lightning in transit between Travis AFB and Hickham, Honolulu. Robin Woolven recalled that 'the lightning had demolished the ASV scanner under the nose and when I opened the hatch to discover why the single line timebase on my radar screen was stuck pointing aft, I could see the stormy Pacific Ocean and no scanner housing. Parts of the plastic radome bent the tips of the propellers on one engine (No. 3) but the flight proceeded safely. A new radome and new propeller blades were delivered to us in Honolulu and we arrived at Christmas Island on 15 October, 13 days after leaving Cornwall.' However the damage to WB826 produced some serviceability problems during the detachment.

The fairly primitive living conditions were recalled by Robin Woolven, a contrast to the comfort of the US bases. Mosquitoes and land crabs could be a problem, so the old hands advised using old wooden packing cases to build waist-high wooden walls to keep the latter out. The difficulty was that the walls kept in intruding rats so to get the rodent out, the wall had to be lifted rather defeating its purpose. On 'rest' days between the average 14-hour sorties there was an opportunity for swimming inside the coral reef, with dire warnings posted of the dangers of straying outside the reef, and for any doubters on this score there was always the illuminated open tent which housed the hospital mortuary, clearly visible from the domestic site. The food on the island was good, according to Robin Woolven, thanks to the NAAFI shop 'even if the prices were extortionate', and convivial evenings consuming the contents of beer cans were, as always, enlivened by sing-songs led by Master Signaller Ted Rose.

Some grew thin!
(CC/206)

Group Captain Laurie Hampson, then Squadron Adjutant, remembered the boredom of standby for SAR 'which was almost totally offset by laying on a contact landline to a tent on the beach, where the crew "stood by" during the slack periods.' 'Skinny-dipping' was the order of the day, with the CO setting the example. Snorkelling and fishing within the reef were popular, although enthusiasm for the former was diminished when a surprised 206 Squadron signaller caught a shark!

When the first Valiant aircraft landed with the task force commander on board, Air Vice-Marshal W. Oulton, it was met by a group of very brown grass-skirted natives who offered the crew a refreshing (and very alcoholic!) beverage tastefully served in half coconuts. Unfortunately, the Valiant Crew Chief recognised one of the 'natives' as a former fellow mess member, whom he knew to be a master navigator on 206 Squadron, otherwise these 'natives' might have been able to prolong the confusion.

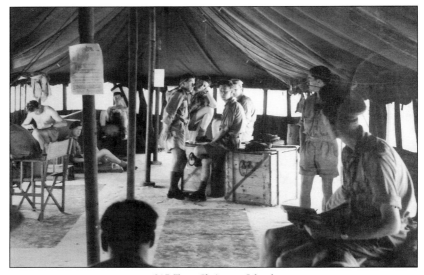

SAR Tent, Christmas Island
(CC/206)

L to R: Air Cdre Weir, Wg Cdr Preston and Gp Capt. Giles.
(CC/206)

There was an intensive flying programme starting with a 'mercy drop' of medical supplies to USS *Glacier* on 12 October, the flagship of the US icebreaking fleet which was en route to Antarctica. Wing Commander Preston and Flight Lieutenant Hampson had to fly to their extreme range in a 14-hour trip deep into the South Pacific to locate the vessel in which a crew member was seriously ill. The drop was successful and a message of thanks was later received from the US Naval authorities. On the 14th the first of several met. sorties was flown by Flight Sergeant Siekierkowski. Other duties included flights to calibrate the local DECCA chain and to locate, report and photograph any vessel straying into the danger area. The aircraft were required to transport passengers and freight from Hickham, which on 18 October brought some problems for Flight Lieutenant Houldsworth and crew when their aircraft developed a 'mag' problem on one engine. This delayed the flight for several days in Hickham.

Other tasks included conveying personnel and equipment from the Atomic Weapons Research Establishment (AWRE) to various locations to monitor the approaching test. The first such trip was to Kwajalein in the Marshall Islands – the first time for many years that an RAF aircraft had landed there, and the first time ever the route, direct from Christmas Island, had been flown. The aircraft had left Christmas Island on 20 October but only arrived at its destination on the 22nd due to the 180 degree meridian en route. The aircraft then flew on to Canton Island in the Phoenix group, to drop some freight where Pan American Airways entertained the crew. Flight Sergeant Siekierkowski transported more AWRE personnel and freight to Aitutaki in the Cook Islands group on the 25th. An unexpected bonus of these flights was that fresh tomatoes and bananas were brought back to Christmas Island on at least one occasion.

With 'D-Day' only days away, safety of personnel had a high priority and safety exercises were carried out, where air and ground personnel were transported to various pre-arranged locations on the island. As the target date for the test approached, 5 November, a Christmas Island danger area was established at midnight on 1 November, and intensive met. flights and SAR sorties were maintained by the Shackletons. Persistent heavy rains and low cloud led to a postponement of the test, as the storms had disrupted some of the electronic equipment although there was a dramatic improvement on 5 November as the day dawned bright and clear. Cloudy conditions prevailed on 'D' minus One on 7 November which was a cause of anxiety and at 2200 hrs Flight Sergeant Siekierkowski and crew took off on a met. sortie to report the latest conditions to the Task Force commanders. In the early hours of 'D-Day' three search/met. aircraft took off captained by Flight Lieutenant Hampson ('search one'), Squadron Leader Craig ('search two') and Wing Commander Preston ('search three').

Squadron Leader Craig and his crew had taken off in WB826 ('search two') at 0300 hrs and at 0358 hrs obtained a radar contact 47 miles south-west of 'Ground Zero' and heading in that direction. This contact was located and illuminated and identified as the Siberian Tanker SS *Effie*. This was a critical situation, as related by Robin Woolven:

'In the dark of night we attempted to contact the crew by radio and Aldis lamp but no reaction was detected as we repeatedly "buzzed" the freighter. We then started firing red Very and 1.75-inch flares and, after what seemed hours, the vessel at last reacted by assuming that we were in distress. Meanwhile we had attempted to load into the flare chutes the metal canisters containing the notice of the danger area in many languages. These were primarily carried in the bomb bay but, on this flight, they were carried internally and it was only when we attempted to load them in the chute that we realised that the metal rings and bomb hooks seemed welded to the canisters and thus were too large to fit in the chutes......A hacksaw was produced and the job was done.' Eventually the ship appreciated the danger but AVM Oulton decided to delay the timing of the bomb being dropped by 30 minutes while HMS *Cossack* steamed at full speed to escort

Effie well out of the danger area. (AVM Oulton had apparently protested to the authorities at home that a warning Notice to Mariners had not been issued in sufficient time.)[7]

At 0850 hrs the weapon burst and the ORB blandly states that of the four Shackletons airborne not one felt any blast or noise effect, although a magnificent view was obtained of the awe-inspiring sight. Robin Woolven recalled this unique experience:

'........With the ships clearing the area we then concentrated on the serious business of preparing ourselves and the aircraft for the imminent nuclear explosion. As the now-delayed drop-time approached we positioned ourselves some 60 miles from Ground Zero (GZ) and, monitoring the countdown from control on the island, we progressively switched off all possible electronic equipment. In fact one of our navigators neglected to switch off the ADF radio compass which unfortunately was ruined by the electromagnetic surge from the nuclear explosion and had to be replaced. As the countdown got to 60 seconds to burst, we drew curtains and covered our eyes with our hands (one pilot retaining control) and, with radios now off, we continued our own countdown. In spite of having my hands across my eyes and being tucked away in the radar tent, I still sensed the flash and we immediately took the briefed actions. Within seconds the dramatic fireball was seen to be rapidly expanding and rising. Equipment was switched on and my ASV13 screen showed the GZ as a solid and expanding mass at a range of 60 miles. There were some very sober and serious thoughts expressed individually and communally on the intercom as we spent the next few hours watching the giant mushroom cloud developing then gradually dispersing over the next eight hours. The priority at the airfield was to land the Valiant and then the Canberra aircraft sampling the atmosphere and the cloud. Their samples were soon despatched to the UK and, in time, the Shackletons were recovered. The parties in the various messes were under way but the mushroom cloud over the south-eastern end of the island remained until after dusk and was a lingering reminder of the successful megaton experiment we had witnessed.'

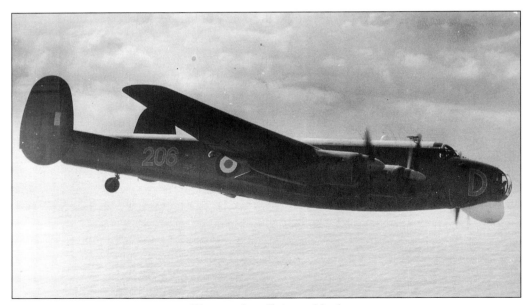

'D' returns from Christmas Island.
(CC/206)

7   Robin Woolven.

Any thoughts of winding down after this episode were soon dispelled when within two days all but two crews were alerted to assist in the search for a Pan American Airways Stratocruiser *Romance of the Skies* which had disappeared midway between Travis and Honolulu. Sadly, no trace of the aircraft was ever found and soon afterwards the Shackletons were ordered to return to the UK. This time, to the disappointment of the crews, triple-tiered bunks in a Quonset transit hut were all that was on offer, and not luxury hotel accommodation.[8] The two remaining captains and crews at Christmas Island, Squadron Leader Church and Flight Lieutenant Foster, continued with SAR work, although the former was detailed to fly the Task Force Commander, AVM Oulton, and his staff to Raratonga in the Cook Islands on 19 November.

The trip home was in the main uneventful for the crews, with the last aircraft VP289 captained by Flight Lieutenant L. Hampson reaching St Eval on 29 November, some nine days behind schedule. *Grapple* was over at least for the moment.

With only a few weeks left at St Eval normal operations resumed, with an SAR for an F-84 Thunderjet which had come down some 100 miles north-east of the Azores, with no result. There was a reminder of the epic events of the previous few weeks when Robin Woolven recalled buying 1957 Christmas cards which featured the H-Bomb explosion in colour together with a map of the Pacific. By this time preparations were well in hand for the move across the valley to St Mawgan in January 1958.

Grapple Z featured in the summer of 1958 when one aircraft MR 3 WR986 and crew was detailed to stand by for a proving flight to Christmas Island on 8 August. The crew was captained by the St Mawgan station commander Group Captain D. R. S. Bevan-John and flew by way of the Azores, Bermuda, Kelly AFB in Texas, San Diego and Honolulu, arriving at Christmas Island on 17 August. At San Diego the aircraft was demonstrated to the US Navy. While at Christmas Island two search sorties were flown prior to the dropping of the H-Bomb. Departure for home was on 24 August via Honolulu, San Francisco, Norfolk in Virginia and Greenwood in Nova Scotia. There was another opportunity to demonstrate the aircraft at Norfolk to the US Navy and by the time the aircraft had returned to St Mawgan on 5 September it had flown 117 hours, 15 minutes, without any major mechanical problems.

Thus 206 Squadron had played its part in the thermonuclear tests of the 1950s which provided Britain with the nuclear deterrent it maintained through the years of the Cold War. It is doubtful if such a task could have been undertaken without the Shackleton, which once again had proved its all-round capability in a difficult environment. Group Captain Laurie Hampson summed up the achievement: '206 Squadron did everything that was asked of it. The serviceability record of the aircraft was outstanding, especially when taking the very basic operating conditions into account. The complex task of arranging the transport of ground crew (suitably subdivided into support crews) and in-flight spares was handled most efficiently at squadron level and was a credit to the 206 maintenance organisation. Furthermore, the close and interdependent relationships generated across all ranks operating under demanding and difficult conditions induced very high morale, which then got an extra boost when the squadron got its new Mk 3 Shackletons soon after returning from Christmas Island.'

---

8   Ibid.

CHAPTER 15

ST MAWGAN 1958-1965

'206 Squadron.........always the bridesmaid – never the bride'.

Wing Commander D. R. Locke on the cancellation of an expected detachment to a warm climate, winter 1963.

Enter MR 3, Exit MR 1

The squadron's settling-in period at the new station in January 1958 coincided with the gradual conversion to the Shackleton Mark (MR) 3. This modified and improved version of the original Shackleton design had been many years in the making and its introduction had been delayed by a tragic accident in 1956 and further testing and production problems.

The main changes from earlier versions included the tricycle/nosewheel undercarriage, of greater strength to accommodate additional payload for new weapons and equipment, and the increased fuel capacity of external wing-tip tanks, bringing the total to over 4,700 gallons. As it turned out the extra weight

First MR3 received by 206 Sqn, WR981, January 1958.
(P. G. Smith)

slightly offset the expected range of the aircraft to less than that of previous versions. The other major changes were to crew facilities, better soundproofing, improved seating and general working environment. The grim dark cabin appearance was replaced by brighter and more welcoming décor.

The first squadron delivery of the MR 3 was to No. 220 Squadron at St Mawgan in the autumn of 1957 (re-numbered as 201 Squadron in October). The turn of 206 came on 21 January 1958 when the squadron received its first MR 3 WR981. By June the squadron had taken delivery of WR982 to WR986, bringing it to full strength of six aircraft.

The process of converting the crews began without delay on 14 January, a few days after the move from St Eval was completed. Crews One, Two and Six captained respectively by Flight Lieutenants K. FitzRoy, D. R. Foster and L. Hampson commenced a lecture programme lasting for two weeks. In the meantime the squadron was settling in to the new surroundings. Robin Woolven was favourably impressed by the more modern and better standard of accommodation compared to St Eval, with squadron offices and crew rooms close to the ATC tower[1] and the Operations facilities at the top of the hill.

The Shackleton MR1s were retained for the time being for normal operations, such

---

1 Air Traffic Control.

as the usual CASEX sorties of which several were flown during January and February while crew familiarisation continued with MR 3 WR981 totalling eight hours' flying time by the end of January. The month ended with the news that Flight Lieutenant Foster had received the Queen's Commendation.

During February eight Long-Range OFEs were flown, and Flight Lieutenant K. McDonald and crew were detached to Malta on an exchange visit for exercises with a submarine in the Mediterranean. Flying hours with the MR 3 were reduced during the month due to unserviceability problems with the hydraulics and the engines which unfortunately persisted in the months ahead, delaying the conversion of crews. Presumably this subject was on the agenda during a discussion about the conversion process at St Mawgan on 21 February with Air Vice-Marshal Saye, AOC No. 19 Group.

Training for Exercise *Dawn Breeze III*, a NATO anti-submarine and close support training exercise scheduled for the end of March, took up much of that month. Robin Woolven recalled this opportunity for another taste of foreign travel as his crew were diverted to the French naval aviation base at Lann Bihou where they experienced a visit to the station barber 'which was a mistake as, although his cut-throat razor was sharp, it was nothing compared with the after shave lotion he used with typical French relish. The Petty Officers' Mess was an education in dealing with several courses on the same large plate.' Captains taking part in the exercise included Squadron Leader J. Moss, Flight Lieutenants C. Campbell and W. Houldsworth and Squadron Leader A. Craig. No sooner was the exercise over but there was an unsuccessful SAR from 29 to 31 March for two Hunters of the Belgian Air Force lost in the North Sea.

Engine failures resulting from problems with the fuel pipe lines led to the MR 3s being grounded from 17 to 25 April except for WR982 which was flown to Avro at Woodford for investigation into the fuel flow problem. However, by the end of April, the remaining MR 1 crews completed the ground course for the MR 3s. Also during the month Wing Commander J. E. Preston relinquished command of the squadron to take up an appointment in Malta. Memorable events under his command included two *Grapple* detachments to Christmas Island and the winning by 206 of the Aird Whyte Trophy in 1957. In the Queen's Birthday Honours of 1958 he was awarded the Air Force Cross. Wing Commander R. T. Billett assumed command from 14 April. Other changes of personnel during May included the departure of Squadron Leader A. Craig for HQ Coastal Command, to be replaced by the new flight commander Squadron Leader Murray B. Spalding

SAR standby commitments continued in the spring and 'Bisto' (Autolycus) sorties. Robin Woolven had mixed feelings about the latter:

'Of the "Signals Leaders" (AEOs were just coming in[2]) I do recall Flight Lieutenant "Hoppy" Hopkinson who had a great thing about the "Autolycus" diesel exhaust detection equipment and led to some really boring ocean searches.' The new improved ASV 21 radar had now replaced the dated ASV 13 and the ability to detect submarine snort targets was greatly enhanced.

On a much lighter note the squadron had seven entrants in the 19 Group Golf Championships at Trevose Golf Club, success being achieved by Sergeants Allen and Roberts. The Coastal Command pentathlon was narrowly lost to No. 228 Squadron when Wing Commander Preston received an eye injury during the final squash tournament, which he had been winning up to that point.

The MR 3s were grounded again for a brief period at the start of May due to a failure of the nose-wheel to lock. But before long exercises with submarines resumed with HM submarine *Alliance* and a CASEX with HM submarine *Thule*, and a Long-Range OFE by

---

2 Air Electronics Officers.

Flight Lieutenant Hampson to the Ocean Weather Ship *Juliet* and Rockall. There was a notable SAR on 16 May when Flight Lieutenant C. Campbell and his crew were scrambled in the early hours of the morning to locate the 600-ton Dutch coaster *Musketeer* which had developed a bad list off Trevose Head in severe gales. To make matters worse the captain had his wife and two children aboard. The aircraft located the vessel and homed the Padstow lifeboat to the coaster, but it proved impossible to transfer the women and children to the lifeboat in the prevailing weather conditions. The aircraft remained in the area but as light improved the weather moderated and as it turned out the ship was able to proceed safely. On its return to base the Shackleton had to land at St Eval due to the cross-wind. Flight Lieutenant Campbell and crew received the well-deserved congratulations of the squadron and station commanders for carrying out this difficult sortie so efficiently. At the end of what had been an eventful month the last Shackleton MR 1 left the squadron on 29 May.

Business as usual

A fresh crisis in the Middle East prompted another trooping standby for the squadron in June 1958 during a time of tension between Colonel Nasser's United Arab Republic of Egypt and the recently established federation of the kingdoms of Jordan and Iraq. In the event the federation collapsed with the murder of King Feisal II of Iraq in July, welcomed by Nasser, which left King Hussein of Jordan isolated in the Arab world. However, the need for trooping on this occasion was not required and 206 Squadron was eventually stood down to continue with routine training during July. One way in which the crisis affected 206 and no doubt other squadrons was the decree that stocks of 1.75 illuminating flares were to be reserved for SAR duties as such flares were required for anti-terrorist operations in the Middle East. At that time 206's former stable-mate No. 42 Squadron was based in Sharjah carrying out bombing operations against local tribesmen in Iraq who were intent on destabilising the peace and order of the region. It was perhaps with such colonial policing duties in mind as a possible future role for 206 that later in the year the MR 3 front turrets were modified for shooting.

Routine operations included 'Bisto' patrols, Long-Range OFEs, one of more than 16 hours' duration, and free-range bombing, with navigation exercises based on the LORAN or 'Long Range navigation' system. On a practice torpedo drop on 17 July a weapon was not recovered but a station board of enquiry exonerated the squadron personnel from any blame. Two crews, captained by Squadron Leader J. A. Moss and Flight Lieutenant P. Clack RCAF, departed during July for No. 103 Joint Unit Course (JUC) at the Joint Anti-Submarine School (JASS) at HMS *Eagle*, Londonderry, with a third crew captained by Flight Lieutenant D. Foster stationed at Ballykelly to act as test and ferry crew for the detachment. Robin Woolven recalled such an occasion:

'In the air we monitored the Royal Navy's HTP powered high speed submarine HMS *Excalibur*[3] and whilst living in barracks in Londonderry we were subject to the idiosyncrasies of the Royal Navy. We SNCOs were required to be inspected before being allowed outside the barracks and, as there was an IRA campaign in progress, we were aware that wandering around the barracks after dark was unwise as heavily armed and camouflaged RM commandos could (just) be seen patrolling inside its walls.'

During August the report of a missing KLM Constellation airliner with over 90 people on board between Shannon and Gander airports led to Flight Lieutenant Donald and Crew Four being directed to a sea search. After only an hour of the search the crew saw

---

3 HTP=High Test Peroxide powered sub. Hydrogen peroxide was dropped on water and a mass of steam was generated – this powered the engines when submerged. The RN had two such subs in the 1960s. (Info from Robin Woolven.)

wreckage and bodies. There were no survivors, but the Dutch Government later commended the squadron for its work in this tragic event.

A new navigational aid *Blue Silk* was tested by a squadron aircraft on 3 August (see below) which was anticipated for use in the forthcoming Christmas Island detachment. The departure of one aircraft for Christmas Island left five aircraft at St Mawgan – by this time all the squadron pilots had now converted to the MR 3. A noteworthy event during the month was a dummy attack by Flight Lieutenant D. R. Foster and crew on the world's first US nuclear-powered submarine *Nautilus* while the aircraft was patrolling west of the Scillies on Tuesday 12 August at 1930 hrs. The crew had caught the sub at periscope depth! Later the captain, Commander William R. Anderson, and crew of the *Nautilus* sent a message of congratulations to Flight Lieutenant Foster and his crew. The vessel was just completing its historic voyage from Honolulu to Portland, passing under the North Polar ice cap, the first submarine ever to achieve this feat.

Light relief intervened on 21 August with Sports Day. It seemed that 206 was contributing more than its fair share with almost the entire flying wing entries composed of squadron personnel!

An opportunity to demonstrate the capabilities of the Shackleton came on 3 September when Major-General Tilmo, the Brazilian Chief of Air Staff, and his aides were flown in an aircraft captained by Squadron Leader M. Spalding. But it was back to the serious business of the autumn NATO exercise series which included *TALLY-HO* and *SHIPSHAPE* in mid-month. For this purpose the squadron moved to its war base at RNAS Culdrose and flew a total of 19 sorties taking up 227 flying hours in all, and returning to St Mawgan on 26 September. There was a busy autumn training schedule of navigation exercises, tactical searches, bombing and gunnery, 'Bisto' tracking and homing, practising sonobuoy tactics and sometimes combining one or more of these with long-range OFEs. On one occasion during October Flight Lieutenant Foster and Crew Three flew a long-range OFE to check the maximum range of the MR 3 without war load. With a fuel load of 700 gallons 2,876 miles were flown in 17 hours, 35 minutes. Another long flight was a visit to Greenwood RCAF base by the CO Wing Commander R. T. Billett with Squadron Leader Spalding and crew for a five-day stay.

On home ground again the Under-Secretary of State for Air, Mr Ian Orr-Ewing, visited the squadron in October, the same Minister who had felt it necessary to stand up in the House of Commons to deny a rumour that the Royal Navy would be taking control of 'Maritime Air' from the RAF.[4] No doubt this was related to the political struggle for rationalisation of the armed forces and cutting the cost of defence spending, at a time when the emphasis was on building up our nuclear deterrent. Thus conscription was ended during 1960 and the conventional forces faced cutbacks, just when it seemed that our responsibilities and interests around the world were as great as ever. One factor in the navy's thinking may well have been the introduction of the Fairey Gannet in the mid-1950s with its anti-submarine capability, and the helicopter for SAR duties, but it became obvious that in neither case could there be any substitute for the all-round and long-range capability of the Shackleton, proven in a multitude of tasks. In the event the pressure was kept up on Coastal Command and by early 1959 its strength was reduced to a low point of 24 aircraft, with the disbandment of No. 228 Squadron and the closure of St Eval.[5] But the Command survived intact, and with it 206 Squadron, but the episode could hardly have improved the morale of the people at the sharp end.

For the rest of 1958 there was the usual co-operation with naval units in anti-submarine exercises including the French and Italian navies. With the Home Fleet

---

4 Ashworth, *RAF Coastal Command*, p213.
5 Ibid. p215.

"NOW REMEMBER CHAPS, THE EFFICIENCY TEAM ARE STILL WITH US"

WITH THE COMPLIMENTS
of No. 206 SQN. ST. MAWGAN

(Cartoon drawn by George Heald via B. Doughty)

valuable training was carried out in various exercises with HM submarines *Sanguine* and *Tabard* and HMS *Blackpool* and HMS *Undaunted*. In November the entire squadron was detached to Luqa in Malta, where exercises were hampered by severe weather and high winds and unavailability of submarines. Back home again there were several routine OFEs, SARAH homings (see Chapter 13), 'shadowing' exercises, and 'Snortex' sorties, mostly in the Portland area. The 'Snort' was the name given to the German 'schnorkel' device used by the Germans in World War Two to enable the U-Boats to run their diesel engines and charge batteries while remaining underwater. The 'snort' could be detected by aircraft radar but this became difficult in high seas. This was experienced by Flight Lieutenant C. Campbell and crew on 10 December as some underwater lights were seen but nothing else, and the exercise was hampered by the high wind and sea state.

There was a novel task in December when the squadron responded to a request by Cornwall County Council to photograph the local beaches to enable the planners to make them safer for the holiday season. For the routine work of the squadron three aircraft were fitted with the *Blue Silk* navigation equipment and various exercises tested the new device. *Blue Silk* was the doppler navigational equipment eventually to be installed in the Shackleton - (the Doppler effect was named after the physicist Christian Doppler to describe the increase/decrease in the frequency of sound, light or other waves as the source and observer move towards/away from each other – a principle adapted to locate one's position accurately). Many other RAF aircraft had a similar system called *Green Satin*. Other operational improvements included the already mentioned ASV Mark 21 radar and a new radio homing device, an example of early avionics, the Instrument Landing System (ILS) which by the end of December 1958 had been calibrated and cleared for practice by the crews. All these were part of the continuing improvement and development of the MR 3 which became known as the 'Phase I' modifications completed during 1959.[6]

The start of 1959 saw two SAR operations, the first on 2 January when there was a call-out to locate the German coaster *Scharlotte* which was drifting rudderless in a North

---

6   Jones, *Avro Shackleton*, pp 102-3.

Sea gale. The ship was found at dusk. In the same month there was a search for two Sea Venoms which it was feared had collided off the Strumble light, but nothing was found. A new SAR 'Duty Squadron' system was introduced later in January, whereby one squadron would be detailed to stand by for a specified period to cover the whole of the United Kingdom for SAR duties or other special operations as required, for example trooping duties. The turn of 206 came from 19 to 31 January. There were the routine naval exercises during the month such as 'Subsunk' – this was an operation so-called when an allied submarine lost contact for a period of time either due to radio problems, a false alarm or worse, a disaster at sea, and failing to surface as a consequence. It was vital to divert a Shackleton to the area and to search for signs of wreckage as soon as possible. The exercise on this occasion took Flight Lieutenant P. Clack and Crew Two to the Mull of Kintyre/Ailsa Craig areas. There was a mishap when the aircraft was struck by lightning but only minor damage was sustained. Other events during the month included the appointment of a new station commander Group Captain W. D. Hodgkinson DFC, and a crew standby for the flight of Prince Philip by Comet on 20 January at the start of his world tour.

There was a detachment to Gibraltar from 7 to 22 February 1959 for Exercise *Whitebait* which was composed of several CASEX and 'SubAir' sorties, the latter providing experience in submarine-air co-operation, with valuable practice in locating and homing. Unfortunately high winds associated with the 'Levanter' led to the cancellation of some sorties, and there was a brief SAR diversion for a missing Stinson between Gibraltar and Tangier which proved unsuccessful. The detachment ended on the high note of a cocktail party given by the squadron for participating naval and local RAF officers.

The remaining aircraft and crew at St Mawgan, captained by Flight Lieutenant D. R. Foster, undertook an endurance flight on 17 February which lasted for a total of 24 hours 21 minutes and covered 3,440 miles – the longest flight by a Shackleton to date, with the aid of a bomb-bay auxiliary fuel tank. The same captain and crew flew a second such flight on 25 February, this time over a range of 3,367 miles in 22 hours 5 minutes.

March and April 1959 were quiet months at St Mawgan with a deployment to RNAS Culdrose for Exercise *Dawn Breeze IV*, a crew at Boscombe Down where new navigational equipment was being fitted and a few personnel at Kinloss. Squadron Leader M. Spalding, and Flight Lieutenants W. Houldsworth and K. McDonald attended No. 107 JUC at JASS in Londonderry.

The personal side of SAR work was brought home to the squadron in May when Flight Lieutenant P. Clack and crew were called out to search for a missing Anson in the Snowdon area of north Wales. A passenger in the aircraft was Group Captain J. E. Preston who had so recently been CO of the squadron. There was no sign of the aircraft even after two other aircraft and crews joined in the search. Wreckage was later found but there were no survivors. There was another unsuccessful search in June for a missing Vampire from St Athan. Wreckage was located but there was no sign of the pilot.

'Phase' improvements and the Aegean detachment

The first of the Phase I modified Shackletons became operational in June 1959, incorporating a number of improvements including the new intercom system and the ASV Mark 21. However there was a severe setback when the order came through to restrict flying on the MR 3 to 20 hours per month. This had come about because a defect in the spar of the MR 1s and MR 2s had been discovered, leading to the fleet being grounded. Coming at a time of the cutbacks already outlined within Coastal Command it must have been a fairly depressing time for the squadron, especially as the 'Fair Isle' detachment to Malta and the Aird Whyte competition were cancelled for September.

However, the flying hours' restriction was lifted in July, a month which also saw the departure from the squadron of Flight Lieutenant D. Foster after three and a half years' service.

A chance to demonstrate the Shackleton and to exercise with NATO forces came at the end of August when four aircraft flew to Elevsis in Greece for co-operation with the Royal Hellenic Air Force. Then came Operation *Medaswex 31* in September when the squadron was detached to Crete to exercise with British submarines and the forces of fellow NATO members Greece and Turkey in the north Aegean. Apart from several CASEX sorties flown it must have been a useful opportunity to spread goodwill in the area, given the political tensions over Cyprus between Britain, Greece and Turkey.

Several aircraft left for No. 49 MU Colerne in October for the Phase I improvements including the fitting of ASV 21 which functioned with input from *Green Satin* Doppler navigation radar (see above), ILS, Mark 10 autopilot, zero reader, radio/radar activated altimeters and the new intercom system. More basic but no less essential were the courses for aircrew at RAF Mount Batten School of Rescue and Survival. A fairly typical example was the experience of Flight Lieutenant Clack and his crew at the end of October, when the calm morning of lectures gave way to an afternoon of dinghy drill in 35 knot winds. A similar exercise held in January 1960 involving Flight Lieutenant G. Acklam and crew was filmed by BBC television, for one of the increasingly popular televised outside broadcasts.

Squadron administration benefited from the appointment of a permanent adjutant Pilot Officer G. E. A. Richards in October, and the modification programme proceeded with a Sonics Ic course at the Royal Aircraft Establishment at Farnborough, attended by two AEOs. Exercise *Squarebash IV* with the Portland Training Squadron was held in the Channel area west of Portland Bill, using Autolycus. By this time all the squadron aircraft were equipped to Phase I standard - WR 977 'A', WR 983 'D', WR 980 'B', WR 978 'E', XF 730 'C' and WR 976 'F'. There was now confidence that these improvements would enable the squadron to meet the technological challenges of the 1960s.

Operation *Grape* took up some time in early December 1959 but there was a potentially serious incident on the 4th during a high speed run by Flight Lieutenant P. Howard and crew in WR 980 when the pilot's canopy blew off and the nose wheel failed to lock down. Fortunately the aircraft made a safe landing. Trials were also held with the Air Torpedo Development Unit (ATDU) whose expertise included recovering torpedoes that had been dropped from aircraft on exercises.

Into the 1960s

The regular 'Fair Isle' detachment to Malta took place in February 1960, which included naval exercises and practice in 'Autolycus'. SAR duties on 5 March involved Flight Lieutenant G. Acklam and Crew Four searching the sea off Skegness for an English Electric P1 which had crashed after the pilot had safely ejected. On the trip home there was a diversion to locate a missing cabin cruiser between Poole harbour and Weymouth – however the boat was later found moored in Poole harbour.

Exercise *Dawn Breeze V* occupied the last six days of March with an emphasis on anti-submarine training and 'camera' attacks. By all accounts it was a successful exercise, with a number of visual sightings of periscopes and radar contacts reported, sonobuoys laid and several simulated depth charges (DCs) being dropped. In addition to the exercise Squadron Leader C. P. Thompson carried out a sortie which comprised eight CASEX 31s[7] with HMS *Urchin*, HMS *Venus* and HMS *Vigilant*.

---

7   The 'Combined Anti-Submarine Exercise' was usually followed by a number to indicate the type of exercise with the resources involved.

Encounter with a Soviet 'W' Class submarine, August 1960.
(CC/206)

Another task for the squadron came in April 1960 with the first of many 'Methop' sorties, dropping mail and other supplies to the weather ships of the British Meteorological Service in the mid-Atlantic. Those were the days before the introduction of weather satellites and supply by air was a very welcome lifeline, especially during the Christmas period. For the airmen it offered a challenging long-range training sortie in which navigation and homing equipment could be tested and a precise 'drop' achieved.[8] The spectacle was often filmed by TV cameras for the news programmes at home. SARs also increasingly provided dramatic material for BBC and ITV outside broadcasts.

The summer of 1960 saw the squadron participating in various exercises comprising *Fastnex*, *Squarebash VII* and a number of *Shadex* sorties were flown. In July there was torpedo-dropping practice. Various official visits included one by the Senior Officers' War Course and on a separate occasion the Chief of the Air Staff Air Chief Marshal Sir Thomas Pike KCB, CBE, DFC was present at a demonstration of the Shackleton's full weapons load – Chief Technician J. H. Swann, Senior Armament NCO, was commended for his efforts. On 26 July there was a change of command with Wing Commander J. E. Bazalgette DFC taking over from Wing Commander R. T. Billett.

In August preparations got under way for Operation *Bolero Bound*, a goodwill visit to Buenos Aires planned from September to October to take part in the 15th Annual Argentine Aeronautical Week and to demonstrate the Shackleton MR 3. Two aircraft were to leave in September on the detachment, commanded by the AOC Air Vice-Marshal L. W. C. Bower CB, DSO, DFC with Flight Lieutenants P. W. Flinn and P. J. Howard and their respective crews.

---

8   Chartres, *Avro Shackleton*, p75.

Autumn exercise *Fishplay V* was followed by *Fallex '60*, the latter NATO exercise being the biggest to date involving over 400 aircraft and 146 ships starting off the Norwegian coast and ending off the Spanish coastline. Exercise *Squarebash 9* in November rounded off a busy period. It was about this time that trials were taking place with the Gee Mark IV receiver, another technical improvement. The end of the year saw a Christmas 'Methop' drop to Ocean Weather Ship (OWS) *Juliet*, accompanied by BBC TV and ITN film crews.

Anti-submarine warfare (ASW) training continued into 1961 with CASEX 43 and CASEX 52 in February and a *FASTNEX* in March – search for a submarine in a known area followed by sonics tracking and bombing. Towards the end of the month another *Dawn Breeze* NATO exercise included naval and air force units from Britain, France, West Germany and Portugal. Routine squadron training continued to include Long Range OFEs, SARAH homings, Autolycus practice and a 'Fair Isle' detachment in June.

The squadron was put on 'trooping' standby in July due to events in the Middle East, this time concerning Kuwait which had just been granted full independence after over 60 years as a British protectorate but retaining a defensive pact with Britain. Its neighbour Iraq, now a left-wing republican regime following the 1958 Revolution there, claimed the territory and tension increased in the region. Fortunately Iraq backed down on this occasion and the trooping facility was not required.

The format of the annual Aird Whyte Competition was changed in 1961 to become a test of anti-submarine tactics, but as usual presented to the squadron crew (one selected from each squadron) gaining the most points in the competition. This comprised a day and a night sortie against a 'tame' RN submarine and points were awarded for detecting and attacking the target. The competition winners would then represent the RAF in a new trophy, the Fincastle Trophy, presented by Mr and Mrs Aird Whyte in 1960 in memory of their son Sergeant Nairn Fincastle Aird Whyte who had been killed as an air gunner in Coastal Command in 1943. This trophy was first competed for in 1961 as a simple bombing competition between maritime crews of the RAF, Royal Australian Air Force, Royal New Zealand Air Force and the Canadian Forces. Until 1969 the four competing crews flew over their home waters and then sent results to an adjudicating committee in London for the selection of the winner. A crew from the RAAF won the trophy in 1961 and the first RAF win was in 1966.

Much of the rest of 1961 was taken up with preparations for a three-aircraft detachment to Cape Town for joint exercising with the South African Air Force (SAAF) at the end of the year. It was in May 1961 that South Africa had formally left the Commonwealth and declared itself a Republic but relations with Britain were still reasonably cordial, especially on the strategic front where a continual watch was kept on Soviet naval forces sailing around the Cape of Good Hope between the Indian and Atlantic Oceans. Also the SAAF had ordered Shackletons in 1957 so there were common bonds between the airmen of both countries.

Phase II modifications for the Shackletons were gradually introduced in the early part of 1962. These comprised the fitting of electronic countermeasures equipment (ECM), the TACtical Air Navigation (TACAN) system, the Mark Ic Sonics system giving the aircraft the facility to drop active as well as passive sonobuoys, and radio updates. The changeover was not without its problems as various 'teething' troubles reduced the number of flying hours during February. The upheavals did not prevent a successful SAR night sortie in January to deliver drugs to a very sick seaman aboard the Swedish MS Portland.

NATO exercises included *Dawn Breeze VII* in the second half of March which was held off Portugal and *Strong Gale* in May, the latter appropriately hampered by poor weather. Several CASEX sorties and two IDEOGRAMS were flown. An unusual

CAPEX 1961
(CC/206)

Return leg from CAPEX 1961. Engine change, Aden.
L to R: Flt Sgt Smith; Sqn Ldr Parry-Davis ('B' Flt Cdr); M/E Johnny Madden; Sgt Roy Higdon; Cpl/T G. Hart; J/T
Tony Middleton.
(CC/206)

Shackleton Mk 3 Phase 2.
(CC/206)

assignment followed on 5 June when Wing Commander Bazalgette and crew searched for and located Mr Francis Chichester on his solo transatlantic voyage. By the end of the month Wing Commander Bazalgette had relinquished command of the squadron to Wing Commander D. R. Locke OBE.

A 'Smashex' exercise – simulation of a submarine sinking so all efforts would be put into locating the vessel and assisting in rescue - and Mark V Radio Altimeter trials followed by Exercise *Cold Road* to the Royal Norwegian Air Force base at Bodo, took up much of July and part of August. Annual block leave during that month led to some unserviceability problems for the aircraft left standing unused during the exceptionally wet Cornish summer. In September there was another detachment to Norway by four aircraft in Operation *Matador*.

Growing Soviet naval activity in the eastern Atlantic increased the number and length of surveillance sorties flown by Coastal Command – often up to 18 hours or more – with the objective not always submarines or warships but the fishing fleets which were to be found in ever-greater numbers often in the vicinity of NATO exercises. Apart from being a source of annoyance to home fishermen these trawlers were also thinly disguised intelligence-gatherers (ELINTS – see below). Of particular interest to Soviet eavesdroppers were the movements of US submarines from the Polaris base at Holy Loch in the Clyde which had opened in 1961. Another favourite spot for these vessels was off Malin Head (north-west point of Ireland) – a good position from which to monitor electronic traffic. Any doubts about the sinister nature of these ship movements were dispelled by the Cuban Missile Crisis of October 1962, arguably the most dangerous crisis of the entire Cold War. All Coastal Command squadrons were put on six hours' readiness, which for 206 Squadron curtailed operational flying for almost a whole week until the situation eased.

The backlog from the previous month plus unserviceability problems, with up to four aircraft in hangars during the worst period, meant that there was much catching up to do in amassing flying hours during November. In the middle of the month Squadron Leader R. E. Cox and crew were tasked with flying the AOC-in-C Air Marshal Sir Anthony Selway KCB, DFC and the C-in-C Home Fleet Admiral Sir Wilfred Woods to the US Navy base at Keflavik in Iceland. The aircraft was specially fitted out for the trip in a manner that would have done credit to BOAC! Another notable episode was an SAR by Flight Lieutenant A. Pasco and Crew Three on the 18th to drop Lindholmes to the crews of two lifeboats sheltering off the Farne Islands with a cloud base of 300 feet and in severe gales. As a result a letter of thanks was later received from the Royal National Lifeboat Institution (RNLI). By the end of the month 50 hours of the flying backlog had been made up and the CO remarked on the encouraging increase in 'submarine time' available to the crews which improved morale and honed training skills. He expressed the hope that each crew should have at least one exercise with a live submarine every month.

SAR standby, Christmas leave from 21 to 27 December and not least, the deteriorating weather in what was to become the worst winter in living memory, reduced the amount of training at the year's end. However two crews were able to carry out submarine exercises in the Western Approaches, one using Active Sonobuoys in successful tracking despite a high sea state. On the 24th the CO and a volunteer crew carried out the Christmas 'Methop' to OWS *India* which included mail, a Christmas tree and a cake, the event being recorded for listeners on the BBC's Home and Light programmes.

New Year 1963.
(Drawn by G. Heald – CC/206)

Problems with the weather lingered into the spring of 1963 but the usual crop of training exercises continued into the early summer, *Vendetta*, *Dreadnought*, *Hallmark 9* (previously *Squarebash*), and *Fishplay VII*, the latter at Aldergrove in May. During the previous month the Mark Ic sonics system had been demonstrated to the New Zealand Defence Minister, Mr Eyre. The squadron seemed to be overcoming serviceability problems and morale was on an upward trend. The latest equipment was put through its paces in a number of trials which included Admiralty ECM trials in Exercise *Tonga*, Mark V Radio Altimeter trials and Exercise *Two-Up*, testing the effectiveness of ASV Mark 21. In June there was an SAR for a fishing craft off the west coast of Eire, which was located and RN helicopters were homed in to pick up the crew.

Not everything went according to plan, though, as in Exercise *Bargold* in July in which the CO criticised indecision and confusion in the handling of this 'war that never was'. However the squadron ended the month 314 hours above the 'line' – Wing Commander Locke's summary of the situation was that 'we shall run out of hours before we run out of squadron spirit'.

Soviet naval activity required constant surveillance, in the North Sea, the Western Approaches and increasingly in the narrow northerly gap from the Norwegian Sea into the Atlantic. Thus Flight Lieutenant Pasco RCAF and crew shadowed a Sverdlov-class cruiser near the Scillies in August 1963, with Squadron Leader R. E. Cox and crew taking over the watch. The Sverdlov-class cruiser was the first of the modern Soviet cruisers, a type which had come into prominence in May 1956 when Commander 'Buster' Crabbe, a Navy frogman, had disappeared in the vicinity of the *Ordzhonikdze* in Portsmouth Harbour. The vessel had conveyed the Soviet leaders Nikita Krushchev and Nikolai Bulganin on a visit to Britain. It was only in June 1957 that Commander Crabbe's headless body was found, ending speculation that he had been captured and held by the Soviets.

The cat and mouse game in August 1963 was played out again when Flight Lieutenants G. W. Abel and J. J. Oakes flew to Kinloss and located a Sverdlov-class vessel, a Kotlin-class destroyer, a W-class submarine and four Soviet trawlers two of which were possibly ELINTS – 'Electronic Intelligence Vessels'. Routine exercises during the month included an Exercise *Torpex*, which required an aircraft to drop an operational torpedo with the warhead replaced with a weight, a recording device and a device to send up a float to aid recovery – usually dropped on Torpedo ranges with RAF Marine craft or the ADTU to recover the weapon. There was also Exercise *Riptide*, consisting of a strike fleet opposed by high altitude bombers with the squadron being assigned an anti-submarine role under the control of HMS *Tiger*.

Surveillance of this type, however vital, was very time consuming in terms of patrol length with often limited results at the end. Once again 50 hours over the target were flown during the month of August but the CO raised the issue of the 'quality' training time this included in the operation of equipment like the Mark Ic sonics system – as without making the contacts there could be no practice in dropping sonobuoys or bombs – this was where CASEX exercises were more useful. The other problem was that overflying often led to unserviceability – a hint perhaps of the ageing of the Shackleton fleet? However in September 1963 the absence of Soviet activity enabled the squadron to resume a more normal training routine with depth charge and torpedo-dropping and bombing practice.

Bill McColl remembers a training sortie during September 1963 which turned out to be anything but routine. He was a crew member in Shackleton WR983 which left St Mawgan on 17 September at 0845 to exercise with a Royal Navy frigate in the Fowey range. Whilst carrying out the radar homing to the ship the aircraft descended to 100 ft. The radar scanner, aft of the bomb bay, had been lowered to the first search position, approximately one-and-a-half to two feet below the fuselage. At about five miles from the ship the aircraft entered a fog bank, and while the crew were looking out for the ship, they failed to notice the gentle descent of the aircraft. As they passed abeam the ship's position, with the crew still distracted, the Shackleton struck the sea tearing off the radar scanner and damaging the camera doors in the rear fuselage. Fortunately the propellers did not touch the sea and the aircraft climbed back to a safe altitude. During the return flight to St Mawgan the crew assessed the damage and the captain carried out a handling check. Hydraulic fluid had been lost when the scanner was damaged, and the undercarriage and flaps had to be operated by the emergency air system. The aircraft landed safely at 1005 hrs.

The squadron was represented by Flight Lieutenant J. J. Oakes in the annual Aird Whyte Competition in October, but he did not win on this occasion. Nevertheless Flight

Lieutenant Oakes was chosen to represent the squadron in the Fincastle Trophy but this was postponed to November due to hydraulic failure. Problems arose again with aircraft unserviceability, this time due to failures in the electronics systems because of heavy rain – there was a call for better waterproofing to protect the equipment. There was a standby for possible internal security (IS) duties in Nassau in the Bahamas – a role previously termed 'colonial policing'. Tension in the area had been rising since Fidel Castro had come to power in Cuba in 1959 with his pro-communist policies and there was concern about Cuban incursions into the territorial waters of the Bahamas, at that stage still a British possession.

Disappointment was expressed towards the end of the year when the expected detachments to the Bahamas and New Zealand were cancelled, dashing the hopes of escaping the winter weather – the CO put into words what must have been widely-felt frustration when he lamented that 'with 206 it seems that where a detachment to a warm climate is mooted it is a case of "always the bridesmaid – never the bride!"'

The year closed in an atmosphere of anti-climax as there were no operational sorties in December – higher authority had reduced the flying programme – instead full use was made of the opportunity to concentrate on frequently neglected ground training.

The start of 1964 saw Exercise *Phoenix*, an evaluation of the new County Class guided missile destroyers in a limited war role. In February there was evidence of ELINT and HYDROLINT vessels in the 19 Group area, the latter ships deploying sensitive hydrophones to detect underwater sound – from ships and submarines. On this occasion no sorties were flown.

Once again feelings had been running high in Cyprus between Turkish and Greek Cypriots since the end of 1963 and various Shackleton detachments were sent to the area for reconnaissance duties – by March 1964 it was the turn of 206 and two aircraft left for Akrotiri under the command of Squadron Leader R. James to patrol the eastern Mediterranean. A threat of war between Greece and Turkey hung over the region until the United Nations sent in a peacekeeping force in April. Even then Turkish fleet movements had to be closely monitored.

A spring detachment to Kinloss for Arctic icefield patrols signalled yet again the growing importance of the northern waters in maritime defence, especially as the Atlantic telephone cable was cut on 20 April – a Russian trawler was suspected.

That along with preparations for the forthcoming detachment to Cape Town in May – Exercise *Capex* – kept the squadron fully occupied. Three aircraft set off for South Africa captained by Squadron Leader R. James, and Flight Lieutenants D. R. Foster and J. J. Oakes and their respective crews, accompanied by the CO. Squadron Leader R. E. G. Payne was placed in temporary command of the squadron. The days of these South African detachments were numbered as the political problems over *Apartheid* came to the fore – the last Coastal Command *Capex* was by No. 42 Squadron in 1966.

Within a few months of his return from the detachment in October 1964, Wing Commander D. R. Locke handed over command of the squadron to Wing Commander H. R. Williams.

Over the years the 'Phase' improvements to the Shackleton had produced extra weight in the form of new equipment which required a strengthened 'tricycle' undercarriage – especially the nosewheel, which itself increased the weight - and this led to the search for additional power and a tougher internal structure. From 1963 tests began which would form the basis of the 'Phase III' developments in the Shackleton fleet.

Rolls-Royce were unable to modify the Griffon engines sufficiently to provide the added performance so an eventual solution was found by fitting two Bristol Siddeley Viper 11 turbojets behind the outboard Griffons. The aim was to provide extra power for a limited period in take-off and for any emergencies in the air. One problem to overcome was the need to avoid two different fuel systems, so the Vipers were modified to operate on high octane (AVGAS) petrol instead of the usual kerosene – the only limitation being that the engines could only run for a short period on full power. The added stress to the aircraft had to be overcome by strengthening the MR3's main spar and wing structure.

The squadron's aircraft were brought up to Phase III standard in the course of 1965, the year that 206's connections with Cornwall were finally severed, except for occasional detachments, and the move to Kinloss in the north of Scotland completed. Another era in the squadron's history had ended with the days of the Shackleton in squadron service numbered.

Flt Lt Ken Maynard and crew with all they need for a sortie.
'I see no packhorses!' or 'It'll be different when we get the Nimrod!'
(CC/206)

CHAPTER 16

KINLOSS AND THE LAST SHACKLETON YEARS 1965-1970

'Life Gets Tedious - *Coastal Command pilots are, reportedly, not amused by the story of the Officer who dreamed he was flying a Shackleton on a maritime reconnaissance patrol - and woke up to find that he was!'*

Flying Review January 1961 reported in 'The Growler', autumn 2000.

The 206 Squadron relocation to Kinloss in Morayshire during July 1965 was part of a strategic reorganisation to concentrate resources in the No. 18 Group area where the Soviet Northern Fleet was potentially the main threat to Atlantic shipping, as already outlined. In March No. 201 Squadron had moved from St Mawgan to Kinloss to join the resident No. 120 Squadron, so 206's move in July completed the all-Shackleton three squadron fleet in the Scottish airfield. To free up the additional accommodation required at Kinloss, the Maritime Operational Training Unit (MOTU) moved to St Mawgan. This unit had replaced No. 236 Operational Conversion Unit (OCU) and No. 1 Maritime Reconnaissance School (MRS) in 1956 – in July 1970 it was redesignated No. 236 OCU. These changes left No. 42 Squadron at St Mawgan as the sole operational unit within No. 19 Group. The remaining components of Coastal Command numbered three squadrons at Ballykelly and one in Gibraltar.

At the start of 1966 there was a three month detachment to RAF Changi in Singapore to assist the Commonwealth forces in the so-called 'Confrontation' with Indonesia. Since 1963 sporadic armed conflict had arisen between the Federation of Malaya (expanded into the Malaysian Federation in 1963) and President Sukarno's Indonesia. Borneo represented the focus of the disagreement, as Sukarno resented the incorporation of British North Borneo (Sabah) and Sarawak in the Malaysian Federation. As Britain and

Detachment to RAF Changi, Singapore, early 1966. Around 70 aircrew plus 50 ground crew.
(Malcolm Morris)

206 Sqn Standard Presentation 28 July 1966.
(Malcolm Morris)

Aerial shot of March-Past after Presentation of Standard.
(CC/206)

Malaya had signed a defence agreement in 1957 and the Sultanate of Brunei (on the Borneo mainland) was a British protectorate, Britain was very much involved from the start and British and Gurkha troops were dispatched along with RAF and Royal Navy units.

In Operation *Hawk Moth* the 206 Shackletons took over patrol of the Straits of Malacca and the waters around Borneo, monitoring the activities of the Indonesian forces. The appearance of some Soviet vessels seemed to confirm suspicions of communist influence behind the leaders of the agitation. However, the growing weakness of the Indonesian economy and disillusion with Sukarno's leadership – with his eventual downfall in 1967 – finally brought the confrontation to an end and a peace treaty was signed between Malaysia and Indonesia in August 1966.

The presentation of the Squadron Standard on 28 July 1966 by HRH Princess Margaret, the Countess of Snowdon, at Kinloss was a memorable day in the squadron's history. King George VI had first introduced Squadron Standards in April 1943 to mark the 25th Anniversary of the formation of the Royal Air Force and squadrons would qualify for the award on completion of 25 years' service. The Queen approved the award of a Standard for No. 206 Squadron in 1963 and the presentation day was a proud event for the squadron. The Standard depicts eight Battle Honours, the maximum permitted, to commemorate notable actions in which the squadron participated. These were: The Western Front 1916-1918, Arras, Dunkirk, the Atlantic 1939-1945, the Channel and the North Sea 1939-1945, Biscay 1941-1944, Fortress Europe 1940-1942 and *Bismarck*. Missing were the other campaigns in which the squadron played a distinguished part: Lys (during 1918), the Invasion Ports 1940, the German Ports 1940 and 1942, the Baltic in 1945 and the South Atlantic in 1982. The motto 'Nihil nos effugit' – 'Naught escapes us' with the octopus motif in the centre is indicative of the squadron's activities in many varieties of work over great distances.

Kinloss 12 Feb. 1967 – one of the crews that took part in round the world flight.
(CC/206)

The Shackleton demonstrated again its long-range capability in February 1967 when two squadron aircraft flew around the world via Canada, the United States, the Pacific, Malaysia and the Middle East. A somewhat more mundane but essential task at home was the requirement to patrol the wreck of the oil tanker *Torrey Canyon* which had run aground off Land's End in March, the object being to pass on reports of the position and extent of the oil slick to enable pollution to be dealt with.

During the same month there was an organisational change at Kinloss with the individual squadron aircraft of Nos 120, 201 and 206 Squadrons becoming part of the 'Kinloss Wing' and instead of squadron numbers being visible on the aircraft there were single-letter codes painted instead – No. 120 Squadron letters 'A' to 'H'; No. 201 'J' to 'Q' and No. 206 'R' to 'Z'.[1]

---

1 Jones, *Avro Shackleton* p105.

In the face of the economic difficulties of the country in the mid and later 1960s the Labour Government's Defence White Paper of 1966 and a Supplementary Statement in 1967 outlined cutbacks in defence spending, the cancellation of various projects, and our intention to withdraw from Aden and South Arabia in 1968 (a date brought forward to 1967) and from the Far East and the Gulf by the end of 1971. Meanwhile in the interim period we still had responsibility for our protectorates in the Middle East and Gulf states which had to be covered by our available forces including Coastal Command – not to mention other tasks like the policing of the oil embargo against Rhodesia. The disbandment of No. 224 Squadron at Gibraltar in 1966 put further pressure on the existing squadrons to cover our commitments at home and overseas. The pressure to reduce defence spending was further complicated by the growth of unrest in the Gulf states and the nationalist uprising in Aden. It was against this background that detachments from 206 Squadron took their turn to be based at RAF Sharjah between late 1967 and 1969, Sharjah being one of the Trucial States for whose defence and foreign policy Britain had responsibility (the Trucial States becoming the United Arab Emirates in 1971). The main task was to mount surveillance sorties to combat arms smuggling – and the base was also a convenient distance from RAF Khormaksar in Aden to assist in covering our withdrawal from the territory.

Tragedy struck at the end of 1967 when Shackleton Mk 3 XF702 crashed on 21 December, all 13 crew members being killed. The aircraft had been flying on a routine training sortie and hit the ground at Creag Bhan, Lochailort, in Inverness-shire in bad weather – the possible causes being turbulence and icing.[2] The dead were Squadron Leader M. C. McCallum, Squadron Leader H. Harvey, Flight Lieutenant B. G. Mackie, Flying Officer R. J. Fonseca, Flying Officer T. C. Swinney, Flying Officer D. J. Evans, Flying Officer J. V. Young, Pilot Officer I. C. Maclean, Flight Sergeant D. J. Harris, Sergeant C. P. Matthews, Sergeant M. B. Bowen, Sergeant K. B. Hurry, Sergeant M. A. Jones.

The routine work of the squadron and the Kinloss Wing continued through the late 1960s – SAR work, anti-submarine exercises and the multifarious roles that had been assigned to the Shackletons. An additional task in 1969 was an oceanographic survey in co-operation with ships of the US Naval Laboratory. But a new era was dawning as the Shackleton was approaching the end of its service life – the reorganisation of the RAF Command structure and the entry into service of the Hawker Siddeley Nimrod. As was later remarked in lighter vein: 'The trouble with the Shack is that no one put a "use by" date on it.'[3]

A rationalisation of the structure of the air force was overdue as the service had shrunk in size over the years and the hope was to make for a 'leaner' and 'fitter' organisation. Hence the old Bomber and Fighter Commands were merged in April 1968 to form Strike Command, and in November 1969, Coastal and Signals Commands were absorbed in the new organisation. Air Support Command had replaced the old Transport Command in 1967 but this was also absorbed in Strike Command in 1972.

No. 18 (Maritime) Group, Strike Command, now replaced the former Coastal Command, with headquarters at Northwood, and the former Nos 18 and 19 Groups became, respectively, HQ Northern Maritime Air Region based at Pitreavie Castle in Fife and HQ Southern Maritime Air Region based at Mount Batten in Devon.[4]

The disbandment parade for Coastal Command, ending 33 years of history, took place at St Mawgan on 27 November 1969. Air Marshal Sir John Lapsley took the salute and two SAR Whirlwinds, nine Shackletons and a Nimrod formed the flypast – representing the present – and the future.

---

2   Chartres, *Avro Shackleton* p88.
3   Quoted in 'The Growler' summer 2001 (Speech by Peter Farr, Shackleton Anniversary celebration March 1989).
4   Ashworth, *RAF Coastal Command* pp222-226.

'Transport late again' – Sharjah November 1967.
(CC/206)

Shackleton Mk3 Phase 3 desert training from Sharjah, 1968.
(CC/206)

The 'Mardet Line', Sharjah March 1969.
(CC/206)

CHAPTER 17

CONVERSION TO NIMROD

'Nimrod, a mighty hunter before the Lord.'

Genesis, Chapter 10.

The next major landmark in the history of No. 206 Squadron was re-equipment with the all-jet Hawker Siddeley Nimrod MR Mk 1, to which crews began conversion at St Mawgan in September 1970.

Since the late 1950s the Air Ministry had been considering the question of an eventual replacement for the Avro Shackleton as the RAF's maritime reconnaissance aircraft. To this end the Ministry issued Operational Requirement (OR) 350 which called for an aircraft combining a high transit speed with the ability to patrol at low speed and at low level. A number of designs were submitted including a version based on the Trident civil airliner, a variant of the Lockheed Orion, and the Avro 776, the latter similar in appearance to the Trident. There were the inevitable delays as the various proposals circulated and the Ministry of Defence issued in 1963 the more precisely defined Air Staff Target (AST) 357 but by the following year there had to be a rethink if the target date of 1968 for the phasing out of the Shackleton and the introduction of the new aircraft was to be met[1]. This appeared to rule out a new design in favour of some interim solution which at the same time had to possess the potential for future development. Thus existing aircraft like the French Breguet 1150 (later the Atlantique) or the American Lockheed Orion were possibilities, or alternatively and more appealing to the politicians, were the proposed maritime versions of British civil designs like the VC10, the Vanguard and the BAC 111. The Royal Air Force preferred a four-engined all-jet solution which would seem to have eliminated the Orion, the Vanguard, the Atlantique and the BAC 111, the latter two aircraft having the disadvantage of being twin-engined.

It was this requirement for a four-engined aircraft which began to swing the argument in favour of a maritime version of the de Havilland Comet. Air Commodore R. W. Joseph (206 OC 1992-94 and station commander at RAF Kinloss 1994-96) later learned something of the hitherto little known background to these events during a conversation with Cyril Bethwaite, at the time Chief Design Engineer at Hawker Siddeley Manchester. The occasion was the 25th Anniversary of the Nimrod's introduction into operational service, held at Kinloss on 11 November 1994 (see also Chapter 21). Cyril Bethwaite described how he was instructed by his Managing Director, Air Chief Marshal Sir Harry Broadhurst, to scrap the design being considered for a version of the Trident 2 airliner, because the company thought that the Atlantique solution was beginning to find favour. Instead a new design was to be based on the successful Comet 4C aircraft, but because of the tight timescale this would have to be done in three days! Needless to say the timescale was met.

Thus in May 1965 Hawker Siddeley were authorised to proceed with the development of the HS801 Comet Maritime Reconnaissance Aircraft. The Air Staff Requirement (ASR) 381 summed up the various tasks of the proposed aircraft. These included the conduct of anti-submarine warfare (ASW), surveillance of sea and land

---

1 Although the Shackleton continued service with No. 8 Sqn in the Airborne Early Warning (AEW) role for many years after that.

forces, area surveillance, the ability to carry out limited air to surface strikes against enemy vessels, the search and rescue role and the ability to carry out emergency trooping. The aircraft design was based on the Comet 4C with four Rolls-Royce Spey turbofan engines. Weapons were to be carried in a ventral pannier running for most of the fuselage length blending with the nose which housed the ASV21 radar, producing the greatest departure from the classic 'Comet' shape. Electronic Counter Measures (ECM) was located in the fairing on top of the dorsal fin and a tail boom was introduced to house the Magnetic Anomaly Detector (MAD) – a structure to keep the equipment at the greatest distance possible from the metallic mass of the aircraft. Other modifications were made to the windscreen panels to improve pilot visibility in low level manoeuvres.[2] The aircraft was capable of a range of 1,000 miles to its patrol area, remaining on station for up to four hours. Its weapons load could include homing torpedoes, depth charges and sonobuoys as well as air-to-surface missiles on wing pylons[3].

A contract was signed for 38 production aircraft with Hawker Siddeley in January 1966 and the flight test programme began at Broughton in 1967 in the charge of J. G. 'Jimmy' Harrison, the Chief Test Pilot at Hawker Siddeley Aviation (HSA) Woodford. In the same year the Maritime Comet was named 'Nimrod' after the biblical figure in the Book of Genesis, chapter ten: 'Nimrod, a mighty hunter before the Lord.'[4] It was an apt description of what was to become the only western turbo-jet maritime aircraft.

The first Nimrod MR1 to be delivered to the RAF was XV230 in 2 October 1969 to the Maritime Operational Training Unit (MOTU) at St Mawgan, where conversion for the aircrew got under way just at the moment when Coastal Command was being replaced by No. 18 (Maritime) Group of Strike Command. It was this aircraft which joined the Shackleton flypast at the closing down ceremony. On 1 July 1970 MOTU was redesignated No. 236 Operational Conversion Unit (OCU). No. 201 Squadron at Kinloss was the first operational squadron to receive the Nimrod in October 1970 with No. 206 following by the end of the year and No. 42 Squadron at St Mawgan in the spring of 1971. Finally No. 203 Squadron at Luqa, Malta, re-equipped in July 1971.[5]

Overall the arrival of the Nimrod Mk 1 brought greatly improved maritime patrol capability. Air Vice-Marshal David Emmerson recalled the better working environment for the crews with more modern equipment, and the more rapid transit speed meant that long range deployments were possible in hours rather than days. Reaction times for operational and SAR incidents were greatly shortened so that the new sensor equipment could be deployed in situations where time was of the essence (as it usually was). The galley facilities and toilet provision approached the standard of the airline cabin as against the more spartan Shackleton environment, with obvious benefits for crew morale and efficiency. While the ASV21 radar represented dated technology, for the first time UK maritime fixed wing aircraft had the capability to locate and track submerged submarines over considerable distances. Air dropped low frequency passive (listening only) acoustic sonobuoys could be deployed in wide area patterns from any altitude and once in the water a hydrophone was activated to a pre-selected depth. The hydrophones transmitted to the patrolling aircraft the frequency patterns created by any noise source. All propulsion units in the water, conventional or nuclear, create unique energy patterns that can be detected and passed back to the aircraft for analysis – some noise emissions travel very long distances and the seas are a noisy environment, which can complicate the workings of the technology.

It is perhaps less well known that the hastily put together Nimrod programme also

---

2   *Comet and Nimrod* by Ray Williams, p26.
3   *Royal Air Force: An Illustrated History* by Michael Armitage p237.
4   *Comet and Nimrod* p27.
5   Ibid. pp28-29.

benefited from the cancellation of the TSR2 aircraft. Some of the modern navigation system avionics were transferred to the Nimrod – which was why the aircraft was one of the first to have a partial inertial navigation system installed. This was not all good news as some of the avionics were prone to overheating and the more experienced and adventurous navigators found that one solution was to transfer the equipment from the navigation crate to the galley cold box for an hour or so – another advantage of having an aircraft with a galley area.[6]

To complement this capability the Nimrod was also fitted with short-range active sonobuoys, which sent out a 'ping' to bounce off the target to provide a range, depth and bearing from the buoy to the target, the possible disadvantage being that the target i.e. the submarine, would be alerted and take evasive action. These Mk1c active buoys were equivalent in cost terms to the price of a Mini car, so dropping them was only practised on rare occasions![7] The Magnetic Anomaly Detector (MAD) equipment mounted in the tail boom was able to pick up small changes in the earth's magnetic field such as those caused by a submarine, although the ranges involved were in yards and not miles – thus the equipment remained effective only at low level and might also detect anomalies such as shipwrecks as well as submarines. Thus to be effective the submarine position had to be known with a fair degree of accuracy but if a signal was detected then the crew knew it was within striking range of the target. In addition the new Electronic Support Measures (ESM) equipment enabled electronic emissions to be detected, for example the radar transmission of a ship or submarine, and a bearing calculated and analysis made of the signal. The signal could then be assessed against known civil and military targets. Thus given good background intelligence combined with crew training and practice the aircraft had the capability to track submarines in transit, and the squadron spent many hours tracking targets for days on end in many parts of the world and around the shores of the UK. All these technologies were refined and upgraded in the succeeding years.

Then as now modern flight simulators proved crucial to crew conversion and training. In fact the flight deck simulators for the Nimrod were the first used within the RAF to be based on digital technology. All aspects of flight, as recalled by David Emmerson, including in-flight emergencies, could now be practised safely on the ground. This saved some 'circuit bashing', to the delight of back-end crews, and provided initial procedural and emergency training during conversion and continuation training for flight deck crews. The visual display for the flight deck simulator consisted of a small camera running along a very detailed model of the local area – consequently, it was not uncommon when coming in to land to meet a very large spider![8]

Plans were afoot for a Maritime Crew Trainer (MCT) before the Nimrod entered service – involving an accurate mock-up fuselage from the beam seats to the tail with a full suite of electronic and navigation equipment to allow a full crew to practise all the potential tasks of the aircraft on the ground, but in a realistic environment. All the actions of the crew would be monitored by instructors and recorded for post-flight analysis. This equipment would have been digitally-powered and a 'first' in the service but it was an idea ahead of its time and the technological problems proved insurmountable. So converting rear crew members had to depend on theory and 'ad hoc' practice equipment. It was ten years before the MCT was introduced and successfully updated to represent the Mk 2 aircraft. The MCT could be coupled to the flight deck 'dynamic' simulator to form a 'Full Mission Simulator' although poor serviceability frequently prevented such a link from being fully productive. Nowadays all crews have to

---

6 Air Cdre R. W. Joseph.
7 Air Cdre Joseph.
8 Air Cdre Stu Butler.

undertake much of their continuation training each month in the MCT.

The main developments in the weaponry arsenal of the Nimrod had to wait for the Falklands War (see Chapter 18) but it is worth mentioning that there were plans for the deployment in Nimrods of nuclear depth bombs (NDBs) in the anti-submarine warfare (ASW) role, principally against the threat from Soviet nuclear submarines. Apparently this was not new, as the Shackleton MR3 was earmarked to carry the US NDB Mk34 codenamed 'Lulu' during the period 1965-1971. Lulu was gradually replaced after 1971 by the B57 NDB just as the Nimrod MR1 was being introduced to the squadrons. The B57 was parachute-retarded and weighed 510lb, with a pre-programmable yield of between 5Kt and 20Kt. It seems that arrangements were made to store NDBs (Lulu and/or B57s) from about the mid-1960s at St Mawgan and later at Machrihanish for use by Shackletons and later Nimrods. In addition there were storage facilities laid on for some ten B57 NDBs at the US Naval Air Station in Sigonella in Sicily, also for possible deployment by UK maritime aircraft. By the mid-1970s Britain had developed an ASW nuclear capability in the form of the WE 177C NDB, developed from the bomb version, with a yield of 10Kt. Frequent checks were made on crews to ensure that they followed NDB checks and procedures to the letter – crew captaincies were won and lost on the outcome of these assessments.

In 1991, following the end of the Cold War, President Bush ordered the withdrawal of the land-based B57 NDBs and it appears that storage at St Mawgan of nuclear NDBs ended by 1992. [9] At the RAF Museum in Hendon there are two NDBs on display – Mk 57s (BDU-11A/E) – presumably drill rounds![10]

The maritime routines which had become well established during the Shackleton era continued much as before. The origins of the Fincastle and Aird Whyte trophies have been discussed in earlier chapters, in particular the former as an annual bombing exercise between anti-submarine crews of the UK and the 'Old Commonwealth' countries of Australia, Canada and New Zealand, in which each aircraft made practice bomb attacks against a towed target to simulate depth charge drops. Until about 1970 Mrs Aird Whyte presented the trophies personally. In the same year the exercise was changed to test a wider range of ASW skills, including localising and attacking a

Fincastle winners 1974 (Flt Lt Hempson).
(CC/206)

Fincastle winners 1977 welcomed home at Kinloss (Flt Lt Earp).
(CC/206)

9 Details from (1) *Nuclear Weapons Databook* Vol V p85 by R. S. Norris et al. and (2) *Jets* (winter 2001) p65.
10 Info from Peter Elliott, Senior Keeper, RAF Museum, Hendon.

submerged submarine, with the sorties being flown from a common venue (unlike previously), rotating between Canada, the UK, Australia and New Zealand. As before, the choice of crew to represent the RAF in the Fincastle was decided by the outcome of the Aird Whyte competition, held annually between the RAF maritime squadrons, with the winning crew going forward for the Fincastle. The Fincastle Trophy of 1970 was the first held under the revised rules, and the first in which the Nimrod participated and won for the RAF, with a 201 Squadron crew. The 1st Navigator of that crew happened to be Squadron Leader David Emmerson, later to be CO of 206 Squadron from 1981 to 1983. No. 206 Squadron won the Maritime Squadrons' Efficiency Trophy (the Aird Whyte) both in 1974 and 1977 which permitted them to go forward for and win the Fincastle Trophy in those years.[11]

206 SQUADRON WINS: AIRD WHYTE/FINCASTLE TROPHY 1954 – 2003

1954	AIRD WHYTE
1967	AIRD WHYTE
1974	AIRD WHYTE & FINCASTLE TROPHY
1977	AIRD WHYTE & FINCASTLE TROPHY
1992	AIRD WHYTE & FINCASTLE TROPHY
1997	AIRD WHYTE
1998	AIRD WHYTE
2003	AIRD WHYTE

206 take the first Nimrod through Gan, March 1971.
(CC/206)

The conversion of the crews proceeded apace, with the last Shackleton sortie being flown on 5 October 1970 by Squadron Leader Matheson, and the first Nimrod sortie on 9 November. By February 1971 all the squadron crews had completed conversion and returned to Kinloss, but intensive training continued. During the spring the CO, Wing Commander J. Wild, took a crew to Australia, New Zealand and Singapore to demonstrate the new aircraft as Hawker Siddeley were anxious to promote export orders. The main competitor in the field was the Lockheed P3B Orion which had already been ordered by a number of air forces due to the cost advantage of this aircraft and the preference for a turbo-prop powered aircraft as against the all-jet Nimrod.

---

11 Info from AVM David Emmerson.

Air Vice-Marshal David Emmerson recalled a number of detachments he spent in Europe, Australia and Canada demonstrating the Nimrod's capabilities:

'I think that people abroad were not convinced that pure jet was a sensible way forward.....More importantly, Lockheed were offering a competitive alternative which wasn't too much slower in transit, had a faster dash potential, was much more economic, had greater endurance and also had a larger flight deck. There were also doubts about our ability to produce on time and to quoted cost.'

Consequently, orders for the Nimrod were confined to the Royal Air Force.[12] The massive increase in oil prices in October 1973 as a direct consequence of the Yom Kippur War between Israel and Egypt allied with Syria, was an added disincentive for potential overseas buyers, as the Nimrod's fuel consumption was relatively high, a feature that was shared with Concorde. Another factor which influenced foreign buyers was the raging inflation in the UK's economy at the time.

As well as continuing the maritime reconnaissance role at home in a critical phase of the cold war, changes in our Far East commitment were to bring about a fresh Nimrod deployment. The Labour Government's 1968 Defence White Paper had announced the UK's proposed withdrawal of British forces from Malaysia and the now-independent Singapore by 1971, leaving only a facility for reinforcement if the need arose. Thus the Far East Air Force (FEAF) was gradually run down and the remaining Shackleton squadron, No. 204, came under the control of No. 18 (Maritime) Group until its return to the UK for disbandment at Honington in April 1972.

In the meantime the new Conservative Government had issued a Supplementary Statement on Defence in October 1970 proposing a small contribution by British forces to the defence of South-East Asia in association with Australia, New Zealand, Malaysia and Singapore. The Royal Air Force element of this was to include a Nimrod detachment in its long-range maritime reconnaissance role. A five-power agreement was signed along with a separate pact between Australia, New Zealand and the UK in what became known as the ANZUK force, based in Singapore. In November 1971 two 206 Squadron crews flew to Tengah, Singapore, for training exercises with the ANZUK forces. Then on 1 January 1972 OC 206 Squadron Wing Commander Jim Wild opened up the Nimrod Maritime Detachment at Tengah with up to four Nimrod MR1s. Apart from maritime reconnaissance the detachment was deployed to other bases for SAR duties for HM The Queen's royal tour of the area. The Far East commitment was short-lived as the Defence White Paper of 1975 of the recently elected Labour Government announced the withdrawal of British forces from ANZUK, ending the Nimrod detachment in the area. This change of policy took place against a background of the oil crisis already referred to and the continuing economic recession – once again defence expenditure was high on the list of Treasury economies.

A dispute between Britain and Iceland erupted as a result of Iceland declaring a 50-mile fishing limit in September 1972. This threatened to drive our deep-sea fishing fleet from the rich cod grounds off Iceland. The Icelanders were in no mood to compromise and by the summer of 1973 were deploying their gunboats to harass British trawlers. The Royal Navy dispatched frigates to the area and the sequence of events became known as the 'Cod War'. The squadron played its part in supporting the Royal Navy and mounting surveillance sorties until an eventual agreement was reached with Iceland by which British trawlers withdrew beyond the 50-mile limit. Air Commodore Joseph recalled that the careers of many Royal Navy ships' commanding officers were saved by the photographs taken by Nimrods, showing that Icelandic gunboat captains were often riding-off RN vessels too closely and collisions resulted. During one sortie in March 1976

---

12 *Comet and Nimrod* p29.

the then Flight Lieutenant Joseph was navigator with captain Squadron Leader Dave 'Bog-H' Baugh when the aircraft ran in with bomb doors open to deter the Icelandic gunboat *Thor* from ramming a RN frigate which was protecting a fishing boat – probably the first ever aggressive act by a Nimrod.

EVENING EXPRESS FRIDAY JUNE 21 1985

NEWS EXTRA
by Colin Craig

THE CRACKDOWN on illegal fishing in the North Sea is being helped by an important "ally" — the Nimrod plane.

Frequent low-level sweeps over the sea by the sophisticated maritime patrol aircraft from RAF Kinloss have been netting valuable evidence to catch offenders.

The aerial fishery patrol to protect stocks is one of the vital missions undertaken by Nimrods from the Moray base.

They regularly photograph every fishing vessel in their path and these are studied by the Department of Agriculture and Fisheries to pinpoint boats and countries ... and whether they are fishing legally.

My host on one such trip was Flight Lieutenant Graham Hillman of 206 Squadron (motto

Nimrod patrols snap up illegal fishers

Mission commander Flight Lieutenant Bob Fox and the crew of the Nimrod.

North Sea net in sky

Nimrods hunt the illegal fishers! – mid 1980s 'Tapestry' sorties.
(CC/206)

After the ANZUK commitment ended there were no further standing detachments but several short deployments around the world including Scandinavia, Germany, France, Cyprus, Gibraltar, Bermuda and the Azores.

A fresh commitment nearer home came in January 1977 when the Nimrod squadrons were called upon to undertake Operation *Tapestry*, which included fishery protection, policing the foreign fishing fleets and protecting North Sea oil-rig installations. Britain was exploiting oil reserves on a massive scale and there was a significant risk from terrorists. Also the question of fishing rights and quotas around UK shores became an important issue which required constant monitoring of fishing boats and types of fishing under way. Much attention was paid to the massive Soviet 'fishing' fleets in evidence and the need for crews to distinguish between the genuine fishing boats and those converted for electronic eavesdropping lurking among them.

Thus the regular patrols, scheduled to take place about three times a week during much of the 1970s and 1980s, involved monitoring and if necessary photographing all the fishing boats in a given area by type and nationality. The patrolling required low level approaches and it was not unusual to visit 150 vessels in a sortie. The three areas designated were - Area 1 from the Shetland Islands to the Malin Head, Area 2 the northern half of the North Sea and Area 3 the southern half.

'The intense helicopter traffic in the North Sea and surrounding areas made this taxing and hazardous work, with many near misses being reported. No wonder squadron crews disliked the mixture of boredom and in-flight incidents, and avoided the "Tapestry" sorties whenever they could.'[13] Pilots, however, always enjoyed the low flying which frequently saw a seven hour sortie with over 95 per cent flown below 500 feet![14] The 'jolly' for the pilots represented very hard work for navigators who had to record

13 AVM David Emmerson, notes supplied 17/5/03.
14 Air Cdre Stu Butler.

each and every contact on the chart and numerous logs, whilst ensuring that details corresponded with the huge number of photographs taken.[15]

MR2 Conversion

The Nimrod MR1 had always been regarded as an 'interim' aircraft and during the production stage modifications were already being introduced to its communications systems. Refits were undertaken by the Nimrod Major Servicing Unit (NMSU) based at Kinloss, for which Hawker Siddeley provided a Contractors Working Party (CWP). This servicing arrangement was controlled by No. 18 Group with a view to keeping under the one roof, so to speak, all the servicing of the Nimrod fleet. The system remained in place until the mid-1990s.[16]

From 1975 there was an extensive upgrading of the avionic and sensor suite in the MR2 development programme overseen by British Aerospace. The main change was the replacement of the ASV21 radar which had been inherited from the Shackleton era with the new EMI Searchwater with its greatly improved capability in range and efficiency. 'All radars suffer from sea returns that become worse as sea states increase, thus masking small targets such as the submarine snort or periscope. Searchwater, however, used sophisticated techniques to cancel out sea returns and was optimised to detect small targets in all sea conditions. Equally important was the fact that radar was configured so that the strength of the transmitted signal, if intercepted by a submarine, did not give any true indication of aircraft range. Thus no longer were submarines able to calibrate their intercept equipment to indicate the range of an approaching aircraft from the power of the radar intercept. Finally Searchwater was able to rapidly assess the direction and speed of movement of a far distant target and also its size. Life was not as predictable as that, but it was still a major advance.'[17]

The AQS-901 acoustics system enabled more accurate analysis to be made of information provided by both passive and active sonobuoys, and a Central Tactical System (CTS) was introduced which supplied a more accurate and stable navigation platform with a Ferranti Inertial Platform, and with Omega replacing Loran C as the long range navigation aid. Electronic Countermeasures (ECM) was replaced by Loral Electronic Support Measures (ESM) which was now carried in new wing pods, making the small pod at the top of the tail fin unnecessary (although this structure was retained). Loral ESM – the overall system being called 'Yellowgate' - provided electronic intercept information over a much broader band width and of a much higher quality. The computing capacity was increased by some 60 times and the crew complement by one to a total of 13 (2 pilots, 1 Air Eng., 2 Navs, 1 AEO, 4 Dry, 3 Wet). In this context 'dry' crew members were those involved 'above the waterline' in radar and ESM, the 'wet' members with 'under the water' operations such as the acoustic system. However some jobs were done by both, for example radio and buoy loading.[18]

No. 206 Squadron was the first to begin conversion to the Nimrod MR2 in December 1979 with the first aircraft delivered for front line use in late 1980. However, on 17 November 1980, there was the first tragedy involving a Nimrod when the fourth MR2 XV256 took off on a conversion flight, carrying a crew of 20 which had been expanded for training purposes (from the Nimrod Conversion Flight), and collided with a flock of sea birds just after take-off from Kinloss, sustaining severe damage to at least three of the engines. The pilots skilfully guided the crippled aircraft to make a controlled crash landing into the forest less than a mile from the end of the runway but the aircraft burst

---

15 Air Cdre R. W. Joseph.
16 Comet and Nimrod p29.
17 AVM Emmerson.
18 *Comet and Nimrod* p30, and notes from AVM Emmerson and Stu Butler.

Crash of 17 November 1980, Nimrod XV256.
(CC/206)

into flames. The 18 crew managed to escape but both pilots were killed, Flight Lieutenant Noel W. Anthony RAAF (captain) and Flying Officer Stephen P. Belcher (co-pilot). The former was posthumously awarded the Air Force Cross and the latter The Queen's Commendation for Valuable Services in the Air.

By April 1981 crews had successfully converted to the MR2, just at the moment Wing Commander R. C. McKinlay handed over command to Wing Commander David Emmerson. During the early months of 1982 the squadron saw the loss of many experienced personnel to form the new Nimrod MR2 Operational Conversion Unit at RAF Kinloss. Bob Joseph was among them and was posted as Chief Navigation Instructor (CNI). In the squadron there was now a settling down period of intensive training and familiarisation with the new aircraft systems but few could have imagined at the time how valuable this interlude would be in the light of events shortly to follow.

First MR2 Fincastle crew, XV254, Sept. 1981. Crew captain Mitch Lees (navigator); Stu Butler First Pilot at front right.
(Stu Butler)

CHAPTER 18

FALKLANDS CAMPAIGN

'.....It was easy to imagine how a goldfish in a bowl feels with a cat looking in.'

Air Vice-Marshal David Emmerson on patrolling off the Argentinian coast, May 1982.

On the morning of 2 April 1982 the news that the Argentine forces had invaded the British colony of the Falkland Islands came as a shattering blow. For many years there had been negotiations between the British and Argentine Governments over the question of the disputed sovereignty of the Islands, but the military 'junta' in power in Argentina, headed by General Leopoldo Galtieri since 1981, had now decided to take matters into their own hands. For the British Government and defence establishment it had been assumed that we would be directing our energies towards NATO and the European scene in the future rather than 'out of area' and colonial-type conflicts, especially now that we had withdrawn from the Middle and Far East. In spite of this there was no hesitation, and a task force was ordered to be assembled and despatched to re-take the Falklands, a total of some 70 ships in all. The operation was termed 'Corporate' and was placed under the command of Admiral Sir John Fieldhouse GCB. The air contingent included Royal Navy and RAF Sea Harriers on HMS *Hermes*, along with support helicopters and transport aircraft like the Lockheed Hercules, BAe VC10s and the Handley Page Victor tankers. Plans were also drawn up to utilise a force of Vulcan V-bombers which incidentally were less than three months away from being scrapped! Also, it was clear that the Nimrods would be an indispensable part of any such force for maritime reconnaissance, anti-submarine warfare (ASW) and search and rescue (SAR).

Vital in the strategic planning was Ascension Island in the South Atlantic. This volcanic speck in the ocean was one of the British St Helena dependencies, some 700 miles north-west of St Helena and annexed to that colony from the Admiralty in 1922.

Wideawake Airfield, Ascension Island, 1982.
(CC/206)

The island was dominated by the US staging airfield curiously named 'Wideawake' (after the sooty tern which inhabits the island in large numbers). If the island had not existed it is difficult to see how 'Corporate' could have been launched as it was approximately half the distance between the UK and the Falklands, albeit some 3,900 miles from the Islands.

As diplomatic negotiations proceeded events were moving rapidly. On 5 April two Nimrod MR1s of No. 42 Squadron left for Wideawake under the command of Wing Commander D. L. Baugh for reconnaissance and SAR duties, the first operational sortie being carried out from Ascension on 7 April. In the meantime at RAF Kinloss No. 206 Squadron under Wing Commander David Emmerson trained hard for possible deployment to a third country in support of the campaign while practising fighter evasion tactics. As 206 was at that time the only squadron fully equipped with the MR2 it was inevitable that their services would be required sooner rather than later.

Considering the vast distances to patrol in the South Atlantic the Nimrod's operating range was not going to be sufficient, so urgent consideration was given to the need for Air-to-Air Refuelling (AAR) of the Nimrod and as early as 14 April an instruction to proceed with the modification was issued by the Ministry of Defence to British Aerospace at Woodford. Amazingly by 25 June 13 Nimrods equipped with ex-Vulcan refuelling probes had been delivered, designated Nimrod MR2P, which extended the endurance of the aircraft up to 19 hours permitting patrol ranges as far as the waters near the Falklands. David Emmerson added: 'Somewhat alarmingly, the fuel line from the new probe entered the aircraft cabin just behind the head of the pilots. The hose was standard bowser refuelling hose and it ran on the floor through the main cabin to amidships in the fuselage before disappearing into the internal fuel tanks. It was treated with great respect!'

In addition the weapons system had to be upgraded, in particular with an air-to-air missile, to combat Argentinian aircraft which were believed to be shadowing the fleet, and to provide an offensive capability to engage the Argentinian Boeing 707 surveillance aircraft identified twice approaching Ascension Island by Nimrods. Thus four wing-mounted AIM-9 Sidewinder air-to-air missiles (AAMs) were rushed from the United States and fitted for defence in enemy air space, and two AGM-84A-1 Harpoon anti-shipping missiles (ASMs), also from the United States, were mounted in the weapons bay.[1] The

Falklands Victor Tanker plus Nimrod.
(Stu Butler)

1   Ray Williams, *Comet and Nimrod*, pp 31-2.

aircraft was also modified to carry Stingray torpedoes and 1000lb retard bombs. There were also improvements made to the navigation system.

On 21 April Wing Commander Emmerson had just landed back from a training sortie when he was met by the station commander to be given two hours' notice to fly to London to attend a briefing at the Northwood Headquarters. It was assumed that the MR2 would replace the MR1s on Ascension and therefore an MR2 squadron commander should be at the island to take command of the detachment. The next day, 21 April, he was travelling overnight to Ascension Island 'as the only passenger on a VC10 freighter sleeping on 10,000 cans of Newcastle Brown destined for the troops in transit to the South Atlantic. Only 9,998 arrived!'[2]

David Emmerson's command at Ascension consisted of between two and five aircraft and crews at any one time, MR2s from Nos 120, 201 and 206 Squadrons, and up to 50 ground crew. Aircraft and crews were rotated at about 10-day intervals and by the end of the detachment about 14 or 15 crews had flown sorties from the island. The system of rotation had the advantage of keeping the aircrew fresh and up to speed on training in the new equipment, as well as ensuring top line aircraft serviceability but there was the disadvantage that the crews 'had only just reached the top of a steep learning curve before leaving the operational theatre.' However, the potential fatigue problem was avoided which might result from flying the equivalent of 200 plus hours per crew per month combined with the crowded and uncomfortable sleeping conditions.[3]

Facilities at Ascension were basic, considering that up to now one aircraft movement per day had been accepted as the average. As the build-up proceeded up to 400 aircraft movements per day became the norm and there could be as many as 30 aircraft on the ground at any one time. Living conditions were cramped and in short supply. Fortunately the Nimrod force was able to claim the only air-conditioned working accommodation normally set aside for visiting US Navy P3 aircraft. For the ground crew tents were sited some three miles from the airfield although later on huts were made available. In due course prefabricated buildings were flown in by the US Air Force which became known as 'Concertina City' since each unit came in flat pack form, fully equipped, and had only to be pulled open like a concertina for the beds to fall into place – each with its own vacuum-packed blanket pack! These, along with portacabins from the UK provided a better range of temporary accommodation. With no transport available improvisation was the order of the day, and the ground crew rescued an abandoned American lorry which they managed to put to use. Two civilian cars were bought, one being designated 'the Squadron Commander's Mini' acquired by Wing Commander Emmerson for $400. A good relationship was built up with the local population of just over 1,000 who opened up their clubs for the servicemen, which were regularly drunk dry! Food was supplied by PAN AM, who ran the airfield for the US Air Force and obtained provisions from US sources, a formidable task considering that throughout the emergency 1,000 servicemen had to be catered for. There was a struggle to maintain aviation fuel supplies and it proved difficult to re-supply the airfield storage tanks from the main fuel storage area in the settlement of Georgetown. Later the Royal Engineers laid on a three-mile pipeline in a record time of three days which solved the problem.

The tasks allocated to the Nimrod detachment included one-hour SAR standby for aircraft in the vicinity of Ascension Island, and airborne SAR when the war got under way during May for the carrier-borne Harrier force and for the Vulcan bombing sorties (codenamed 'Black Buck'), the first of which took place on 30 April to Port Stanley airfield. There was also the need for surface surveillance in advance of the naval task

---

2 AVM D. Emmerson, *My Unforgettable Ascension Island*.
3 Ibid.

force in case Argentinian warships were in the transit area. On occasions mail and spares were dropped to ships and hunter/killer nuclear submarines (SSNs) on their southward progress. Another perhaps less well known task was surveillance up to a radius of 200 nautical miles around Ascension Island (commonly known by the crews as ASI 400) to check on shipping as there was some concern that the Argentinians might launch a diversionary attack to disrupt our supply lines – such being the importance of the Island in the entire operation. Occasional Argentinian ships were identified as well as some Soviet intelligence vessels, but in the event this threat did not materialise.

Long-range sorties were made possible by the in-flight refuelling equipment which was fitted to some Nimrods from 10 May after an intensive three weeks of designing, fitting and testing the equipment, a huge achievement by engineers considering that the peacetime schedule would have been up to two years. The run-up period was recalled by Dick Scrivener who had recently joined Andy Melville-Jackson's Crew Three as 1st navigator, his first stint in this capacity on the Mk 2. On 6 May the crew were detailed for a long flight to check the effects of such a sortie on aircraft and crew. As well as the usual crew of 13 they had an extra navigator and flight engineers along with an additional pilot, Squadron Leader Tony Banfield from Boscombe Down, to fly the three in-flight refuelling operations during the flight – bringing the crew total to 17. They took off at 2300 hrs on Thursday 6 May and landed at 1900 on the 7th – 20 hours' flying of which only one was night. 'Memories of hearing the Victor tanker engines above our own noise and the pilot (Tony Banfield) becoming slightly disorientated during the first prod and being talked to by M-J (Melville-Jackson) to overcome it – stand out. Apart from loo overload I don't think many problems were revealed.'[4]

The 20-hour crew, 6/7th May 1982. G=Guest.
Back row L to R:
G, G, Marcus Wilson, 'Gunner' Graham, Al Rennett, Neil Benton, Tom Holden, Tony Banfield (G), Simon?, Mo Smith (G), Jeff Spencer, John Healey (G)
Front:
Steve Skinner, Wally Alloway, Andy Melville-Jackson, Dick Scrivener, Steve Griffin
(Richard Scrivener)

4   Dick Scrivener, email of 9/4/03.

For the aircrew it was only possible to provide the barest minimum of training before the first AAR ASW was flown on the 11th by Flight Lieutenant Ford and Crew Five to provide cover for the task force approaching the Falklands some 2,750 miles south-south-west of Ascension. The sortie lasted for 12 hours. Other sorties were now flown to areas off the Argentinian and Falklands coastline, remaining in the patrol area for five or six hours watching for hostile ships emerging from Argentinian ports and for submarines at sea. The first operation of this type was flown by Wing Commander Emmerson and a 201 Squadron crew on 15 May in XV232, a sortie which lasted for $19^1/_2$ hours and without the protection of the Sidewinder which was not yet fitted, making the aircraft especially vulnerable in the daylight hours close to the Argentinian coast. The aircraft landed back at Ascension after three refuellings having covered a distance of 8,300 miles, the longest sortie undertaken by a Nimrod to date. On 21 May the same Nimrod, this time with a 206 crew, set a new record for a long-distance operational reconnaissance mission of 8,453 miles in 18 hours and five minutes. David Emmerson recalled one of the more interesting aspects of these sorties:

'On the night prior to the landing by British troops, to our surprise we found we could still see the lights of Port Stanley blazing fiercely despite the war activities. That said, any sortie within the Argentinian air defence cover kept crews alert and the adrenalin flowing. The risk of interception was low but when flying off the Argentinian coast on a sunny cloudless day it was easy to imagine how a goldfish in a bowl feels with a cat looking in.'

The Nimrod became an essential component of the Vulcan sorties acting as a 'shepherd' and using the Searchwater radar to guide the returning Vulcan to its waiting Victor tanker after completing the bombing run – trials had been carried out to ensure that the radar would detect Vulcan/Victor IFF. These episodes were not without hazard as on 3 June Wing Commander Emmerson recalled watching a Vulcan attempting to refuel, breaking its probe and having to divert to make an emergency landing at Rio de Janeiro, Brazil. 'In this case, we accompanied the Vulcan to about 100 miles from the Brazilian coast where we waited until the aircraft landed safely. R/T contact was maintained until after the Vulcan had landed.'

Andy Melville-Jackson's crew deployed to Ascension late in May and flew one sortie operationally using refuelling among the ten flights totalling 75 hours they completed. As well as Dick Scrivener the crew consisted of co-pilot Steve Skinner (later to be OC 206), 2nd navigator Steve Griffin and Wally Alloway (AEO). Among the other crew members were Al Rennett and Gunner Graham.[5]

Given the brief training time available, air-to-air refuelling tested aircrew skills to the limit, as occasionally Victor tanker crews would warn 'too close, back off!' and there were some instances of Nimrod crews making several attempts before a successful contact with the refuelling basket was made. The ground crews worked incessantly to keep the aircraft serviceable for the tasks required, with the additional challenge of maintaining the MR2 aircraft avionics which were new, complex and demanding of spares and servicing time. Requests for advice, spares and equipment to the home base were usually answered within 24 hours but little would have been achieved without the years of training, abundant common sense, teamwork and the obligatory sense of humour. This last quality was tested in late April when 100 people were persuaded to pay $1 for a dance on the hospital ship *Uganda* which was moored for two weeks off Ascension Island. Everyone arrived at the jetty eagerly anticipating a lively evening with the nurses on board ship, only to be told that the event was a spoof for charity – all of which was taken in good part.

---

5   Ibid.

As it turned out no casualties or losses were suffered by the squadron during the conflict and none of the weapons fitted were used in anger but over 70 sorties were flown by 206 – a total of 531.10 hours of operational sorties out of a total of 1,299.10 hours flown by all four maritime squadrons. Also, as mentioned previously, aircraft and crews were tested to their limits over unfamiliar waters. The difficulties were immense; the lack of a secure communications link with the UK which left personnel with a feeling of isolation from the big picture, and the need to co-ordinate operations procedures with the Victor tankers. There had to be precise and accurate debriefing of crews who might already have been on duty for 24 hours. The myriad fishing vessels off the South American coast had to be distinguished in their electronic emissions from Argentinian warships, occasionally causing false alarms and wasted time in investigation, usually by submarines. Fighter evasion was a necessary part of the training – stimulating for the pilot but stomach-churning for the rest of the crew.

The part played by the Nimrods in the campaign is less well-known than other aspects of the air war, for very understandable reasons, but the support and surveillance role was crucial and an outstanding vindication of the years of training and quality of the aircraft and its systems. This was recognised by the award of the Air Force Cross to the detachment commander Wing Commander Emmerson and the Falklands Medal to the members of the squadron who took part, including the then Flight Lieutenant Stu Butler who later became OC 206 Squadron and subsequently the final Air Commodore Maritime before the Nimrod force was truly integrated with other Intelligence, Surveillance and Reconnaissance aircraft. Another Battle Honour was added to those earned in the long history of the squadron. By the time the conflict had ended all the Nimrods had been brought up to MR 2P standard, after which the 'P' suffix was dropped in the designation.

Sqn Ldr Taylor presenting Wg Cdr Emmerson with a painting of a Shackleton in September 1982, to commemorate the 30th anniversary of the re-formation of the squadron at St Eval.
(CC/206)

South Atlantic Medal Award Ceremony, December 1982. Dick Scrivener being awarded the South Atlantic Medal by the CO, Wg Cdr Emmerson. In foreground is Glyn Davis, ex-Phantom, Jaguar and Hunter ace. On Dick's right is Neil Hamilton, navigator.
(Richard Scrivener)

CHAPTER 19

HIGHS AND LOWS 1982-1990

'Only 40 minutes or so earlier, we had been enjoying the relative comforts of the Officers' Mess and now we were en-route to what would become one of the biggest disasters in UK living memory.'

Gp Capt. G. R. Porter on the Piper Alpha disaster, July 1988.

206 Squadron, March 1983.
(CC/206)

There was a return to the routine of a maritime squadron after the end of the Falklands conflict. In April 1983 Wing Commander David Emmerson AFC relinquished his post as commanding officer of the squadron and was replaced by Wing Commander B. Johnson. The experience gained and the aircraft modifications were to stand the squadron in good stead over the coming years, especially the long-range capability. On 23 January 1984 a Nimrod from the squadron flew non-stop from the Falklands to RAF Brize Norton, covering a distance of 8,047 miles in 17 hours 15 minutes. On board were the Secretary of State for Defence, Michael Heseltine, and the Vice-Chief of the Defence Staff Air Chief Marshal Sir Peter Harding.

A major Cold War task for the Nimrods was the tracking and monitoring of Soviet nuclear submarines, as described by David Emmerson: 'These vessels exercised in the north Atlantic and also off the west coast of Scotland. They also transited past the UK to the Mediterranean. There were long periods (it was often weeks) when the Nimrod fleet mounted 24-hour coverage sorties to track these targets, normally having been alerted by long range acoustic intelligence. After the fitment of in-flight refuelling we were able to visit the Barents Sea and observe the Soviets in their own back yard.'

The year 1986 marked the 70th Anniversary of 206 Squadron and a reunion weekend was held at Kinloss in June to mark the occasion. Wing Commander Brian J. Sprosen was at the time commanding officer. During that year there were the usual

At the North Pole, 3 May 1988. Nimrod meets nuclear-powered submarines HMS *Turbulent* and HMS *Superb*. (CC/206)

number of exercises in which the squadron aircraft participated. Two crews were maintained at Gibraltar and there were detachments to Cyprus, Sigonella in Sicily and Lann Bhioue and Keflavik in Iceland. Flight Lieutenant Alan Hughes, as display pilot, took part in air displays in the UK and air fairs at Comox, Vancouver Island and Abbotsford in Washington State, USA. Many hours were flown in training for the anti-submarine and anti-shipping roles.

During the following year, 1987, there was a detachment to Homestead AFB, Florida for ASW weapon training. Valuable time was spent during the three weeks of the detachment flying sorties over the deep sea weapon range off the Florida coast. In October Wing Commander C. M. 'Mike' Sweeney took over command of the squadron.

A memorable episode began at midday on 3 May 1988 when two Nimrods captained by Flight Lieutenants Russ Williams and Gary Porter took off from Kinloss to provide support for two Royal Navy nuclear-powered submarines HMS *Turbulent* and HMS *Superb* which had surfaced at the North Pole. The aircraft were in the patrol area for four hours at low level and in close formation, practising air-to-air refuelling and specialist navigation techniques. After a sortie which lasted for 14 hours both aircraft returned safely to Kinloss – the first time that any RAF aircraft had operated for a lengthy period over the North Pole, and the first occasion that two Royal Navy submarines had been at the Pole together. Once again, the aircraft's capability was demonstrated in a remote environment and at considerable distance from the home base.

On a very tragic note on 6 July 1988 news was received from the Rescue Co-ordination Centre at Pitreavie of a major oil rig disaster in the North Sea. Within 40 minutes the first Nimrod at the scene was MR2 XV228 captained by Squadron Leader G. R. Porter with 1st Pilot Major G. Barth CAF and Flight Lieutenant G. Woodhouse (AEO).

An awesome sight greeted the crew as the aircraft levelled off at 15,000 feet with a bright light visible in the night sky marking the position of the burning oil rig Piper Alpha some 80 miles away. It was quite clear that this was no routine operation but had all the makings of a major catastrophe. Co-ordination and control of the search and rescue was the complex task ahead and through the gaps in the cloud 'we were all too aware of the fire-storm raging on the burning rig, occasionally supplemented by explosions of awesome power.'[1]

Gradually the rescue and support vehicles gathered, one being the rig support vessel *Tharos* which was capable of taking helicopters and possessed some medical facilities. There were a few fishing vessels and commercial helicopters ready to assist but it was not until about 30 minutes after the Nimrod's appearance that the RAF and Coastguard helicopters from Lossiemouth and Sumburgh were able to get the rescue operation into top gear. As the night wore on further RAF, Royal Navy and commercial assets became available making the task of co-ordination even more complex to manage. Several oil rigs in the vicinity had helipads but their aviation fuel reserves could not be guaranteed so one task for the Nimrod was to ascertain their availability to ensure that the helicopters 'were in the right place with the right amount of fuel, ready for the right task at the right time.' At any one time the Nimrod crew was responsible for up to a dozen helicopters – 'some were conducting searches of the datum, like moths around a camp fire, whilst others raced against time to deliver burns victims to the Aberdeen Hospital and further afield.'[2] At least the weather conditions were favourable with good visibility below the cloud base. The boats on the surface were organised in lines to look for survivors, a risky operation as the fire continued to rage unpredictably. Squadron Leader Porter was relieved two hours after daybreak on 7 July by another Nimrod and landed at Kinloss after a flight lasting 8 hours, 35 minutes. In all three 206 Nimrods would attend the rescue operation over a period of 24 hours. The aircraft had the task of co-

Piper Alpha, 6 July 1988.

1 Gp Capt. G. R. Porter.
2 Ibid.

ordinating up to 25 rescue vessels and 10 helicopters and at the same time maintaining communications with Kinloss and Pitreavie. Only 61 personnel survived the disaster out of a total of 167 killed. Later Squadron Leader G. R. Porter (now Group Captain and Station Commander at RAF Kinloss) was awarded the Queen's Commendation for Valuable Services in the Air, for his work in the initial response to the disaster.

A fitting end to the decade was the dedication of a memorial window to the squadron in St Columba's Church, RAF Kinloss, on 28 May 1989. Nos 120 and 201 Squadron already had memorial windows and there was a third blank window available. Funds were raised and the work was undertaken by the local Benedictine monks from Pluscarden Abbey. The finished window depicted the surrender of a German U-Boat to a Liberator of 206 Squadron during May 1945. The service of dedication took place during a squadron reunion organised by the recently formed 206 Squadron Fortress Liberator Association, whose secretary was Alan Smith.

The close of the decade witnessed the formal ending of the Cold War, a process which had begun with the coming to power of Mikhail Gorbachev in the USSR in 1985. A greatly improved atmosphere prevailed between East and West which led to substantial Soviet arms reductions and the eventual withdrawal of Soviet formations from Eastern Europe. The dismantling of the Berlin Wall by the end of 1989 was only the start of a remorseless chain of events which would lead to the dissolution of the Soviet Union itself as Eastern European states seceded, and the eventual collapse of the Warsaw Pact. The full story had not yet unfolded by the summer of 1990 but the trend was unmistakable. There was no doubt that a re-think about the strength and structure of our armed forces was imminent. This came with *Options for Change*, a document presented to Parliament on 25 July 1990 which outlined a plan for cuts and restructuring of the armed forces – for the Royal Air Force it meant a cut in front-line strength and a reduction of almost 16 per cent in personnel, to the lowest figure since 1938[3]. The full implications of this did not work themselves out until the early 1990s but in the meantime any optimism about a 'new world order' was ironically dispelled only a week after the announcement, when Iraq invaded Kuwait in August 1990.

---

3 Armitage, Michael, *The Royal Air Force: An Illustrated History* pp 269-70.

CHAPTER 20

OPERATION *GRANBY* AND AFTERMATH 1990-1991

'Nobody there (at Nimrod Ops) knew anything.....it was only when we got back to the hotel at 4 a.m. that the wire service machine in the lobby confirmed that bombs were falling in Baghdad.'

Flight Lieutenant Duncan Milne, 206 Squadron pilot, 17 January 1991.

In April 1990 Wing Commander Brian G. McLaren had taken command of the squadron just a few months before a new crisis erupted in the Gulf, with the sudden and unprovoked Iraqi invasion of the neighbouring state of Kuwait on 2 August 1990. The Iraqi dictator Saddam Hussein had been cast in the role of a new 'Hitler' since he had waged an eight-year war on Iran following his attack on that country in 1980, and ruthlessly persecuted the Kurds and anyone else who opposed him. This latest outrage prompted a UN resolution to isolate Iraq and the formation of an international coalition led by Britain and the United States to oust Iraq from Kuwait. There was an immediate military build-up in the Gulf as the diplomats attempted to solve the crisis before a decision was made to use force. The Middle East was and remains of crucial strategic importance to the world economy as the source of much of its oil, and Saddam's aggression threatened the stability and peace of the whole region.

At this stage it was by no means clear what role there might be for the Nimrod Wing at Kinloss, Nos 120, 201 and 206 Squadrons, and No. 42 Squadron at St Mawgan. There was no threat to coalition forces from hostile submarine activity. However, the crews were by no means unfamiliar with the area as for the previous eight years Nimrod detachments had been sent to Oman as part of a deployment codenamed 'Magic

'It's either the rations or the weapon!'
Crew 8 in a vain attempt to reduce their all up weight.
(CC/206)

Roundabout' after the BBC children's TV series of the time – the name reputedly chosen because of the large clocktower and roundabout in Muscat. The aim of the deployment had been to maintain a British presence in the area and to support the Sultan of Oman and his armed forces in surface surveillance of shipping.[1] Britain's long-standing links with the Gulf had been reinforced at the start of the Iran/Iraq war in 1980 with the Royal Navy's Operation *Armilla* – the Armilla Patrol – whereby warships had been diverted to the area to ensure the safety of British-registered ships in the Gulf. The Nimrod detachments had assisted in the Navy's work.

Within days of the invasion a plan emerged to send a Nimrod detachment to the Gulf, to assist in the enforcement of United Nations Security Council Resolutions designed to ensure a naval blockade of Iraq. Aircrew and accompanying ground crews had to be chosen, and the aircraft and equipment made ready for an early departure. Three 120 Squadron crews departed for Seeb in Oman (Muscat airport) on 12 August, but very soon all the squadrons would be involved as a rotation system for the crews and aircraft was put into operation, much as had been the case during the Falklands conflict. There was no need to re-paint the aircraft in desert camouflage as the drab

The first 206 Squadron crew deployed to Seeb, Oman, following Iraq's invasion of Kuwait –
Crew 3 captained by Flt Lt Hardy.
(CC/206)

marine colouring was considered adequate for protection. For most of the period 206 Squadron was contributing two crews to the detachment which comprised three aircraft and four crews in total.

Seeb was a shared military and civilian airport on the coast of Oman, controlled by the Sultan of Oman's Air Force, somewhat removed from what became the main centres of action during the war and consequently largely overlooked by the media. Thus there

---

1   Allen, Charles, *Thunder & Lightning*, p36ff

was little press coverage of the activities of the Nimrod detachments both during and after the conflict, a situation which suited the Omanis as they had no wish to have their active participation advertised around the world! Also there was the safety and security of the detachment personnel to consider.

Within a week the detachment had grown to about 100 people all of whom were billeted at first in Muscat's luxurious Inter-Continental Hotel, although working conditions at the airfield left much to be desired with only a basic building, a telephone, coffee bar and insufficient electric wiring for the computers. A lot of work had to be done before the facilities were brought up to standard.

The Nimrods usually flew two sorties a day initially in the Gulf of Oman rather than the Arabian Gulf itself, with the task of locating, reporting and communicating with all the merchant shipping in the area. Any suspicious vessels were reported to the US Navy for possible interception. By the end of August Nimrod operations were extending into the Arabian Gulf but keeping well south of the Kuwaiti border and away from the Iranian coast. In this crowded region encounters could include American aircraft, Iranian and Soviet aircraft, and to the east of Hormuz a number of Soviet vessels were usually on station as intelligence-gatherers. Great care had to be taken on patrol up the west side of the Gulf, staying outside Iranian territorial waters, a zone of 12 miles plus a three-mile buffer zone, and then the detailed search would continue down the west coast. It has been estimated that a total of 6,500 ships were challenged between mid-August 1990 and mid-January 1991.

The climate in the area could produce problems for an aircraft used to operating in colder conditions although detachments to the Gulf were by no means new. The electronic systems could fail due to condensation from the humidity, and the only way to prevent this was by constructing a 'gutter' system over the navigators to divert the moisture away from the equipment.[2]

Flight Lieutenant Duncan Milne recalled his time in the Gulf as co-pilot in Glenn Macey's crew (206 Squadron Crew Five). They arrived at Seeb on 24 November 1990 and quickly settled in to the very pleasant accommodation in the Muscat Intercontinental Hotel. Duncan had been on the Nimrod fleet for only a year before the crisis erupted. He had previously been an instructor on the Northumbrian Universities Air Squadron and before that a Canberra pilot based at RAF Wyton. The task was now to carry out comprehensive surveillance of both the Gulf of Oman and the Arabian Gulf:

'On a given day, one aircraft would take off early and fly across Oman and the United Arab Emirates (UAE), letting down to the north of Abu Dhabi and then patrol the entire Arabian Gulf roughly south of the latitude of Al Jubail. This aircraft would exit the Gulf at low level via the Straits of Hormuz, and return to Seeb. The second aircraft would take off later in the morning and complete the search of the Gulf of Oman. All significant vessels (merchant ships) would be identified and reported and listed ships photographed and interrogated from the air. The idea was to complete a comprehensive plot of shipping movements in and out of the Gulf, with a view to enforcing the UN sanctions against Iraq. Sanctions breakers would, of course, be intercepted by coalition warships and boarded if necessary.' Although the task was routine there was the continual problem of keeping clear of, or at least being positively identified by, twitchy warships who did not like aeroplanes heading towards them at low level! There was a four-day working cycle – flying in the Gulf of Oman, then in the Arabian Gulf, one day on an hour's standby at the hotel (sunbathing mostly) and a day free. Little disturbed the standby days as a rule although there was the occasional SAR incident which did not involve the 206 crew.

---

2 Ibid. p42.

At the start of January 1991 the diplomatic effort was seen to be breaking down and war became inevitable. The seriousness of the situation was outlined by the Prime Minister John Major himself during a visit to the unit in early January as part of his tour of British forces and friendly Arab states. Duncan Milne recalled the occasion:

'Although you might not think of John Major as a charismatic figure, close up talking to a relatively small group he was very much at ease and in command of the situation. He left us in no doubt that things were about to change and that UK assets would soon be closely involved in the forthcoming conflict.' Inevitably, rumours about the 'war role' for the Nimrods were legion, compounded by the fact that higher authority had only worked out fairly late in the day what that task would be. Duncan Milne's crew had a minor drama on 6 January while participating in a medium scale Maritime SAR exercise in the Northern Gulf, and landing at Bahrain to refuel: 'Unfortunately when we came to leave we found that one of the engines would not start due to a sheared starter-motor drive. At that time, Bahrain was literally covered in aircraft, British Tornados and Victor tankers, Italian Tornados, US Marine Corps C130 tankers and innumerable transport aircraft and helicopters. We were told either to get out or be towed out to the desert to make room. Luckily, permission from Group HQ was forthcoming for a three-engine ferry take-off, and we made it back to Seeb without difficulty.'

In the middle of January, only days before the deadline to Saddam was due to expire, there was a complete change in tasking, as Duncan recalled:

'We now found ourselves operating at night in the northern Arabian Gulf, often within sight of Iraqi-occupied Kuwait City. The brief was to compile a comprehensive large scale radar plot of the shallow waters around the Iraqi and Kuwaiti coasts. All fixed objects such as wrecks, buoys, channel markers, rigs, wellheads and sandbanks were marked on charts so that any changes from the normal could be spotted immediately. The plan was to use the Nimrods, with our far superior radar capability, in the night hours while the US Navy P3Cs covered the daylight. This system guaranteed 24-hour protection for forward units of the coalition navies against attack by small craft and missile boats.'

On the 17th the air war started, Operation *Desert Storm* or *Granby* in British parlance, but nobody bothered to tell the Nimrod detachment, as Duncan related:

'On only the second such sortie flown by our crew, the Gulf War officially started all around us although nobody told us it was happening! Everything had seemed normal, the only unusual part of the pre-flight preparation being the reading of a signal from General de la Billière (C-in-C UK forces) telling us what wonderful chaps we were etc. In the small hours of 17 January our controlling ship (I think it was USS *Yorktown*) cleared us to depart an hour or so early. Needing no further bidding, we headed off for the 90-minute transit back to Seeb. As we headed south, we noted that two enormous American battleships had moved closer to the coast and had taken up line abreast formation (to allow for cruise missile firing as it turned out) and we could see large formations of aircraft (tanker and fighter packages) heading the other way, though this was not all that unusual since exercises were being conducted on an almost daily basis at this stage. It was only when we arrived back in Seeb at about 3 a.m. and saw that every single one of the 30 or so Muscat-based US Air Force tankers was airborne that we really understood what was going on.'

'Nonetheless, on going to Nimrod Ops to debrief the mission, nobody there knew anything. Even the Detachment Commander had been at an Embassy function and was now tucked up in bed. It was only when we got back to the hotel at 4 a.m. that the wire service machine in the lobby confirmed that bombs were falling on Baghdad. We phoned the Ops staff to let them know the news!'

The emphasis was now on the detection of hostile vessels, principally Iraqi Fast

Patrol Boats (FPBs), which now posed a direct threat to warships in the northern Gulf. 'Over the opening couple of weeks of the air campaign, Nimrods detected a good number of missile attack craft attempting to achieve a launch position against the frigates, destroyers and battleships on station off Kuwait. The results were always the same – the rapid vectoring of a fighter-bomber to the target and the destruction of the intruder before they could achieve their aim. An example would be the night of 23 January when our radar operator detected a fast moving vessel leaving the Iraqi waterways and heading directly for one of the battleships (possibly USS *Wisconsin*). An A6 Intruder on Surface Combat Air Patrol (SUCAP) was called in by the controlling ship and vectored by us to the target. Using equipment rather clumsily known as the Target Recognition/Attack Multi-sensor (TRAM) infra-red turret, the A6 crew identified our contact as an OSA-class missile boat (a Russian-built vessel) and destroyed it with a Skipper (rocket boosted guided bomb). Although a success for us, the fact that the OSA had a crew of 30 or more, and that the hapless Iraqi sailors never really had much of a chance of either achieving their mission or of being picked up after the sinking, this episode left us quiet and reflective rather than jubilant.'

'On clear nights we could see well inland and had a great view of artillery fire, particularly the spectacular launches of American multiple launch rocket system (MLRS) rockets, but the greatest spectacle we witnessed was a co-ordinated Scud attack on the Dhahran area. This occurred as we were going home, and initially appeared as some sort of airborne catastrophe because the first we saw was a massive explosion in the sky way off to the right and above. This was followed by a trail of flaming debris heading earthward, and I personally thought there had been a mid-air collision (a real possibility given the number of aircraft in the sky). Soon afterwards there came more explosions (I counted five altogether), together with the sight of bright flashes on the desert floor around the city. We only later realised that the multiple flashes were the motors of the Patriot surface-to-air (SAM) missiles as they left their box launchers, and the mid-air explosions were the successful intercepts of Scuds. On CNN afterwards, the Patriot was hailed as the ultimate answer to the Scud threat but that was mostly propaganda. Certainly the interception of the Scuds was impressive, but the Patriot batteries had fired about every round they had to get those few Scuds. In any case, the damaged missile booster casings, with or without warheads, still had to come down somewhere and the potential for destruction on the ground was still there.'

'Soon after the start of the air campaign, as a security measure, we all had to move out of the "Intercon". This was a sad day, particularly as our new home was the Omani naval base at Wudam (about 40 miles up the coast from Seeb) and a whole crew of 13 had to move into a three-bedroom Omani family quarter. Still, the mess facilities at Wudam were very good, alcohol was still freely available and we were still working a routine of two nights flying, one day on standby (because of the distances involved the standby crew stayed at the Omani Air Force HQ at Lansab near Seeb) and a day free (now mostly spent sleeping off the tiring night sorties).'

Meanwhile a lot of hard work was being done installing various modifications to the Nimrod, as Duncan Milne noticed a few days after the air war began: 'Another piece of excitement came on about 21 January, when an aircraft appeared on the ramp with a whole lot of new equipment. These so-called "Granby mods" had been rushed through as a set of Urgent Operational Requirements (UORs) and were designed to enhance our operational capabilities, as well as provide a good measure of self-protection. This new gear included the Sandpiper infra-red (IR) turret and a rudimentary datalink fit (Link 11, receive only). More impressively, the aircraft now sported modern Bofors Z series (BOZ) pods under each wing, two fitted to each aircraft. These carried both large quantities of chaff ("window" in World War Two parlance) and powerful IR decoy flares. There was also the missile approach warning system (MAWS) sensors, and most radical of all, the world's first operationally deployed Towed Radar Decoy (TRD) system. On the 22nd, after some ground lectures, we flew a short familiarisation flight with the new kit, under the guidance of specialists from the Standards Unit at Kinloss. The firing of the very powerful BOZ decoy flares (at night over the Gulf of Oman) was very impressive, but resulted in UFO sightings all along the coast and headlines in the next day's papers!'

There was a tremendous effort on the part of the ground crews to keep the aircraft and new equipment 100 per cent serviceable.

At the start of February it was clear that the conflict in the air and at sea was going the Coalition's way and the ban on crew change-overs which had been in force since before the conflict was lifted and Duncan Milne and Crew Five were allowed to return home. Tom Cross and Crew Six of 206 Squadron stayed on for much longer and saw the war to its conclusion.

When the ground war started on the night of 24 February the Nimrod crews had grandstand seats and could view the entire war as it progressed – an awesome sight. After the ceasefire patrols continued along the Kuwaiti coast when the smoke from the burning oil wells dominated the horizon 'like something out of a Lowry painting'[3]. There was always the chance of a last desperate Iraqi strike. The final *Granby* sorties were flown in March 1991 by which time the veterans had mainly returned home, to be replaced by fresh crews and aircraft from Kinloss and St Mawgan. In the 'Octopus News' of March 1991 Wing Commander McLaren paid tribute to the first class job done by all the personnel during the detachment.

However British involvement in the region continued with UK participation in the multinational enforcement of UN Security Council Resolutions. The Armilla Patrol was maintained as part of an international effort to enforce the trade embargo against Iraq under the terms of various Security Council Resolutions, and Nimrod detachments continued to be called upon to reinforce maritime interdiction operations. Quite apart from oil and the need to defend free trade in the region, the UK has special interests in the area which include investments, defence exports markets and a large expatriate community.

---

3   Ibid. p51.

CHAPTER 21

1990-2001

'Work Hard, Play Hard.....'

In September 1990 the squadron participated in the Canadian International Air Show in Toronto. The detachment was led by the OC 206 Wing Commander Brian McLaren. There they met up with the ex-OC, now an Air Vice-Marshal, David Emmerson, who had been invited to open the Sunday display. AVM Emmerson returned to Kinloss with the crew via CFB Greenwood, Nova Scotia, on what was to be his last flight in a Nimrod as a serving officer.

With *Granby* successfully concluded normal operational routine at Kinloss resumed although detachments to the Middle East were by no means at an end. The 75th Anniversary of the squadron was held in June 1991 hosted at Kinloss by Wing Commander McLaren and organised by Flight Lieutenant Andy Robson.

Aird Whyte 1991
Flt Lt Macey and Crew 5 before the Competition.
No. 42 Sqn were the winners!
(CC/206)

At the end of that historic year the Soviet Union was dissolved but there was no respite for the Nimrod crews in ASW training. The Russian fleet remained active and great vigilance was still required in the northern waters. With the breakdown of the old East-West power blocs a series of new conflicts were emerging which would have implications for international security.

Several special events made 1992 a memorable year for the squadron. In March an epic tour was completed by squadron crews in the Caribbean and Central America en route to Chile to participate in FIDAE 92, the largest air and aerospace display held in South America. The year also saw a crew flying to the North Pole once again to rendezvous with US and Royal Navy submarines.

The Aird Whyte Trophy held on 14 May 1992 was won by Flight Lieutenant John 'Grimbo' Grime with Crew Five, competing against each Nimrod squadron and the Nimrod Conversion Unit – the first success of the squadron since 1977. The crew went on to represent the RAF in the inter-Commonwealth Fincastle Competition which was held at Kinloss in October with competing nations Canada, Australia and New Zealand. The crew duly won the competition for the RAF in two busy weeks of intense rivalry in the air and no doubt at the bar as well – a proud moment for the squadron.

A new Squadron Standard was presented in a parade at Kinloss by HRH Prince Philip, Duke of Edinburgh, on 21 May. Pouring rain all day did not prevent the ceremony

POLEX '92.
(CC/206)

Nº 206 SQUADRON

ROYAL AIR FORCE

PRESENTATION

OF THE

SQUADRON STANDARD

BY

HIS ROYAL HIGHNESS
PRINCE PHILIP THE DUKE OF EDINBURGH

AT

ROYAL AIR FORCE KINLOSS

THURSDAY 21st MAY 1992

Presentation of the new Squadron Standard by HRH Prince Philip, Duke of Edinburgh, on 21 May 1992.
(CC/206)

Wg Cdr Brian McLaren, OC 206, leads parade through Forres on Saturday 6 June 1992, on the occasion of RAF Kinloss being awarded the Freedom of Moray.
(CC/206)

'Back seat driver' gets command of Nimrod

THE first woman to captain an RAF maritime patrol aircraft took command of her crew yesterday as a "back seat driver".

Flt Lt Sarah Heycock, 30, has been a navigator on 206 Squadron's Nimrod MR2, based at RAF Kinloss, Morayshire, for three years.

In that time she has plotted the aircraft's course through everything from routine maritime patrols around Scotland's shores to United Nations operations in the former Yugoslavia.

And because the captain of a Nimrod does not have to be the pilot, Flt Lt Heycock has been promoted to take charge of the £70 million aircraft with its crew of 11 men and one other woman.

"The job of a navigator on this aircraft is probably one of the best in the RAF," she said at the start of a sea and air exercise.

"It is very demanding as a tactical navigator. There are two navigators on the aircraft and when you are in the tactical seat you effectively run the show,

Picture: PA

In command: Flt Lt Sarah Heycock on board her Nimrod aircraft yesterday

Flight Lieutenant Sarah Heycock, 206 Squadron.
(CC/206)

passing off well and the day was concluded with a rousing barn dance. The old Squadron Standard was laid up in Kinloss Parish Church on 19 July. On 6 June the station was honoured with the Freedom of Moray, and the squadron formed the heart of the parade through Forres. The *Forres Gazette* commented on the occasion:

'.....The Freedom is being conferred in recognition of the Nimrod airfield's outstanding service to the country both in peace and war and its contribution to the richness of life in Moray........Irrespective of nationality or whether the casualty is civilian or military, the presence of an RAF Nimrod overhead in times of emergency at sea is one of the most reassuring sights people in danger will see. Thousands of people, from light plane pilots and yachtsmen to fishermen and cargo ship crews owe the men and women of RAF Kinloss an incredible debt.....Every time a Nimrod flies, it takes a little bit of Moray with it.'

The month of July saw the retirement of Master Air Electronics Operator (MAEOp) Mick Muttitt after 40 years' service in the RAF – earlier in the year on 6 January Mick had completed 15,000 flying hours. In August 206 became the first front line squadron to be joined by a female crew member, Flight Lieutenant Sarah Heycock, who had started training as a navigator in 1989 when the RAF opened its doors to female aircrew. She was now in post as second navigator, later to achieve another record as the first female Nimrod captain in October 1996.

At the start of September Flight Lieutenant 'Grimbo' Grime, the display pilot, along with Crew Five deployed to Toronto for the Canadian International Air Show. Air Commodore Joseph commented about the occasion:

' "Grimbo" Grime was one of the most popular squadron members who successfully balanced a larger than life character with excellent piloting and captaincy skills. During the Toronto airshow, he and Crew Five decided to put the foreign fast-jet display teams in their place by making the notorious video "A Day in the Life of a Nimrod Display Pilot" and playing it at a major aircrew briefing event, with the prior permission of the UK Assistant Chief of the Air Staff (ACAS) who was in attendance. Needless to say, the video was designed purely to lampoon the other display crews, which it did most successfully. The only condition laid down by ACAS was that the video (and all copies) was to be destroyed afterwards – it was!'

As usual this event was combined with charity work, visiting the Sick Children's Hospital in Toronto to raffle Scottish goods (mostly Scotch) to raise money for essential equipment. Over Ca $6,000 was raised in what was a very worthwhile occasion.

The logical working through of *Options for Change*, mentioned earlier, and the parallel restructuring and retrenchment of the armed forces were beginning to be felt at the sharp end. One sign of this was the consolidation of the Nimrod force at Kinloss. Thus in October 1992 additional personnel and an extra seven aircraft arrived at Kinloss as No. 42 Squadron at St Mawgan was disbanded. Instead No. 236 Operational Conversion Unit (OCU) was renamed the Nimrod Operational Conversion Unit No. 42 (reserve) Squadron and was now based at Kinloss. The task of winding up No. 42 Squadron fell to Wing Commander R. W. Joseph, a navigator, who proceeded to replace Wing Commander Brian McLaren as CO of 206 Squadron on 23 October. A new station commander was appointed at RAF Kinloss, Group Captain Andrew Neal.

Towards the end of 1992 there was a new deployment, to the Naval Air Station at Sigonella in Sicily in Operation *Sharp Guard*, previously known as *Maritime Guard*, to operate in the Adriatic enforcing the United Nations arms embargo of the Federal Republic of Yugoslavia. After the death of President Tito, Yugoslavia had begun to fragment into its various national groupings and Serbia and Montenegro had formed a new Federal Republic of Yugoslavia in 1992. Under Slobodan Milosevic the new republic had undertaken military adventures in neighbouring states including Bosnia-Herzegovina as part of a scheme of creating a 'Greater Serbia' – with all the horrors of 'ethnic cleansing'. This had led to the UN embargo which was the start of many multinational deployments to the region, of which the Nimrod detachments were part. As the name suggests *Sharp Guard* was in response to a deteriorating situation in the region and maritime patrol aircraft (MPA) began to fly armed with warshot torpedoes and defensive aids. The first 206 deployment took place from 17 November to 2 December 1992 with Wing Commander Joseph as detachment commander. Bob Joseph recalled that he arrived back at Kinloss with Squadron Leader 'H' Nockolds and Crew Six to a blaze of publicity with reporters and television crews present on the tarmac. The deployment was shared with the US Navy and Portuguese P-3 Orions and continued into 1993, 1994 and 1995. Many vessels were challenged by 206 crews with some being boarded by UN inspectors or escorted into Italian ports to have their cargoes searched.

Later in December 1992 Wing Commander Joseph flew General S. F. Rodrigues, the Indian Chief of General Staff, on a Nimrod sortie and, on 5 January 1993, a 206 Squadron crew captained by Flight Lieutenant 'Rick' Richards flew media reporters and cameramen to the wreck of the *Braer*, an oil tanker that came ashore on the Shetland islands and spilt thousands of tons of oil into the sea and on to the northern beaches with a tremendous impact on the local wildlife. The 206 Squadron pictures made the front pages of all the national newspapers and the television footage was beamed around the globe.

In April 1993 Exercise *Rum Punch* was held at Jacksonville Naval Air Station in Florida, USA, from which the squadron practised at the Atlantic Undersea Test and Evaluation Centre (AUTEC) range in the Bahamas. Live tracking was carried out against a Royal Navy nuclear submarine culminating in the deployment of Sting Ray torpedoes (live but without warheads!). During May Exercise *Linked Seas* took place in Gibraltar and a variety of displays were on the agenda for the display pilot Flight Lieutenant Duncan Milne and his crew throughout the year, including the Confederate Air Force Display in Midland, Texas, later in the year.

The history of the squadron was not neglected during a period of many 50th anniversaries associated with the Second World War, one being that of the Battle of the Atlantic held in Liverpool during May 1993 in which the squadron association participated. Wing Commander Joseph commented: 'The memories of the march through the streets of Liverpool and the magnificent service in the Anglican Cathedral will remain with us forever.' Bob Joseph continued: 'Whilst at Liverpool, the then Air Officer Commanding 18 Group, Air Marshal Sir John 'Win' Harris, had presented me with a unique challenge which was to get on board the visiting Russian Sovremennyy class destroyer *Gremyashchy* and present a framed colour picture of the ship taken by 206 Squadron as she transited south. The mission was successful.'

On 1 July 1993 Bob Joseph was promoted to group captain but remained on the squadron as CO, a fairly unusual situation but one that was very popular with squadron members who regarded a group captain 'boss' as having extra 'top cover', something which proved vital after the squadron party to celebrate the promotion, as Bob Joseph recalled: 'During the party, the squadron mini metro car was introduced into the coffee bar with lights flashing and horn blazing. Needless to say, the car sustained slight damage (actually on the way out) and the Police Report of 2 July made an interesting read – squadron morale was extremely high at this point.'

It was during this period that Group Captain Joseph instigated a 206 Squadron affiliation with Alastrean House, the RAF Benevolent Fund residential home at Tarland in Aberdeenshire. This relationship remains strong today with the squadron regularly visiting the veterans to boost their morale and provide the occasional party. Closer to home efforts were being made to establish liaison with the town of Nairn to reinforce already very good relations with the area in general.

The 365-day per year commitment to Search and Rescue, shared with the other two squadrons at Kinloss, produced many incidents which did not always hit the headlines. In February 1994 six crews from the squadron flew a 36-hour mission when the MV *Christinaki* sank 240 miles south-west of Cornwall. In what were later described as the worst conditions ever seen there were no survivors.

In March Group Captain Joseph commanded a deployment to the Falkland Islands, designed to practise the Nimrod's ability to support the Islands in times of crisis. This was a welcome task for the crews as their

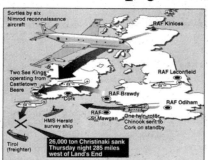

Sea rescuers brave eye of a hurricane to find empty raft

By Paul Stokes

THE 27-man crew of a cargo ship were feared drowned last night after a dramatic search by RAF reconnaissance aircraft and helicopters found nothing but a broken liferaft and empty survival suits.

Battling against heavy seas and a "hurricane", six RAF Nimrods and two helicopters, assisted by the Royal Navy survey ship Herald and the Austrian freighter Tirol, scoured an area of the Atlantic 285 miles south-west of Land's End for the 26,000-ton Christinaki.

But rescuers said it was unlikely the crew of the Greek-registered ship would have been able to live for more than a few minutes unless they were in survival suits, rafts or boats.

Two orange suits were recovered yesterday afternoon by one of the Nimrods. Debris, including a lifebelt, an empty liferaft and the remains of a smashed lifeboat, was seen in the water.

The ship, with 22 Filipino and five Greek crew on board, was carrying scrap metal from Liverpool to Veracruz, Mexico, when she sent out a mayday on Thursday afternoon saying she was shipping water after losing a hatch cover. Rescue operations began within minutes, but were hampered by 40 ft-high waves and winds of up to 70 mph.

Ms Jenny Mountstephens, spokeswoman for RAF Brawdy, said helicopter pilot Sqdn Leader Jerry English and his three crew had experienced the worst conditions they had ever known.

"When they came back, all they could talk about was the 50 ft swell and huge waves on top of that and the wind was force 12. Quite simply, they flew straight into the eye of a hurricane," Lights seen in the water by the Tirol and one of the Nimrods overnight are now thought to have come from the ship's empty liferaft.

Cdr Tim Sewell, captain of the Herald, said last night the search would continue even though there was little hope of finding survivors. He said: "The Tirol found an empty liferaft and we have come across small amounts of debris."

A Falmouth coastguard said last night the search area had been extended with the use of a French Air Force long-range reconnaisance aircraft.

SAR to the *Christinaki*, February 1994. There were no survivors.
(CC/206)

presence usually coincided with the deployment of other Royal Navy surface and sub-surface assets. Whilst there Bob Joseph flew in a Tornado F3 and intercepted Flight Lieutenant 'Stumpy' Davies and Crew Nine!

A memorable event took place on 8 April when Squadron Leader Bill Speight, Air Engineer Leader, achieved his 10,000 hours in the air (he later clocked up 15,000 hours in August 2003). On the operational side Group Captain Joseph commanded, as task force commander, the Nimrod Wing's first ever deployed Tactical Evaluation exercise (TACEVAL) at RAF St Mawgan, with crews from all three Kinloss squadrons and other RAF units. This was the first large-scale deployed TACEVAL undertaken by the RAF which involved the bringing together of several units and capabilities at a remote 'bare-base' site simulating a location far overseas. The exercise was successful and 'little did we know the extent to which RAF operations would become involved in deployments of this sort in the years to come.'[1]

In July Wing Commander S. D. 'Stu' Butler, an ex-206 man, took over command of the squadron from Group Captain Joseph who now became station commander at Kinloss. It was another year of 'work hard, play hard' as squadron routine was combined with many social functions, according to *Octopus News* 1995.

Various anniversaries were celebrated – the Nimrod's 25th at RAF Kinloss on 11 November 1994, attended by senior British Aerospace (BAe) representatives. During the celebration dinner Kevin Smith, then Managing Director of the BAe Military Aircraft Systems Division, presented the station with a magnificent sterling silver Nimrod MR2 model. Earlier that day Kinloss had been presented with the Wilkinson Sword of Peace by the Chief of the Air Staff Air Chief Marshal Sir Michael Graydon. This award was in recognition of the work of the station in 'enhancing the good name of the Royal Air Force in the field of humanitarian activities' due to the SAR role and the work of the Mountain Rescue Team. Nor was the squadron's own history neglected when on 15 November a Nimrod carried out a flypast at Sumburgh 50 years to the day when Jack Frost landed his battle-damaged Liberator there in 1944, having gallantly fought off three Me 110s (see Chapter 9).

On the operational side November 1994 saw another Exercise *Magic Roundabout* detachment to Seeb in Oman. This involved patrols of the Omani Exclusion Zone and assisting Anglo-Omani relations, not to mention a lively mixed-ranks guest night close to the swimming pool of the Seeb Intercontinental Hotel which resulted in several damp aircrew, including the CO! The team effort involved in these detachments was reinforced by improved liaison with the Nimrod Line Squadron (NLS) North or 'lineys', one of two servicing lines at Kinloss. The outcome of these links was a closer understanding between air and ground crews as each gained a better insight into mutual problems.

The annual routine towards the end of 1994 included anti-submarine exercises like *Jolly Roger*, deployed to Gibraltar in conjunction with the Dutch and Americans. Another *Rum Punch* in Florida involved four crews in October and November summed up by the CO as 'being about as good as it gets for real anti-submarine training' with the Royal Navy 'volunteering' a submarine to be tracked and ultimately attacked using real torpedoes (minus warheads!).[2]

Christmas and Hogmanay 1994 was a busy period for SAR activity, with eight of the nine squadron crews being scrambled. Two crews were detached under the command of the CO to RAF Lyneham when poor weather was forecasted for Kinloss. In fact the predicted snow missed Kinloss altogether and fell at Lyneham!

After 14 accident-free years there were two during 1995. On 16 May a Nimrod R1

---

1 Air Cdre R. W. Joseph.
2 *206 Squadron Octopus News* August 1995, Wg Cdr S. D. Butler.

Crash in Moray Firth of XW666, May 1995.
(Stu Butler)

A Nimrod provides top cover in transfer of a sick Russian sailor from a Victor III-Class
submarine to a Sea King helicopter, February 1996.
(CC/206)

XW666 of No. 51 Squadron ditched in the Moray Firth when both starboard engines caught fire during a test flight. The aircraft was normally based at RAF Waddington but had been operating out of Kinloss. All seven of the crew were rescued in an incident which was a testimony to the skill of the captain and crew as well as the tough and enduring quality of the by now aged Nimrod's airframe. Wing Commander Butler, CO of the squadron, was appointed President of the resulting Board of Inquiry. The loss of XW666 came at an unfortunate time, just as the R1 fleet was engaged in monitoring the no-fly zone over Bosnia and urgent steps had to be taken by British Aerospace to modify another aircraft for the role.

On 2 September MR2 XV239 of 120 Squadron captained by Flight Lieutenant D. Gilbert crashed into Lake Ontario during the Canadian International Airshow at Toronto. The aircraft sank immediately and tragically all seven of the crew were killed. The losses were felt keenly by all at Kinloss.

Mindful of the ASW role of 206, the end of the Cold War had not banished the Russian fleet from the northern waters. A surprising reminder of this was the scrambling

Sonia Nancy SAR, January 1998. Nimrod crew commended by the Spanish.
(CC/206)

of Crew Six in failing February light during 1996 to assist in the 'medivac' of a Russian sailor with appendicitis from a Victor III-class nuclear-powered submarine 200 miles north-west of Scotland. When the sub had reached the agreed rendezvous point the Nimrod monitored the winching of the sick sailor to a Sea King helicopter and escorted the boat away from UK shores. The incident even reached the Russian newspapers!

History once again came to the fore in the 80th Anniversary reunion of the squadron held at Kinloss at the end of August 1996, when the squadron gained the first of its '206 Anniversary Tails' with three aircraft ultimately getting a new, yet temporary, paint job. Many friends and former squadron members attended in what was a memorable gathering. In December there was once again a change of command with Wing Commander Butler handing over to Wing Commander S. N. Skinner, to spend a year away in Australia before returning as OC Kinloss.

The ability to handle successfully an emergency in the air was tested in February 1997 when Crew Six captained by Flight Lieutenant Chris Ouston, Air Electronics Officer (AEO), was returning from a Mediterranean detachment and the aircraft suffered a severe hydraulic failure and other serious problems. On the flight deck were 1st pilot Flight Lieutenant Sid Vallance with co-pilot Flight Lieutenant Kev Hughes and engineer Flight Sergeant 'Leakey' Lomax. The decision was made to divert to Lyon International Airport where a successful landing was made. Later the crew received flying awards for their skill and airmanship.

Also during 1997 Flight Lieutenant Seymour-Dale won the ASW Competition and Aird Whyte Trophy, subsequently going on to represent the RAF in the Fincastle Trophy at Comox, Vancouver Island, in October. The crew came a very close second to an aircraft of No. 5 Squadron, Royal New Zealand Air Force, but earned much admiration for the enthusiasm and spirit they showed throughout the event. In 1997 and 1998 regular detachments overseas included Sicily, the Falklands, Iceland, Oman, Canada and Gibraltar.

The start of the year 1998 was marked by two remarkable SAR missions, the first which began on 31 December to assist the bulk carrier MV *Oak* whose cargo above decks had shifted and was listing up to 40 degrees in atrocious weather. The vessel was 600 miles west of Shannon with a crew of 26. The captain was concerned that his ship might capsize if the vessel turned to beam in the high sea state. Three sorties were flown as 'top cover' and stand-by should the need arise for dinghy drops. At last at 0916 a.m. on 3 January the captain sent a message of thanks and congratulations to the crews that all was now well.

On Sunday 4 January the Spanish trawler *Sonia Nancy* began to take in water and had lost engine power. The fishing boat with its crew of 10 were 200 miles south of Cork and once again the weather conditions were appalling with 100 ft waves and an 80-knot wind to contend with. The squadron flew a total of three sorties to the stricken vessel dropping some dinghies and vectoring a Sea King helicopter from RAF Chivenor to the scene. It was a remarkable feat for the Sea King crew to winch off the crewmen safely in such conditions. Both these incidents brought great credit and praise for the efforts of the crews involved, with personal letters of thanks from Glenda Jackson MP, Parliamentary Under-Secretary for Transport, the Rt Hon. George Robertson MP, the Secretary of State for Defence, and the Spanish Ambassador. In addition Flight Lieutenant Kev Hughes and Crew Six, the first crew to arrive at the incident, received a Commendation for their actions from the Air Officer Commanding-in-Chief.[3]

Also in January 1998 a deployment was ordered of one crew to Florida for SAR duties, to provide cover for a detachment of GR7 Harriers on their return to the UK via Bermuda and Lajes, Azores. From 9 to 26 April two crews were deployed together with supporting ground crew to San Diego, California, for Exercise *Joint Fleetex 98-1*. The crews were captained by Flight Lieutenants Dave Harris and John Meston and were deployed by way of Halifax, Nova Scotia, where one crew was forced to spend a weekend under heavy snow due to a technical problem. With the aircraft finally at San Diego sorties were flown in support of the carrier USS *Abraham Lincoln* in a scenario based on a possible Gulf War. Well over 30 ships took part, mainly US Navy, including four Los Angeles-class nuclear submarines along with multinational maritime patrol aircraft (MPA) from Australia, Canada and the United States. The exercise was a unique opportunity for the Nimrods to work with a multinational force of MPA as well as the US Navy.[4]

The 'work hard, play hard' ethic was again demonstrated on 26 April when ten members of the squadron including the CO Wing Commander Steve Skinner participated in the London Marathon to raise money for a group of charities including the Malcolm Sargent Cancer Fund for Children. All the runners completed the course and a total of £5,000 was raised including £700 from the 206 Squadron Association.

For the second year running Flight Lieutenant Seymour-Dale won the RAF ASW Competition and the Aird Whyte Trophy, going on to represent the RAF in the Fincastle Competition which was held at RAAF Edinburgh in Adelaide, South Australia from 7 to 14 November. Two aircraft set out (one as back-up), XV231 and XV245, but on this occasion the competition was won by the New Zealand team flying a P-3K Orion. However valuable training experience was gained in a round the world tour taking in far-flung locations such as Hawaii, Fiji, Guam, Japan, Manila, Singapore and the Maldives.

Training detachments during 1998 and 1999 provided essential experience in both ASW and Anti-Surface Unit Warfare (ASUW). Such deployments included Sicily, Oman, Gibraltar, Crete and Lann Bihoue in Lorient, France. SAR cover was provided for Tornado F3 fighters based in the Falklands. However Exercise *Rum Punch* was the most notable

---

3   *Octopus News* July 1998, Wg Cdr Steve Skinner.
4   *Royal Air Force News* 26 June 1998.

event involving five crews deploying to Florida to practise their ASW skills on the American Underwater Training Evaluation Centre in the Caribbean.

Probably a less welcome but equally essential event in the 206 calendar was the Annual Standardisation Visit from the 'Trappers' in June 1999. This appeared to be successful with a number of above average assessments being given. Crew Six, now captained by Flight Lieutenant Mark Bradshaw, was classed as 'Combat Ready Advanced' (the same as the former B Cat. Crew). Two other captains, Squadron Leaders Richie Ross and Simon Collier, were recommended for A Cat. status. Only a month later, in July, Wing Commander Tom Cross took over command of the squadron from Wing Commander Steve Skinner, now promoted to the rank of group captain and destined to take over from Group Captain Butler as OC RAF Kinloss.

The 12-month period from July 1999 to July 2000 saw 206 Squadron amassing over 3,000 flying hours by participating in 11 operations, 22 exercises and 7 overseas SAR deployments. In addition there were 15 SAR missions from Kinloss. The exercises included two in Norway, one of which was termed 'Partnership for Peace' as it included many of the former communist Eastern Bloc nations such as Poland. Other deployments took 206 crews to the United Arab Emirates, Oman, Sweden , Brazil, the Caribbean and Malaysia. The Malaysian detachment took three crews to participate in Exercise *Flying Fish* during June 2000. The destination was Penang via Sicily, Oman and Sri Lanka and the exercise itself involved maritime units from Malaysia, Singapore, Australia, New Zealand and the UK. Much of the flying took place over the South China Sea and valuable experience for air and ground crew was gained as well as colourful memories of night life on Penang Island! Closer to home was the Joint Maritime Course series of exercises which enabled crews to hone their ASW and ASUW skills and provided valuable training time liaising with naval vessels.

One of the notable SAR missions during the period was flown on 13 March in support of the Stornoway Coastguard Helicopter which had been called out to pick up a sailor suffering from an eye injury from the French fishing vessel *Bisson* 178 miles west of Stornoway. Flight Lieutenant Iain Macmillan and Crew Two were first on the scene and located the vessel, vectoring in the helicopter to the limit of its range, providing top cover while the rescue took place and shadowing the helicopter until it was safely back in Stornoway.[5]

The diversity of the squadron's activities was well illustrated by events during the 12 months from August 2000 to August 2001. The core skills of a maritime unit like 206 continued to centre around ASW, ASUW and SAR and various deployments around the world gave ample scope for these tasks. As always, training time with vessels from the Royal Navy and other European navies proved valuable although it was often difficult to procure submarines in the right place at the right time, which often resulted in the need to transit to the South West Approaches and the Channel to fulfil training schedules. Once again over 3,000 hours were flown by the squadron in the 12-month period, including 8 operations, 21 exercises, 8 overseas SARs and 20 SARs around UK shores. The 1999 Wilkinson Sword of Peace was presented to RAF Kinloss once again in a ceremony on 5 October 2000, an honour shared by all the squadrons there.

From 14 October to 1 November 2000 two aircraft and crews headed for Jacksonville, Florida, to take part in the annual Exercise *Unified Spirit*. En route one aircraft had to make an emergency descent to Bangor, Maine, due to smoke in the cabin but the trip was successfully completed the following day. The exercise took in almost the entire eastern seaboard of the USA with the aim of practising tactics in attack and defence. The Nimrods provided direct support to a carrier battle group headed by the

---

5   *Octopus News* July 2000, Wg Cdr Tom Cross.

Harry S. Truman and useful training was gained in ASW and ASUW skills. Other skills in singing and drum work were practised in 'The Harmonious Monk', a watering hole favoured by the Nimrod crews.

In March 2001 two crews were involved in the rescue of fishermen from the Spanish fishing vessel *Hansa* which had begun to take in water late one evening and had sunk by midnight. Life rafts were dropped by the crews to survivors in complete darkness and a nearby ship was directed to the location. Also top cover was provided for an RAF Sea King helicopter. Ten out of sixteen fishermen were saved – one surviving for several hours until spotted by a 201 Squadron aircraft.

The overseas deployments included visits to Spain, the USA, Canada, Norway, Oman, Bahrain and the Caribbean. Every opportunity was taken on these expeditions to train with the new aircraft equipment such as the Link 11 data-link system and the new acoustic processor. Exercise *Blue Game* off the coast of Norway provided training in ASUW skills close inshore against fast patrol boat targets – the type of task increasingly demanded of the squadron. There was also the regular Exercise *Magic Roundabout* in Oman helping the authorities there police the Exclusion Zone. Experience gained in that area of the world was to have immense value as events were soon to prove. The Caribbean deployment involved three crews for six weeks and offered a useful opportunity to work closely with US and Dutch allies as well as Royal Navy vessels.

One of the highlights of 2001 was the 85th Anniversary reunion held at Kinloss in May. Participation was also being planned for an August trip to Archangel in Russia to coincide with events commemorating the Arctic convoys of the Second World War. The plan was for a 206 Squadron Nimrod to carry out a flypast at the war memorial dedicated to those who died in the convoys.

Further deployments during the year were planned for the Falklands and Iceland but the events of 11 September 2001 ('9/11') overshadowed all our lives and added another dimension in what was termed the 'War Against Terror', a struggle which continues today and whose final chapter is yet to be written.

Wing Commander Tom Cross, soon promoted to group captain, relinquished command of the squadron at the end of the year, being replaced by Wing Commander Andy Flint who took up his post in January 2002. The squadron was in excellent shape and ready to meet some very daunting challenges in the period which lay ahead.

CHAPTER 22

THE FUTURE 2002 -

'We were on our way to Saudi Arabia, via RAF Akrotiri, to complete the most taxing and dangerous operations since the Nimrod's introduction in the 1970s.'

Wing Commander A. P. Flint, OC 206 Squadron and Operation *Telic* Nimrod Detachment Commander, March to April 2003.

The aftermath of 11 September 2001 produced the greatest operational effort 206 Squadron had experienced in many years. The global war on terrorism and Operation *Veritas* or *Enduring Freedom*, led to the deployment of all the crews at different times to the Gulf region – usually two crews at any one time. The crews are no strangers to harsh living conditions but to describe them as 'basic' would be an understatement. Daytime temperatures could rise to 45 degrees celsius and crews of 13, including females, would often be living in one tent without air-conditioning. Later on portacabins were introduced with comfortable beds and improved washing and toilet facilities. Operational sorties include patrols over the Gulf of Oman, the Arabian Sea and Afghanistan in support of coalition forces.

The concept of an 'Expeditionary Air Force' has been demonstrated yet again in many parts of the world, where deployments have been made to locations as diverse as the Caribbean, the Falkland Islands, and Bahrain. The annual round of exercises in ASW and ASUW techniques continued. Exercise *Dogfish* in the spring of 2002 held at the Naval Air Station Sigonella in Sicily once again involved ships and aircraft from many other NATO countries. Crews gained useful experience in using the new acoustic processor. Later in the spring the ASW exercise *Rum Punch* took place at the underwater range in the Bahamas, assisted by the participation of a Royal Navy submarine.[1]

SAR duties had to be combined with all these commitments, tasks which stretched all personnel of the squadron to the full. On a pleasant note Flight Lieutenant Duncan Milne was selected to captain the Nimrod flypast during the Queen's Golden Jubilee Flypast over Buckingham Palace on 4 June 2002.

Earlier in the year everyone associated with the squadron were saddened by the death of Alan Smith on 5 March 2002, the secretary of the Association, whose work over so many years had helped to create the family atmosphere among past and present members of the squadron and their families. Moving tributes were paid to him in a Service of Thanksgiving held at St Clement Danes, the Central Church of the Royal Air Force, on 12 September. The squadron later conducted a 'Scattering of Ashes' ceremony over the Pentland Firth as a fitting tribute to Alan's life and work. In addition Wing Commander Andy Flint decided to perpetuate Alan's memory by awarding an annual trophy to be called the 'Alan Smith Trophy' to the best ASW crew in the squadron. It was also sad to record the death of Life Vice-President Wing Commander J. C. Graham DFC and Bar on 19 July, a staunch supporter of the Association over the years and source of much advice and inspiration to Alan Smith. The author is much indebted to 'JC's' hospitality and advice in the preparation of this book, which included an informative joint visit to the Public Record Office at Kew (now the National Archives).

---

1   *Octopus News* July 2002, Wg Cdr Andy Flint.

Parade at St Omer, Remembrance Day 11 November 2002.
Back row L to R:
Sgt Paul Chadwick; Sqn Ldr Graham House; Sgt Paul Palmer; Flt Lt Gary Laing; Sgt Paul Marr; Sgt Colin Denby;
Flt Lt Duncan Milne
Front row:
Flt Lt Pete Deeney; Lt Dave Simms RN; Sgt Adrian Flanagan; Sgt Ian Sinski; Sgt Adrian Cooper; Sgt Saul 'Jake'
Thackeray; SAC Mat Brown; Flt Lt Tom Talbot; Sgt Mark Walker

In keeping with the squadron motto 'Naught Escapes Us' some 13 squadron members led by Squadron Leader Graham 'Sheds' House, Flight Lieutenant Tom Talbot, squadron historian, and Flight Lieutenant Duncan Milne, paid a visit to St-Omer in the Pas-de-Calais from 7 to 11 November, to participate in Remembrance Ceremonies in the town and to visit some of the sites associated with the early history of No. 6 (Naval) Squadron/No. 206 Squadron RAF in the Great War. The journey began in brilliant sunshine at Dover, the original birthplace of the squadron, and a Nimrod performed a flypast as the SeaFrance ferry plied its way across the Channel. The story seemed to have come full circle!

Towards the end of 2002 serious operational matters once again came to the fore, this time with the increased tension in the Middle East over Saddam Hussein and Iraq. As the country looked forward to the 2002 festive season the squadron at Kinloss were preparing crews for standby for deployment to the Gulf region. Pre-deployment activities included gun firing practice and equipment checking and training. In particular there was intensive Nuclear, Biological and Chemical (NBC) training and to ensure full medical fitness of all crews, the required vaccinations were given including, at the choice of personnel, anthrax.

The preparations went ahead in double quick time, allowing the squadron little opportunity for Christmas festivities. The heightened state of readiness continued during the prolonged period of political uncertainty in early 2003. No deployment could take place until the go-ahead was given by the government. Also there was at this stage no base in the Gulf where it had been agreed that the crews and aircraft could deploy. Thus an intensive period of preparation and training was interwoven with inactivity and anticipation. Wing Commander Flint continued:

'By the time the order was received, I had assumed command of the detachment and eventually – after a great deal of "on-the-bus-off-the-bus" – the first of the aircraft to deploy to the Gulf region left RAF Kinloss on 4 March 2003. The remaining aircraft arrived in theatre a few days later and by 8 March the Nimrod force was ready and able to enter the fray (in Operation *Telic*). We were on our way to Saudi Arabia, via RAF Akrotiri, to complete the most taxing and dangerous operations since the Nimrod's introduction in the 1970s. Fitted with a new electro-optical device, the WESCAM MX-15, under the starboard wing, the crews had only managed one flight each with the new equipment to familiarise themselves with its operation prior to deployment. Indeed, I remember as I transited over the Nile reading on the manufacturer's operating instructions for the new kit – "Congratulations on your purchase of the WESCAM MX-15...."'

The inactivity experienced at home continued for a time at the new base in Saudi Arabia where the detachment found itself at some distance from their usual operating area. There had been a rush to deploy but little formalised mission planning had been possible. Thus the first few days were spent trying to integrate the Nimrod force into Operation *Southern Watch*, an operation which had been in place since the 1991 Gulf War whose primary aim was to patrol the southern no-fly zone over Iraq. Eventually, after a number of frustrations, the mission plans were finally being completed, as Wing Commander Flint relates: 'The complicated and very busy airspace was successfully negotiated and the crews experienced an extremely steep learning curve to get to grips with the airspace control procedures and the tactics involved with our new capability.'

On the night hostilities broke out, 19 March, the detachment personnel were glued to the TV, much as the families and the rest of the nation were at home, to watch the events unfolding in Baghdad. The Nimrod's mission was a vital one, as is indicated by the following example, summarised by Wing Commander Flint:

'The crew was tasked to provide support to UK Ground Forces as they entered Iraq by searching for, and reporting, any enemy activity. On arrival in the area it was quickly ascertained that there were targets of interest, and that vehicles deemed to be hostile were moving south. The enemy activity was urgently relayed and air strikes were conducted against these targets by coalition aircraft. Also during this time, the Nimrod was able to identify and report friendly forces, signified by "counter fratricide" symbols, thus preventing any possible blue-on-blue incident from taking place. As the war progressed the Nimrod found itself in the most inhospitable environment in which it had ever operated, flying over land with a clear and present threat from beneath them. On a number of occasions the aircraft patrolling high above Iraq came under fire from both ground artillery and unguided surface-to-air missiles, fortunately with little effect. That said, there were many ashen faces from the returning crews who had experienced fire for the first time. Despite this, all crews operated with professionalism and fortitude in the face of enemy activity.'

Fortunately the war was drawing to a close – a lot sooner than many had thought likely – and after much discussion it was decided that the Nimrod presence in theatre would no longer be required. In the middle of April, the aircraft and crews returned to a warm welcome from family, friends, colleagues and the press in Kinloss.

The Nimrod deployment had lasted for just short of two months in a hostile and entirely alien environment, the normal environment being of course the sea and not the land. The aircraft had proved its worth in a high intensity war zone, as testified by Wing Commander Flint: 'All crews from RAF Kinloss, including those from 206 Squadron, had acquitted themselves with great honour and fortitude. My personal memories are many and diverse. The protracted deployment was understandable given the political sensitivities; however, once integrated into the overall mission many quickly saw the great advantage that our new capability provided. The austere settings were quickly got to grips with and all pulled together to provide a service to forces on the ground. But equipment aside, as with any campaign it was the individuals, from the ground crew to the aircrew pulling together, who were the key in ensuring that the mission was completed and that the Nimrod was covered in glory during the operations. It goes without saying that I was relieved to return with the same number of personnel as I deployed with. The experience has been a highlight of my 20 years in the Royal Air Force, one which I have no wish to repeat but am grateful to have had the opportunity.'[2]

The future – Nimrod MRA4

At the time of going to press there are great hopes for the latest version of the Nimrod, the MRA4, which is eagerly awaited at Kinloss. The story of the MRA4 has its origins in Staff Requirement (Air) SRA420 in 1992 for a replacement maritime patrol aircraft (RMPA). Entries in the ensuing competition included Lockheed's upgraded P3 Orion, now designated Orion 2000, Loral's Valkyrie, and BAe's Nimrod 2000 based on the present Nimrod airframe and basic layout. The Nimrod 2000 was selected and the contract was signed to produce 21 of the aircraft, designated the MRA4 in 1997. Initially the fuselages of three aircraft in store at Kinloss were flown to FR Aviation Ltd in Bournemouth for structural rebuilding before being transported to BAe at Warton for the fitting of the avionics systems being developed by Boeing and for flight testing. Rolls Royce were contracted to supply the BR 710 Turbofan engines.

The changes in the new Nimrod incorporate some of the latest developments in aviation technology. The MRA4 is to be heavier than the present aircraft due to the greater fuel capacity of the larger wing which, combined with the greater fuel economy of the new engine, will produce an endurance of between 12 and 14 hours.

Probably the most sweeping change is on the flight deck with the 'glass' cockpit, operated by the flight deck crew of two, eliminating the need for a flight engineer. The crew will monitor the flight and engine data by means of various screens which will enable them to manage aircraft performance, assimilate weather trends, tactical data and communications, including the Traffic Collision Alerting System and Enhanced Ground Proximity Warning System. The mission crew of eight will consist of five sensor operators, a communications manager and two Tactical Coordinators (TACCOS). The team will manage the integrated suite which comprises radar, ESM, and acoustics. The latter will have two workstations which will enable the operators to monitor up to 64 sonobuoys compared with 16 in the MR2. In addition the crew will manage the Electro Optical Detection System (EOSDS), Magnetic Anomaly Detection (MAD), the latter being the only system retained from the MR2, and the Defensive Aids Sub-system (DASS). This latter device integrates missile and radar warning systems with chaff and flare dispensers and a towed radar decoy, which will provide better self-defence than for any previous MPA. The integrated design permits each of the sensors except for the acoustics to be accessed from any of the five workstations. A new communications system has been designed and the aircraft's offensive capability improved with a greater emphasis on an 'anti-surface' attack role with up to nine Stingray torpedoes, two Harpoon anti-ship missiles or 11 dinghies in the bomb bay, not to mention missile-carrying capacity. Hence the designation 'MRA' – 'Maritime Reconnaissance and Attack' which has been chosen for the new Nimrod.[3]

BAe were contracted to have the first MRA4 entering service by April 2003, but due to technical difficulties and the increase in costs the earliest expected date was put at 2005, and in more recent days 2007, with the number of aircraft in line for modification reduced from 21 to 18.[4] It is planned that No. 120 Squadron will be the first to convert, with 206 the last.

From the perspective of 2004, eighty-eight years does not represent much time in terms of the span of human history, but it requires a gigantic leap in the imagination to compare the technology of the Nimrod MRA4 with that of the Nieuport Scout, the first aircraft flown by No. 6 (Naval) Squadron from 1916-1917, with its 110 horse-power Le Rhone engine and maximum speed of 107 mph, and single Lewis machine-gun for armament!

---

2   I am indebted to Wg Cdr A. P. Flint MSc, BA for this report, dated Sept. 2003.
3   'Nimrod MRA4' article in 206's 85th Anniversary journal, May 2001, by Flt Lt Jon Bowland.
4   Sunday Telegraph report 3/11/02.

POSTSCRIPT

THE 206 SQUADRON ASSOCIATION, REUNIONS AND ANNIVERSARIES

Squadron Reunion, 1970.
(CC/206)

After the squadron was disbanded in 1920 there were a number of reunions of veterans under the title 'No. 6 Squadron RNAS & No. 206 Squadron RAF, OCA (Old Comrades' Association).' A typical one was the Fifth Annual Reunion on 13 October 1928 at W. H. Hill & Son's Restaurant, Ludgate Hill, London EC4 at 7 p.m. The cost was a princely six shillings and six pence per head, exclusive of drinks, but members were encouraged to subscribe as much as they could afford. There was a fund available for those unable to bear the full cost of dinner and travel. Members were 'allowed to bring male guests, numbers to be subject to approval of the Committee.' The letter was signed 'Walter T. Ganter.' Further information on this early association has not come to light.

After the Second World War one of the early squadron reunions was in 1952, as a result of a number of meetings held in March and April of that year at the 'White Horse', Rupert Street, London W1. The death of the King led to the postponement of the planned reunion dinner, but on 17 May a get-together was held from 6 to 9.30 p.m. at the Church House Restaurant, Great Smith Street, Westminster. A charge of five shillings per head was made to cover the cost of a buffet bar, and it was requested that the remittance be forwarded to the then Hon. Treasurer, Tom Dalton.

From the available records it appears that a formal association was not established until the 1980s, and the driving force behind this enterprise was Alan Smith. Alan had retired from the Royal Air Force as a squadron leader in 1967 after seeing service in the

Original 'Fortress/Liberator Association'

Far East, during the Berlin Airlift and in the Suez crisis. Like many of his contemporaries he took up a career in civil aviation and joined British European Airways, flying with them until 1979. Then, after a two-year spell with British Midland, he became Senior Training Captain at Manx Airlines from 1982 until his retirement in 1987.

In 1983 he decided to find the members of the crew he had flown with for over two years from 1943, both on Fortresses and Liberators in Benbecula, the Azores, St Eval and Leuchars, finally finishing at Oakington when they were operating on the route to the Far East: 'So I started by writing to the RAF Record Office and I got the addresses of quite a few of my crew including Wing Commander Graham who was in South Africa, Wing Commander L. F. 'Sid' Banks who was in London and various others, wireless operators and navigators. Will Paynton was in Canada and others were in the UK. One I couldn't find was Frank Stubbs but it turned out that he had returned to his home town of Kingston-upon-Hull to get married and we had lost touch. So in August 1983 I phoned Humberside Radio and asked them to put out a message for Frank whom I had not seen since 1944. The next day Frank's son phoned me, having heard the message, and he put me in touch with his father.'

Encouragement in these early days also came from Bill Thompson who should have flown with Guilonard that tragic day in April 1945 but was in hospital having a minor operation at the time.

From then on the pace of events quickened. Wing Commander 'JC' Graham knew David Beaty, who also had a crew get-together from time to time. 'Jack' Frost had an annual reunion with his crew on 10 November each year, the day they were 'jumped' by three Me110s off the coast of Denmark and fought them all the way back to Sumburgh in the Shetlands. JC suggested that a '206 Squadron Fortress/Liberator Association' be formed with Alan Smith as secretary and that everyone should meet up at the RAF Club in London on an annual basis. For the next two years more people were getting in touch and the first reunion luncheon was held in 1986. Subsequently many of them went to Kinloss for the 70th Anniversary of the squadron on 27 to 29 June of that year, hosted by the CO Wing Commander Brian J. Sprosen. There was some discussion there that it would be more appropriate to call the association the 'The 206 Squadron Association' as enquiries were being received from people who had flown Ansons before the war and Hudsons at Bircham Newton. The idea of a 206 Squadron Memorial

70th Anniversary Reunion June 1986 at Kinloss, jointly organised by Alan
Smith and the squadron.
(Sid Banks)

David Beaty, Betty Beaty and Alan Smith at 75th Anniversary, Kinloss 1991.
(CC/206)

Window at RAF Kinloss was proposed and it was Wing Commander Sprosen's successor, Wing Commander Mike Sweeney, who carried forward this project. The Memorial Window in the station church at RAF Kinloss, designed and installed by the Community of Monks at Pluscarden Abbey, was formally dedicated during the squadron reunion weekend on 26 to 29 May 1989. By the time of the 75th Anniversary Reunion at RAF Kinloss in June 1991 the title '206 Squadron Association' had been adopted, and it was during this event that the first annual general meeting was held. Office-bearers elected included the president, Air Chief Marshal Sir David Parry-Evans, Captain Ian C. Grant as chairman, and as secretary, Captain Alan D. B. Smith. Frank Stubbs became treasurer and G. Hart membership secretary. Wing Commander Brian McLaren, now squadron CO, hosted the reunion.

By now the Association was well established and during 1993 Air Vice-Marshal D. Emmerson CBE, AFC (squadron CO 1981-83) was elected president. During that year a reunion was planned of the members of the Association 'who flew either Fortresses or Liberators', at the RAF Club on 10 April at a cost of £18-00 per head. It was anticipated

Battle of the Atlantic 50th Anniversary, Liverpool 1993.
L to R (front) Ludovic Kennedy, Bill Balderson, Alan Smith. Rear (standing on right) Jim Glazebrook.
(CC/206)

that arrangements could be discussed for the planned 50th Anniversary of the Battle of the Atlantic, to be held in Liverpool from 26 to 31 May of that year, an event of particular importance to the crews of those aircraft. There has always been contact with other squadron associations, such as the 210 Squadron Association through Bill Balderson. Bill and Alan Smith joined together at the 50th Anniversary of the Battle of the Atlantic organised by the Royal Navy. It was important that Coastal Command was involved in this event due to the important work the Command did in that battle and, sadly, no arrangements had been made for Coastal Command's representation. So, the two squadron associations, 210 and 206, represented Coastal Command and, as a direct result, the Coastal Command and Maritime Air Association was set up. Ultimately, and of great significance, John Cruickshank VC, ex-210 Squadron, carried the Book of Remembrance in the Liverpool Cathedral service attended by Their Royal Highnesses the Prince and Princess of Wales.

The events surrounding the Berlin Airlift were recalled in 1994 when a number of Association members including the secretary Tommy Trinder, representing the 206 Squadron Airlift veterans, and Peter Laird, visited Berlin in May for the 45th Anniversary of the ending of the Blockade. The month of September was marked by the official German government farewell to the Allied Forces in Berlin. These events were a poignant reminder of the deaths of five members of the squadron during the Airlift when an Avro York crashed after an engine failed on a night take-off from RAF Wunstorf.

Two Life vice-presidents were elected during the AGM in April 1995 at the Newquay reunion, Wing Commander J. C. Graham DFC and Bar, and Squadron Leader David Beaty MBE, DFC and Bar. The former had gained his first DFC while flying with the squadron and as the Association's inaugural chairman had contributed much to its success. David Beaty had a distinguished war record with the squadron as well as being the author of over 20 books, many of which related to the squadron's role of submarine-hunting and he had been awarded the MBE in recognition of his pioneering work on the human factors in aircraft accidents. This led to redesigned cockpit layouts and changed operating and training procedures. In addition David Beaty had greatly contributed to the success of the Association.

In May of the same year a reunion visit was organised to RAF Benbecula and in the following year, 1996, the 80th Anniversary of the squadron was held at RAF Kinloss from 30 August to 1 September – it was during this event that Alan Smith was awarded the Commendation of the Air Officer Commanding 18 Group. Memories of the days at RAF Oakington, by now occupied by the 1st Battalion The Royal Anglian Regiment, were revived by a visit there during the annual reunion held at Cambridge in April 1997. A further invitation was extended to the Association to visit RAF Benbecula in September 1997 on the occasion of the Battle of Britain Commemoration.

The epic days of protecting the Russian convoys were recalled by the presentation of 50th Anniversary Medals of the Great Patriotic War to several members of the Association and ex-members of 210 and 269 Squadrons by Mr Yuri E. Fokine, the Ambassador of the Russian Federation. This took place during 1998 at a reception at the embassy in Kensington Palace Gardens, and Association members honoured included Alan Smith, Wing Commander J. C. Graham and Wing Commander L. F. Banks. Other Association members eligible for the honour included Flight Lieutenant M. J. Frost DFC, Group Captain E. E. Lake, and Flight Lieutenant J. E. Bury. In May 2000 Alan Smith was among a number of veterans invited to visit Moscow by the Russian Ministry of Foreign Affairs on the occasion of the 55th Anniversary of the Victory. Alan represented the Coastal Command squadrons which had provided air cover to the Russian convoys. This event culminated on 9 May 2000 in a military parade and procession of over 1,800 war veterans of the Great Patriotic War in Red Square followed by a ceremonial reception and banquet in the Kremlin. As a follow-up Ekaterina Filippova, attaché at the Embassy of the Russian Federation, was invited to the annual luncheon of the Association in October.

The work of the Association was not confined to reunions and anniversaries during those years. In the summer of 2000 contributions were raised to support Group Captain S. N. Skinner in his Hospice in Moray Marathon Fund Appeal. Group Captain Skinner managed to raise a total of around £3,600 in the course of three marathon runs!

The impending closure of RAF Benbecula was marked in September and early October 1999 by a third and final visit there by members of the Association, to attend the Battle of Britain Commemoration at the invitation of the station commander, Squadron Leader P. Buttery. Fifteen members of the 206 Association and three of the 220 Association were able to attend and the then AOC, Air Vice-Marshal Burridge, himself an ex-206 Squadron member, reviewed the formal parade. There was a Service of Remembrance at Nunton Cemetery and the party included Wing Commander Jim Romanes who had been squadron CO at Benbecula from July 1941 to October 1943.

Another landmark was the official opening in May 2001 of the National Arboretum at Alrewas in Staffordshire by the Duchess of Kent, a Millennium Project which had been the inspiration of the late Group Captain Lord Cheshire VC, OM, DSO, DFC. Alan Smith, as chairman of the British Berlin Airlift Association, attended the ceremony to dedicate the 39 trees representing the British Airlift casualties. The squadron played an important part in that episode flying Avro Yorks from Wunstorf near Hanover to Gatow in Berlin. Also on that occasion the squadron was represented by Squadron Leader Graham House, 206 flight commander. Within the Arboretum Memorial there are groves for the Navy, Army and RAF. Within the RAF Grove there are various Wings which include the Commands. In the Coastal Command Wing space is made available for 50 trees. So far RAF stations Kinloss and St Mawgan are represented and squadron trees include Nos

206, 210, 211, 216, 217, 218, 220, 221, 222 and 228 Squadrons and the Indian Flying Boat and Beaufort Squadron Associations.

During the war the squadron included about 40 Canadians and an equal number of New Zealanders and Australians. The Association made a point of keeping in touch and appointed a North American secretary to look after the Canadians and the few Americans. Over the years Joe Griffith acted as the North American secretary and he recently handed over to Don Lancaster who flew with Shackletons after the war and who later joined Air Canada. Joe flew with Willis Roxburgh and has attended many functions in the UK and like Don Lancaster, joined Air Canada after the war. Active Association members in Canada also included Abe Shamas. Similarly there was an Antipodean secretary, Doug Riley, and he kept in touch with the New Zealanders. Freddie Pearce, radar leader during the war, now lives in Sydney and is a stalwart of the Association there.

The Association has also worked alongside a number of other Coastal Command associations. These include the Coastal Command and Maritime Air Association which was formed after the 206 Association, with the aim of keeping all the Coastal Command associations in touch. The Coastal Command Maritime Air Trust was a committee set up under Air Chief Marshal Sir John Barraclough to establish a suitable Coastal Command Memorial. The idea for the memorial was first suggested by the late Tony Spooner, a renowned World War II veteran, and followed a feasibility study during 1999/2000 chaired by David Emmerson. The Patron of the Appeal is HRH Prince Philip Duke of Edinburgh. The unveiling of the 'Commemorative Tribute' by Her Majesty The Queen took place on 16 March 2004 in front of a full congregation in Westminster Abbey, which included many present and former 206 Squadron members. The OC of the squadron Wing Commander Flint was also present, and he had been an active member of the Appeal Steering Group.

The Association has also kept in touch with 269 Squadron Association as Wing Commander J. C. Graham was at the time the treasurer. There is also good liaison with 220 Squadron Association, 206's sister squadron – the only other squadron in Coastal Command which flew Fortresses. The two squadrons flew them together in Benbecula and at Lagens (now Lajes) in the Azores and prior to that they operated Hudsons at Bircham Newton in Norfolk. No. 220 Squadron was disbanded in 1957. The 220 Squadron Association secretary was Joe Ayling and he attended a combined reunion at Benbecula and other 206 functions. He has now handed over to Jack Hobbs who suggested that the two associations join together because of reduced membership. The first combined reunion was held in York in May 2002.

Another contact is with 547 Squadron which was based at Leuchars with Liberators at the same time as 206, being disbanded at the end of the war. Bob Denwood is the link with that association and he frequently attends the 206 luncheons and is in touch with organisations including the U-Boat museum in Hamburg which supplies information on U-Boat history if that is required. There is also 333 (Norwegian) Squadron – Armand Jonassen who lives in Calgary in Canada is the contact and he has paid several visits to the UK. He attended the 50th Anniversary of the Battle of the Atlantic in Liverpool as did eight other members of 333 Squadron. They flew out of Leuchars during the war but also operated seaplanes which were based in the Tay at Dundee.

There are also strong links with 311 (Czech) Squadron, who flew Liberators with Coastal Command operating out of Tain, joining with 206 in combined operations. Four former members of that squadron living in the UK were present at the 50th Anniversary of the Battle of the Atlantic in Liverpool. Other Coastal Command squadron contacts include Nos 228 and 240 Squadrons. Nos 120 and 201 Squadrons are based at RAF

Kinloss with 206 Squadron, and 201 Squadron has a healthy and active Association, with president Air Vice-Marshal George Chesworth. No. 120 Squadron has no formal Association but does hold five-yearly reunions to celebrate important birthdays.

In Kinloss personnel on the squadrons tend to rotate between all three so there is always good contact and healthy rivalry among the units there, including No. 42 Squadron (the OCU/ 42 Reserve Squadron).

The work of the Association goes on, in spite of the death of Alan Smith on 5 March 2002. Having been secretary for so many years, Alan's loss was keenly felt by all the members and their families, as well as members of many other squadron associations. Among other deaths recorded during that year was that of Wing Commander 'J. C.' Graham DFC and Bar on 19 July, who had been Life vice-president and a staunch supporter of the Association. Air Vice-Marshal David Emmerson kept the Association alive with much hard work and dedication until new officers could be elected at the 2003 Annual General Meeting held at Stratford-upon-Avon:

Hon. President – Air Commodore R. W. Joseph BSc, CBE, RAF; Chairman – Air Commodore S. D. Butler RAF; Secretary/Treasurer – Wing Commander D. P. E. Straw RAF (Retd); Entertainments – David Fellowes.

APPENDIX I

BIBLIOGRAPHY AND SOURCES

PRIMARY AND UNPUBLISHED SOURCES

Documentary sources

<u>Public Record Office</u>, Kew (now the National Archives)

1.   Station Operations Record
     Bircham Newton inc. Appendices (AIR 28/70-77, 900)

2.   Operations Record Books (Form 540): No. 206 Squadron.
         AIR 27/1221   Nov. 1917 to Feb. 1920
         AIR 27/1221   June 1936 to Dec. 1939
         AIR 27/1222   Jan. to Dec. 1940
         AIR 27/1223   Jan. to Dec. 1943
         AIR 27/1224A   Jan. 1944 to June 1945
         AIR 27/1224B   July 1945 to April 1946
         AIR 27/2706   Oct. 1952 to Dec. 1957
         AIR 27/2833   Jan. 1958 to Dec. 1960
         AIR 27/2834   Jan. 1959 to Dec. 1960 (Operational Orders)
         AIR 272987   Jan. 1961 to Dec. 1962
         AIR 27/2988   Jan. 1963 to Dec. 1965

<u>206 Squadron Archives, RAF Kinloss</u>
Photograph archive: acknowledged in the text.
Army Forms W. 3348 Combats in the Air (World War One).
History of 206 Squadron (Unfinished): Compiled from Official Records, RAF St
Mawgan 1958.

<u>Misc.</u>
Report on 'The Aeroplane Postal Services' organised with the British Military Services
in France, Flanders and Germany 1918-1919. (Maj. E. E. Gawthawn OBE, DCM, OC RE
PS, Aerial Mails, Cologne, September 1919: RAF Museum)
Britain's First Aerial Mails (MS) by L. W. C. Pearce-Gervis. (RAF Museum).
Air Historical Branch (RAF) Ministry of Defence: History of 206 Squadron (AHB
5/206S).
Ministry of Defence (Navy) - *German Naval History: The U-Boat War in the Atlantic
1939-1945* (HMSO 1989).

Personal reminiscences
(see also **JOURNALS & ARTICLES**)
<u>1. WORLD WAR ONE</u>
Sgt W. S. Blyth DFM: personal log book and letters. (206 Sqn Archives, RAF Kinloss)
Lt J. B. Heppel, Croix de Guerre, Observer 206 Sqn RAF 1918/1919: personal narrative.
(206 Sqn Archives, RAF Kinloss)
Lt B. H. Rook, Recording Officer, 6 RNAS & 206 RAF 1918/1919: personal narrative.
(206 Sqn Archives, RAF Kinloss)
Capt. M. E. Spinney, Chaplain to the Forces, 206 RAF 1918: personal narrative. (206

Sqn Archives, RAF Kinloss)
Sgt Observer Horace Walter Williams: memorabilia 1917-1919. (206 Sqn Archives, RAF Kinloss)

2. BETWEEN THE WARS
Bill Parkes, *Bircham Newton*. (206 Sqn Archives, RAF Kinloss)

3. WORLD WAR TWO
Vernon Buckman, *Memories of Life with 206 (GR) Squadron, December 1938 until September 1942.*
G. V. Donald, *Notes on 206 Squadron Coastal Command, based at Bircham Newton.* (1991)
Jim Glazebrook, *War Time Memories of a B24 (Liberator) Pilot.* (206 Sqn Archives, RAF Kinloss)
Jack Holywell, *Memoirs of Life with 206 Squadron 1940-1941.* (206 Sqn Archives, RAF Kinloss)
Frank MacManus, *'Piece of Cake': Memoirs of 6 Years in the RAF 1940-1946.*

4. 1945-PRESENT
'Keeping Off the Q-Form' by Betty Beaty. An article originally written for the WRAF Officers' Gazette.
Wing Commander J. D. Beresford OBE, RAF (Ret'd), CO 206 Sqn 1952-1954.
Squadron Leader C. H. Taylor RAF (Ret'd), 206 Sqn at St Eval 1952-1955.
Squadron Leader Robin Woolven, Sergeant Air Signaller, 206 Sqn 1957-1959
Lewis M. Glanville, Sergeant AG, 206 Sqn 1952-1953.
Group Captain Laurie Hampson, 206 Sqn Adjutant 1957, in Operation *Grapple*.
Air Vice-Marshal David Emmerson CBE, AFC, CO of 206 Sqn 1981-1983, *My Unforgettable Ascension Island.*
Squadron Leader (later Group Captain) G. R. Porter, 'Search and Rescue at the Piper Alpha Oil-Rig, July 1988.'
Wing Commander A. P. Flint, OC 206, on the work of the squadron from 2002.
Other recollections include those from Air Commodores R. W. Joseph and S. D. Butler, Wing Commander D. P. E. Straw (RAF Ret'd) and Flight Lieutenant Duncan Milne.

Commonwealth War Graves Commission (CWGC): database, No. 6 (Naval) Squadron/206 Squadron RAF.

SECONDARY SOURCES

Books
206 SQUADRON 1916-1986 (70th Anniversary booklet)
206 SQUADRON 1916-1991 (75th Anniversary booklet)
206 SQUADRON 85th Anniversary booklet (May 2001)
ALLEN, CHARLES, *THUNDER & LIGHTNING: THE RAF IN THE GULF* (Warner Books 1995)
ARMITAGE, Michael, *THE ROYAL AIR FORCE: AN ILLUSTRATED HISTORY* (Arms and Armour 1994)
ASHWORTH, Chris:
AVRO YORK IN ROYAL AIR FORCE SERVICE 1942-1957 (*Aviation News* Mini-Monograph: Hall Park Publications Ltd)
RAF COASTAL COMMAND 1936-1969 (Patrick Stephens Limited 1992)

BARNETT, Correlli, *ENGAGE THE ENEMY MORE CLOSELY: The Royal Navy in the Second World War* (Hodder and Stoughton 1991)

BOWYER, Chaz:

COASTAL COMMAND AT WAR (Ian Allan Ltd 1979)

MEN OF COASTAL COMMAND 1939-1945 (William Kimber, London 1985)

BEATY, Betty Campbell, *WINGED LIFE: A biography of David Beaty MBE DFC* (Airlife 2001)

BEATY, David, *LIGHT PERPETUAL: Aviators' Memorial Windows* (Airlife 1995)

CHARTRES, John, *AVRO SHACKLETON* (Postwar Military Aircraft 3: Ian Allan Publishing 1999)

FRANKS, Norman L. R., *SEARCH FIND AND KILL* (Aston Publications 1990)

GLAZEBROOK, Flight Lieutenant Jim, *A WAR HISTORY OF NO. 206 SQUADRON, ROYAL AIR FORCE* (Private publication 1946)

GUNN, Peter B., *BIRCHAM NEWTON: A NORFOLK AIRFIELD IN WAR AND PEACE* (2002)

HALLEY, James J.:

RAF AIRCRAFT BA100-BZ999 (Air-Britain 1985)

RAF AIRCRAFT EA100-EZ999 (Air-Britain 1988)

RAF AIRCRAFT KA100-KZ999 (Air-Britain 1990)

FAMOUS MARITIME SQUADRONS OF THE RAF Vol I (Hylton Lacy Publishers Limited 1973)

HENDRIE, Andrew, *LOCKHEED HUDSON IN WORLD WAR II* (Airlife, England 1999)

HENSHAW, Trevor, *THE SKY THEIR BATTLEFIELD: ALLIED AIR CASUALTIES IN THE FIRST WORLD WAR* (Grub Street 1995)

HOBSON, Chris, *AIRMEN WHO DIED IN THE GREAT WAR 1914-1918* (J. B. Hayward & Son 1995)

HUGHES, Mike, *THE HEBRIDES AT WAR* (Canongate Books Ltd 1998)

JONES, Barry, *AVRO SHACKLETON* (The Crowood Press Ltd 2002)

MIDDLEBROOK, Martin, & EVERITT, Chris, *THE BOMBER COMMAND WAR DIARIES* (Viking 1985)

MOYES, Philip J. R., *BOMBER SQUADRONS OF THE RAF AND THEIR AIRCRAFT* (Macdonald: London 1971)

NASH, Jeremy, & WARRENER, Paul, *ON THE STEP: A History of 201 Squadron* (1990)

O'CONNOR, MIKE, *AIRFIELDS AND AIRMEN – Somme* (Leo Cooper – Pen & Sword Books Limited 2002)

PRICE, Alfred, *AIRCRAFT versus SUBMARINE* (Jane's 1980)

RAWLINGS, John D. R. *COASTAL, SUPPORT AND SPECIAL SQUADRONS OF THE RAF AND THEIR AIRCRAFT* (Jane's 1982)

FIGHTER SQUADRONS OF THE RAF AND THEIR AIRCRAFT (Crécy Books 1993)

RAWLINGS, John D. R. (Consultant), *HISTORY OF THE ROYAL AIR FORCE* (Temple Press 1984)

SHOLTO DOUGLAS with WRIGHT, Robert, *YEARS OF COMMAND*, HarperCollins Publishers Ltd 1966)

STURTIVANT, Ray, *ANSON FILE* (Air-Britain 1988)

STURTIVANT, Ray, and PAGE, Gordon: *DH4/DH9 FILE* (Air-Britain 1999)

ROYAL NAVY AIRCRAFT SERIALS AND UNITS 1911-1919 (Air-Britain 1992)

TERRAINE, John, *BUSINESS IN GREAT WATERS: The U-Boat Wars 1916-1945* (Octopus 1989)

THETFORD, Owen, *AIRCRAFT OF THE ROYAL AIR FORCE SINCE 1918* (Putnam 1988)

THOMAS, Richard, *TOWARDS THE SUN* (novel based on 206 Squadron during World War II) (Richard Thomas 2000)

WILLIAMS, Ray, *COMET AND NIMROD (Images of Aviation)* (Tempus Publishing Limited 2000)

JOURNALS & ARTICLES

AEROMILITARIA, Air-Britain Military Aviation Quarterly (No4 1979)

AIR PICTORIAL, Vol 24 No. 5 May 1962 pp172-173, History of 206 Squadron by J. D. R. Rawlings.

CROSS & COCKADE, INTERNATIONAL: Journal of the Society of First World War Aviation Historians:

Sans Escort, Reminiscences of 206 Squadron RAF by Major J. S. Blanford DFC (Part I Vol 7, No. 4 1976; Part II Vol 8, No. 1 1977).

206 Squadron RAF – Some Australian Connections by Alan Rowe (Vol 28, No. 1 1997).

Captain I. N. C. Clarke: An Experienced Australian Bomber Pilot with Nos 5 and 6 Squadrons RNAS & 206 Squadron RAF by Alan Rowe.

THE GROWLER – Journal of the Shackleton Association.

OCTOPUS NEWS – 206 Squadron Annual Newsletter, from March 1991.

SCALE AIRCRAFT MODELLING, Vol 1 No. 1 October 1978 pp 26-28, No. 206 Squadron Royal Air Force.

APPENDIX II

COMMANDING OFFICERS

December 1916	Sqn Cdr J. J. Petre DSC, Croix de Guerre (France), RNAS
April 1917	Sqn Cdr C. D. Breese RNAS
November 1917	Sqn Cdr C. T. MacLaren RNAS
May 1919	Maj. G. R. M. Reid RAF
15 June 1936	Sqn Ldr A. H. Love
13 July 1936	Wg Cdr F. J. Vincent DFC
22 October 1936	Wg Cdr H. O. Long DSO
9 May 1938	Sqn Ldr H. H. Martin
July 1938	Wg Cdr J. L. Findlay RNZAF
September 1938	Sqn Ldr H. H. Martin
13 January 1939	Sqn Ldr N. H. D'Aeth
19 June 1940	Wg Cdr J. Constable-Roberts
20 February 1941	Wg Cdr D. C. Candy RAAF
11 August 1941	Wg Cdr A. F. Hards
15 June 1942	Wg Cdr H. D. Cooke
29 June 1942	Wg Cdr J. R. S. Romanes DFC
16 May 1943	Wg Cdr R. B. Thomson DSO
23 March 1944	Wg Cdr A. de V. Leach DFC
9 January 1945	Wg Cdr J. P. Selby
24 July 1945	Wg Cdr T. W. T. McComb OBE
17 November 1947	Sqn Ldr F. C. Blackmore
15 March 1948	Sqn Ldr J. C. Blair
12 July 1948	Sqn Ldr E. Moody
1 November 1949	Sqn Ldr E. A. Rockliffe
27 September 1952	Sqn Ldr J. D. Beresford
8 December 1954	Sqn Ldr E. K. Paine
10 April 1956	Wg Cdr J. E. Preston
14 April 1958	Wg Cdr R. T. Billett
26 July 1960	Wg Cdr J. E. Bazalgette DFC
25 June 1962	Wg Cdr D. R. Locke OBE
27 October 1964	Wg Cdr H. R. Williams
15 August 1966	Wg Cdr S. G. Nunn OBE, DFC
1 October 1968	Wg Cdr D. R. Dewar
29 May 1970	Wg Cdr J. Wild
25 November 1972	Wg Cdr M. J. W. Pierson MBE
1 January 1975	Wg Cdr G. K. Peasley AFC
7 April 1977	Wg Cdr G. H. Rolfe MBE
18 April 1979	Wg Cdr R. C. McKinlay MBE
April 1981	Wg Cdr D. Emmerson AFC
April 1983	Wg Cdr B. Johnson
March 1985	Wg Cdr B. J. Sprosen
October 1987	Wg Cdr C. M. Sweeney
April 1990	Wg Cdr B. G. McLaren
October 1992	Wg Cdr R. W. Joseph
July 1994	Wg Cdr S. D. Butler
December 1996	Wg Cdr S. N. Skinner
July 1999	Wg Cdr T. Cross
January 2002	Wg Cdr A. P. Flint

APPENDIX III

SQUADRON BASES

Abbreviation: **Det.** detachment

1 November 1916	Formed as No. 6 Squadron RNAS at Dover.
December 1916	Moved to Petite Synthe, Dunkirk area, France, where the unit expanded to full squadron complement (Nieuport Scout).
March 1917	La Bellevue, France, to commence patrols at front.
April 1917	Chipilly, France.
April 1917	Flez, France.
June 1917	Bray Dunes, Dunkirk area, France (Sopwith Camel).
July 1917	Frontier Aerodrome, Bray Dunes. Disbanded there August 1917.
January 1918	Squadron re-formed at Dover as day-bomber unit from personnel of Walmer Defence Flt & No. 11 Sqn RNAS (DH4 & DH9).
January 1918	Petite Synthe, France.
March 1918	Ste Marie Cappel, France.
1 April 1918	Squadron transferred from No. 5 Wing RNAS to 11th (Army) Wing, RFC, and became No. 206 Squadron, RAF.
11 April 1918	Boisdinghem, France.
15 April 1918	Alquines, France.
29 May 1918	Boisdinghem, France.
5 June 1918	Alquines, France.
5 October 1918	Ste Marie Cappel, France.
24 October 1918	Linselles, France.
26 November 1918	Nivelles, Belgium.
20 December 1918	Bickendorf, Germany.
27 May 1919	Maubeuge, France.
June 1919	Alexandria & Heliopolis, Egypt.
27 June 1919	Helwan, Egypt.
1 February 1920	Squadron re-numbered No. 47 Sqn.
15 June 1936	Squadron re-formed at Manston from C Flight, 48 Sqn (Anson) as No. 206 (General Reconnaissance) Squadron.
30 July 1936	Bircham Newton.
August 1936	Squadron transferred to Coastal Command (No. 16 Group)
	Det. Carew Cheriton
	Hooton Park
	Aldergrove
	St Eval
March 1940	Squadron began converting to Hudsons.

30 May 1941	St Eval, Cornwall
12 August 1941	Aldergrove, N. Ireland.
	Det. Wick
	St Eval
	Chivenor
	Stornoway
	Donna Nook
1 July 1942	Benbecula, Outer Hebrides.
	Det. St Eval
	Thorney Island
August 1942	Squadron converted to Fortresses.
October 1943	Thorney Island, Hampshire.
8 October 1943	Lagens, Terceira, Azores.
31 March 1944	Davidstow Moor, Cornwall.
April 1944	Re-equipment with B-24 Liberators.
12 April 1944	St Eval, Cornwall.
	Det. Tain
11 July 1944	Leuchars, Fife.
	Det. Tain.
June 1945	Squadron transferred to 301 Wing, Transport Command.
1 August 1945	Oakington, Cambridgeshire.
25 April 1946	Squadron disbanded at Oakington.
17 November 1947	Squadron re-formed at Lyneham, Wiltshire (Avro York)
1948	Detachment to Wunstorf, for Berlin Airlift (Operation PLAINFARE).
20 February 1950	Disbanded at Lyneham.
27 September 1952	Squadron re-formed at St Eval (Shackleton).
14 January 1958	St Mawgan, Cornwall.
7 July 1965	Kinloss, Morayshire.

APPENDIX IV

EQUIPMENT

NIEUPORT SCOUT

This became the standard equipment of No. 6 Squadron Royal Naval Air Service in December 1916 until June 1917. Serials included: N3101, N3189, N3192, N3199, N3208, N3209, N5865.

SOPWITH F1 CAMEL

The squadron became the first naval squadron to equip with this aircraft from June to August 1917, when the squadron was disbanded.
Serials included: B3821, B3882, B6228, B6318, B6356, B6447, D1873, E7177, F5188, N6341, N6356, N6371, N6379.

During this period the squadron's equipment appears to have been supplemented in July 1917 with the **SOPWITH 1½ STRUTTER** and the **SOPWITH TRIPLANE.**

DE HAVILLAND DH4

The squadron was re-formed as a day-bomber unit in January 1918 and was equipped with the DH4, probably for training only from January to March 1918. Examples include B9499, D1751, N6404.

AIRCO DE HAVILLAND DH9

Re-equipment followed with the DH9 from February 1918 until January 1920. Examples include B7583, B7586, B7600, B7617, B7618, B7668, B7678, B9345, C1166, C1177[1], C6170, C6220, C6289, D460, D1022, D1024, D1663, D1687, D1689, D2783, D5722, D7222, D7227.

DH9A

Examples include E9742, F1051, F1080, H5881(?)

AVRO ANSON

The squadron was equipped with the Anson when being re-formed at Manston in June 1936 until re-equipment with the Hudson in June 1940. The Squadron number was carried on the side of the Ansons from 1937 onwards. Late in 1938 the code letters 'WD' were applied until the outbreak of war when they were changed to 'VX'.

Mark I

K6159		
K6167	WD-C	VX-C
K6175		
K6176	VX-J	
K6177	VX-K	
K6178	VX-L	
K6179	WD-A	VX-A

---

1 This DH9 was from a production batch of 300 built by G & J Weir at Glasgow, Scotland. It crashed with 98 Sqn on 2 March 1918, was repaired and re-issued. Eventually issued to 206 Sqn and crashed and destroyed 29 June 1918 (see account of Lt Eaton).

K6183	Missing from anti-sub search to Dutch coast 5/9/39
K6184	VX-P
K6185	Hit trees on night approach at Bircham Newton (BN) 22/4/39
K6186	VX-M
K6187	VX-E: Lost in sea on patrol off Calais 9/9/39
K6188	
K6189	VX-R: Missing from N. Sea patrol 6/12/39
K6190	VX-M
K6191	VX-B
K6192	
K6193	
K6194	
K6195	Struck Off Charge (SOC) 21/7/40
K6196	VX-G
K6207	Wrecked in forced-landing, Morston, Wells-next-the-Sea 26/1/40
K6208	
K6211	
K6225	
K6288	VX-D
K6289	
K8745	VX-O
K8754	
K8755	
K8756	VX-U
K8757	Hit boundary hedge on approach BN 16/12/38
K8814	VX-N
K8824	
K8836	On night approach nav. exercise flew into sea in bad weather off Flamborough Head, Yorks 1/11/38
K8837	VX-F
L7973	
L7974	
L7975	
L9157	VX-R
N4912	
N9897	VX-N: Collided with Blenheim L9256 (235 Sqn) on t/o BN 25/5/40
N9898	
R3312	

LOCKHEED HUDSON

Re-equipment with the Hudson began in March 1940 at Bircham Newton.
Mk I: March 1940 to August 1942
Mk II: April 1941 to August 1942
Mk III: April 1941 to August 1942
Mk IV: April 1941 to August 1942
Mk V: October 1941 to August 1942

Mark I

N7273	
N7275	Later *Spirit of Brussels*
N7278	

N7293	
N7299	Flew into runway at BN when flarepath extinguished 29/6/40
N7300	Flew into wood in fog, West Raynham Hall 19/11/40
N7302	
N7312	Tyre burst on landing, swung, u/c collapsed 25/4/40
N7318	
N7319	Damaged by Me109s off Elbe estuary; belly-landed BN 3/5/40
N7327	
N7329	Failed to Return (FTR) from Hamburg 18/5/40
N7331	
N7333	Crashed after t/o from BN 20/12/40
N7343	
N7351	Hit trees on t/o: belly-landed Docking 3/9/40
N7353	Shot down by Me109s N of Baltrum off German coast 12/5/40
N7362	FTR 14/10/40
N7363	FTR from Hamburg 20/5/40
N7367	Swung on t/o & u/c collapsed. Fire & bombs exploded BN 1/9/40.
N7368	FTR from ASR for Hampdens off Texel 4/7/40
N7369	
N7376	
N7378	
N7379	
N7392	
N7393	
N7395	Overshot, swung & u/c collapsed, bombs exploded BN 7/8/40
N7396	
N7400	FTR from Hamburg 18/5/40
N7401	Control lost after t/o; dived into ground Sunderland Farm, Docking 14/8/40
N7402	FTR Recce off German coast 22/5/40
N7403	Crashed on landing at BN. Blew up 25/4/40
P5120	Hit ridge on approach BN. Stalled & u/c collapsed 20/6/40
P5133	Stalled after steep turn, hit ground & blew up, Syderstone, Norfolk 5/8/40
P5137	
P5140	
P5141	
P5143	
P5148	
P5153	Crashed on landing. Bombs exploded BN 6/8/40
P5162	FTR from ASR for Hampdens off Texel 4/7/40
T9272	Heavy landing, Aldergrove 5/8/40 DBR (Damaged Beyond Repair)
T9274	
T9276	Stalled on landing to avoid Hurricane, BN 7/9/40
T9281	
T9282	FTR 3/8/40
T9283	
T9287	Hit barn low flying near Langham 1/1/41
T9288	
T9289	FTR 12/2/41
T9300	
T9302	

T9303	FTR 16/10/40
T9304	Crashed at Castle-on-Dinas 21/4/41
T9310	
T9311	
T9324	Crashed on beach N Sheppey in forced landing 17/5/41
T9331	FTR 4/2/41
T9332	
T9346	Abandoned in fog off Sarclet, Caithness 12/2/41
T9348	
T9350	Abandoned in fog off Caithness 12/2/41
T9357	Hit hedge landing at Docking 10/10/40. DBR

Mark II

T9368	
T9382	Damaged by AA and abandoned off Birchington 10/11/40
T9383	
T9384	

Mark III

T9421	
T9431	Crashed on t/o Aldergrove 8/4/42
T9433	
T9434	
T9443	
T9444	
T9451	
T9453	
T9454	
T9463	

Mark IV

AE609	FTR from patrol 1/7/41
AE611	Dived into ground at night Aldergrove 20/3/41
AE612	FTR from ASR 13/6/41
AE613	Ditched on anti-sub patrol 8/7/41
AE614	FTR from ASR 12/6/41
AE615	
AE617	
AE619	
AE620	
AE622	
AE623	
AE624	
AE625	
AE626	
AE628	
AE629	
AE630	
AE631	SOC 10/11/42
AE632	

AE633
AE634

Mark V

AE648	
AM581	
AM587	
AM588	Flew into hill at night NE of Ladyhill, Co. Antrim 16/8/41
AM603	
AM604	Hit trees low flying near Aldergrove 1/2/42
AM605	
AM606	FTR 26/6/42
AM612	
AM613	U/c collapsed on t/o Aldergrove 1/2/42
AM622	Crashed on t/o Aldergrove 14/2/42.
	(Fire resulted: Ted Nelson WOp/AG – survived)
AM634	Ditched on patrol 11/12/41
AM635	
AM648	
AM650	
AM664	Stalled on approach Aldergrove 24/9/41
AM689	
AM690	DBR 31/1/42
AM706	Crashed on overshoot, Aldergrove 5/2/42
AM711	
AM722	
AM734	
AM762	FTR 26/6/42
AM785	
AM788	
AM792	
AM801	
AM805	FTR 28/7/42
AM822	
AM837	FTR 21/12/41
AM875	

BOEING FORTRESS

The squadron replaced its Hudsons at Benbecula in August 1942 and its aircraft moved to Lagens, Azores, on 18 October 1943.

SQUADRON CODE

When re-equipment took place with the Fortresses at first no markings were carried but later the numeral '1' denoted 206 Squadron.

Mark I

AN519	
AN520	
AN530	SOC 11/9/43
AN531	

Mark II

FA695
FA696
FA699
FA700
FA702
FA703
FA704   Ditched in N. Atlantic 11/6/43
FA705   Missing on patrol 6/1/44
FA707
FA708
FA710
FA711   SOC 14/8/44
FA713

Mark IIA

FK184
FK186
FK190
FK191
FK195   SOC 27/4/44
FK198
FK199   SOC 14/6/45
FK208   Crashed in sea off Carnero Point attempting to land at Gibraltar 29/11/43
FK210
FK211
FK213
FL451
FL452
FL453   Missing 14/12/42
FL454   Stalled avoiding another aircraft and crashed in sea, Benbecula 6/10/42
FL455
FL457
FL458
FL459
FL460

CONSOLIDATED LIBERATOR

On 18 March 1944 the squadron returned to the UK to convert to Liberators.
Mk VI: April 1944 to April 1945
Mk VIII: March 1945 to April 1946

SQUADRON CODE

With the coming of the Liberators the code became '**PQ**'.

Mark V

BZ760
BZ869

Mark VI

BZ961	Hit high ground on approach, Leuchars, 14.9.44
BZ972	
BZ975	
BZ981	
BZ984	
BZ986	
BZ999	
KG827	
KG856	
KG859	
KG861	PQ-L
KG862	
KG863	
KG867	
KH241	
KH377	
KH380	
KH381	
KK226	
KK255	
KK257	
KK260	
KK342	
KK375	
KK377	
KL351	
KL494	
KL503	
KL595	Sank back on t/o & crashed & burst into flames, Melsbroek 13.10.45. Damaged Beyond Repair (DBR)
KL622	
KL623	
KL637	
KL641	
KL664	(approx May 1946). Converted to transport and used on Far East routes
KL665	
KL666	
KL669	
KL670	
KL672	
KN705	
KN750	
KN777	

GR.VI

EV828	
EV872	
EV873	Crashed on t/o and blew up, Leuchars, 20.7.44.
EV874	

EV882
EV884
EV885   Missing on patrol 29.9.44
EV887   Caught fire and crashed, St Andrew's Bay, Fife, 2.12.44
EV888
EV898
EV943
EV944
EV947   Missing on patrol 16.7.44
EV954
EV955
EV985
EV988
EV998
EW288   Lost 15.11.44
EW298
EW301
EW310
EW311
EW313
EW322

Mark VIII

KG959
KG961
KG979
KG982
KG988
KH131
KH180
KH259   Undershot landing at Lydda & nosewheel collapsed.
KH415
KH418
KK250
KK253
KK256
KK259   Missing from patrol 9.4.45
KK261
KK262
KK263
KK264
KK291
KK292
KK293
KK323
KK324
KK335
KK410   Failed to return 20.4 .45
KN737
KN811
KN833

AVRO YORK

November 1947 to February 1950.

SQUADRON CODE

The Yorks probably carried no markings.

C. I

MW270 Crew abandoned take-off at Wunstorf 10/11/48 due to airspeed indicator failure. U/c raised to prevent overrun and a/c declared Cat.E1. and SOC as scrap.
MW253 Cat.B damage 25/1/49.
MW286 Cat.B damage 25/3/49.
MW303 Cat.AC damage 2/3/49.*

*Category of damage:
A/AC – Repairable on unit.
B – Repairable by second-line unit.
D – Repairable by industry.
E – Beyond repair.
SOC – Struck off Charge.

DOUGLAS DAKOTA

January 1950 to February 1950 at Waterbeach.
Believed uncoded.
KN367, KN369, KN573, KN608, KN701

HAWKER SIDDELEY (AVRO) SHACKLETON

SQUADRON CODE

The Shackletons at first carried the letter 'B' and then the number '206'. There was also an emblem on a white shield on the fin.
MR 1: September 1947 to May 1958.
MR 2: February 1953 to June 1954.
MR 3: January 1958 to October 1970
Representative aircraft:

MR1

VP263, VP289, VP293, VP294

MR1a

WB821, WB826, WB828, WB832, WB836, WB851, WG508, WG510, WG526,WG528, WG529

MR2

WG557, WG558, WL742

MR3

WR980, WR981, WR982, WR983, WR984, WR985, WR986, XF707

HAWKER SIDDELEY (DH) NIMROD

SQUADRON CODE

Nimrods, as Wing aircraft, only carry the squadron emblem occasionally as on the occasion of the 80th Anniversary of the squadron in 1996.

MR1: November 1970 to April 1981.
MR2: April 1980 to present.

Aircraft available to the squadron as part of the Kinloss Wing, 1990:
Nimrod MR2, MR2P (last 2 digits of serial in black on fin)
XV227, XV228, XV229, XV230, XV232, XV233, XV234, XV235, XV236, XV238, XV239, XV240, XV241, XV242, XV243, XV244, XV247, XV250, XV251, XV252, XV254, XV255, XV260, XV284.
Source: *United Kingdom Air Arms 1990* (Blackbird Aviation Publications in association with Mach Three Plus 1990)

Aircraft available, Kinloss Wing, 2002:
Nimrod MR2
XV226, XV227, XV228, XV229, XV230, XV231, XV232, XV235, XV236, XV240, XV241, XV243, XV244, XV245, XV246, XV248, XV250, XV252, XV254, XV255, XV260.
(Comprises Nos 42(R), 120, 201 and 206 Squadrons).
Source: *United Kingdom Air Arms 2002* (MACH III PLUS 2002).

APPENDIX V

DECORATIONS AND AWARDS

WORLD WAR I

Officers of the Order of the British Empire – Military Division

Maj. C. T. MacLaren (Squadron Commander)

Bar to Distinguished Flying Cross

Capt. R. N. G. Atkinson MC, DFC

Distinguished Flying Cross

Capt. R. N. G. Atkinson MC
Capt. E. Burn
Capt. L. R. Warren
Capt. T. Roberts
Lt L. A. Christian
2/Lt J. S. Blandford
2/Lt (Hon. Capt.) W. A. Carruthers
2/Lt A. J. Garside
2/Lt G. A. Pitt

Distinguished Flying Medal

Sgt Mech. W. W. Blyth
Pte 1st Cl. (later Sgt) J. Chapman
Sgt G. Betteridge
Cpl H. W. Williams
Sgt L. H. Rowe

Bar to Distinguished Flying Medal

Sgt J. Chapman

La Croix de Guerre (French)

Capt. T. Roberts DFC
Lt A. M. Bannatyne

Le Medaille Militaire (French)

AC1.AGL. R. A. Hollingsbee

Chevalier De L'Order De Leopold II

Sgt G. Betteridge DFM

La Croix de Guerre (Belgian)

Maj. C. T. MacLaren OBE
Capt. R. N. G. Atkinson MC, DFC
2/Lt (Hon. Capt.) W. A. Carruthers DFC
2/Lt A. J. Garside DFC

2/Lt J. B. Heppel
2/Lt H. McLean DFC
Sgt G. Betteridge DFM
Sgt J. Chapman DFM
Sgt W. S. Blyth

Mentioned in Despatches

Capt. R. G. St John DSC
Lt B. H. Rook
Lt M. G. Penny
Lt J. S. Common
2/Lt J. D. Russell
2/Lt J. B. Heppel
2/Lt C. O. Shelswell
2/Lt R. Ramsay

WORLD WAR II

Notes: Names appear alphabetically (with date of award).
All ranks stated are those held at time of award.

Distinguished Service Order

Wg Cdr A. F. Hards 7/7/42

Distinguished Flying Cross (* indicates Bar awarded later)

Flt Lt L. F. Banks 27/7/45
Flt Lt A. D. Beaty* 10/10/44 & 17/2/45
Flt Lt W. H. Biddell 22/7/41
Fg Off. T. M. Bulloch 22/11/40
Fg Off. P. F. Carlisle 1/10/44
Flt Lt J. F. Clark 28/8/43
Fg Off. L. G. Clark 9/7/43
Fg Off. R. L. Cowey 15/5/43
Sqn Ldr C. N. Crook 7/7/42
Plt Off. F. J. Curtis 13/9/40
Flt Lt B. O. Dias 13/9/40
Flt Lt A. D. S. Dundas 30/6/44
Flt Lt Elviss RCAF 27/7/45
Flt Lt E. V. Fisher RAAF 27/7/45
Fg Off. M. J. Frost 3/12/44
Plt Off. D. Gauntlett 22/9/42
Plt Off. J. J. V. Glazebrook 17/2/45
Sqn Ldr J. C. Graham* 20/3/45
Plt Off. C. A. S. Greenhill 16/1/40
Plt Off. R. H. Harper 20/2/40
Plt Off. S. R. Henderson 1/1/40
Fg Off. J. L. Humphreys 28/8/43
Flt Lt E. N. Jennings 17/2/45
Plt Off. R. T. Kean 10/7/40
Fg Off. R. L. Kelly 15/5/43
Fg Off. P. E. Laird 27/7/45
Flt Lt D. P. Marvin 28/1/41
Fg Off. (later Sqn Ldr) R. C. Patrick* 15/9/41 & 5/5/44

Sqn Ldr A. J. Pinhorn 5/1/44
Flt Lt J. R. S. Romanes 30/7/40
Flt Lt W. Roxburgh 9/7/43
Wg Cdr R. B. Thomson DSO 28/8/43
Plt Off. G. P. Watson 21/10/40
Fg Off. F. S. Wills 25/5/43

Distinguished Flying Medal

Sgt C. R. Alexander 30/7/40
AC1 L. J. Britton 16/1/40
LAC W. D. Caulfield 6/6/40
Sgt W. J. Coldbeck 1/7/41
LAC N. Deighton 13/9/40
Sgt E. A. Deverill 10/7/40
AC1 R. Field 5/4/40
LAC K. F. Freeman 6/6/40
Sgt F. Garrity 17/1/41
Flt Sgt M. S. Gollan 3/12/44
Flt Sgt Hoyle 1/10/44
Flt Sgt J. A. Nicholson 3/12/44
Flt Sgt G. Whitfield 7/7/42

Croix de Guerre

Flt Lt L. F. Banks 23/6/45

Polish Cross of Valour

Sqn Ldr W. H. Biddell 22/7/41

British Empire Medal

Flt Sgt E. A. Hartwell 8/6/44

Mentions-in-Despatch

Fg Off. K. J. Ayrton 1/1/46
Fg Off. G. C. Bassett RAAF 1/1/46
WO J. R. Bolton 8/6/44
Fg Off. T. M. Bulloch 1/1/41
LAC G. Collins 8/6/44
Cpl R. S. Cooke 1/1/41
Fg Off. G. R. Cowdrey 24/9/41
Flt Lt C. N. Crook 11/6/42
Plt Off. J. Custerson 1/1/41
Wg Cdr N. H. D'Aeth 1/1/41
WO F. Davies 8/6/44
Flt Sgt A. A. G. Dent 11/6/42
Flt Lt I. Donald 8/6/44
Flt Sgt C. Dunkerley 20/2/40
LAC A. E. Foreman 20/2/40
Flt Lt D. R. Fray 1/1/46
Flt Sgt W. E. Gamble 24/9/41
Sgt T. Gardiner 1/1/45
WO N. A. H. Garnham 8/6/44
Sgt D. Gauntlett 11/6/42

Sqn Ldr J. C. Graham 20/3/45
Flt Lt I. C. Grant 1/1/46
Fg Off. E. M. C. Guest 24/9/41
Flt Sgt H. Harris 8/6/44
Flt Lt L. S. Harrison 27/6/45
Cpl J. C. Higgs 2/6/43
Fg Off. B. H. Leonard RNZAF 1/1/46
Sgt A. G. Mann 11/6/42
AC2 D. Mannion 1/1/41
Flt Lt S. C. Pearce RAAF 27/6/45
Fg Off. N. G. Reading 8/6/44
Cpl E. J. Reynolds 8/6/44
Sgt G. Roberts 24/9/41
A/Wg Cdr J. R. S. Romanes DFC 14/1/44
Flt Sgt E. Stevens 14/9/41
Cpl G. A. Turner 2/6/43
Sgt G. Whitfield 11/6/42
Flt Lt J. R. Wilkes 1/1/46
Sgt F. T. Willett 24/9/41
Flt Sgt R. W. Wilson 24/9/41
WO T. H. Yallis 8/6/44

POST-WAR TO FALKLANDS CAMPAIGN

Members of the Order of the British Empire

Flt Lt (formerly Sgt) C. R. Alexander 12/6/46
Flt Lt I. Donald 12/6/46

Distinguished Flying Cross

Flt Lt R. G. Gray 23/10/45
Flt Lt D. A. Jones 5/3/46
Fg Off. King 8/6/45

Air Force Cross

Flt Lt Noel W. Anthony RAAF 11/80
Flt Lt G. R. Haggas 12/6/46
Flt Lt L. A. Mather 7/48
Wg Cdr J. E. Preston 6/58

Air Efficiency Award

Flt Lt D. H. Bryon 3/46
Flt Lt M. J. G. Frost 21/3/46
Flt Lt L. R. Gore 18/4/46

Queen's Commendation for Valuable Services in the Air

Fg Off. Stephen P. Belcher 11/80

FALKLANDS CONFLICT

Air Force Cross

Wg Cdr D. Emmerson

APPENDIX VI

GRAVES, MEMORIALS, MEMORABILIA

Source: Database of The Commonwealth War Graves Commission (March 2001)

WORLD WAR I

No. 6 SQUADRON, ROYAL NAVAL AIR SERVICE

Belgium

LARCH WOOD (RAILWAY CUTTING) CEMETERY – Ieper, West-Vlaanderen
Kendall, Flt Sub-Lt Edward Hext, RNAS. 12 July 1917. Age 22.
Shot down in flames in Sopwith F1 Camel N6350 from 13,000 ft by Albatros nr Slype.
(Grave Ref: I. B. 10)

OOSTENDE NEW COMMUNAL CEMETERY – Oostende, West-Vlaanderen
MacLennan, Flt Cdre George Gordon, Croix de Guerre (France), RNAS. 21 July 1917.
Age 31. Graduate of Toronto Univ. Shot down in Sopwith F1 Camel N6360. (Grave
Ref: A. 18)

RAMSCAPPELLE ROAD MILITARY CEMETERY – Nieuwpoort, West-Vlaanderen
Strathy, Flt Sub-Lt Ford Stuart, RNAS.
From Toronto, Canada. Shot down in air combat while flying Sopwith Camel N6334
over enemy lines near Zevecote, 17th August 1917. Age 19. (Grave Ref: VI.D.1)

France

ARRAS FLYING SERVICES MEMORIAL – Pas de Calais
Reeves, Flt Lt Fabian Pember, RNAS. 6th June 1917. Age 21.
Flying a Nieuport Scout (Nieuport 17) (N3204) as part of a formation which was
attacked by several enemy aircraft. Last seen being pursued by an Albatros Scout
enemy aircraft near Cambrai. Wings of the Nieuport reportedly came off in pursuit.

AUBIGNY COMMUNAL CEMETERY EXTENSION – Pas de Calais
Walker, Flt Sub-Lt Frederic Cloete, RNAS. 17th March 1917. Age 18.
From St John's Wood, London. Killed while flying a Nieuport (N3201). (Grave Ref:
V.A.36)

BRAY MILITARY CEMETERY – Somme
Berridge, Flt Sub-Lt Raymond Winchester, RNAS, attd. 14th Wing, Royal Flying Corps.
Killed whilst flying 3rd May 1917. Age 19.
Pilot of a Nieuport Scout (N3195). (Grave Ref: II.G.21)

CAYEUX MILITARY CEMETERY – Somme
Thorne, Flt Sub-Lt A. L., RNAS. 9 April 1917. Killed in Nieuport Scout N3205. (Grave
Ref: I. C. I.)

CERISY-GAILLY MILITARY CEMETERY – Somme

Petre, Sqn Cdr John Joseph, DSC, Croix de Guerre (France), RNAS. 13 April 1917. Age 23.
First CO of the squadron. Killed in flying accident while doing aerobatics in Nieuport Scout N3206. Native of Ingatestone, Essex. (Grave Ref: I.D. 39)

HAZEBROUCK COMMUNAL CEMETERY – Nord
Oakeshott, Flt Sub-Lt Leonard England, RNAS. 31 March 1918. Age 18.
Crashed in DH9 B7622 making flat turn into wind. Also Flt Sub-Lt H. W. Day. Both died of injuries. (Grave Ref: III E. 4)

Italy

OTRANTO TOWN CEMETERY
Begg, Flt Sub-Lt R. G., 6th Wing RNAS. 17th July 1917. British Adriatic Squadron.
Hilton, Air Mech. 1st Class Harry, 6th Wing RNAS. Died of sickness 8th September 1917. Age 37. British Adriatic Squadron.
Planterose, Sub-Lt E. A., 6th Wing RNAS. 17th July 1917. British Adriatic Squadron.

PADUA MAIN CEMETERY
Gorman, Flt Lt Joseph, 6th Wing RNAS. Died of accidental injuries while transiting to 6th Wing Otranto, 17th December 1917. Age 28. Northern Squadron.

No. 206 SQUADRON ROYAL AIR FORCE

Belgium

HARLEBEKE NEW BRITISH CEMETERY – Harelbeke, West-Vlaanderen
Prime, 2nd Lt H. L., 6th October 1918. (Grave Ref: XII.E.6)
Pilot, shot down in DH9 B7678 on 5 October. Became PoW but died of wounds. Observer 2nd Lt C. Hancock unhurt: PoW.

HOOGE CRATER CEMETERY – Ieper, West-Vlaanderen
Mathews, Capt. J. W. 1st August 1918. (Grave Ref: II.H.9)
Killed with observer Lt W. A. John in DH9 D2855 on bombing operation. Last seen over Menin. Probably shot down by enemy aircraft. Lt John also buried in cemetery but not on CWGC list. Native of Chile.

SANCTUARY WOOD CEMETERY – Ieper, West-Vlaanderen
Sangster, 2nd Lt Albert Burnett. 13th August 1918. Age 18. (Grave Ref: V.M.27)
Killed with Lt C. S. Johnson (see below: Bailleul) in DH9 D5590 on bombing operation.

Egypt

CAIRO WAR MEMORIAL CEMETERY
Berry, AC2 William Arthur. 1st November 1919. Age 19.

France

ANZAC CEMETERY, SAILLY-SUR-LA-LYS – Pas de Calais
Bray, 2nd Lt Cyril Ivor. Killed whilst flying 7th July 1918. Age 18. (Grave Ref: III.M.3)
Harington Lt J. R., 7th July 1918. (Grave Ref: III.M.4)
Killed together in DH9 D1730. Shot down during Line reconnaissance patrol.

ARNEKE BRITISH CEMETERY – Nord
Desmond, 2nd Lt Sidney Maurice. Killed 6th September 1918. Age 24. (Grave Ref: VIII.A.19)
Helliwell, Air Mech. 1st Class Alfred, 6th September 1918. Age 27. (Grave Ref: VIII.A.20)
Killed together in DH9 D3249. Crashed in thick ground mist and aircraft completely wrecked.

ARRAS FLYING SERVICES MEMORIAL – Pas de Calais
Brock, 2nd Lt Frederick Albert, MM, 7th August 1918. Age 22.
From Swinton, Rotherham. Pilot, killed on bombing operation with Cpl Cullimore (below) in DH9 C6289. Last seen Neuve Eglise.

Collins, 2nd Lt Frederick Ferdinand, 19th May 1918. Age 25.
Observer, killed with Lt Dunford (below) on bombing operation in DH9 C6159 NW of Roulers. 'Kill' claimed by Lt Paul Strahle, Jasta 57.
Teacher and member of Surrey (NW) National Union of Teachers in civilian life: Shaftesbury School, Bisley.

Cullimore, Cpl Charles Hulbert, 7th August 1918. Age 18.

Dunford, Lt Bertram Fred, 19th May 1918. Age 19. Pilot.

Heron, 2nd Lt Francis Turretin, 25th July 1918. Age 19.
Pilot, killed with 2nd Lt C. J. Byrne (Burne?) (observer) in DH9 C6121 on bombing operation. Last seen two miles north of Gheluve. Probable combat with enemy aircraft. Byrne's burial place unknown.

Howell-Jones, 2nd Lt Athol Cuthbert, 19th May 1918. Age 18.
Killed with 2nd Lt F. G. Reddie (below) on bombing operation in DH9 B7594. Victim of enemy aircraft near Menin.

Pacey, Sgt (Observer) Joseph Woodley, 29th July 1918. Age 21.
Killed with his pilot Lt Galloway Cheston, US Air Service (attached 206 Sqn RAF), in DH9 B7668 on bombing operation near Courtrai. Possibly shot down by enemy aircraft. Lt Cheston is buried in Flanders Field American Cemetery, Waregem, Belgium.

Reddie, 2nd Lt Francis Graham, 18th May 1918. Age 18.

Slinger, 2nd Lt Albert, 3rd May 1918. Age 19.

Steel, Lt Arthur Edward (RAF & 21st Bn Middlesex Regt), 3rd May 1918. Age 19.
Both killed in DH9 C2157. Last seen going down in flames Bailleul-Kemmel, on bombing raid to Armentières.

BAILLEUL COMMUNAL CEMETERY EXTENSION (NORD) – Nord
Johnson, Lt C. S., 13th August 1918. (Grave Ref: IV.A.6)

BOUCHOIR NEW BRITISH CEMETERY – Somme
Cutmore, Lt William Cecil, 24th June 1918. Age 18. (Grave Ref: ?)
Duncan, 2nd Lt William Gardiner, 24th June 1918. Age 33. (Grave Ref: V.C.30)
Killed together in DH9 D1012 east of Montdidier on Line reconnaissance. Enemy aircraft claimed 'kill'.

LINSELLES COMMUNAL CEMETERY – Nord
Bailey, Lt Eric Henry Platt. Killed in action 11th August 1918. Age 20. (Grave Ref: D5)
Milne, Lt R., 11th August 1918. Age 20. (Grave Ref: D4)
Killed together in DH9 C2199 on Line recce. HA (hostile aircraft) made claim of 'kill' north of Lille.

LONGUENESSE (ST OMER) SOUVENIR CEMETERY – Pas de Calais

Anketell, 2nd Lt Charles Edward, MM (RAF & Royal Fusiliers), 11th May 1918. Age 23. Killed in DH9 B7587 on bombing operation in combat with two enemy aircraft near Armentières. Shot up and made forced landing. Lt G. A. Pitt (observer) unhurt. (Grave Ref V. B. 5)

Binnie, Lt William Harold, Observer (7th Royal Scots), killed in action 22nd July 1918. Age 26. (Grave Ref: VC100)
Killed in DH9. From Durban, South Africa. Not listed in CWGC database.

Calvert, 2nd Lt Ernest. 14th August 1918. Age 19.
From Middlesborough. Died of wounds received in DH9. (Grave Ref: VD53)

Morgan, Lt Edward Percival, 22nd May 1918.
Pilot, from Kilburn, served with Canadian Infantry. Killed with 2nd Lt Taylor (below) in DH9 D1695. Aircraft stalled on turn after take-off, crashed and burnt out. (Grave Ref: VB26)

Paget, 2nd Lt Frederick James. Observer, died of wounds received in aerial combat, DH9 D1015, 6th August 1918. Age 23. (Grave Ref: VD34). From Barrow-in-Furness. 2nd Lt J. F. S. Percival (pilot) wounded. Later died but not as result of this incident (1919) – see below (St Pancras, Middlesex).

Robinson, Lt Ralph, 12th April 1918. Age 19. (Grave Ref: VA35)
Pilot, from Northampton. Killed in DH9 B7617. Aircraft crashed near aerodrome on landing, caught fire and bombs exploded. Air Mechanic I. G. Woodgate (observer) escaped unhurt.

Taylor, 2nd Lt Frederick Charles, 22nd May 1918. Age 19.
Observer, from Queenborough, Kent. (Grave Ref: VB25)

Y FARM MILITARY CEMETERY, BOIS-GRENIER – Nord

Jackson, 2nd Lt William Vernon, 30th October 1918. Age 19. (Grave Ref: A.13)

Germany

COLOGNE SOUTHERN CEMETERY – Koln, Nordrhein-Westfal

Cumming, Lt Charles Linnaeus, 31st January 1919. Age 30.
DH9A E8877 caught fire in air, Buschbell. Cumming and 2nd Lt Waters (below) both killed.

Gibbs, Lt Stanley, 14th May 1919. Age 27.
Killed with A. Page (below) in DH9 D7380.

Page, Cadet A. B., 14th May 1919.

Waters, 2nd Lt Andrew John, 31st January 1919. Age 19.

United Kingdom

BIRMINGHAM (LODGE HILL) CEMETERY – Warwickshire

Pollard, 2nd Lt Wilfred Walter, 5th July 1918. Age 19.

ST PANCRAS CEMETERY – Middlesex

Percival, Flt Lt John Frederick Spencer, Mentioned in Despatches, 1st March 1919. Age 29.

UPTON-CUM-CHALVEY (or SLOUGH) (ST MARY) CHURCHYARD – Buckinghamshire

Pullen, 2nd Lt William Stanley, 206th Training Depot Station, RAF, 12th June 1918. Age 18.

Graves of Lt Cumming and 2/Lt Waters, Cologne.
(CC/206)

WORLD WAR II

Azores

LAJES WAR CEMETERY
Neil, AC1 Stewart Semple, RAFVR. 18th December 1943. Age 22.

Belgium

BRUSSELS TOWN CEMETERY – Evere, Vlaams-Brabant
Alderton, Fg Off. Harry Thomas Walter, RAFVR (WOp/AG), 13th October 1945. Age 33.
Connor, Fg Off. Bernard, RAFVR (Nav.), 13th October 1945. Age 23.
Freckleton, Fg Off. John Dolphin, RAFVR, 13th October 1945. Age 22.
Green, Flt Lt Peter, RAFVR, 13th October 1945. Age 26.
Nightall, Flt Sgt Dennis George, RAFVR (Flt Eng.), 13th October 1945. Age 20.
Rivaz, Sqn Ldr Richard Charles, DFC, 13th October 1945. Age 37.

Denmark

AARESTRUP CHURCHYARD
Emery, WO Kenneth, RAFVR (AG), 21st April 1945.
Gale, Plt Off. Windsor Thomas Henry, RAFVR (Flt Eng.), 21st April 1945. Age 24.
Harding, Fg Off. Alan James, RAFVR (Nav./Bomber), 21st April 1945. Age 28.
Laycock, Flt Lt Peter Stevens Leinthall, RAFVR (WOp/AG), 21st April 1945. Age 24.
Long, WO George Charles Kenneth, RAFVR (AG), 21st April 1945.
Orritt, Flt Sgt Frederick Ralph, RAFVR (WOp Mech./AG), 21st April 1945. Age 21.
Smith, Fg Off. Anthony Richard Tenison, RNZAF, 21st April 1945. Age 23.
Spencer, WOI Walter William, RCAF (WOp/AG), 21st April 1945. Age 22.
Theaker, WOI Thomas Keith, RCAF (AG), 21st April 1945. Age 25.
Topliff, Plt Off. George Henry, RAAF, 21st April 1945. Age 20.

SKAGEN CEMETERY
Heatlie, Fg Off. John Adam Wilson, RAFVR (Nav./Bomber), 9th April 1945. Age 24.
Mollard, Fg Off. Lloyd Bemister, RCAF (Pilot), 15th July 1944. Age 30.

Egypt

HELIOPOLIS WAR CEMETERY
Bradshaw, Flt Lt Ronald Thomas (Flying Instr.), 4th November 1942. Age 34.
Brown, Sgt Max Otto (WOp/AG), 4th November 1942. Age 27.
Holland, LAC Frederick, RAFVR, 4th November 1942.

France

NANTES (PONT-DU-CENS) COMMUNAL CEMETERY – Loire-Atlantique
Durrant, Sgt James William (WOp/AG), 21st December 1941. Age 20.
Rawes, Plt Off. Errington Douglas, RAFVR, 21st December 1941. Age 25.
Terry, Flt Lt Ian Wingate, RNZAF (Nav.), 21st December 1941. Age 25.
Watts, Sgt Ronald Leslie, RAFVR (WOp/AG), 21st December 1941. Age 19.

Germany

HAMBURG CEMETERY
Cooke, Wg Cdr Humphrey Desmond (Pilot), 26th June 1942.
McGlynn, Flt Sgt Griffiths (WOp/AG), 26th June 1942. Age 22.
Watson, Plt Off. James Cameron, RCAF (Air Obs.), 25th June 1942.

KIEL WAR CEMETERY
Crook, Sqn Ldr Cyril Norman, DFC (Pilot), 26th June 1942. Age 29.
Hubbard, Flt Sgt Robert Albert William, RAFVR (WOp/AG), 26th June 1942. Age 22.
Payze, Sgt Robert William, RAFVR (WOp/AG), 26th June 1942. Age 22.
Phillips, Plt Off. David Thomas Williams, RAFVR (AG), 26th June 1942. Age 22.
Wright, Flt Sgt Kenneth Douglas, RAFVR (Pilot), 26th June 1942. Age 22.

SAGE WAR CEMETERY
Moore, Sgt Montague (Pilot), 12th May 1940. Age 26.

Gibraltar

GIBRALTAR MEMORIAL
Brown, WO Donald Brooke, RAFVR, 29th November 1943. Age 22.
Burnett, Flt Sgt Robert Alfred Charles, RAFVR, 29th November 1943. Age 21.

Coutts, WO David Strang, RAFVR, 29th November 1943.

Mitchener, Flt Sgt Denis John Anthony, RAFVR, 29th November 1943. Age 21.

Moule, Fg Off. Arthur Edward, RAFVR, 29th November 1943. Age 24.

Senior, Sgt Ronald Andrew, RAFVR, 29th November 1943. Age 23.

Stones, Flt Sgt James, RAFVR, 29th November 1943. Age 23.

Wilson, Flt Sgt John, RAFVR, 29th November 1943.

Sweden

KVIBERG CEMETERY

Ellison, Sgt George Arthur, RAFVR, 8th-9th April 1945.

Thailand

KANCHANABURI WAR CEMETERY

Lawless, WO Cormac, 9th July 1943. Age 23.

United Kingdom

AMBLE WEST CEMETERY – Northumberland

Riddell, Sgt Norman Grey (WOp), 20th December 1940. Age 21.

BIRMINGHAM (WARSTONE LANE) CEMETERY – Warwickshire

Meller, LAC William Arthur, 1st January 1941. Age 20.

BISPHAM (ALL HALLOWS) CHURCHYARD – Lancashire

Titchener, Sgt Reginald, RAFVR (Pilot), 11th February 1941. Age 28.

BRIDEKIRK (ST BRIDGET) CHURCHYARD – Westmoreland

Hayston, Plt Off. Thomas Lunson, RAFVR (Pilot), 16th August 1941. Age 27.

BRIGHTON AND PRESTON CEMETERY – Sussex

Allen, Plt Off. John Buttemer, RAFVR, 1st January 1941. Age 24.

BRISTOL (CANFORD) CEMETERY – Gloucestershire

Bracher, Sgt William Alan, RAFVR (Pilot), 11th February 1941. Age 20.

CADDER CEMETERY – Lanarkshire

Dobbie, Plt Off. Kenneth James, RAFVR, 20th December 1940.

CAMBRIDGE CITY CEMETERY – Cambridgeshire

Fuller, Plt Off. Richard James, RAFVR, 20th March 1941. Age 25.

CAMBRIDGE CREMATORIUM – Cambridgeshire

Skeats, Fg Off. Herbert Arthur, RAFVR, 19th November 1940. Age 25.

CARNWATH NEW CEMETERY – Lanarkshire

Nimmo, Sgt Hislop, RAFVR, 14th September 1944. Age 19.

CITY OF LONDON CEMETERY – Essex

Warren, Plt Off. Maurice Kingsley, 20th March 1941. Age 25.

COWES (NORTHWOOD) CEMETERY – Isle of Wight

Kettle, Sgt Geoffrey Taylor, RAFVR (WOp/AG), 1st February 1942. Age 23.

CRYSTAL PALACE DISTRICT CEMETERY – Kent

Wiseman, Sgt Norman Peter, RAFVR, 28th July 1943. Age 23.

DERBY (NOTTINGHAM ROAD) CEMETERY – Derbyshire
Mannion, Sgt Dennis (WOp/AG), 5th August 1940. Age 21.
Reeves, Sgt George Verney, RAFVR (Obs.), 21st April 1941.

FARNHAM (ST MARY) CHURCHYARD – Essex
Greenhill, Sgt Charles John, RAFVR, 20th July 1944. Age 22.

FENCE-IN-PENDLE (ST ANNE) CHURCHYARD – Lancashire
Wilkinson, Sgt Edmund Harrison RAFVR (Flt Eng.), 14th September 1944. Age 22.

FULWOOD (CHRIST CHURCH) CHURCHYARD – Yorkshire
Hancock, Flt Lt James Douglas, RAFVR, 20th July 1944. Age 24.

GLENAVY ROMAN CATHOLIC CHURCHYARD – County Antrim
Morgan, Flt Sgt Bernard, RAFVR (Pilot), 24th September 1941. Age 24.

GREAT BIRCHAM (ST MARY) CHURCHYARD – Norfolk
Ballantyne, Plt Off. Herbert Gregory, 14th August 1940. Age 22.
Featherstone, Fg Off. Henry Edward Middleton, 1st January 1941. Age 27.
Meridew, AC1 George Alexander, 1st January 1941. Age 23.
Moss, Sgt John Herbert, RAFVR (WOp/AG), 19th November 1940. Age 20.
Rustom, Plt Off. Robin, 5th August 1940. Age 20.
Stephenson, Plt Off. John Oscar Lloyd, 14th August 1940. Age 25.
Townend, LAC Ernest (AG), 3rd May 1940. Age 28.
Ward, Plt Off. Richard, 20th December 1940. Age 22.

GRIMSBY (SCARTHO ROAD) CEMETERY – Lincolnshire
Walker, Fg Off. Roy, RAFVR (WOp), 14th September 1944.

HAVELOCK CEMETERY – Middlesex
Allen, Flt Sgt Frederick (WOp/AG), 21st April 1941. Age 21.

HIGHGATE CEMETERY – London
Handley, Sgt Christopher Thomas, RAFVR (WOp/AG), 21st April 1941. Age 25.
Jaeger, Sgt James Cleveland Harold, RAFVR (Pilot), 6th October 1942. Age 31.

HINDHEAD (ST ALBAN) CHURCHYARD – Surrey
Kiralfy, Fg Off. Dennis Maurice Gerald, RAFVR, 1st January 1941. Age 27.

HODDESDON CEMETERY – Hertfordshire
Conway, Sgt Kenneth David, RAFVR, 15th November 1944. Age 19.

HORNCHURCH CEMETERY – Essex
Girling, Sgt George Alfred, RAFVR (Flt Eng.), 20th July 1944. Age 21.

HORSFORTH CEMETERY – Yorkshire
Braithwaite, Sgt Dennis, RAFVR (Nav./Bomber), 20th July 1944. Age 21.

ILFORD (BARKINGSIDE) CEMETERY – Essex
Alabaster, Fg Off. Reginald Alfred, RAFVR, 14th September 1944. Age 21.

ISLINGTON CEMETERY – Middlesex
Brace, Sgt Patrick Lewis, RAFVR, 19th November 1940. Age 20.

KILLEAD (ST CATHERINE) CHURCH OF IRELAND CHURCHYARD – County Antrim

Dunn, Sgt Frederick, RAFVR (Pilot), 24th September 1941. Age 22.
Fry, Sgt Philip Alexander, RAFVR (WOp/AG), 1st February 1942. Age 23.
Gihl, Sgt Geoffrey Clarence, RAFVR (WOp/AG), 8th April 1942. Age 21.
Linhart, Sgt Geoffrey Owen, RAFVR (WOp/AG), 24th September 1941.

KINGSTON-UPON-THAMES CEMETERY – Surrey
Curry, AC2 Leslie George, RAFVR, 20th May 1940.

LANGTOFT CEMETERY – Lincolnshire
Plowright, Sgt Robert Arthur, 1st January 1941. Age 20.

LEEDS (HAREHILLS) CEMETERY – Yorkshire
Carlton, Sgt Robert Wilson, RAFVR (WOp/AG), 28th April 1943. Age 20.

LEICESTER (GILROES) CEMETERY – Leicestershire
Pegg, LAC Arthur Alexander, RAFVR, 15th December 1944. Age 32.

LEICESTER (WELFORD ROAD) CEMETERY – Leicestershire
Holyoake, Sgt Frank Leslie, RAFVR, 20th March1941. Age 26.

LEUCHARS CEMETERY – Fife
Bayard, Fg Off. John William, RCAF, 14th September 1944. Age 24.
Dunn, Fg Off. Geoffrey James, RAFVR (Nav.), 14th September 1944. Age 21.
Forbes, WO George John, RNZAF (WOp/AG), 14th September 1944. Age 30.
Tulloch, Fg Off. Archie, RCAF, 20th July 1944. Age 23.

LOWER MITTON (ST MICHAEL) CHURCHYARD – Worcestershire
Thomas, Flt Sgt William Arthur, RAFVR (WOp/Mech.AG), 20th July 1944.

LUND (ALL SAINTS) CHURCHYARD – Yorkshire
Ellerington, Sgt George Raymond (WOp/AG), 20th December 1940.

LUTON CHURCH BURIAL GROUND – Bedfordshire
Tearle, Plt Off. Raymond John, RAFVR, 17th May 1941. Age 25.

MICKLEOVER (ALL SAINTS) CHURCHYARD – Derbyshire
Bradley, Sgt Sidney, RAFVR (AG), 19th November 1940. Age 24.

NEW HUNSTANTON CEMETERY – Norfolk
Kean, Plt Off. Raymond Thomas, DFC, 5th August 1940. Age 22.

NEWCASTLE-UPON-TYNE (ALL SAINTS) CEMETERY – Northumberland
Watson, WO Albert William Hood, RAFVR (Nav./Bomber), 14th September 1940. Age 35.

NEWTON & LLANLLWCHAIARN CEMETERY – Montgomeryshire
Hilton, Plt Off. Norman, RAFVR (WOp/AG), 15th July 1944. Age 23.

NORWICH (THE ROSARY) CEMETERY – Norfolk
Fitzgerald, Sgt Eddie (WOp/AG), 14th August 1940. Age 21.

NORWICH CEMETERY – Norfolk
Funnell, Sgt Cecil Henry (WOp/AG), 20th March 1941. Age 21.

NUNTON CEMETERY – Benbecula
Davis, Sgt A. J., 11th May 1943. Age 18.

Delarue, Fg Off. J. E., RAAF (Pilot), 6th October 1942. Age 26.
Guppy, Sgt J. F., RAAF, 6th October 1942. Age 20.
Taplin, Flt Sgt J. B., RAAF, 6th October 1942. Age 27.

PLYMOUTH (EFFORD) CEMETERY – Devon
Edwards, AC2 Rupert Henry, RAFVR, 9th November 1941. Age 21.

PORTSMOUTH (MILTON) CEMETERY – Hampshire
Mansell, Plt Off. Roy McKenzie, RAFVR (Pilot), 1st January 1941. Age 22.

PRESTATYN (COED BELL) CEMETERY – Flintshire
Knight, Sgt Arthur Gordon (WOp/AG), 17th May 1941. Age 20.

READING (HENLEY ROAD) CEMETERY – Oxfordshire
Hayward, Flt Sgt Victor Charles Donald, RAFVR (WOp/AG), 24th September 1941. Age 20.

RUMNEY (ST AUGUSTINE) CHURCHYARD – Monmouthshire
Thompson, Plt Off. Walter Horace, RAFVR (WOp), 14th September 1944. Age 26.

RUNNYMEDE MEMORIAL – Surrey
Abbott, Sgt Edward, 18th May 1940. Age 25.
Acheson, Fg Off. James Glasgow Irwin, RAFVR, 14th October 1940.
Alpe, Sgt Bertram Lawrence, 11th February 1941.
Arnott, Sgt Albert James, 11th February 1941. Age 25.
Atkinson, Fg Off. Norman, RAFVR, 2nd December 1944. Age 29.
Bagley, LAC John Charles, 6th December 1939. Age 22.
Ball, Fg Off. Thomas Manning Curzon, 28th September 1944. Age 24.
Barton, Plt Off. Anthony James, RAFVR, 9th April 1945.
Beckett, Sgt Thomas, RAFVR, 12th February 1941. Age 33.
Bendix, Fg Off. John Frederick, 1st July 1941. Age 20.
Bentley, Sgt Rupert, RAFVR, 14th December 1942. Age 32.
Bisson, Sgt Keith Cecil, RAFVR, 12th June 1941. Age 19.
Blackett, Plt Off. Anthony Rex, 4th February 1941.
Bouwens, Plt Off. Adrian, 18th May 1940.
Britton. LAC Leonard James, DFM, 22nd May 1940. Age 27.
Brown, Sqn Ldr Ralph, RAFVR, 6th January 1944. Age 33.
Bushell, Sgt Keith Stephen, 4th July 1940. Age 21.
Carlisle, Fg Off. Peter Francis, DFC, RAFVR, 28th September 1944. Age 24.
Charters, Plt Off. William, RAFVR, 2nd December 1944. Age 32.
Clark, Plt Off. John Allen, 22nd May 1940. Age 22.
Cleland, Plt Off. Andrew McNeill, RCAF, 28th September 1944.
Cockayne, Cpl Harold John, 6th December 1939. Age 20.
Crowe, Flt Sgt Eric, RAFVR, 14th December 1942. Age 25.
Dale, Plt Off. Sydney Herbert, RAFVR, 13th June 1941.
De Keyser, Plt Off. John Lionel, 15th October 1940. Age 25.
Duncan, Fg Off. Joseph Henry, RAFVR, 6th January 1944. Age 24.
Durant, AC1 John Leslie, 18th May 1940. Age 19.
Echlin, Fg Off. Allan Grant, RCAF, 15th July 1944. Age 25.
Eckersley, Flt Sgt Thomas, RAFVR, 6th January 1944. Age 31.
Edgar, Flt Sgt Robert John, RCAF, 28th July 1942. Age 24.
Elliott, Flt Lt Kenneth George, RAFVR, 2nd December 1944. Age 32.
Fabian, Sgt Robert, RAFVR, 6th January 1944. Age 24.
Farlowe, Sgt James Thomas, RAFVR, 14th October 1940. Age 22.

Fitch, Sgt Ronald, RAFVR, 15th July 1944. Age 19.

Forsyth, Fg Off. Alexander, RCAF, 15th July 1944.

Fox, WO Kenneth David, RAFVR, 28th September 1944. Age 24.

Gannon, Sgt Benjamin Peter, RAFVR, 3rd August 1940. Age 22.

Garstin, Sgt Richard Elleker, 14th October 1940. Age 22.

George, Plt Off. Anthony Frederick, RAFVR, 13th June 1941. Age 24.

Gilbert, Plt Off. John Allan, 3rd August 1940.

Giles, Plt Off. Malcolm John, 22nd May 1940.

Gill, AC1 Benjamin, 12th May 1940.

Gillett, Sgt John Alfred, RAFVR, 28th September 1944. Age 32.

Goldsmith, Sgt George Howard, 4th July 1940. Age 22.

Gordon, Plt Off. Alexander Lindsay, RAFVR, 12th June 1941.

Gray, Plt Off. Ian Lowrie, 12th May 1940. Age 21.

Grimes, Plt Off. John Henry, 6th December 1939. Age 21.

Gumbrill, Cpl Royston Ewart, 18th May 1940. Age 32.

Hall, WOI Frederick Russell, RCAF, 2nd December 1944.

Harper, Sqn Ldr Robert Howard, DFC, RAFVR, 2nd December 1944.

Heard, WOI Donald Luther, RCAF, 6th January 1944. Age 35.

Henderson, Plt Off. Selby Roger, DFC, 4th July 1940. Age 22.

Hildred, Sgt Robert Nockold, RAFVR, 14th December 1942. Age 21.

Howell, Flt Lt Brian Lloyd, RAFVR, 9th April 1945. Age 24.

Hoyle, Flt Sgt William Royston, DFM, RAFVR, 28th September 1944. Age 23.

Hutchesson, Fg Off. George Derrick Osmund Le, 18th May 1940. Age 26.

Ireland, Plt Off. William Arthur Leslie, RAFVR, 28th July 1942.

Jerome, Flt Sgt Michael, 9th April 1945. Age 21.

Johns, Sgt Eric, RAFVR, 13th June 1941. Age 27.

Johnston, Sgt William Logan, RAFVR, 3rd August 1940. Age 20.

Jones, Sgt William, 19th May 1940.

Judge, Sgt Ernest Albert, 19th May 1940. Age 24.

Keddy, WOI Oliver Ambrose, RCAF, 6th January 1944. Age 24.

Kennett, Sgt John Thomas, RAFVR, 4th February 1941.

Kent, Sgt William, 15th October 1940. Age 24.

Lascelles, Fg Off. John Richard Hastings, 14th October 1940. Age 20.

Lennox-French, Plt Off. Robert James, RAFVR, 18th May 1940. Age 28.

Lester, Plt Off. Stanley John, 4th July 1940. Age 26.

Lewis, Sgt Kenneth Everitt, RAFVR, 4th July 1940. Age 31.

Lewis, WO Wilfred George, RAFVR, 28th September 1944. Age 24.

Mackinnon, Plt Off. James Elmer, 4th July 1940. Age 21.

Macmillan, Sgt Victor Donald, 6th December 1939.

Marshall, Flt Sgt George Stanley, RAFVR, 2nd December 1944.

Mason, Sgt Anthony William Alfred, RAFVR, 9th April 1945.

Mason, Plt Off. Miles Arthur George, 11th February 1941. Age 25.

McDonald, Flt Lt John Edward, Mentioned in Despatches, RAFVR, 8th April 1945. Age 23.

McKinnon, Plt Off. Lloyd George, RCAF, 28th September 1944. Age 28.

McRobb, Flt Sgt Charles, 15th July 1944.

Metcalfe, Cpl Anthony John, 19th May 1940.

Mewett, AC1 Henry Charles, 19th May 1940.

Mills, Sgt Ronald David, RAFVR, 13th June 1941. Age 27.

Morris, Sgt Ralph Brettell, RAFVR, 12th February 1941.

Nadeau, Plt Off. Joseph Albert, RCAF, 28th September 1944. Age 22.

Noble, Plt Off. Hugh William, 4th February 1941. Age 25.

North, Sgt Ronald, RAFVR, 28th July 1942. Age 20.

Owen, Fg Off. John, RAFVR, 14th December 1942. Age 21.

Oxley, Sgt John Alan, RAFVR, 12th June 1941. Age 21.

Parnell, Sgt William James, RAFVR, 14th December 1942. Age 22.

Peats, Flt Sgt Roberts, RAFVR, 2nd December 1944.

Peel, AC1 James Francis, 22nd May 1940. Age 23.

Phillips, Sgt John, RAFVR, 11th February 1941. Age 21.

Pinhorn, Sqn Ldr Anthony James, DFC, 6th January 1944. Age 28.

Poole, WO Fred, RAFVR, 9th April 1945. Age 25.

Preston, Fg Off. William Winwood, RAFVR, 15th July 1944. Age 24.

Quilter, LAC John, 5th September 1939. Age 22.

Reed, Sgt John Henry, 11th February 1941.

Roberts, Fg Off. Francis Dennis, RAFVR, 6th January 1944. Age 34.

Robinson, Flt Sgt Frederick Arthur, RAFVR, 6th October 1942. Age 29.

Sawyer, Sgt Leonard Eustace, 12th February 1941. Age 20.

Shanks, Sgt Walter, RAFVR, 14th December 1942. Age 21.

Sharp, Plt Off. Andrew Fanshawe, RAFVR, 12th June 1941. Age 20.

Sheffield, AC1 Geoffrey, 5th September 1939. Age 18.

Sloan, LAC Reginald James, 12th May 1940.

Smith, Sgt Douglas Harry, RAFVR, 1st July 1941. Age 20.

Smith, Sgt John Fulford, RAFVR, 1st July 1941.

Soppitt, Sgt Alfred, 4th February 1941.

Stares, WO Ronald Norman, RAFVR, 6th January 1944. Age 25.

Stass, Fg Off. Albert George, RAFVR, 9th April 1945. Age 23.

Steel, Sgt James, 15th October 1940. Age 20.

Strachan, Plt Off. Ian Maxwell, RAFVR, 1st July 1941. Age 23.

Sumner, Sgt Gordon Clifton, 4th July 1940.

Swinson, Sgt Patrick William, 3rd August 1940. Age 20.

Taylor, Fg Off. John Elliott, RCAF, 15th July 1944. Age 26.

Teden, Plt Off. Derek Edmund, RAF (Aux. AF), 15th October 1940.

Thynne, Fg Off. Brian Winslow, RAFVR, 15th July 1944. Age 31.

Tomlinson, AC1 Walter Austin, 18th May 1940.

Tulloch, Fg Off. Stewart, RCAF, 2nd December 1944. Age 23.

Tupma, Flt Sgt Charles, RAFVR, 9th April 1945. Age 22.

Turner, Flt Sgt Geoffrey Arthur, 18th May 1940. Age 25.

Walker, WO Eric Andrew, RAFVR, 2nd December 1944.

Wallace, Sgt Joseph, 11th February 1941. Age 21.

Waterman, Plt Off. John Ross, RAFVR, 11th February 1941. Age 22.

Williamson, LAC John Lindsay, 4th July 1940. Age 22.

SOLIHULL CEMETERY – Warwickshire
Hull, Sgt Frederick Herbert, RAFVR, 5th August 1940. Age 22.

STANLEY NEW CEMETERY – Durham
Taylor, Fg Off. Raymond, RAFVR, 14th September 1944. Age 22.

THURROCK (CHADWELL ST MARY) CEMETERY – Essex
Gilder, LAC Kenneth Charles George, 1st January 1941.

WELLINGBOROUGH (DODDINGTON ROAD) CEMETERY – Northamptonshire
Cooper, Plt Off. Leslie Ernest Henry, RAFVR, 17th May 1941.

WOKING (ST JOHN'S) CREMATORIUM – Surrey

Tanner, Fg Off. Richard Lloyd, RAFVR (Pilot), 21st April 1941. Age 21.

WOODRISING (ST NICHOLAS) CHURCHYARD – Norfolk

Ramsay, Sgt Robert Elliott, RAFVR (WOp/AG), 18th August 1941. Age 20.

MEMORIAL WINDOWS

1. Saint Columba's Church, Royal Air Force Kinloss, dedicated on 28 May 1989. Designed by Benedictine Monks Brother Gregory Carling and Brother Michael de Klerk of Pluscarden Abbey, near Kinloss, Morayshire. The window depicts the surrender of a German U-Boat to a 206 Squadron Liberator during May 1945, in addition to the Squadron Crest and Battle Honours. *(See colour section)*

2. Memorial to the late Squadron Leader David Beaty MBE, DFC and Bar at St Mary's Church, Slindon, dedicated on 29 June 2003.

(Kenneth Beere & Betty Beaty)

MEMORABILIA

(Dr Charles Eaton)

Memorial display honouring the late Group Captain Charles 'Moth' Eaton in the Parliament House, Darwin. He served with 206 Squadron on the Western Front in 1918 but crashed behind enemy lines and was taken prisoner. After several daring attempts at escape he finally succeeded. After the war he and his family settled in Australia where he became a pioneer aviator in the Northern Territory in the 1920s, earning his sobriquet 'Moth' after flying the first metal DH Gipsy Moth in the Great Air Race from Sydney to Perth in 1929. Later he served as as the first commander of the RAAF in the Northern Territory in 1939. After the war he became a distinguished diplomat, making a significant contribution to Indonesia's eventual independence. He died in November 1979.

Memorabilia of the late Squadron Leader Peter Laird DFC, AFC at No. 11 (Fighter) Group Museum, RAF Uxbridge. (By kind permission of Chris Wren, Curator, and Brenda Laird, Peter's widow)

SQUADRON LEADER PETER LAIRD DFC AFC

PETER LAIRD SERVED IN THE ROYAL AIR FORCE FROM 1941 UNTIL 1961. BETWEEN 1941 AND 1945 HE SERVED IN COASTAL COMMAND, FLYING AS A WOP/AG ON WHITLEYS, WELLINGTONS, BEAUFIGHTERS, LIBERATORS AND FORTRESSES. HE WAS COMMISSIONED IN 1943.

WITH A CHANGE OF BREVET TO SIGNALLER, IN 1948/49 HE FLEW ON YORKS DURING THE BERLIN AIRLIFT. HE WAS THEN POSTED TO THE FAR EAST AND SERVED ON SUNDERLANDS DURING THE KOREAN WAR AND THE MALAYAN STATE OF EMERGENCY.

IN 1954 WITH A FURTHER CHANGE OF BREVET TO AIR ELECTRONICS OPERATOR, HE SERVED IN BOMBER COMMAND, FLYING IN VALIANTS AT RAF GAYDON.

MEDALS

DISTINGUISHED FLYING CROSS. AIR FORCE CROSS. 1939/45 STAR. ATLANTIC STAR. AFRICA STAR. VICTORY MEDAL. KOREAN MEDAL. UN MEDAL. MALAYAN MEDAL. AIR EFFICIENCY MEDAL. MALTA GEORGE CROSS MEDAL.

HE ALSO RECEIVED A MEDAL FROM THE RUSSIAN FEDERATION IN 1995 TO COMMEMORATE THE 50TH ANNIVERSARY OF THE VICTORY IN THE GREAT PATRIOTIC WAR 1941 - 1945

INDEX

Note: Page numbers in *italic* refer to illustrations.